The Farm Kitchen

The Farm Kitchen

Abby Allen of
PIPERS FARM

Seasonal Recipes from Field,
Coast & Garden

For Jack and Kaia, always remember the importance of our natural world.

First published in Great Britain in 2025 by
Kyle Books, an imprint of
Octopus Publishing Group Ltd
Carmelite House
50 Victoria Embankment
London EC4Y 0DZ
www.octopusbooks.co.uk

An Hachette UK Company
www.hachette.co.uk

The authorized representative in the EEA is Hachette Ireland, 8 Castlecourt Centre, Dublin 15, D15 XTP3, Ireland
(email: info@hbgi.ie)

Text copyright © Abby Allen 2025
Photography copyright © Matt Austin 2025
Design & layout copyright © Octopus Publishing Group 2025

Distributed in the US by Hachette Book Group, 1290 Avenue of the Americas, 4th and 5th Floors, New York, NY 10104

Distributed in Canada by Canadian Manda Group, 664 Annette St., Toronto, Ontario, Canada M6S 2C8

All rights reserved. No part of this work may be reproduced or utilized in any form or by any means, electronic or mechanical, including photocopying, recording or by any information storage and retrieval system, without the prior written permission of the publisher.

Abby Allen asserts the moral right to be identified as the author of this work.

ISBN 978 1 80419 307 5
eISBN 978 1 80419 308 2

A CIP catalogue record for this book is available from the British Library.

Printed and bound in China.
10 9 8 7 6 5 4 3 2 1

Publisher: Joanna Copestick
Senior Managing Editor: Sybella Stephens
Copy Editor: Emily Preece-Morrison
Art Director & Design: Yasia Williams
Photographer: Matt Austin
Senior Production Manager:
  Katherine Hockley

Contents

Introduction 6

Spring 11
Summer 66
Autumn 117
Winter 167

Index 220
Acknowledgements 224

INTRODUCTION

'It is just as rude to arrive early as it is to arrive late.' My granny's voice rang in my memory as I sat waiting, heart pounding, until the clock struck exactly 2pm. Little did I know that this day would change my life forever.

Tottering up the uneven drive, pounding on the farmhouse door with more force than I had intended, fate began her work of setting plans in motion. I was standing outside the door of Pipers Farm, preparing for a job interview. The advert had been vague, requiring a multitude of skills, some of which I had and some of which I definitely did not. That's the thing about youth – it arms you with a confidence that anything is possible, and at that moment in my life the only real experience I had was knowing how to sell, and what is an interview if it is not an assignment to sell yourself?

The interview didn't go that well. We shook hands, mine grasping once again with unintended force. Given my slight frame, the firmness of my handshake has often taken its recipient by surprise. As I drove back down the pothole-filled lanes, a mixture of bewilderment and intrigue rose from my belly. Looking back now, those feelings were entirely appropriate for the rollercoaster ride I was about to embark upon.

A few days later, an email landed in my inbox from Will, son of co-founders Peter and Henri, and managing director 'in training' or 'in transition' of Pipers Farm (it's always hard to put your finger on these things when it comes to shifting a family farming business down the line). 'Job Offer' was the subject line. A directness that, in time, I would come to love and appreciate from Will.

I had spent the last five years working in sales and marketing for a variety of media companies alongside co-founding my own business running networking events for chefs. I had decided that I needed a new challenge and, boy, was I about to get what I was asking for. After some 'contract negotiations', I accepted the role with complete and utter naivety and with no real thought of the future. Thirteen years on and it is extraordinary how significant that day was, and how much my life has changed.

In many ways, I truly believe I would have eventually found my way to working with nature in some form or other. My connection to the countryside is deeply rooted, thanks to an idyllic childhood in rural Devon, where my mum and grandparents nurtured my love of animals, the outdoors and cookery.

Spring was spent in the greenhouse with my beloved Grampy, sowing tomato seeds and listening to his majestic stories of growing up in rural Berkshire with the backdrop of the war never far from his consciousness. I always particularly enjoyed the stories that included Jessica the goat, and Terrence his beloved pig. Summers were filled with Famous Five-style adventures – trying to catch trout in the River Exe, building campfires and climbing trees, spending every minute outside from dawn until dusk with my sister and our dog Bess. Autumn, my favourite season of all, was harvest time. Blackberry picking, pie making, jamming, pumpkin carving and enjoying the fruits of the year's labour. There would always be the last of the sunflowers in a jug to brighten up any rainy September days. Winter was spent defrosting

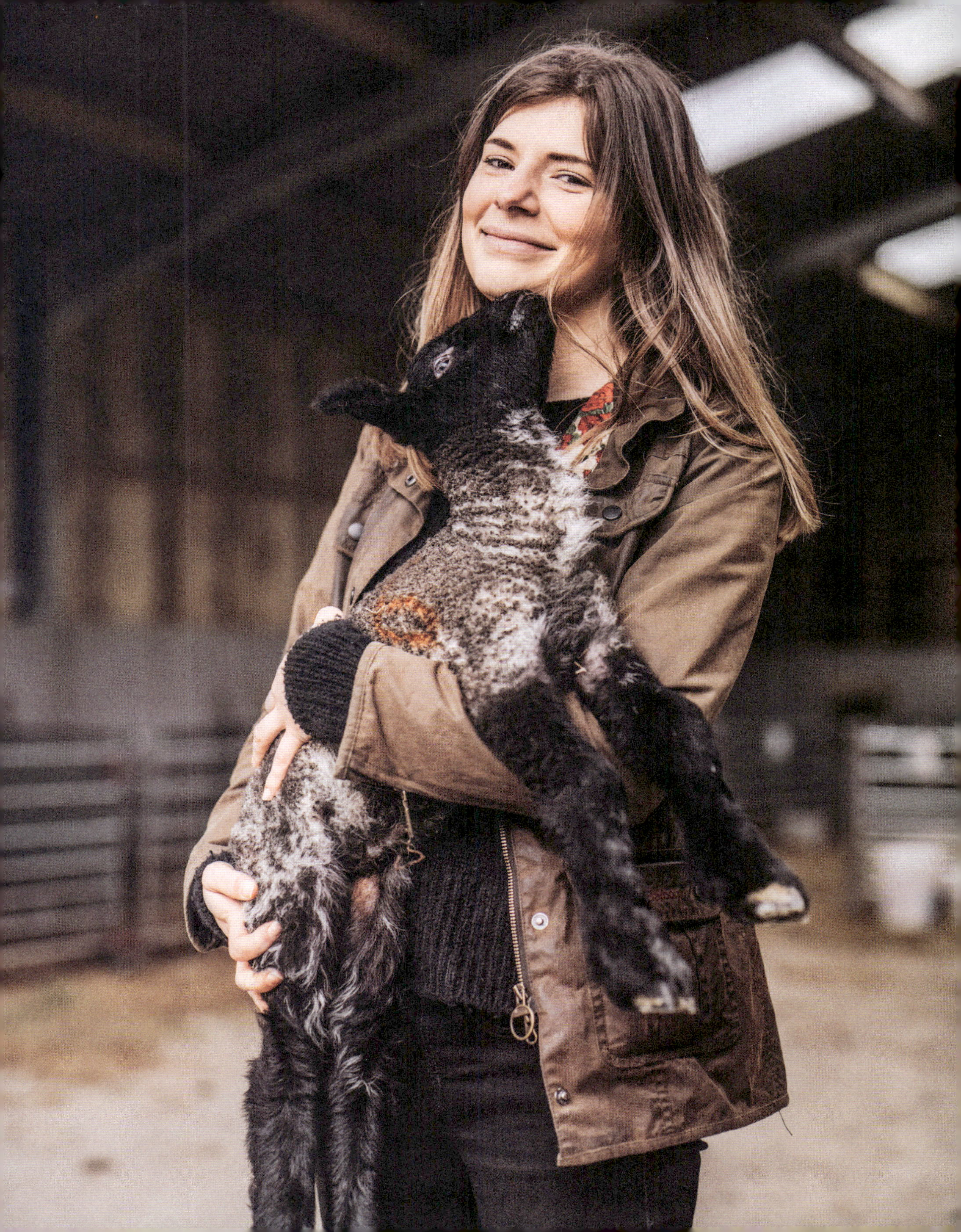

frozen fingers by the Aga and warming up by making soups or stews, or baking with Mum and Granny. It was a good life and provided me with knowledge of and respect for the natural world that was the backdrop to my imagination.

For the last decade plus, during what I refer to now as 'the longest agricultural degree in history', I have been immersed in food and farming. I have been lucky enough to meet and work directly with some of the most inspirational people who are committed to finding solutions for the ever-growing list of challenges laid at the door of agriculture. Broadening my knowledge and seeing first-hand what it really means to farm the land and produce food during a time of unprecedented change. During this time, not only did I fall wildly in love with farming, but with Will, too.

In 2017 Will and I took over the running of Pipers Farm, the business his parents Peter and Henri Greig founded over 35 years ago. We wanted to continue their mission of building a beautiful, living, breathing tapestry of small-scale farms, supporting each family to produce food in harmony with nature, by providing them with a secure and fair route to market.

It is through a life connected with nature, a deeply rooted love of the natural world, of food, of the many wonderful people I have met along my journey's path that drives me to share my vision of a kind, more harmonious world, where eating can become a positive act, not just a human necessity.

For most of us, home is where we lay our head at night. It's the walls that protect us from the elements and the place we keep our belongings. A private space where we eat, sleep and live. However, our home is more than just our house and our belongings. It is the air that we breathe, the water that laps against our shores and runs through our rivers. It's the trees that provide us with shade and the hedgerows that provide shelter.

We are responsible for not just our home, but for the many homes of the billions of living beings around us, from the bird's nest made in an unflailed hedge in the spring, to the nutrient-rich cowpat that the dung beetle burrows deep inside to feed upon. The choices we make are not just contained within our own four walls; they echo across our landscape and permeate our planet.

The more we are able to understand the natural cycles that surround us, that we are part of, makes the answer what should we be eating more obvious, and brings into focus just how dangerous a tightrope we have been walking over the past few decades.

Our connection with nature, with seasons, with the knowledge and skill that are required to grow and prepare food has slowly been severed and, in its place, we have been promised convenience, 'cheap' food and silver bullet solutions in the form of chemicals to fix the malnourished planet and ever-increasing list of health issues we have unwittingly created.

When we started thinking of food as convenient, we started thinking we could have whatever we wanted at any time. Instead of waiting for the first bright green spears of asparagus to burst through the soil in the spring, enjoying and appreciating every mouthful during their fleeting season, we began flying asparagus around the world from countries such as China and Peru to fulfil our insatiable appetite for eating what we wanted on demand, 365 days a year.

Our food system encouraged us to become spoilt and lazy and disconnected from natural systems to such an extent that many people no longer know what is in season and when. We stopped thinking of food as something meaningful, something worth waiting for and worth working for.

The truth is, in order to alter the trajectory on which we are heading, we must find a deeper connection with nature. We must rebuild the knowledge that is fading fast. We must put people at the heart of our food system, valuing their skills and appreciating their work. We must think of more than within our own four walls.

As a wise sheep farmer once told me when discussing coppicing an ancient woodland, 'When we allow light in, it's amazing what can grow.' I like to think that hope is that light. When we allow hope in, we can reimagine our future. But how do we grow hope? It starts with you at home.

This is your awakening. Join me as I share the notes from my farm kitchen in these pages, to help you reconnect with the land and with the people who care for it, to make all our homes a better place.

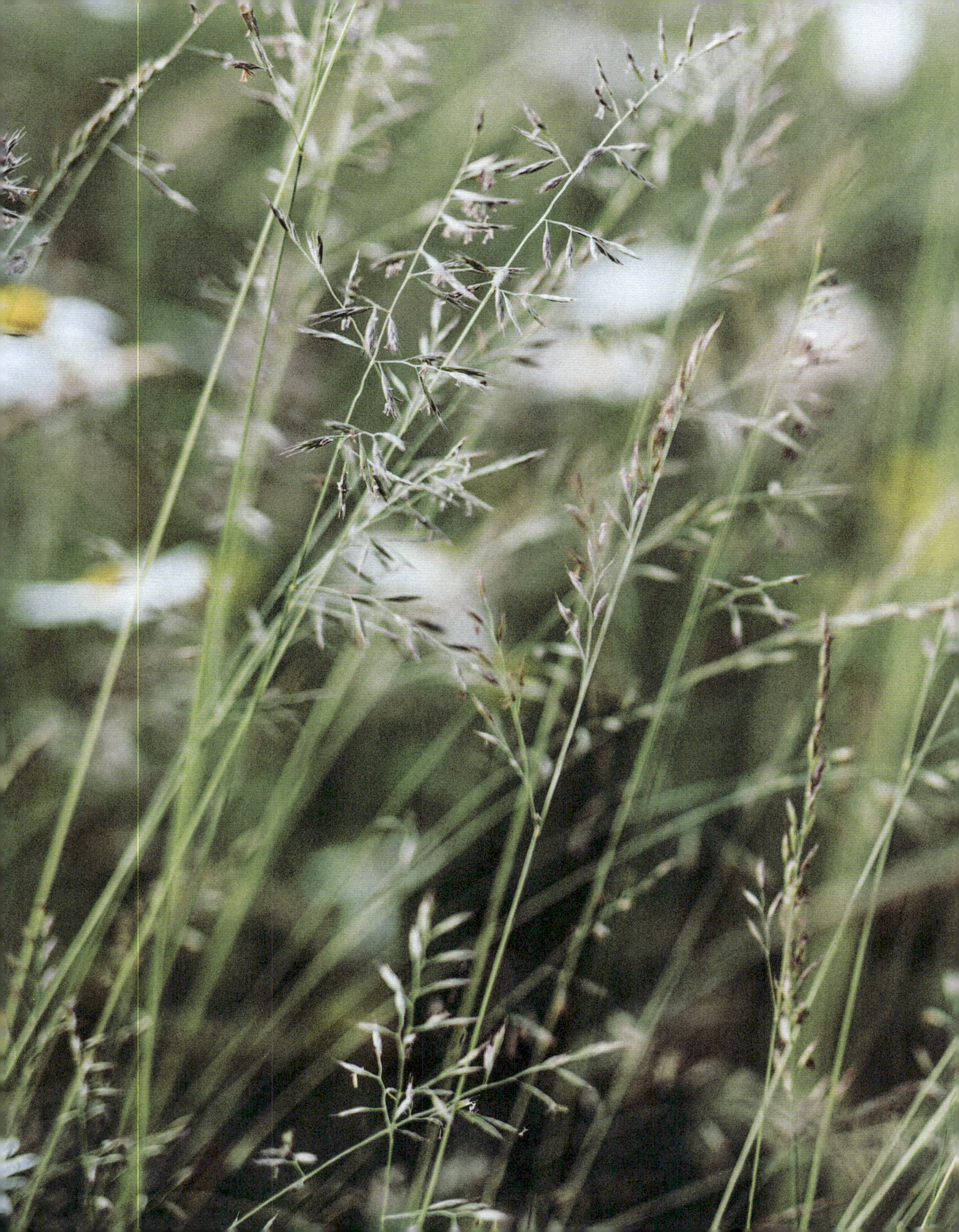

Spring

SPRING

Spring, a tale of two halves. As winter holds her grip tightly, indecisive as to when she will return to her slumberous state, it can be difficult to pinpoint the exact moment of spring's arrival. You see, while there are clear signs – those optimistic days, filled with brilliant white light and the warmth of the long-lost sun on one's face, cheering on the chorus of garden birds and persuading flowers to push their heads through the last centimetres of soil – as generously as Mother Nature gives, she can take away, throwing an almighty tantrum, bringing gales, deluge and even snow whenever she pleases.

Gardening at this time of year is a little like playing a game of chess. You must always stay one step ahead of an opponent's next move. Tender young plants could be smashed like pawns by one quick frost. While losing a few pawns here and there is not the end of the world, and for any seasoned gardener is to be expected, what must be prevented is the loss of the 'key pieces', the structure and backbone of this season's garden, such as the dahlias, lilies, cosmos and the like. Choosing when to plant out is a test of courage and connection to the shifting season.

As the natural world slowly awakens, new precious life can be seen all around us. Just like in the garden, nature's increasing volatility can play havoc with the rhythm and flow at this important time of year. The jelly-like frogspawn gathered around the edges of algae-filled ponds is always the first indicator that clement weather is on the horizon. Next, it's the sound of the rooks, busily swooping and calling to their mates that nest building is on the agenda. Finally, the first wobbly legged lambs can be seen bouncing and skipping through the pasture, never too far from the warmth and sustenance their mothers provide.

With all four seasons often apparent within a matter of hours, the unpredictability of this crucial time of year is a reminder to us all that the delicate balance of nature is a perilous thing. Get it right and abundance will ensue. Get it wrong and hardship will follow.

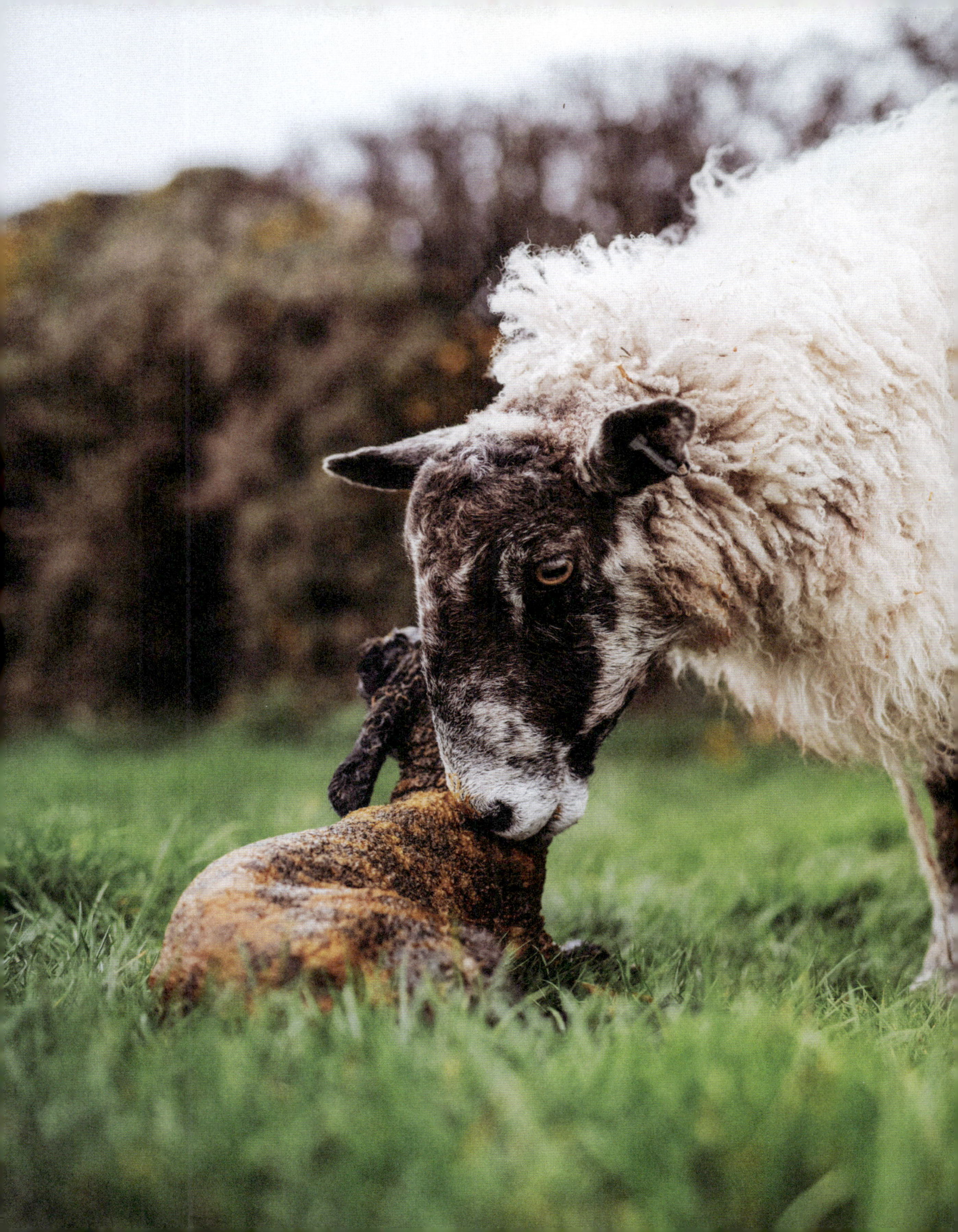

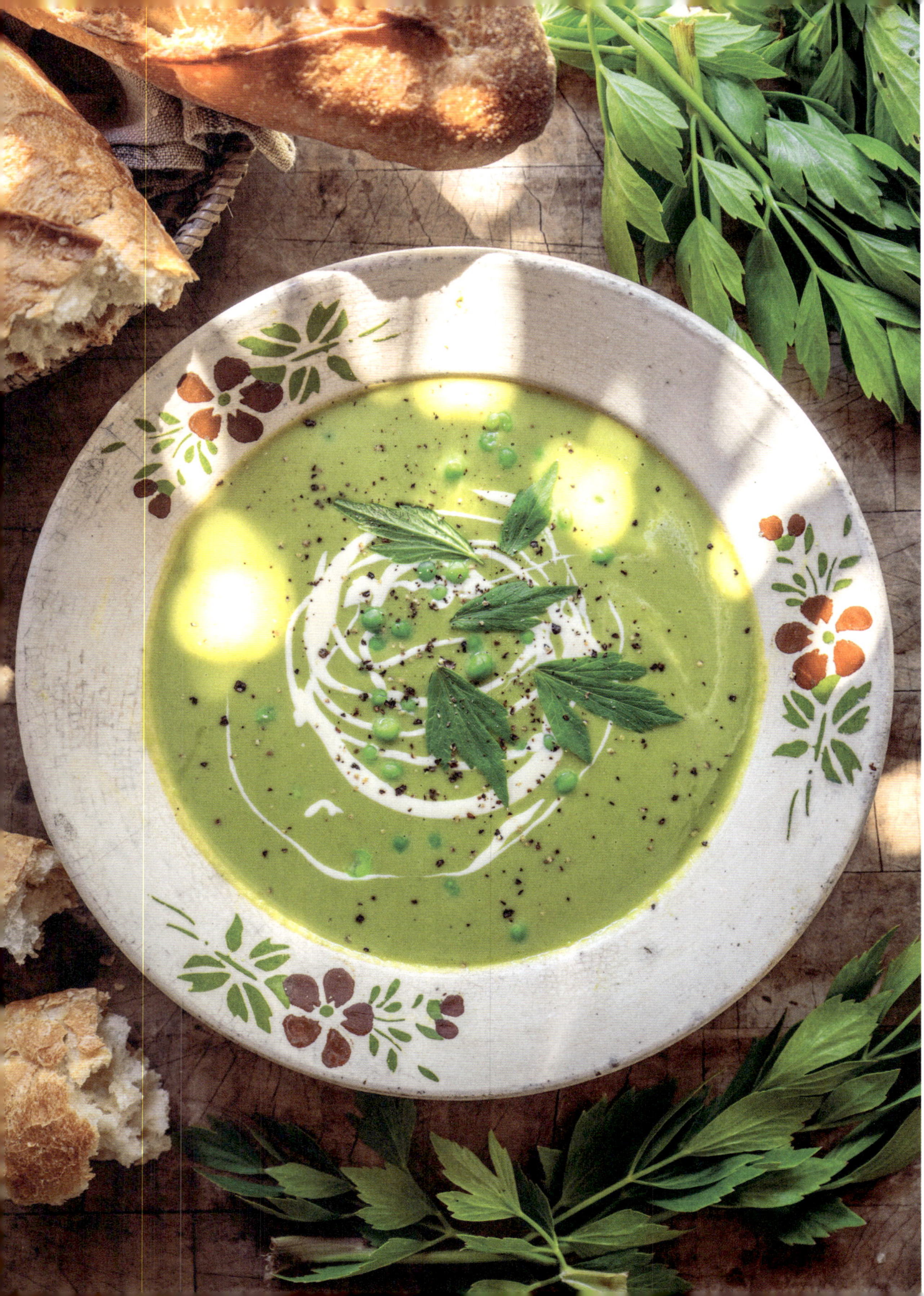

SERVES 2   Spring

Hot or Cold Pea & Lovage Soup

Of all the seasons, spring often has a propensity to be the most fickle when it comes to the weather. Mother Nature has a canny ability to lull you into a false sense of security with balmy, sun-drenched days, yet she can cruelly cast them aside in the blink of an eye, and in their place come bitter winds and monsoon rains. I like to think this recipe keeps you one step ahead of these curveballs, as it is equally good eaten chilled on a beautiful temperate day, as it is served warm with butter-laden, crusty bread on a chilly, drizzly day.

a knob of grass-fed butter, for frying
1 large onion, finely diced
2 garlic cloves, finely sliced
600ml (20fl oz) vegetable stock
750g (1lb 10oz) peas, fresh or frozen
2 tablespoons chopped lovage leaves, plus a few extra sprigs to garnish
juice of ½ lemon
200ml (7fl oz) double cream, plus extra to garnish
flaky sea salt and freshly ground black pepper

Heat the butter in a saucepan, then add the onion and garlic along with a pinch of sea salt and sweat down until they have become translucent, around 6–7 minutes.

Pour in the vegetable stock and bring to the boil. Once boiling, add the peas and simmer for around 2–3 minutes. Remove the pan from the heat and stir in the lovage, lemon juice and double cream. Set aside to cool.

Once cooled, transfer to a blender and whizz until completely smooth. (If you want to retain some texture, reserve a few spoonfuls of peas to add back into the soup later.) Check the seasoning, adding a pinch of black pepper and more salt if required.

Serve chilled or warm with crusty bread, drizzled with a little extra cream and garnished with a few lovage leaves and a twist of black pepper, if wished.

Broad Bean, Pea, Mint, Viola & Sheep's Cheese Toasts

It was a picture-perfect spring day in the countryside, with blossom and blooms everywhere. The farm was to be the backdrop for a party I was hosting to celebrate a friend's forthcoming nuptials. I remember so clearly thinking about how to capture her spirit in the menu for the day, so I set upon an idea that every dish should be bursting with colour, florals and fresh flavours. And so these delicious, delicate toasts were born. We have since made these special toasts to celebrate weddings, engagements, new babies and many other joyful moments.

110g (4oz) broad beans
150g (5½oz) peas
zest and juice of ½ unwaxed lemon
extra virgin olive oil, for drizzling
90g (3¼oz) sheep's cheese
1 bunch of mint
4 slices of sourdough bread
1–2 garlic cloves, peeled
a small handful of viola flowers
flaky sea salt and freshly ground black pepper

Place a pan of cold salted water over a high heat and bring to the boil. Tip in the broad beans and peas and simmer for around 1 minute. Lift them out with a slotted spoon and plunge them straight into cold water. Drain well and pat dry.

Pod the broad beans, removing the bitter outer skin, leaving you with bright green beans. Tip most of the podded beans and peas into a mixing bowl, reserving a few to garnish the toasts later. Add a pinch of salt and pepper, the lemon zest and juice, a small drizzle of olive oil and most of the sheep's cheese, again reserving a little for garnish. Using the back of a fork, carefully press the peas and beans, mashing them and mixing them with the other ingredients while still holding onto some of their texture.

Roughly chop the mint, reserving a few whole leaves for garnish, then mix the chopped mint with the smashed beans.

Drizzle the sourdough bread with a little olive oil, then toast on a hot griddle pan or a barbecue. Once golden and crisp, rub a garlic clove over the toasts and slice to size.

Pile up the toasts with the smashed peas and beans and drizzle with a little more olive oil. Garnish them with the reserved whole peas, beans, crumbled sheep's cheese and mint leaves, and add some viola flowers.

Serve on a pretty platter with a glass of something fresh and sparkling.

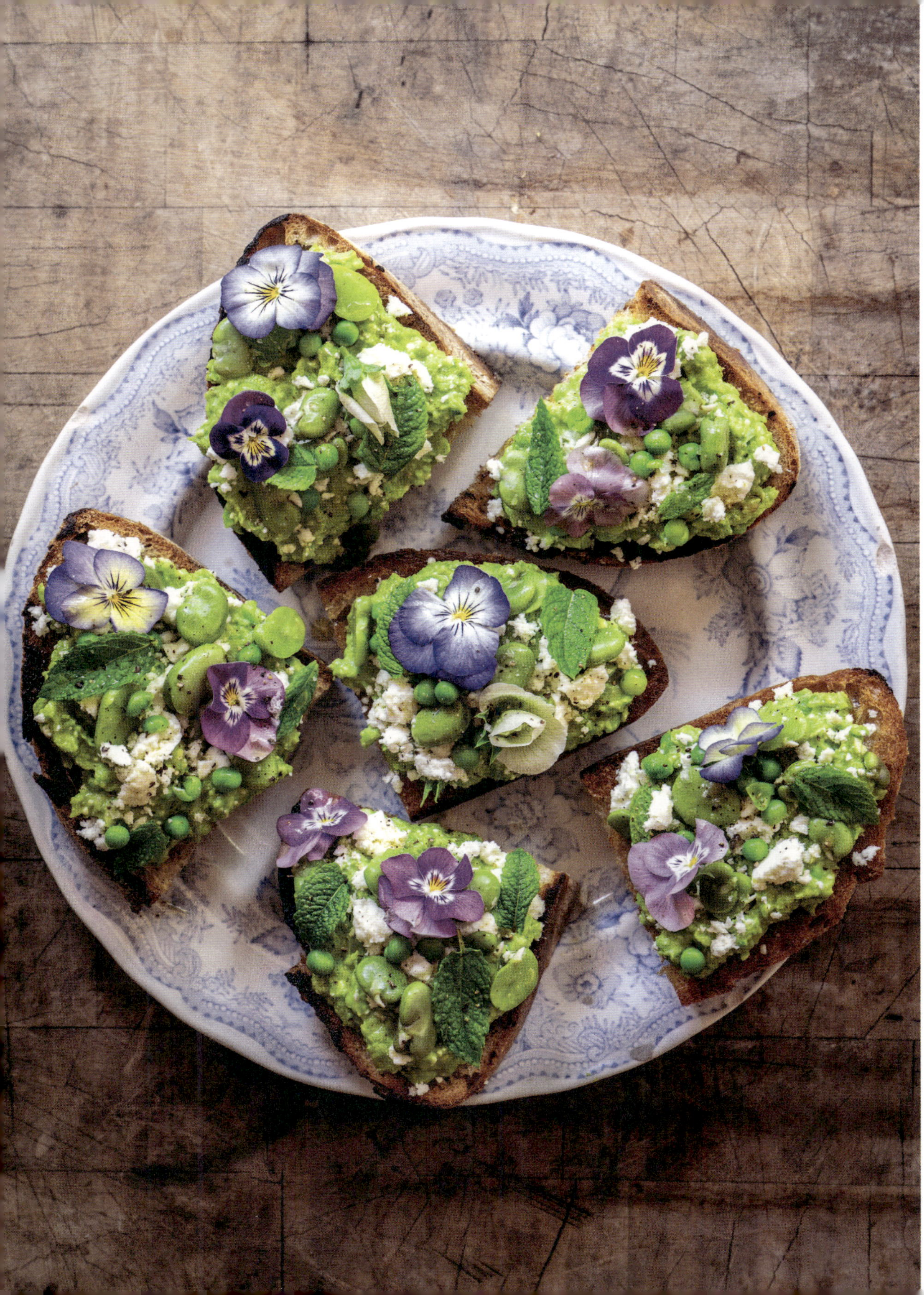

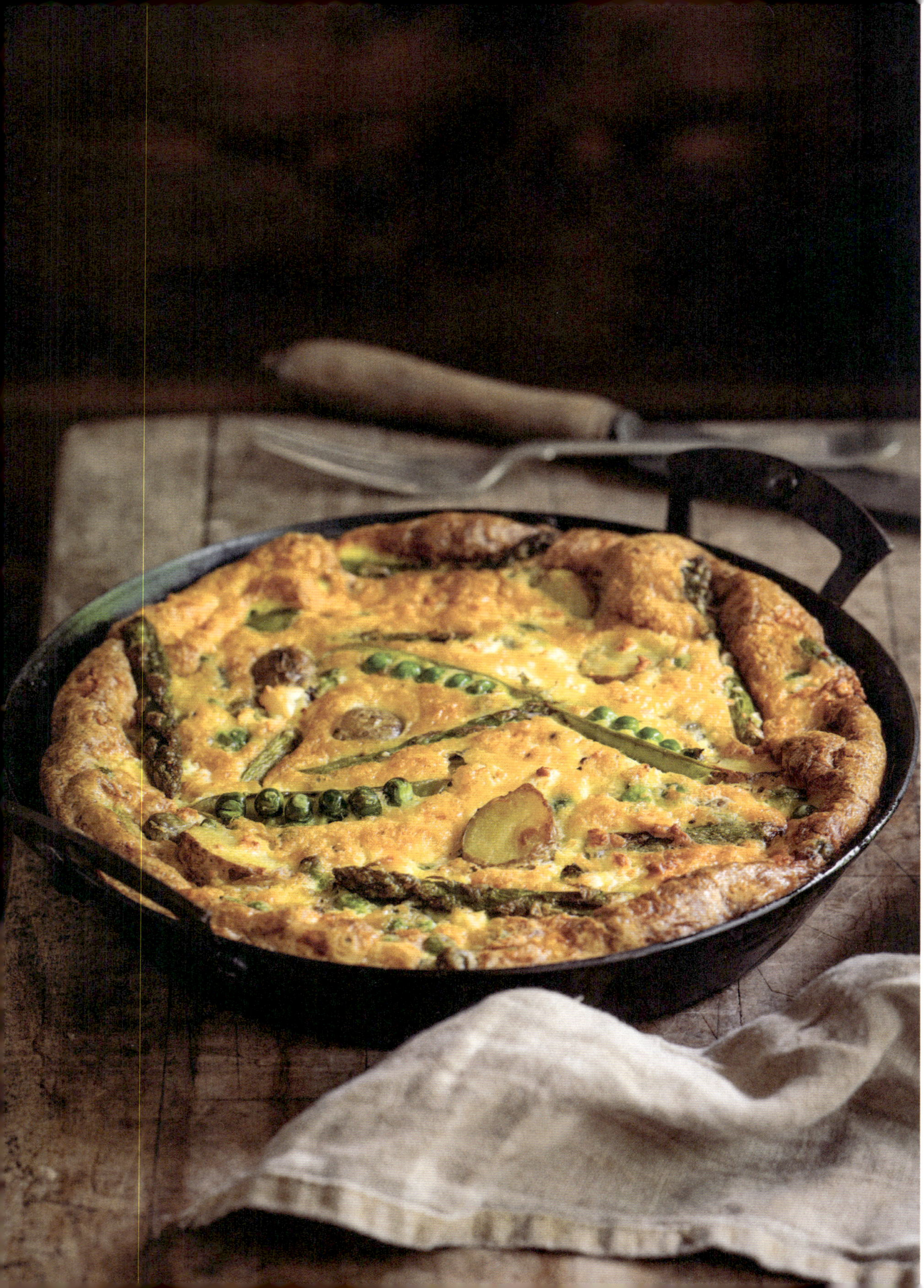

New Potato, Sheep's Cheese, Asparagus, Pea & Mint Frittata

Eating with the seasons is fundamental to how I live my life. It is an innate part of my existence, where my biological clock starts to crave produce that is coming into bloom. Because of this, you will find lots of my recipes are flexible and interchangeable. For example, once the fleeting asparagus season is over, you could move onto courgettes, or perhaps as the summer rumbles on, swap in tomatoes and basil; squash and red onions make a lovely autumnal version; in winter, spinach or kale pair with maincrop potatoes. The principle of this frittata remains the same throughout the year, but the joy comes from swapping the delicious, ever-changing veg.

100g (3½oz) new potatoes, scrubbed (I like to use Charlotte potatoes)
5 asparagus spears, trimmed
150g (5½oz) peas
a knob of grass-fed butter
1 small onion, finely sliced
a drizzle of organic rapeseed oil
6 large organic and/or free-range eggs
2 tablespoons double cream
200g (7oz) sheep's cheese, crumbled
100g (3½oz) mint, roughly chopped
2–3 spring onions, sliced
flaky sea salt and freshly ground black pepper

Preheat the oven to 190°C/375°F/gas mark 5.

Quarter the potatoes, then tip them into a saucepan of cold salted water and bring to the boil. Once boiling, cook for 4–5 minutes until they are tender but still with some bite. Strain, then leave the potatoes in the saucepan to steam for a few minutes.

In a second saucepan filled with salted boiling water, add the asparagus and cook for about 1 minute, then add the peas and cook for a further minute. Drain the veg, then plunge into cold water and set to one side.

Place a cast-iron frying pan over a medium heat and add the butter. Add the onion with a pinch of salt and sweat down until it has become translucent. This should take around 6–7 minutes.

Turn the heat up and drizzle in a little rapeseed oil. Tip in the potatoes, season well and allow them to caramelize on one side. This will take around 5–6 minutes.

Meanwhile, whisk the eggs and double cream together in a mixing bowl. Add half of the crumbled sheep's cheese along with a big pinch of black pepper, a generous pinch of sea salt and most of the mint, reserving a little to scatter over the top of the frittata once finished.

Give the potatoes and onions a mix, then scatter over the blanched asparagus and peas. Sprinkle in the spring onions, then pour in the creamy egg mixture. Scatter the remaining sheep's cheese over the top.

Bake in the oven for around 30–35 minutes. Once the frittata is set, I like to pop it under a very hot grill for the last 2–3 minutes so it gets a nice bubbly crust.

Scatter over the remaining mint and serve with a sharply dressed leafy salad.

Granny's Cheese & Bacon Swirls

My wonderful grandparents were not materialistic, they were both brought up in humble surroundings by families who were deeply connected to the land and their local community. My granny's mother was a dressmaker for the fashionable women of the 1920s, and my grampy's father was a chauffeur for the family living in the 'big house', Downton Abbey-style. They lived through the war, starting their married life at a time when so much was still needing to be rebuilt. They never talked much about what happened during the previous decades and instead focused their energy on what needed to be done now. My granny was the sort of soul who would do anything for another person. Her home was always warm and welcoming. No matter how brief your visit, you were never without a hug, a plate of biscuits and a hot drink. When it was time to gather as a family, in celebration or commiseration, she would put on the most wonderful spreads, never without a plate of her famous cheese and bacon swirls. This is my family silver, so to speak, but I know Granny would have no qualms with me giving it away; she would have given you her last shilling. I love the thought of you incorporating one of our special family recipes into your own repertoire, and creating your own memories as you catch up over a plateful of these, cup of tea in hand.

a knob of grass-fed butter
1 onion, finely chopped
4 rashers of smoked streaky bacon, chopped
2–3 spring onions, finely chopped
1 teaspoon wholegrain mustard
200g (7oz) clothbound Cheddar, grated
2 organic and/or free-range eggs
flaky sea salt and freshly ground black pepper

For the rough puff pastry
400g (14oz) stoneground unbleached white flour, plus extra for dusting
200g (7oz) grass-fed butter, fridge-cold and diced
1 tablespoon flaky sea salt
200ml (7fl oz) water

See overleaf for method.

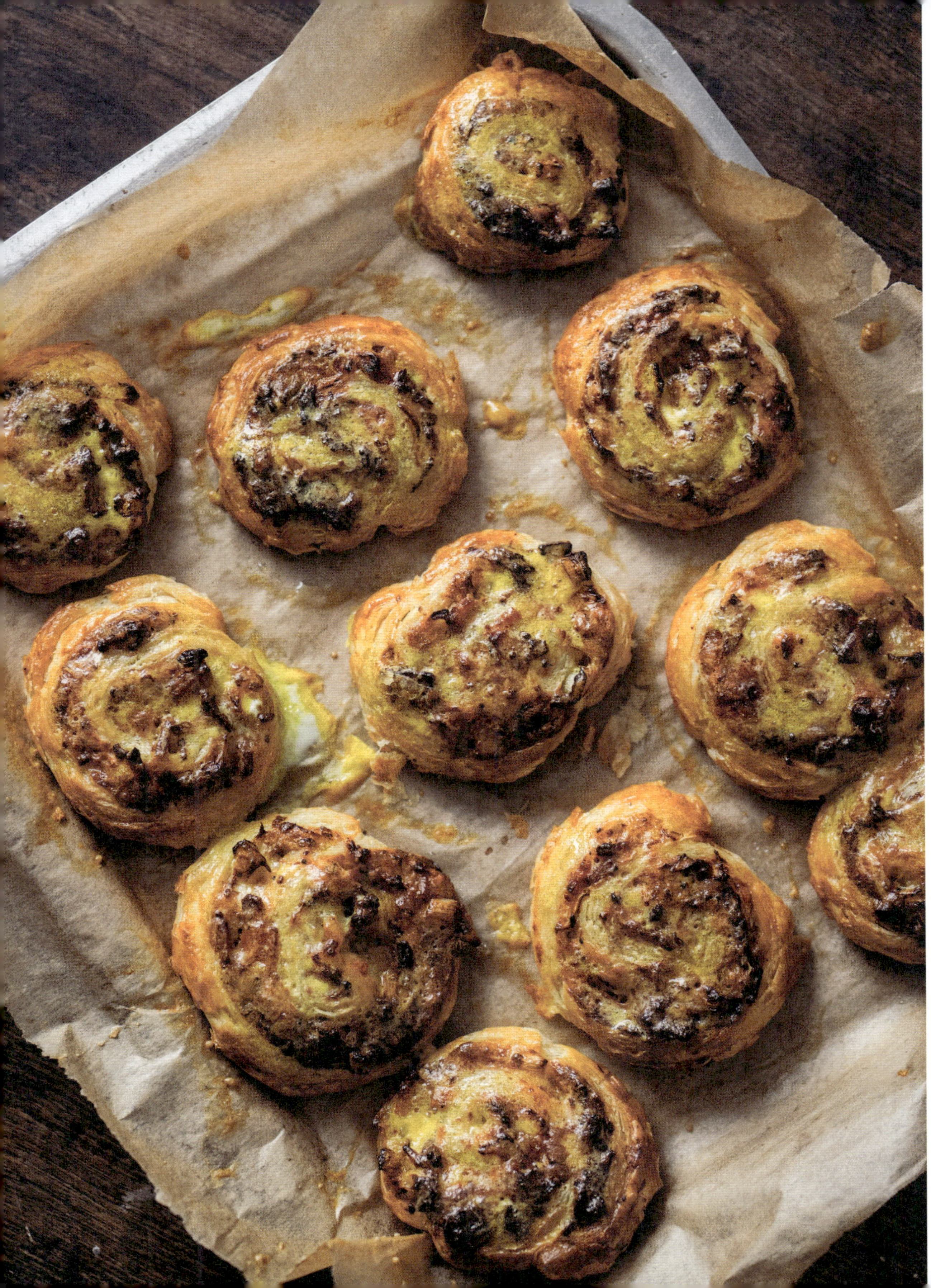

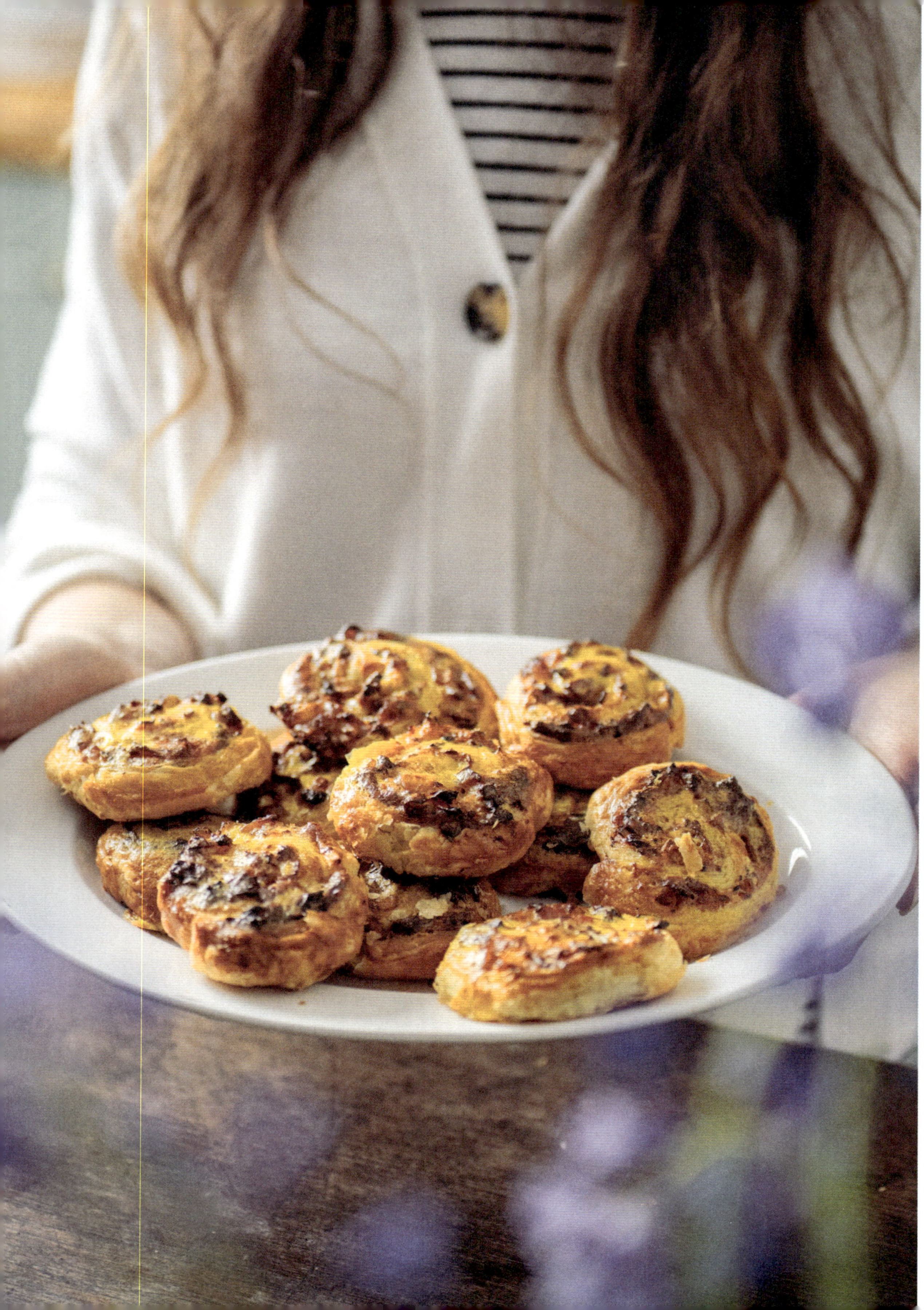

Preheat the oven to 180°C/350°F/gas mark 4. Line a baking tray with greaseproof paper.

First, make the pastry. Place the flour in a mixing bowl and add the cold, diced butter and salt. Slowly pour in the water, gently mixing together without breaking up the butter, then form into a rough dough (it will feel quite dry). Wrap in baking parchment and place in the fridge to chill for 1 hour.

Remove the dough from the fridge. On a flour-dusted work surface, roll it into a rectangle 1cm (½in) thick. Fold either end to the centre, then fold in half top to bottom. You should end up with something that looks a little like a book. Turn the pastry 90 degrees, then roll out and repeat the process once again. This is called laminating. Place the pastry back in the fridge and leave for another hour.

Remove the dough from the fridge and repeat the laminating process with two more folds. Roll, fold, roll, fold. You should have folded the pastry four times in total. Place the pastry back in the fridge for another hour, and then it's ready to use.

To make the filling, set a cast-iron frying pan over a low–medium heat and add the knob of butter. Once sizzling, add the onion along with a pinch of salt and sweat for 7–8 minutes, or until it has become soft and translucent. Tip the onion into a mixing bowl and set to one side.

Increase the heat, then fry off the bacon until the fat has rendered and the lardons are crispy and golden. Tip the bacon into the bowl of onions.

Add the spring onions to the mixing bowl along with the mustard and grated Cheddar.

Once the mixture is completely cool, add 1 egg and mix well to combine. Season with a pinch of salt and pepper.

Whisk the second egg in a separate bowl to create an egg wash.

Dust the worktop with a little flour and roll out the pastry into a thin rectangle.

Spoon the filling mixture into the centre of the pastry and spread it out evenly across the surface, leaving a 1cm (½in) border along one long edge. Roll the pastry from the other long edge to form a log. Egg wash the pastry border and seal the log. Place the log in the fridge and chill for 1 hour to allow the pastry to firm up.

Once chilled, use a sharp knife to cut the log into discs 1cm-width (½ inch) and lay each swirl onto the lined baking tray. Egg wash the top and sides of each swirl. Bake in the oven for 25–30 minutes, or until the pastry is beautifully golden and crisp.

Slide the swirls onto a wire rack and leave to cool for 10 minutes or so.

Pack up to take with you on a picnic, or serve them as part of an afternoon tea or any gathering needing delicious snacks. The swirls are great to make ahead. You can freeze them at the raw stage, then defrost and bake them later. Or you can freeze them once baked and all you'll need to do is defrost them and gently warm through in the oven. They will keep well in either state, wrapped in greaseproof paper and stored in an airtight container in the freezer, for up to 6 months.

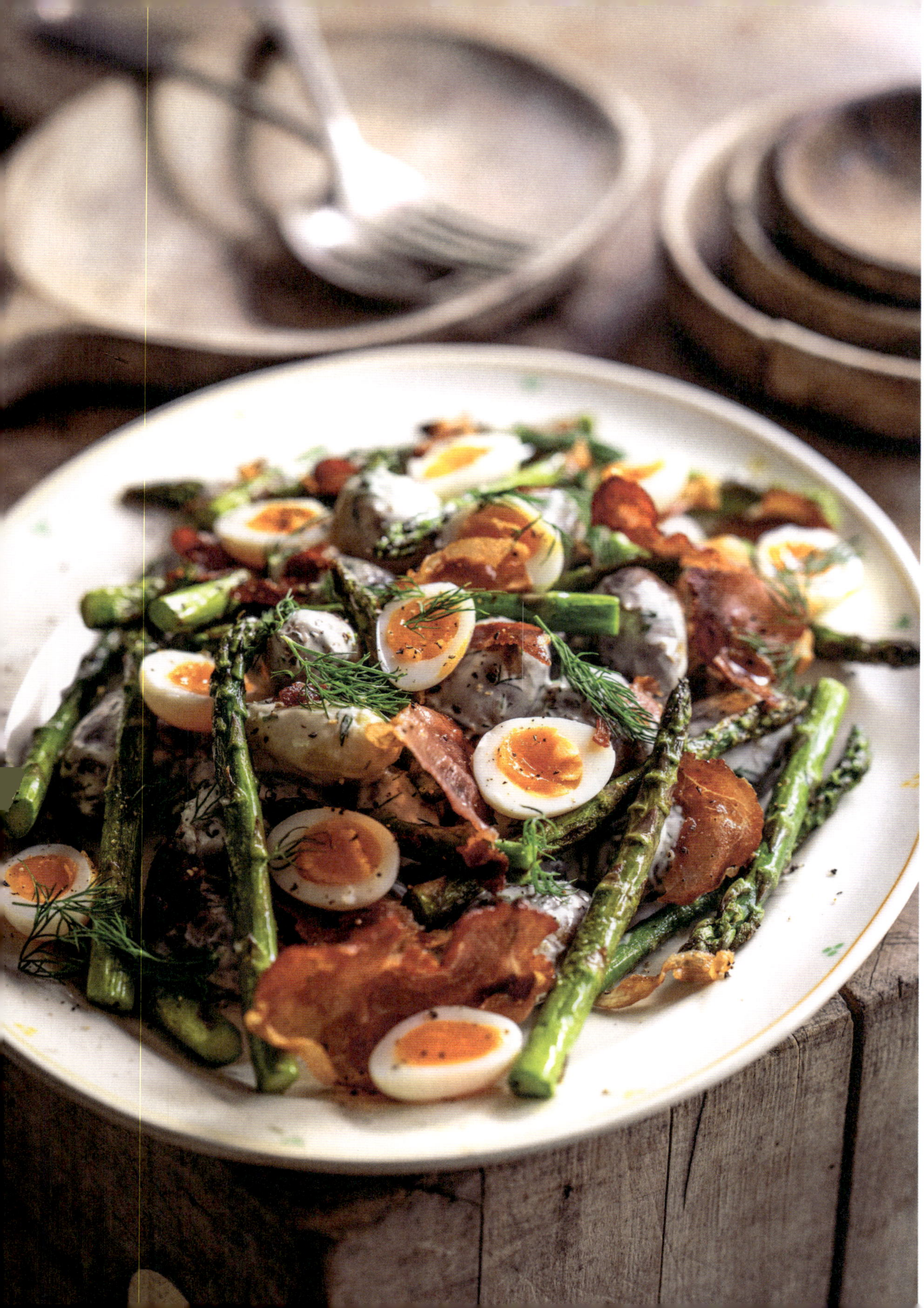

SERVES 4   Spring

Jersey Royals with Quail's Eggs & Asparagus

Having been born in Guernsey and lived on the very point of the island, I'm *au fait* with a salty sea breeze. In fact, where I spent my formative years would have been ideal growing ground for the famous Jersey Royal. You see, it's the saltiness in the air and soil, as well as the seaweed hauled up from the beaches below for use as a fertilizer, that make the Jersey Royal so special.

Sadly though, these days the king of new potatoes is mistreated by corporations, who are more interested in profit than taste. Most Jersey Royals are sold suffocated in plastic bags with their fine soil mercilessly washed away. This treatment does nothing to enhance their texture. If you can find them in retailers sold in paper bags, do hoover them up with relish.

300g (10½oz) Jersey Royal potatoes, scrubbed and any larger ones halved
a knob of grass-fed butter
6 quail's eggs
1 bunch of asparagus, woody ends trimmed
6 slices of air-dried ham
a few sprigs of fresh dill, roughly chopped
flaky sea salt

For the dressing
3 tablespoons mayonnaise
3 tablespoons organic natural yogurt
a small bunch of dill, roughly chopped
2 tablespoons lemon juice, plus extra to finish
flaky sea salt and freshly ground black pepper

Fill a medium saucepan with cold water, add a pinch of salt and set over a high heat.

Add the potatoes, bring to the boil and simmer for around 20 minutes, or until tender. Once cooked, drain the potatoes into a colander and leave them to steam while you prepare the dressing.

To make the dressing, add the mayonnaise, yogurt, dill, lemon juice and a pinch of salt and pepper in a large bowl and mix thoroughly. Check the seasoning and adjust as necessary. You want this dressing to be quite salty and sharp, as it will season all the other ingredients.

Tip the cooked potatoes into the dressing bowl and stir through, allowing each potato to become generously coated. Set to one side.

Preheat the oven to 190°C/375°F/gas mark 5.

Fill a small saucepan with boiling water and place over a medium–high heat. Carefully lower in the quail's eggs. Boil for 2 minutes, then remove and immediately plunge into cold water. Allow to cool and then peel and slice each egg in half.

Take a frying pan and set over a medium heat. Add a knob of butter and allow it to sizzle, then throw in the asparagus along with a pinch of salt. Allow and the spears to caramelise for around 4 minutes, ensuring they retain some bite and have a nice colour.

Line a baking tray with greaseproof paper. Spread out the air-dried ham and place in the oven. After exactly 2 minutes, check the ham is beautifully crisp; if it needs a little longer, carefully watch it, as it doesn't take long for it to catch and go too far. Once crispy and golden, remove from the oven and leave to cool.

To assemble the dish, tip the dressed potatoes onto a large platter. Scatter over the asparagus spears, quail's eggs, crispy ham and dill. Finish with a squeeze of lemon, and serve immediately.

Baked New Potatoes with Chives, Cornish Yarg & Hot Cheese Sauce

One of life's most simple and arguably best delights is freshly pulled potatoes from the garden in springtime. There is something magical about the smell of warm earth and the anticipation of the treasures that are waiting for you below. While you cannot beat a new potato treated simply with a smidge of butter, some robust sea salt and perhaps a few mint leaves, I love potatoes so much that I feel they need to be celebrated – elevated even – so here is my super-indulgent, jubilant ode to the humble new potato.

300g (10½oz) new potatoes, scrubbed (I like to use Charlotte potatoes)
a drizzle of organic rapeseed oil
3 tablespoons cider vinegar
grass-fed butter
150g (5½oz) Cornish Yarg cheese, sliced
40g (1½oz) chives, flowers picked and stems chopped
flaky sea salt and freshly ground black pepper

For the cheese sauce
2 organic and/or free-range egg yolks
300g (10½oz) crème fraîche
70g (2½oz) clothbound Cheddar, grated
50g (1¾oz) Old Winchester cheese, grated
a small pinch of nutmeg

Preheat the oven to 190°C/375°F/gas mark 5.

Tip the new potatoes into a roasting tray, drizzle with a generous glug of oil and a big pinch of sea salt, then give everything a shake to ensure the potatoes are well covered. Bake in the oven for around 45–50 minutes.

Remove the potatoes from the oven and leave to cool for just a few minutes. Slice them down the centre, not quite all the way through, season the flesh with salt and pepper, then douse with a generous splash of cider vinegar. Add a little knob of butter to each potato, then take a slice of Cornish Yarg and wedge it into the centre, scattering over the chopped chives as you go. Set aside.

To make the cheese sauce, set a pan of simmering water over a high heat and place a heatproof bowl over the pan, making sure the bowl doesn't touch the water. Add the egg yolks and crème fraîche to the bowl and whisk vigorously until the mixture thickens. Remove the bowl from the heat and tip in the grated cheeses, a pinch of salt and pepper and a small pinch of nutmeg and carefully mix to combine.

Serve immediately, dunking the vinegary potatoes into the rich, hot cheese sauce or drizzling it over them.

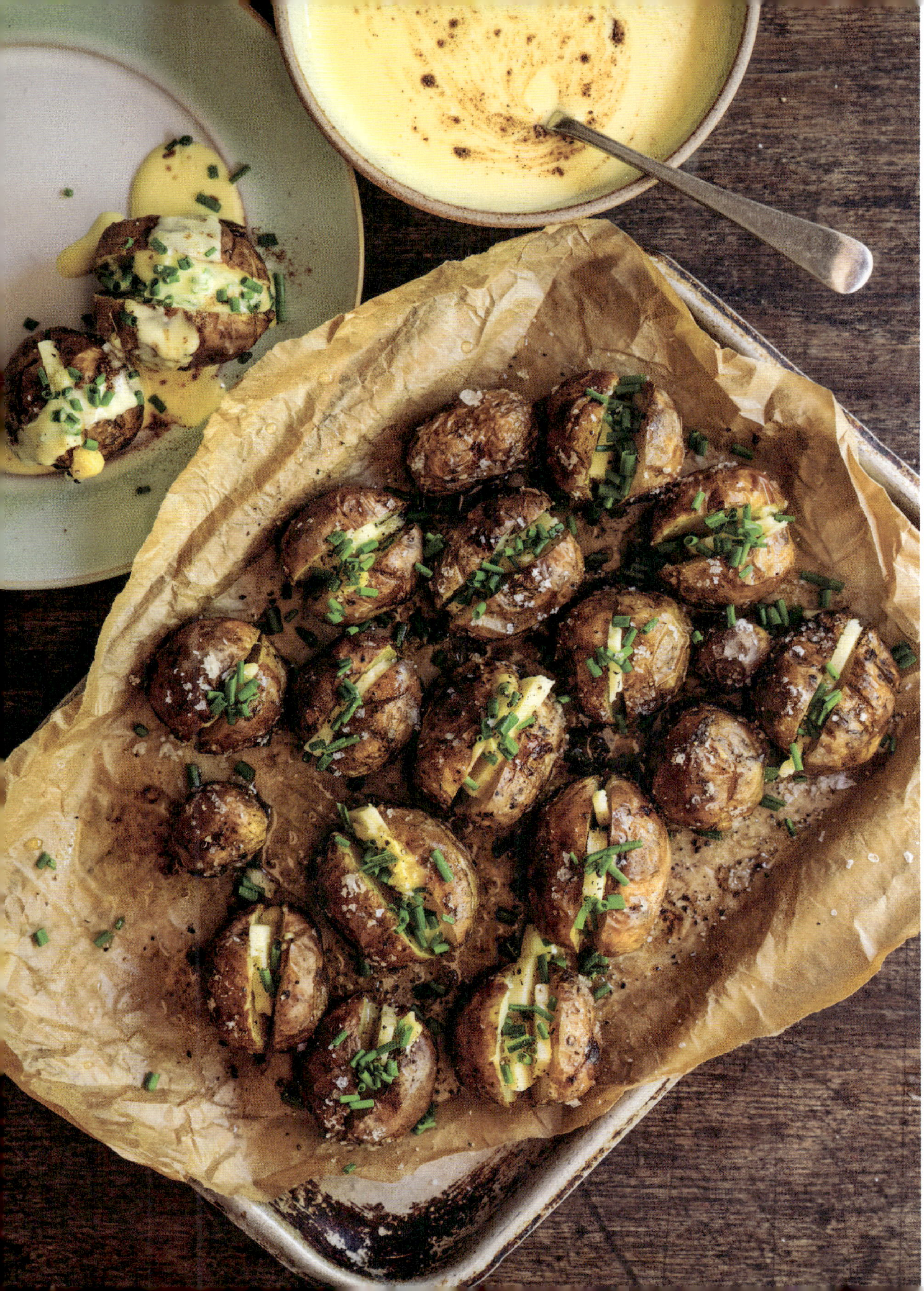

Growing Our Own Food

The urge to grow your own food is instinctive. I have had it for as long as I can remember, and often refer to it as my 'call to the wild'. When life becomes out of kilter, the call becomes louder, there is a primal longing to reach for nature and put my hands in the soil. It truly is the best medicine, no matter what the ailment.

Growing up in rural Devon, during a time before the internet and the immense connectivity that wraps around our lives today, my childhood was filled with simple pleasures – climbing trees, walking the dog, catching fish in the river and growing food in our garden. Living a life spent outside more often than in undoubtedly gave Mother Nature a hand in raising me. I noted when the first blackberries were ripe for picking, how the wisteria would gently scent an early summer morning, the moment the first snowdrops were brave enough to push through the frozen soil in bleak mid-winter. None of these natural phenomena escaped my fascination. The rhythms of nature, understanding her ways and witnessing how changes in the weather affected the usual order of things has provided me with useful tools to navigate my life today.

Tending to plants has helped me through some of my most difficult times. Gardening has provided me with a sense of purpose, knowing that my crops' survival relies upon my care and attention. When the world seems so big and full of so much complexity, being able to rely on nature to remind you what is truly important in life is a gift that none of us should ever take for granted.

It is, of course, wonderful to have a big garden with a greenhouse and all the tools required to cultivate the land, but no matter where I have lived, or what stage of life I have been at, I have always gravitated to finding a patch of earth, or just a few pots to grow things. Don't let the pull of social media with its glorified images of perfection put you off; there are many ways to connect with the land, no matter whether you are urban or rural, have vast amounts of space or just a few window boxes here and there. Growing your own is accessible to everyone.

I know I'm not alone in the desire to roll up my sleeves and get my hands in the soil. Over the last few years there have been rising numbers of people signing up for allotments. In some areas, waiting lists can be up to ten years. The number of domestic seeds sold per year in the UK has been increasing rapidly, and 'pick your owns', from flowers to pumpkins, have been popping up around the country, often with queues down the farm track.

Growing your own food not only has countless benefits for your mental and physical wellbeing, it has a huge impact on our diets, too. Households who grow their own consume on average 40% more fruits and vegetables per day, often enjoying plants that are not accessible in the mainstream market, and putting more diversity, good bacteria, and a greater range of vitamins and minerals into their bodies. However, even with all this activity around self-sufficiency, we are a long way off times gone by. During the 'Dig for Victory' campaign of World War II, over 20% of food consumed was homegrown, yet today this stands at just 2.5%. Most of the food consumed in the UK comes out of the factories and facilities owned by just a handful of large companies around the world.

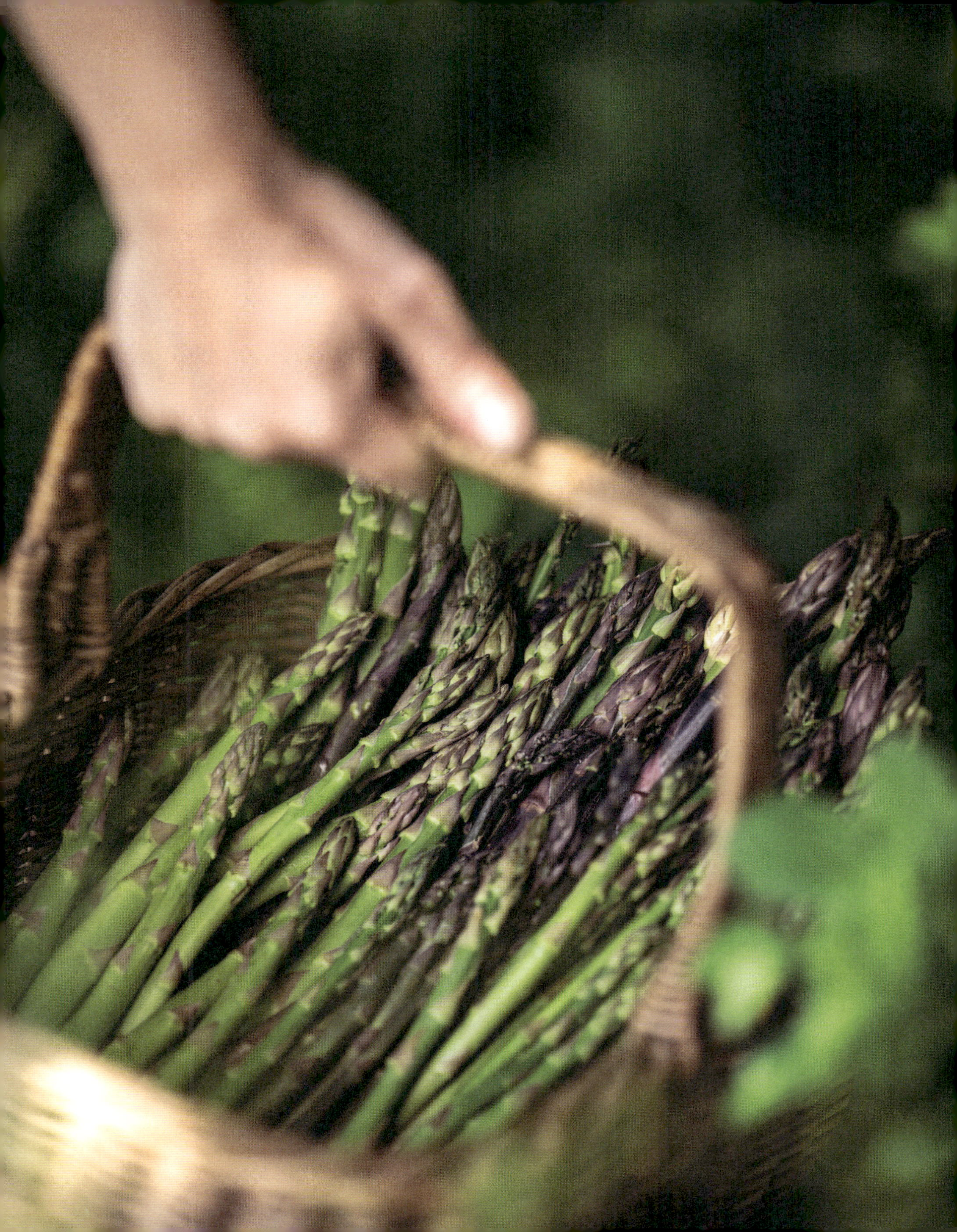

With the acceleration of climate shocks and natural disasters, and the persistence of structural inequality within the UK and globally, food has become an emblem of the troubles around us. Growing your own food is one of the ways we can reclaim our food sovereignty, as outlined by an organization close to my heart, the Landworkers Alliance: 'Food sovereignty is the right of peoples to healthy and culturally appropriate food produced through ecologically sound and sustainable methods and their right to define their own food and agriculture systems. It puts the aspirations and needs of those who produce, distribute and consume food at the heart of food systems and policies rather than the demands of markets and corporations.'

Over the last 50 years, we have moved to a food system where just about all the food found in supermarkets is now not only processed and packed in a small number of facilities, but also distributed through highly centralized networks. Much of what happens is controlled by organizations outside the UK, which don't have the British grower's or consumer's interests at their heart. In a world of shady economics, where the polluter doesn't pay the environmental and social costs, these systems make good economic sense to big business. As a result of all this, the actual story of where our food comes from is hidden from most shoppers.

Not only is there a lack of transparency in these conflated global supply chains, much of the produce that is imported is misaligned with our seasons. You see, supermarkets require straightforward, risk-free supply chains. They have self-selected to enforce a litany of expensive hurdles for producers to jump through to reduce any reputational risk from a poor harvest. They want food on their shelves all year round at the lowest price they can get away with paying. This means small growers, diverse varieties and seasonal eating simply do not stand a chance in their highly geared environment. With their eyes fixed on 'simpler' large-scale European and worldwide producers they have our British growers by the scruff of their necks, demanding that they either scale up or step out. Sadly, all too often it has been the latter.

Working in a cool, wet and hilly island nation, British farmers are unable to supply year-round strawberries, asparagus or tomatoes, or even to grow popular ingredients, such as oranges, avocados and lemons, meaning an element of imported food will always be required. However, Britain imports 46% of its fresh vegetables and 86% of its fruit. While, according to figures from the National Farmers' Union (NFU), 82% of British beef production, at times, has been exported to the EU. Our diets have become misaligned not only with what we are capable of producing domestically, but also with the time of year we should be consuming it.

In the UK, we produce some of the finest food in the world: pasture-fed beef, lamb, hogget and mutton that is nutrient-dense and full of flavour, meaning a little can go a long way; freshly landed seafood, from sparkling white fish to bountiful crabs, rope-grown mussels and seasonal treats, such as clams; nutrient-rich veg, such as kale, cauliflower, leeks, carrots, cabbages, beetroot, mushrooms, sprouts, swede, peas, beans, pumpkins and parsnips – I could dedicate a ballad to each, as I love them so dearly. With herbs and spices, from soft to woody, spicy to aromatic, there is always something available to add depth and nourishment to a meal. There is luscious milk, cream, yogurt and cheese, all rich in good bacteria as well as protein. And there are wild foods, such as game birds, venison, mushrooms, berries, nuts and seeds.

There is so much to tickle our tastebuds at any time of the year – although due to the way our seasons shift some times are more abundant than others. Needless to say, we could and should be eating a diet that is far more connected to British growing seasons, for our own health as well as the health of the planet.

We must begin to take note and reconnect with our landscapes. Notice what is in abundance and when, preserving and using wisely those precious ingredients that may be required for leaner times.

As much as we may adore a summer breakfast of avocado on toast, perhaps we could switch it up with minted smashed peas instead. Or that beautiful asparagus risotto we may crave in midwinter could become purple sprouting broccoli risotto, rich in fibre, vitamins and minerals that our body would far prefer at this time of year. There are so many seasonal swaps we can make to shift our diet in the direction of one that is more appropriate to our landscape.

While I believe we must return to sustainable diets, where the majority of what is consumed can be produced on either our shores or those of our close neighbours', it is impractical to believe we will consume only food with limited food miles. Eating seasonally doesn't always mean eating only British produce. While locally grown fruit might be in abundance during warm summer months, eating only British would mean giving up juicy citrus fruit in the depths of winter, when our bodies require additional vitamins and minerals to flourish. Buying a small amount of well-sourced imported produce can help bring variety into the months of endless root veg and brassicas; the challenge comes from understanding where and how the produce you buy is grown. How do you tell if the tomatoes you're buying are supporting small-scale farmers or exploiting migrant workers? The answer is to buy from somewhere that has transparency within its supply chain. Buying through local farmshops, farmers' markets or box schemes can be a great way to find local, seasonal and organically grown produce. However, it's worth doing some investigation into the outfit you shop from to understand how it operates, as buying 'locally' doesn't automatically mean your fruit and vegetables have been grown locally or produced seasonally.

By reconnecting with the seasons, growing more of our own food and seeking out small-scale, independent farms or networks of producers, we are creating a grassroots movement that breaks the dominance of global corporations. Money is transferred around the local community ensuring that it prospers. Diversity in what is produced and by who begins to flourish once more. Human and planetary health are improved.

We each have the power in our hands to vote for the food system we believe in. Transitioning to a system built around the idea of food sovereignty will unquestionably improve our environment, food security and public health.

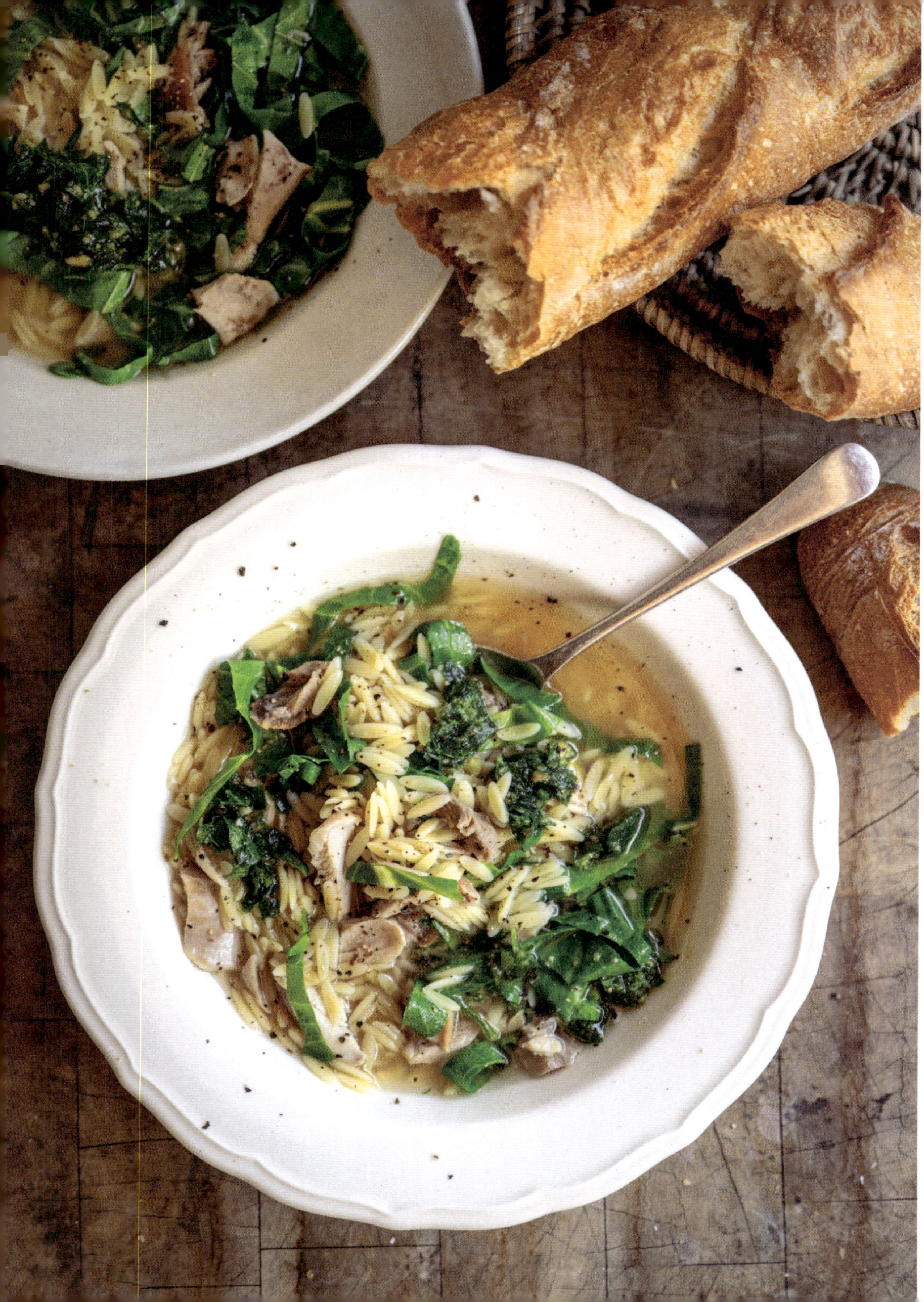

Chicken, Spring Greens & Orzo Broth

The garden has been refreshed after two days of non-stop rain, leaving the sweet scent of earth in the air. Brilliant white spring light illuminates the countryside, showing off glistening green leaves heavy with glassy raindrops. The deluge has washed away the hard edge of winter's grip, allowing a few daring bulbs to push their heads up. After a long winter, during which time the important vitamins and minerals every living being needs to survive are in short supply, my body needs a little nourishment, just like the plants in my garden warming up to spring's glow. Soothing and restorative chicken broth, rich with collagen, is the perfect base for iron-packed, mineral-rich greens, tempered by starchy, slippery pasta. A bowl filled to the brim with vitality.

3–4 free-range chicken thighs or leftover roast chicken
125g (4½oz) orzo
300g (10½oz) spring greens, tough stalks removed and leaves finely shredded
flaky sea salt and freshly ground black pepper

For the stock
1 free-range chicken carcass
2 onions, skin on, quartered
1 leek, chopped into 3 pieces
1 fennel bulb, halved
3–4 bay leaves
a handful of parsley stalks, chopped
½ teaspoon black peppercorns
a pinch of flaky sea salt
3 tablespoons cider vinegar

Preheat the oven to 180°C/350°F/gas mark 4.

Begin by making the stock. In a large stockpot, add the chicken carcass, vegetables, herbs, peppercorns and a good pinch of salt. Fill the pan with cold water, cover with a lid and bring to the boil over a medium heat. Once boiling, skim off the scum that has risen to the top, then turn the heat down to a simmer and leave to bubble gently for around 3 hours. Top up the water level if you need to and skim off any more scum that has risen.

Once the broth has simmered, strain it through a sieve, catching the liquid in a bowl below. Discard the carcass and veg left in the sieve. Add the cider vinegar to the stock, then pour into a saucepan and place over a low heat.

If you are not using leftover roast chicken, season the chicken thighs generously and place on a baking tray. Roast in the oven for 20 minutes. Once cooked, leave to cool until you can handle and shred the meat.

Add the shredded meat to the stock along with the orzo, then turn the heat up and bring the broth to a simmer. Simmer gently for 12 minutes, or until the orzo is almost tender. Add the spring greens for the last 3 minutes of cooking, then taste and adjust the seasoning before ladling into bowls.

Serve with some crusty bread.

Pot-Roast Chicken with Bacon & Barley

Spring — SERVES 4–6

Many moons ago, we worked with a wonderful farm located deep in a Devon valley. It was the perfect location for one of our first free-range poultry enterprises, as its sheltered site made it much harder for airborne diseases to blow over from intensive chicken factories that are an epidemic in this part of the world.

Here we had a breeding flock that lay the eggs which would hatch on the same farm and grow slowly to become the chickens that we sold in both our butcher's shop and through our website. In the breeding flock the hens lived to a good old age, then eventually would finish their lifecycle of laying and become spent. We would sell these old hens at the butcher's counter as 'boiling fowl' – a rather crude name, but one that indicated their purpose.

In this recipe I should be recommending you seek out boiling fowl instead of the chicken advised, but it would be a fool's mission, since in this day and age they simply do not enter the food chain. The sad truth is that most spent hens are slaughtered young and are used as protein meal or oils for animal feed. Millions of birds a year are wasted in this way thanks to a system that is so dysfunctional, I would argue it is now dystopian.

250g (9oz) smoked bacon lardons
2 onions, finely chopped
1 leek, finely sliced
2 garlic cloves, finely chopped
a knob of grass-fed butter
500g (1lb 2oz) mushrooms, sliced
240g (8¾oz) pearl barley
2 bay leaves
2 sprigs of rosemary
3–4 sprigs of thyme
600ml (20fl oz) chicken stock, warmed
1.7kg (3lb 11oz) organic or free-range chicken
100ml (3½fl oz) double cream
a handful of fresh herbs (tarragon, chives or parsley work well here)
flaky sea salt and freshly ground black pepper

Preheat the oven to 190°C/375°F/gas mark 5.

Set a large, cast-iron pot over a medium–high heat. Add the bacon lardons and render down until crispy and golden brown – around 6–7 minutes. Turn the heat down and add the onions, leek and garlic, along with a small pinch of salt, and sweat gently for 7–8 minutes, until softened.

Turn the heat up and add a knob of butter along with the mushrooms. Allow them to caramelize slightly, then tip in the pearl barley, bay leaves, rosemary and thyme and the warm stock. Season the chicken well and place on top of the pearl barley, then cover with foil and roast for 45 minutes.

Remove the foil and roast the chicken for a further 15 minutes, adding a splash of water if needed. Once the chicken is beautifully golden and cooked through, carefully lift it out and leave to rest on a carving board.

Meanwhile, add a little double cream and some fresh herbs to the pan of steaming pearl barley and mix through.

Carve the chicken, giving each person a little bit of both the breast and the leg meat.

Serve with a generous helping of barley and bacon, and perhaps some buttery kale.

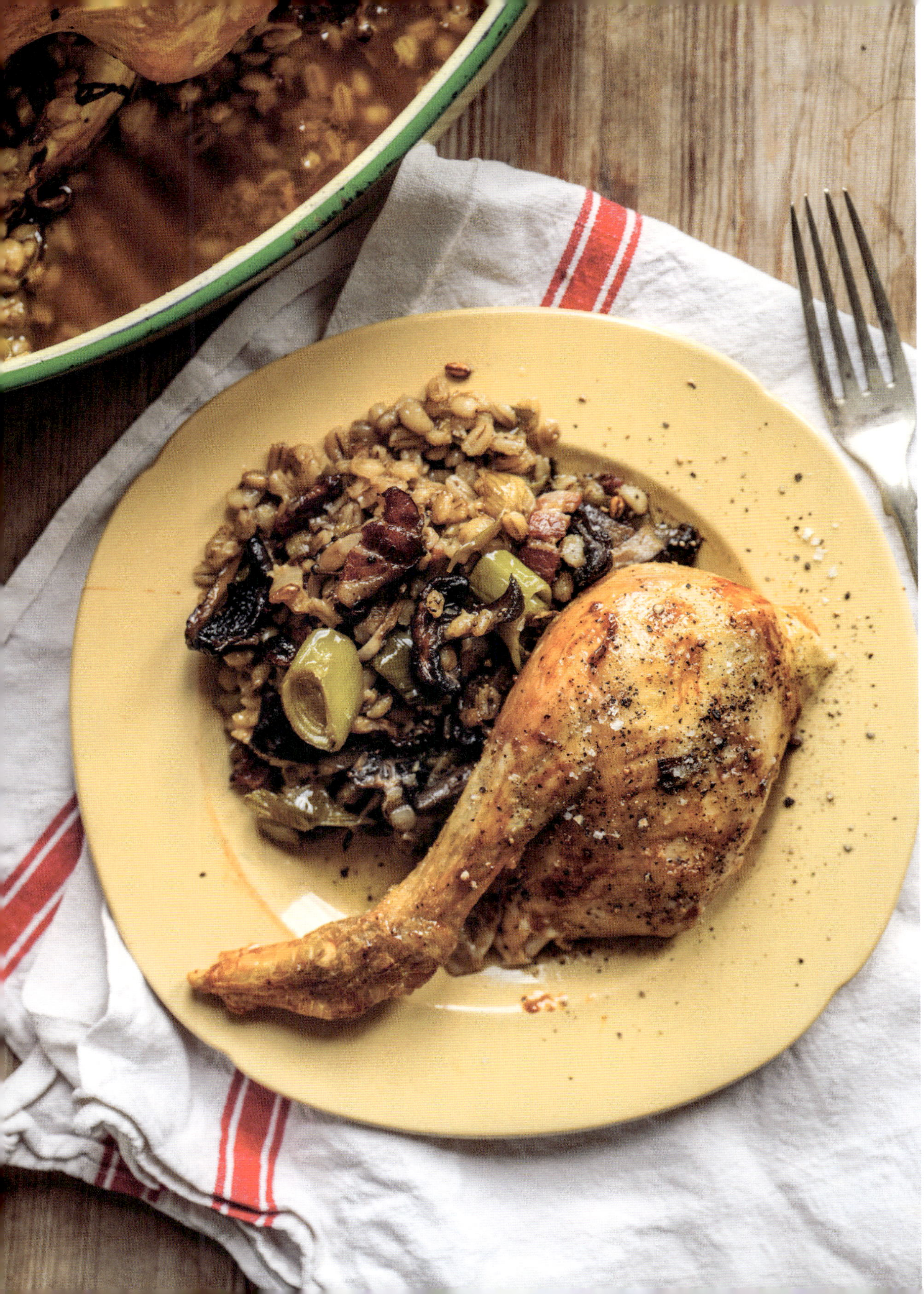

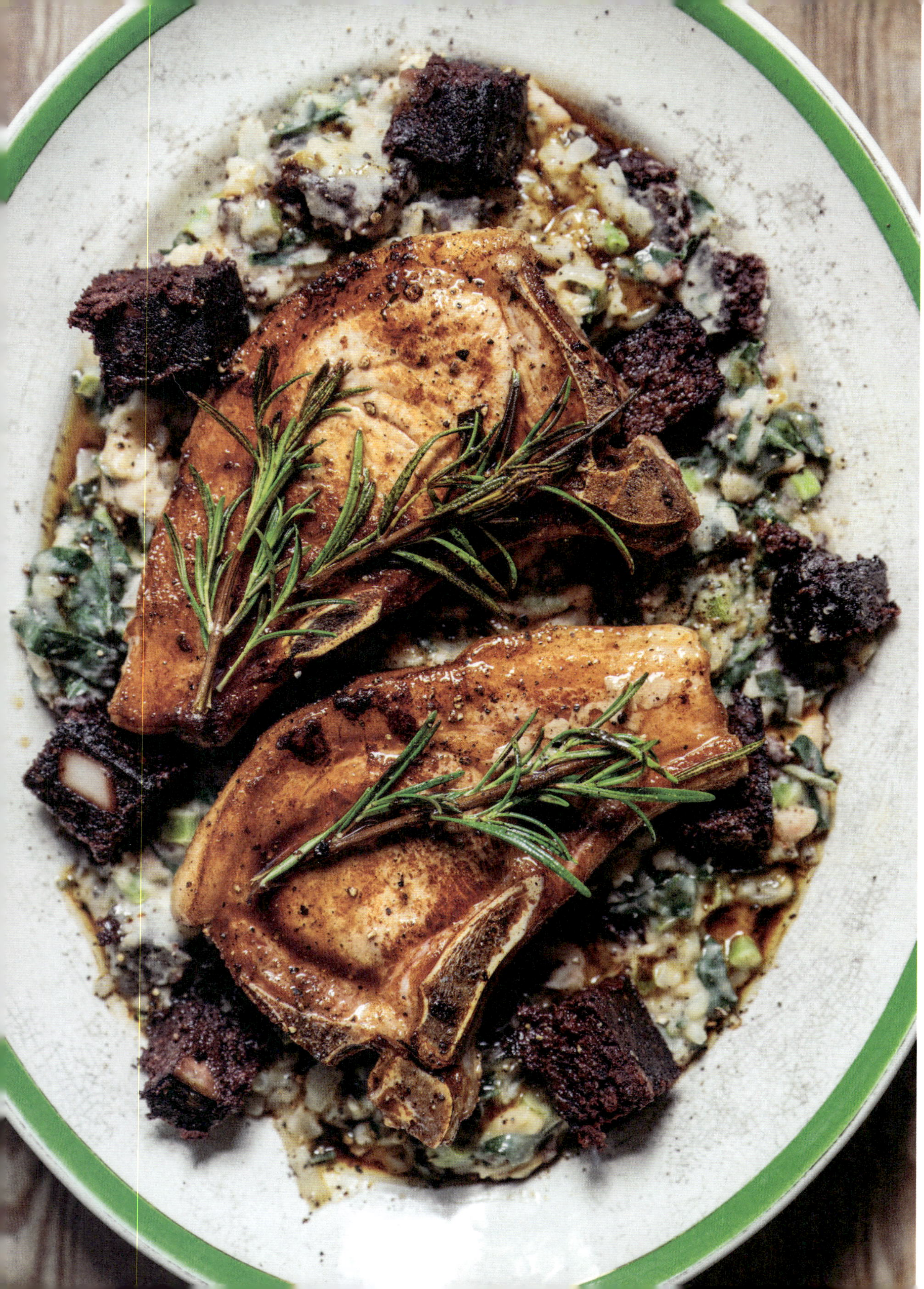

Pork Chops with White Beans, Black Pudding, Kale & Crispy Sage

The landscape is waking up from its deep winter slumber, gently thawing and replacing the frigid silence with the first whispers of spring. Although there is little to shout about in the vegetable garden, most produce having been harvested by now or lost to a lethal combination of weather and pests, what I do have is kale; mountains of the stuff that – come wind, come rain, come several frosts – still stands tall and abundant. There are moments when magic happens in the kitchen. With luck more than judgement, the coming together of this handful of early spring ingredients is divinely satiating.

3–4 kale leaves
a drizzle of extra virgin olive oil
2 garlic cloves, grated
100g (3½oz) black pudding
400g (14oz) can of cannellini, haricot or butter beans, drained but liquid reserved
grated zest and juice of 1 unwaxed lemon
1 tablespoon tahini
2 sprigs of rosemary
flaky sea salt and freshly ground black pepper

For the pork chops
a drizzle of extra virgin olive oil
6 sage leaves
2 free-range pork chops
a knob of grass-fed butter
1 sprig of rosemary

Prepare the kale by rinsing it well in the sink, then pat dry to remove any excess moisture. Pull the leaves away from the stalks. Chop the stalks into 2mm (1/16in) rounds and shred the leaves.

Set a cast-iron frying pan over a medium heat. Drizzle in a little oil and add the kale stalks and grated garlic, let them sizzle for a few seconds, then crumble in the black pudding and gently caramelize. Tip in the white beans, then add the shredded kale leaves, lemon zest and rosemary. Stir well and cook for 2–3 minutes. Add the lemon juice, 1–2 tablespoons of the reserved bean liquid and the tahini and cook for a further 1–2 minutes. Season the beans well with salt and pepper. Using the back of a fork or a potato masher, gently mash the beans to a thick, creamy consistency. Set to one side and keep warm.

Place another cast-iron frying pan over a medium–high heat and drizzle in a little olive oil. Once sizzling, toss in the sage leaves. Fry for 1–2 minutes until aromatic and crispy, then remove from the pan and place on a chopping board lined with a sheet of kitchen paper.

Generously season the chops with salt and pepper, then place them in the hot pan and fry for 2–3 minutes. Turn them over and fry for 2 minutes on the other side. Using a pair of tongs, pick each chop up and press the fat into the pan, holding it there for a couple of minutes, or until the fat crisps and renders. Add a generous knob of butter to the pan along with the rosemary and baste the chops with it for a further 2–3 minutes. Leave to rest for 5–6 minutes.

Spoon generous piles of the creamy beans onto warm plates, then top with a pork chop, along with a spoon of cooking liquor and the crispy sage leaves. Sprinkle the dish with a generous pinch of black pepper and serve.

Malloreddus with Sausage & Fennel Seed Ragu

I first enjoyed a steaming bowl of this perfect marriage between gnocchi and pasta when I was high up a hill in Italy. We had been driving through a particularly beautiful vineyard when the heavens opened. We decided to pull over and take refuge in a pretty trattoria, which on a better day would have had far-reaching views of acres of vines. Inside, the wood fire was lit, and the restaurant was filled with the scent of woodsmoke and cooking. Tables were packed with families and groups of men. Red wine flowed freely. It was heaven.

The name *malloreddus* loosely translates to 'fat little calves', describing the wonderful shape of these perfectly starchy sauce vessels.

400g (14oz) semolina flour or finely ground durum wheat flour, plus extra for dusting
200ml (7fl oz) warm water
a drizzle of extra virgin olive oil
1 onion, finely chopped
3 garlic cloves, chopped
1 teaspoon fennel seeds
½ teaspoon smoked paprika
2 bay leaves
1 sprig of rosemary
4 pork sausages, removed from their skins
100ml (3½fl oz) good red wine
400g (14oz) Preserved Tomatoes (see page 71)
3 tablespoons whole milk
flaky sea salt and freshly ground black pepper
hard cheese, grated, to serve (I like to use pecorino or an English hard cheese, such as Old Winchester)

To make the malloreddus, tip the flour into a mound on a clean work surface and add a pinch of salt. Make a well in the centre large enough to contain the water, then gently pour the water into the well. Using your fingers, gradually mix the flour into the water, slowly incorporating the flour from the sides of the well. As the mixture thickens, use a scraper to scrape up all the flour and add it to the dough. Knead the dough for around 8–9 minutes, until it becomes springy. Once smooth and bouncy, wrap the dough and leave to rest for about an hour.

Once the dough has rested, it's time to shape the malloreddus. Cut off a piece of dough and roll it into a thin cylinder, around 7mm (⅜in) in diameter. Chop this into pieces around 2.5cm (1in) long. Repeat this process until you have used all the dough. Using a ridged gnocchi board, drag the dough pieces down the board with your thumb, one at a time, creating ridged little curls. Leave the shapes to dry out on a tray sprinkled with semolina flour while you make the ragu.

To make the ragu, set a cast-iron casserole pan over a medium-low heat. Drizzle in a glug of olive oil and sauté the onion and garlic along with the fennel seeds, paprika, bay leaves and rosemary for 7–8 minutes, or until the onions are soft and translucent.

Turn the heat up to medium and add the sausage meat, allowing it to sizzle and brown. Turn the heat up a little more, then add the wine and watch it bubble and evaporate for a few minutes.

Turn the heat back down to medium–low and add the tomatoes, followed by the milk. Season with salt and pepper and simmer gently for 25–30 minutes, or until the sauce has thickened. Set to one side and keep warm while you cook the pasta.

Set a pan of heavily salted boiling water over a high heat. Once it reaches a rolling boil, add the pasta to the pan. The shells will float to the top of the pan once cooked, which should take around 3 minutes.

Drain the pasta, add to the ragu and toss through the sauce. Ladle generous servings into warmed bowls. Finish with a drizzle of really good olive oil and a grating or two of hard cheese.

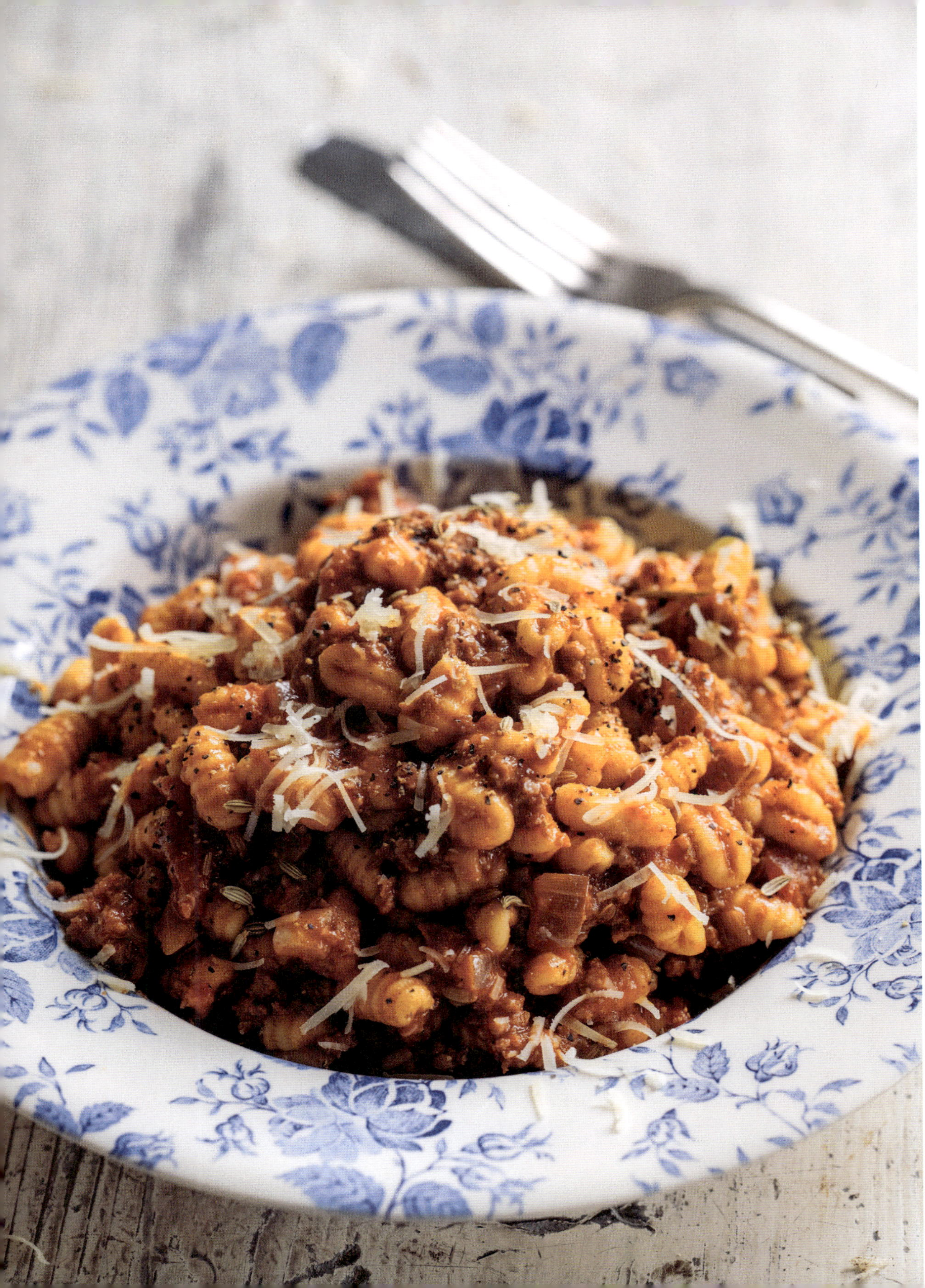

Hogget Liver on Toast with Creamed Nettles

Nettles are one of the greatest gifts for anyone who values seasonal and highly nutritious fresh ingredients. For us gardeners, though, they can be a bit of a plague, springing up with reckless abundance as soon as the ground thaws from its winter slumber. Spring is the moment to enthusiastically pick nettles; the young growth of March and April provides a delicious iron-rich flavour without the toughness you find as the season ticks on. Pick only the tips – the first four or six leaves on each spear – and you are guaranteed to get the most tender and flavourful part of the plant. To gather nettles and avoid their vengeful sting, grab a pair of washing-up gloves, or thick gardening gloves, make sure your arms and legs are well covered and snip away. As soon as you drop your haul into boiling water, the sting will abate, and you'll be left with a wonderful ingredient that can be used in place of spinach or chard.

200g (7oz) nettles
a drizzle of extra virgin olive oil
4 anchovy fillets
3 garlic cloves, 2 finely sliced, 1 left whole
a few sprigs of rosemary, leaves picked and finely chopped
100ml (3½fl oz) double cream
½ teaspoon ground nutmeg
300g (10½oz) grass-fed hogget liver, sliced
1 tablespoon stoneground plain flour
2 slices of sourdough bread
flaky sea salt and freshly ground black pepper

Begin by washing the nettles. Pick out any organic matter, such as grasses or critters that have got caught on the leaves, and discard any tough stalks, keeping only the younger, more supple stalks attached to the leaves. Bring a large pan of well-salted water to the boil, throw in the nettles and blanch for a couple of minutes, then drain. Once cool enough to handle, squeeze the nettles to extract as much water as possible, then chop finely. Set to one side.

Place a cast-iron frying pan over a medium heat. Drizzle in a little olive oil, then add the anchovies, the finely sliced garlic and the rosemary. Sizzle away for a few minutes until the anchovies have all but collapsed, the rosemary is fragrant and the garlic has lightly browned. Add the double cream and leave it to bubble away and reduce by half. Season with the nutmeg and a generous pinch of salt and pepper, then add the blanched nettles. Give everything a good stir, then remove from the heat and set to one side.

Season the liver well with salt and pepper. Place the flour in a small bowl, then dust each piece of seasoned liver until it is lightly coated in flour.

Add a drizzle of olive oil to a separate frying pan and set over a medium–high heat. Once the pan is hot, add the slices of liver in batches. Cook each piece of liver for 1 minute (30 seconds on each side). If the pan dries out, keep adding a little drizzle of oil here and there until all the liver has been cooked.

Toast the bread, then drizzle it with a little olive oil and rub it with the remaining whole garlic clove. Pile on the creamed nettles and top with the slices of liver. Serve straight away.

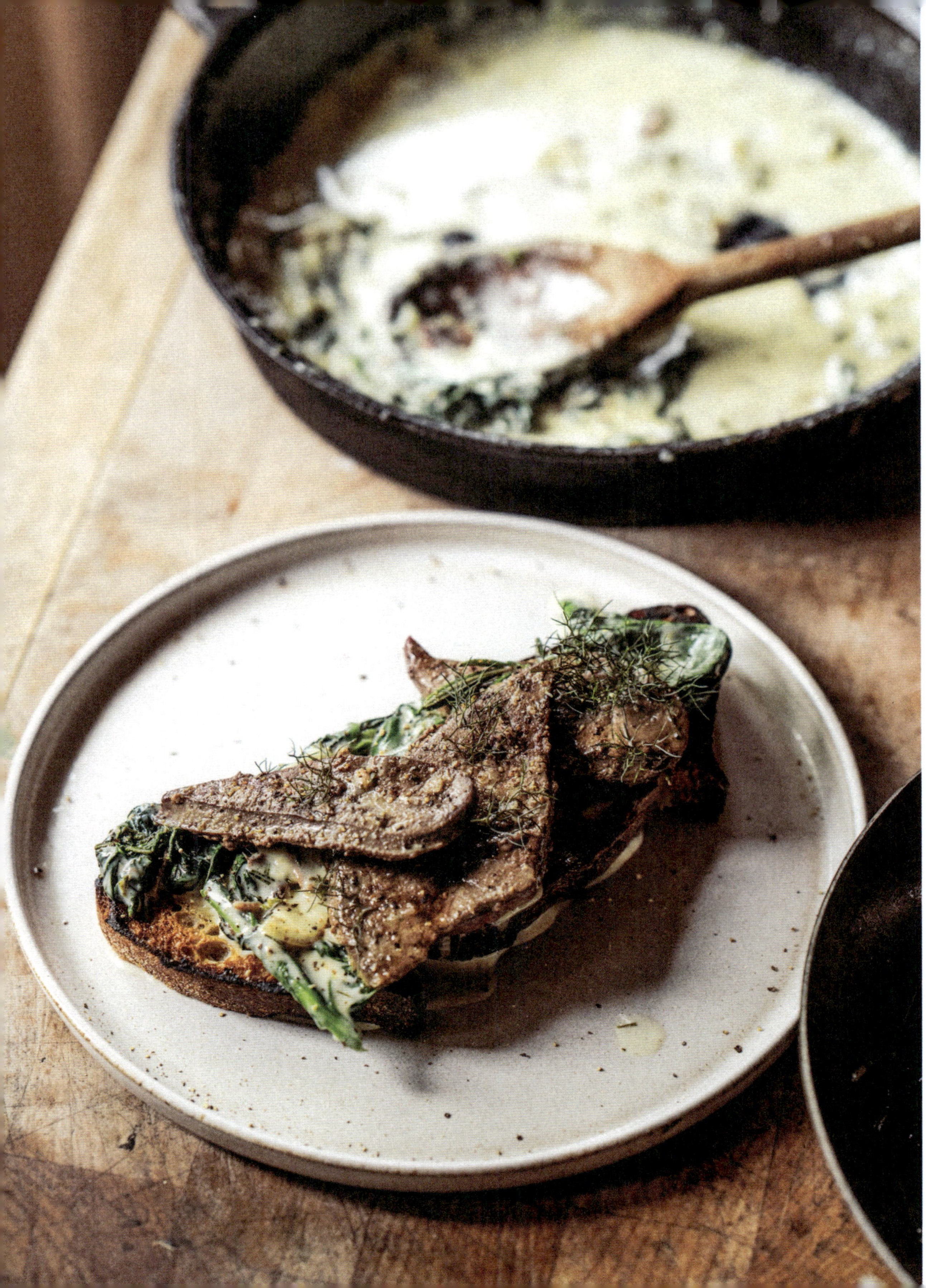

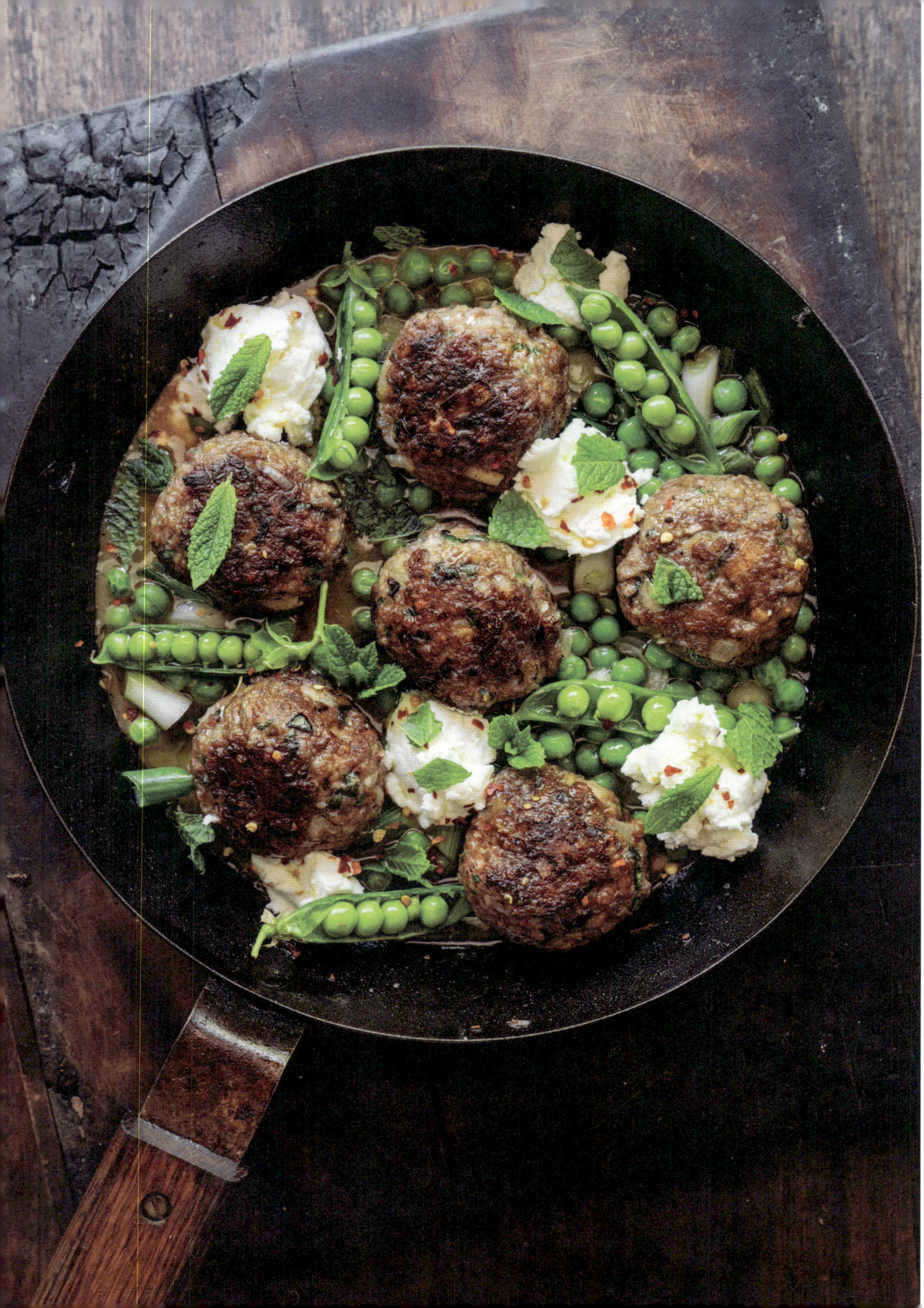

Minted hogget meatballs with Peas & Goat's Curd

The lamb season is over, it's now the time when British hogget comes into its own. Hogget is a sheep aged between one and two years old. With an older animal that has had more time to graze diverse pastures and put some mileage on the clock, you get a real ovine flavour. For me, hogget is the best example of a pasture-raised sheep.

The most important point to note, however, is that from March/April British lamb is totally out of season – crazy when almost all of us associate the Easter feast with a plate of roast lamb in some form or other. What will be sold on supermarket shelves is imported and will have been wrapped in plastic for its journey, in order to 'mature'. This is a million miles, quite literally, from a British pastured hogget that has been hung on the bone to dry-age.

a drizzle of extra virgin olive oil
1 small onion, finely chopped
2 garlic cloves, finely chopped
500g (1lb 2oz) hogget mince
a small bunch of parsley, finely chopped
a small bunch of mint, leaves picked and finely chopped
25g (1oz) breadcrumbs
½ teaspoon chilli flakes
1 egg, beaten
flaky sea salt and freshly ground black pepper

For the sauce
a drizzle of extra virgin olive oil
2 garlic cloves, finely sliced
200ml (7fl oz) chicken stock
grated zest of ½ unwaxed lemon
120g (4¼oz) peas, fresh or frozen
4 spring onions, chopped

To finish
100g (3½oz) goat's curd
a small bunch of mint, leaves picked and roughly chopped
a small bunch of parsley, stalks removed and roughly chopped
grated zest and juice of ½ lemon

Place a cast-iron pan over a medium heat and drizzle in a little olive oil. Add the onion and garlic, and cook gently until both have softened, about 6–7 minutes. Set aside to cool.

In a mixing bowl, combine the mince, herbs, breadcrumbs, chilli flakes and a pinch of salt and pepper with the cooled onions and garlic. Add the egg and mix well to thoroughly combine. Shape the mixture into golfball-sized meatballs.

Place a cast-iron pan over a medium heat, drizzle in a little more oil and fry off the meatballs, being careful not to overcrowd the pan. Once browned on all sides, remove the meatballs from the pan and set to one side.

For the sauce, add a little more oil to the same pan along with the garlic and sizzle gently. Increase the heat, add the chicken stock, season with salt and pepper, then add the lemon zest. Once the stock is bubbling, return the browned meatballs to the pan and simmer for around 8–10 minutes. Tip in the peas and spring onions and cook for around 1–2 minutes. Remove the pan from the heat.

To finish the dish, dollop in generous spoonfuls of creamy goat's curd, scatter over the chopped herbs and a little lemon zest and juice. Check the seasoning and adjust as necessary.

Roast Mutton Leg with Walnut & Mint Pesto

Last year, we planted a special walnut tree on the farm. I will be well into my 60s, nudging 90 even, before the tree reaches full splendour. I hope to have a few nut harvests in my lifetime, but the tree is not there for my benefit. While we may access land for a time, we must remember, no matter what any deed states, that we are simply custodians, not owners, of our natural landscape. It will go on into others' hands long after we are gone, and we must expect that it will continue to shift and change. What I believe to be important is that, in our lifetime, we put in more than we take out. Through the decisions we make, we have the power to leave what we touch better than we found it.

1kg (2lb 4oz) roasting potatoes
2 tablespoons beef dripping
1 whole leg of mutton
2 garlic bulbs
3–4 rosemary sprigs, leaves picked
a few thyme sprigs, leaves picked
flaky sea salt and freshly ground black pepper

For the walnut and mint pesto
100g (3½oz) walnuts
1 bunch of mint, leaves picked
1 bunch of chives
1 bunch of flat-leaf parsley
5–6 tablespoons extra virgin olive oil
2 tablespoons cider vinegar
flaky sea salt and freshly ground black pepper

Preheat the oven to 200°C/400°F/gas mark 6.

Peel the potatoes, cut them up into large pieces and tip them into a saucepan. Cover with plenty of cold, salted water and set them over a medium heat. Bring to the boil, turn down the heat and simmer for 8–10 minutes, or until just tender. Drain in a colander and leave to steam for at least 5 minutes. It's well worth tumbling the potatoes around in the colander once or twice to rough up their edges, as this makes them even crisper.

Meanwhile, spoon the beef dripping into a large, heavy-based roasting tray and place it in the oven to heat up. Once lovely and hot, carefully tip the potatoes into the tray. Use a spatula to turn them through the beef fat, making sure they've all got a little space, then generously season with salt and pepper. Place the potatoes into the oven for 15 minutes.

Season the leg of mutton with salt and slice the garlic bulbs in half. Add the mutton leg to the roasting tray with the potatoes, along with the garlic. Place the tray back in the oven for 20 minutes.

Remove the tray from the oven and use a potato masher slightly squish the potatoes. Add the rosemary and thyme to the tray. Turn the oven down to 180°C/350°F/gas mark 4 and cook for a further 25 minutes per kg of the weight of the mutton leg. For best results, use a meat thermometer: insert in the thickest part of the joint (not next to the bone) – the target temperature is 55°C/130°F.

Remove the mutton from the oven and leave to rest for 20 minutes. Remove the garlic from the roasting tray and set to one side, as you'll need this for the next step.

While the mutton is resting, make the mint pesto. Lightly toast the walnuts in a dry frying pan. Once toasted, add them to a blender, followed by the mint, chives, parsley, roasted garlic cloves squeezed from their skins, extra virgin olive oil, cider vinegar and a pinch each of salt and pepper. Give everything a good blitz until a perfect pesto consistency has formed.

Serve the crispy potatoes alongside thick slices of mutton with generous dollops of pesto.

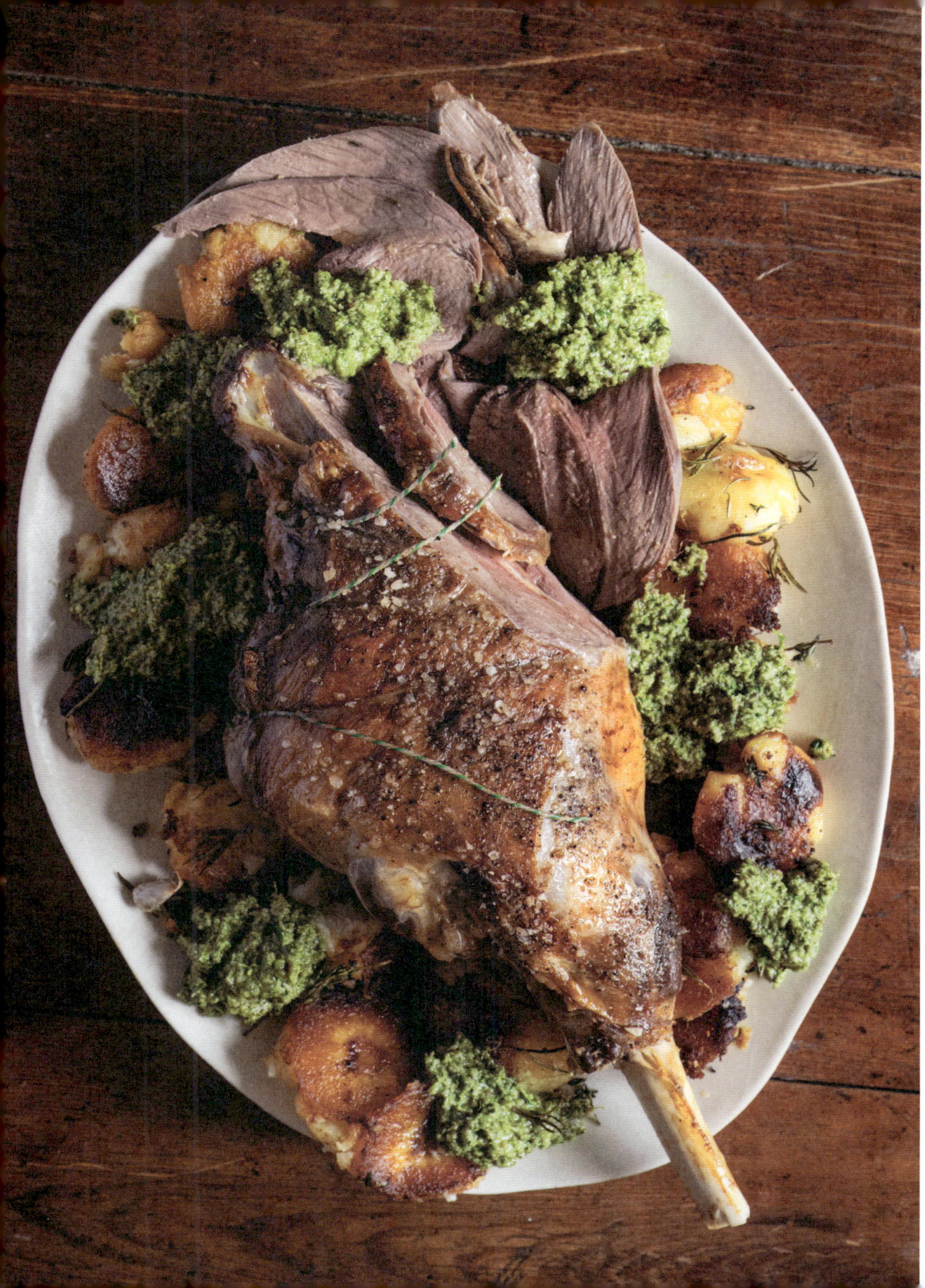

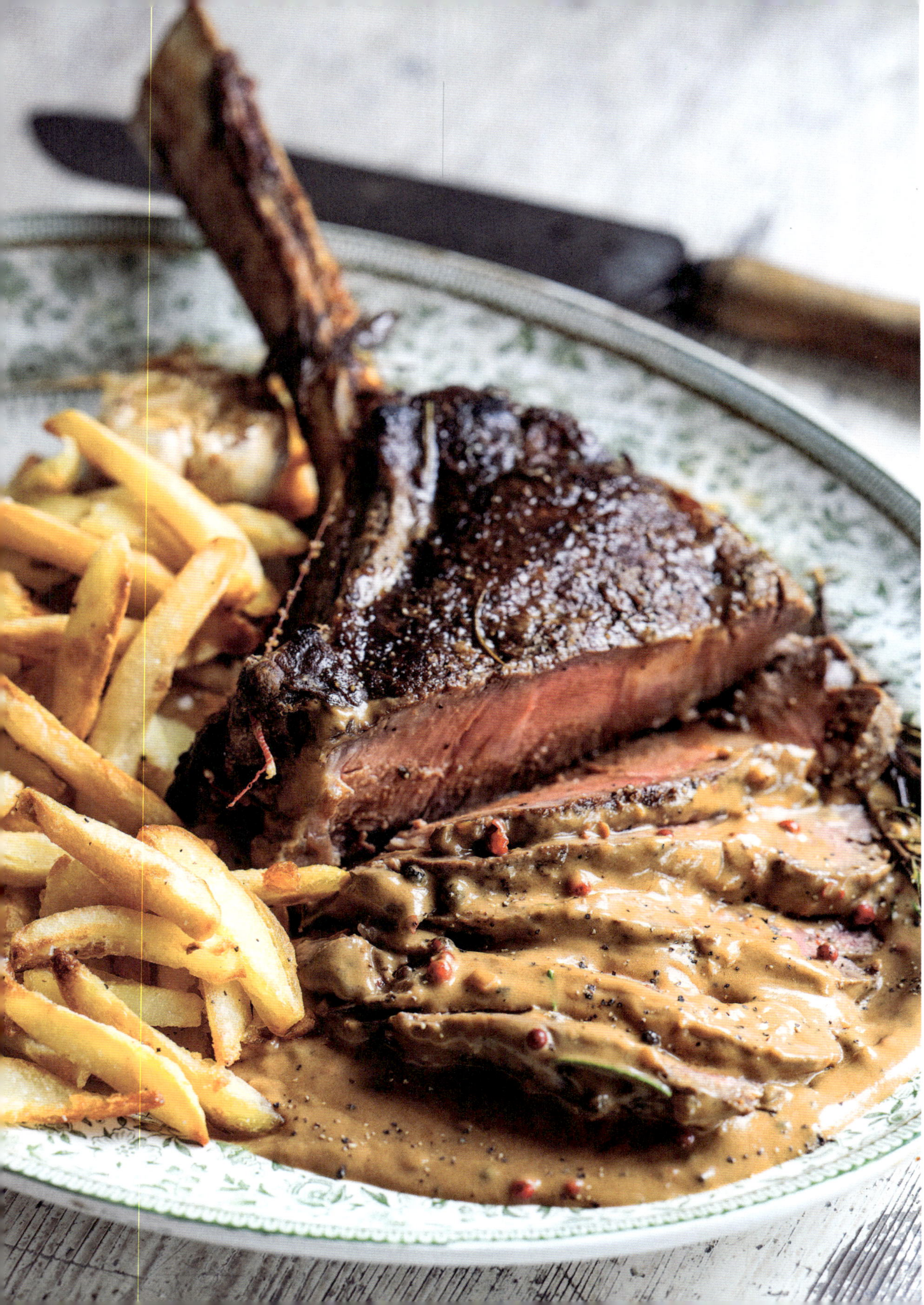

SERVES 2   Spring

Côte de Boeuf with Peppercorn Sauce & Beef-fat Chips

For many, this dish may rank near the top of your 'last supper' meals. A medium-rare steak glistening with buttery fat, served with crisped-to-perfection chips and the greatest of all steak accompaniment – a fragrant peppercorn sauce, rich with cream and brandy.

1 grass-fed côte de boeuf
1 teaspoon beef dripping
a knob of grass-fed butter
2 garlic cloves, bashed
2 sprigs of rosemary
1 teaspoon capers
flaky sea salt and freshly ground black pepper

For the beef-fat chips
50g (1¾oz) beef dripping
1kg (2lb 4oz) floury potatoes (I use Desiree), peeled and cut into thinnish chips
2 sprigs of rosemary, leaves picked
2 sprigs of thyme, leaves picked

For the peppercorn sauce
40g (1½oz) grass-fed butter
2 large shallots, finely chopped
50ml (2fl oz) Somerset cider brandy
150ml (5fl oz) beef stock
200ml (7fl oz) double cream
1 tablespoon green peppercorns
1 tablespoon roughly chopped flat-leaf parsley

Preheat the oven to 200°C/400°F/gas mark 6. Remove the steak from the fridge, pat dry and allow it to come up to room temperature.

Meanwhile, make the chips. Set a saucepan of salted boiling water over a high heat, tip in the potatoes and cook for 3–4 minutes. Drain in a colander and leave to steam for a minute or two.

Spoon the beef drippping into a roasting tray and place into the oven to heat. Once it's sizzling hot, remove the tray from the oven and carefully tip in the potatoes. Stir them through the fat, then scatter over the rosemary and thyme. Place the tray back in the oven and cook for 40 minutes.

While the potatoes are cooking, make the peppercorn sauce. Set a saucepan over a low–medium heat, add the butter and the shallots and cook for a couple of minutes, until soft. Increase the heat, add the cider brandy and simmer until it has reduced by two-thirds. Add the stock and reduce it by two-thirds. Pour in the cream and simmer until the sauce has thickened. Stir in the peppercorns and parsley. Season, if necessary. Turn the heat right down to keep the sauce warm while you cook the steak.

Reduce the oven temperature to 180°C/350°F/gas mark 4.

Season the steak well with salt and pepper. Set a cast-iron frying pan over a high heat and spoon in the beef dripping. Once the fat is sizzling hot, add the steak to the pan. Leave it to sizzle on one side for 4–5 minutes, until a proper caramelized crust has formed, then turn it over and repeat the process. Add the butter, garlic, rosemary and capers and allow it to foam up, then baste the steak for a minute or two. Transfer the pan to the oven and and cook for 15 minutes. If you have a meat thermometer, aim for 48–52°C (118–125°F) for rare; 52–58°C (125–136°F) for medium; for well done, don't bother cooking this beautiful cut. Leave to rest for 10 minutes.

Slice the steak and serve it with the crispy chips and a generous amount of peppercorn sauce, perhaps also with a sharply dressed green salad to cut through the richness.

Venison Steaks with Honeyed Carrots & Spiced Chickpeas

Here I have amplifed the fudgy, candy-like quality of the humble carrot to create the perfect counterbalance to mineral-rich venison. Venison lacks fat, so one of my favourite ways to cook it is in a pan full of butter. I find this helps to develop a light crust that is otherwise harder to achieve. Cook it rare, perhaps medium-rare, but no further, and then enforce a resting period; this gives the juices time to return home. What you should end up with is something akin to fillet steak. A little of the rich venison goes a long way, so a fresh, zippy sheep's cheese is a welcome addition.

500g (1lb 2oz) carrots, sliced in half lengthways
2 red onions, cut into wedges
3 garlic cloves, peeled and bashed
rapeseed oil, for drizzling
2–3 tablespoons runny local honey
2 wild venison steaks
a knob of grass-fed butter
flaky sea salt and freshly ground black pepper

For the spiced chickpeas
2 teaspoons smoked paprika
2 teaspoons cumin seeds
1 teaspoon chilli flakes
125g (4½oz) cooked chickpeas, drained
2 tablespoons pumpkin seeds
2 tablespoons sunflower seeds
a drizzle of rapeseed oil

To serve
100g (3½oz) chervil, chopped
a few sprigs of thyme
150g (5½oz) Wooten White sheep's cheese

Preheat the oven to 200°C/400°F/gas mark 4.

Add the carrots, red onion wedges and bashed garlic cloves to a medium roasting tray. Drizzle over a generous glug of rapeseed oil and liberally season the veg with salt and pepper. Drizzle over a tablespoon of honey, then shake the tray to ensure everything is thoroughly coated. Roast in the oven for 25 minutes.

To make the spiced chickpeas, begin by grinding the spices using a pestle and mortar. Pour the spice mix into a mixing bowl. Add the chickpeas and seeds, along with a drizzle of oil and a good pinch of salt. Stir to combine, then set aside.

Remove the roasted veg from the oven and give everything a good shake. Add the spiced chickpeas and seeds to the roasting tray and drizzle over a little more oil and a further tablespoon of honey. Place it back in the oven and roast for a further 15–20 minutes, until the veg is beautifully tender and caramelized.

Season the venison steaks with a good pinch of salt and pepper. Place a cast-iron pan over a high heat. Add a drizzle of oil, then lay the steaks in and cook for 2–3 minutes on each side. For the last minute of cooking, add a small knob of butter and toss around the pan, coating the steaks. Remove them from the pan and set aside to rest for 8–10 minutes.

Decant the roasted veg, chickpeas and seeds onto a large platter. Scatter over the herbs. Break apart the sheep's cheese and scatter chunks through the warm veg. Slice the rested venison steaks, then lay them on the top of the veg, pouring over any juices from the pan. Finally, drizzle the dish with a little more oil and serve straight away.

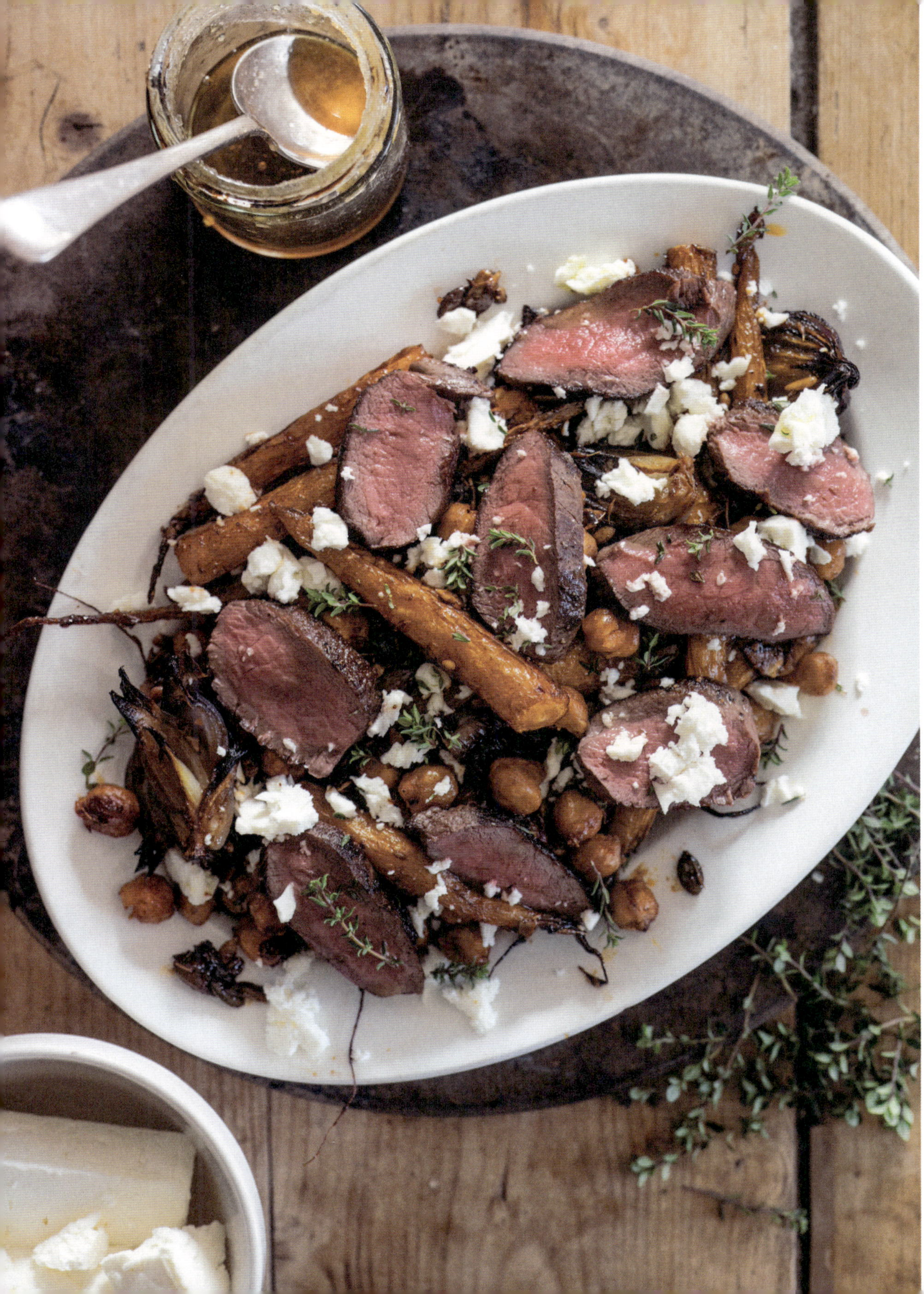

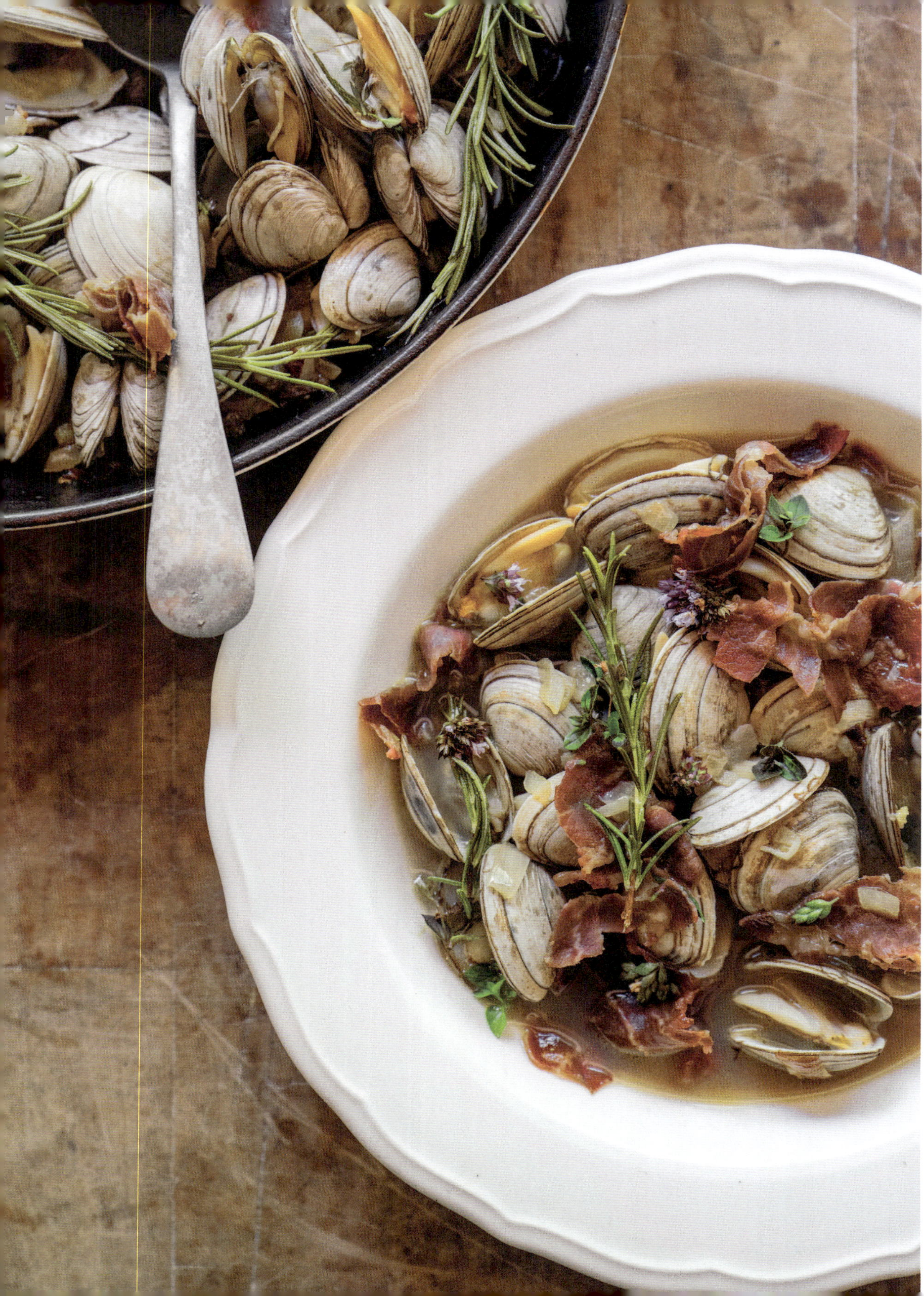

SERVES 4   Spring

Dorset Clams with Coppa, Somerset Cider & Brandy

With two eager spaniels in the back of the car and my faithful Jack Russell, Minnie, poised on the passenger seat, we are heading off on a special reconnaissance mission. It's March and a disappointingly grey day. However, typical British weather will not be dulling our spirits; I have been given word that there is treasure to collect. After a short half-hour drive along one of my most loved scenic roads, we cross the border into Dorset, where incomers are greeted by Thomas Hardy's picture-perfect Wessex. Pretty stone cottages flank the winding lanes, until roads stretch out with everlasting views of cliff edges and rough seas. Buckets, spades and rakes are unloaded before unleashing the dogs to zoom across the empty beach. We head to a gravelly, muddy tidal flat, and there I begin scavenging for treasure. I strike gold and manage to carry a decent haul of 'palourdes', or clams, back to the car, along with three sodden, yet gleeful, dogs.

In a delightful coalescence of my local landscapes, I have crafted this recipe in celebration of the wonderful adventures I frequently enjoy in my neighbouring counties. A reminder to get out and explore what is right on your doorstep.

500g (1lb 2oz) Dorset clams
1 tablespoon extra virgin olive oil
a small knob of grass-fed butter
1 small onion, very finely chopped
50g (1¾oz) coppa ham, sliced into small pieces
3 garlic cloves, finely chopped
100ml (3½fl oz) Somerset cider brandy
a small handful of thyme, leaves picked

Rinse the clams in a colander and ensure you discard any that are open and do not close when tapped sharply.

Take a medium-sized, lidded pan and place over a medium heat. Drizzle in the olive oil and add the butter, then add the onion and sweat for about 5–6 minutes, until it has softened. Add the ham and garlic and cook for 1 minute.

Increase the heat and tip in the clams, along with the cider brandy and most of the thyme, bringing it to the boil. Place the lid on and cook for 5 minutes, or until the clams have opened. Discard any that haven't opened.

Finish with a few more fresh thyme leaves and serve immediately with butter-laden crusty bread.

Pouting, Leek & Tarragon Pie

Living as I do, surrounded by some of the finest coastal waters in the world, means I'm never short of beautiful seafood for my larder. There are few experiences better than eating fresh fish landed from a stone's throw away, other than perhaps catching your own. When I drive by a small fishing village and pick up the catch of the day, I know how lucky I am to have ingredients so sparklingly fresh. The last thing I want to do is to mask the delicate sweet flavour that you find only in really good seafood. A cream and herb sauce is all that's needed here, allowing the seafood to be the star of the show.

4 sustainably caught fillets of pouting or other white fish, such as hake, ling, whiting or coley
2 small leeks, sliced
700ml (1¼ pints) whole milk
3 bay leaves
6 peppercorns
50g (1¾oz) grass-fed butter
60g (2oz) plain flour
a small bunch of tarragon, chopped

For the topping
a bunch of dill, finely chopped
zest of 1 unwaxed lemon
400g (14oz) breadcrumbs
200g (7oz) grass-fed butter
flaky sea salt and freshly ground black pepper

Start by removing the skin from your pouting fillets and cut them into smaller pieces.

Place the fish in a large saucapan along with the sliced leeks. Add the milk, bay leaves and peppercorns and bring to the boil. Reduce the heat and leave to simmer, very gently, for about 3–4 minutes, until both the fish and leeks are almost cooked. Turn off the heat but put a lid on the pan.

Preheat the oven to 180°C/350°F/gas mark 4.

To prepare the topping, place the dill in a mixing bowl. Add the lemon zest along with the breadcrumbs. Season with a good pinch of salt and pepper and mix well.

In a small pan, melt the butter, then pour it over the crumbs. Stir to coat everything thoroughly.

Remove the fish and leeks from the milk, discarding the peppercorns and bay leaves, but reserving the milk.

Melt the 50g (1¾oz) of butter in a cast-iron casserole dish, then stir in the flour to make a roux. Gradually ladle in the reserved milk and whisk the sauce together. Add the tarragon to the sauce, then the fish and leeks and season lightly. Scatter the buttered breadcrumb mixture over the top and bake for around 25 minutes until golden and crisp.

Spoon into warmed bowls and serve as it is or with a little buttered kale on the side.

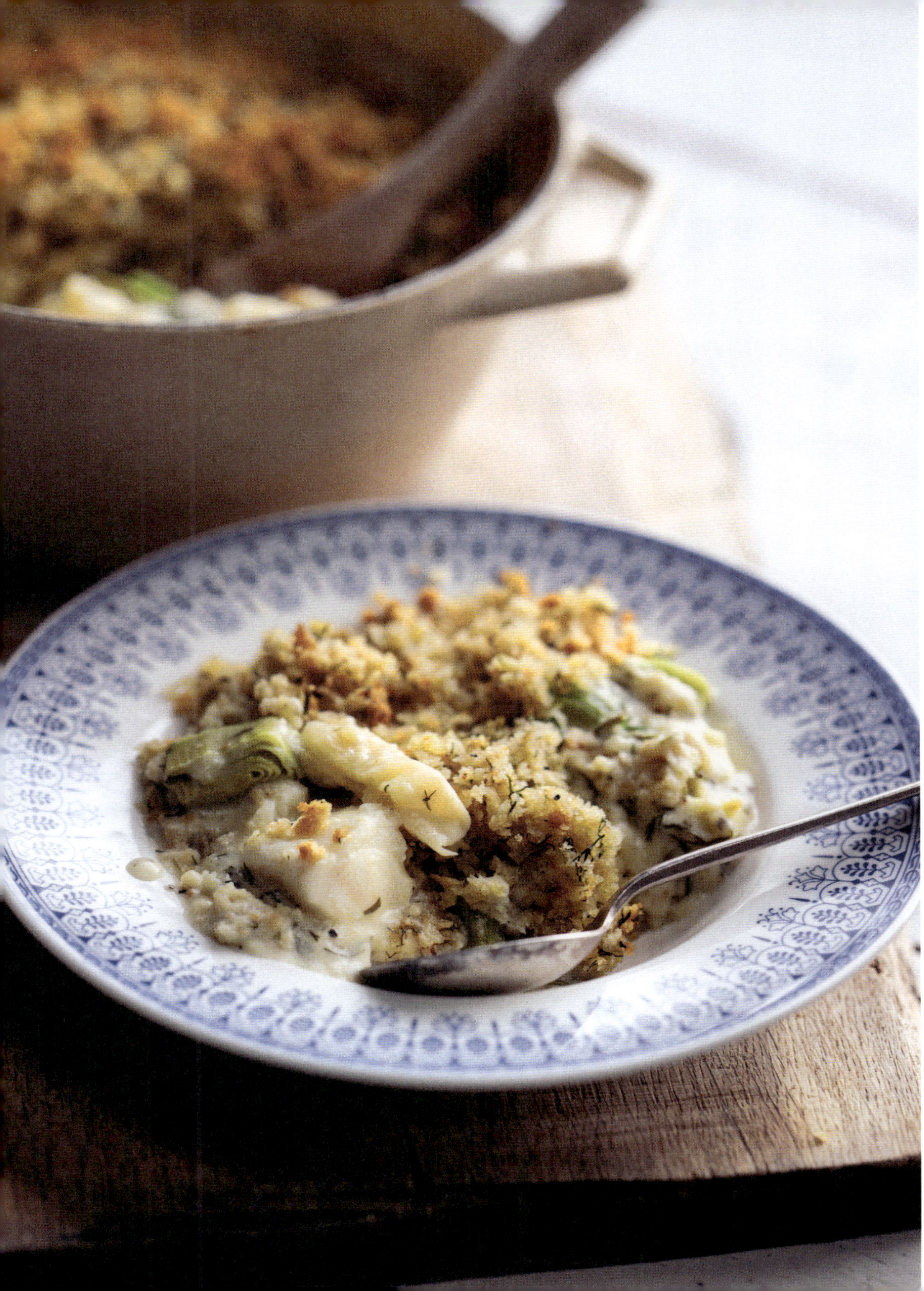

Spring   SERVES 1–2

Canned Sardines on Toast with Wild Garlic Chimichurri

Sardines (also known as pilchards) are small, silvery fish related to herring, which shoal in waters around the Cornish coast. Sardines are in abundance in British waters; regular surveys show that stocks are vast, with little danger of overfishing. The fish are located using sonar fish-finding equipment with extraordinary accuracy, and caught using ring nets. The main season for landing Cornish sardines is August to January, although they are sometimes caught outside this period as by-catch. One of the great benefits of these fat, silvery fish is that they are perfect for canning – one of the best methods of preserving this abundant species. Steamed and laid into cans filled with olive oil within hours, sardines are a great ingredient to use during weeks when boats are struggling to catch fresh fish due to adverse weather conditions.

60g (2¼oz) wild garlic
30g (1oz) mint leaves
30g (1oz) flat-leaf parsley
2–3 spring onions
1 small green chilli, to taste
grated zest and juice of 1 lime
4 tablespoons red wine vinegar
5–7 tablespoons extra virgin olive oil
1 teaspoon flaky sea salt
125g (4½oz) canned Cornish sardines, drained

To serve
olive oil, for drizzling
2 slices of sourdough toast
1 garlic clove, peeled

To make the chimichurri, finely chop the herbs, spring onions and green chilli and place in a bowl. Alternatively, you can blitz them together in a food processor. Add the lime juice and zest, plus the red wine vinegar, then loosen with 5–7 tablespoons of the olive oil. Add the salt and check the flavours, adjusting if you like a little more heat or a little more sharpness. Set aside.

Take a cast-iron pan and place it over a medium heat. Drizzle in some of the olive oil, then fry the sardines for around 5 minutes, or until crisp. Remove the sardines from the pan and set aside.

Drizzle some more oil over the sourdough, then place in the pan used to cook the sardines and cook until crisp.

Rub the warm toasts with the garlic clove, then stack the sardines on top. Spoon over the chimichurri and dig in.

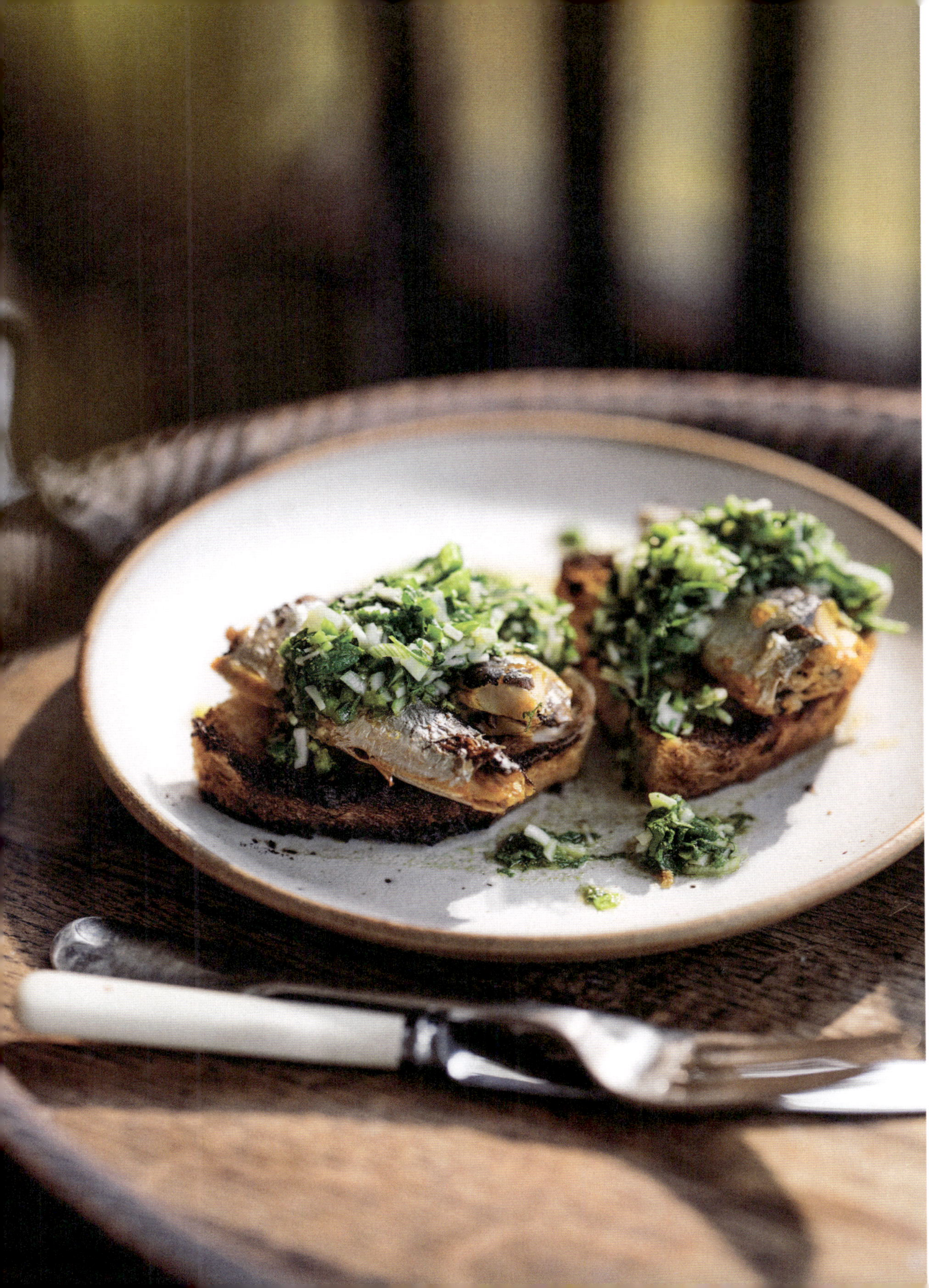

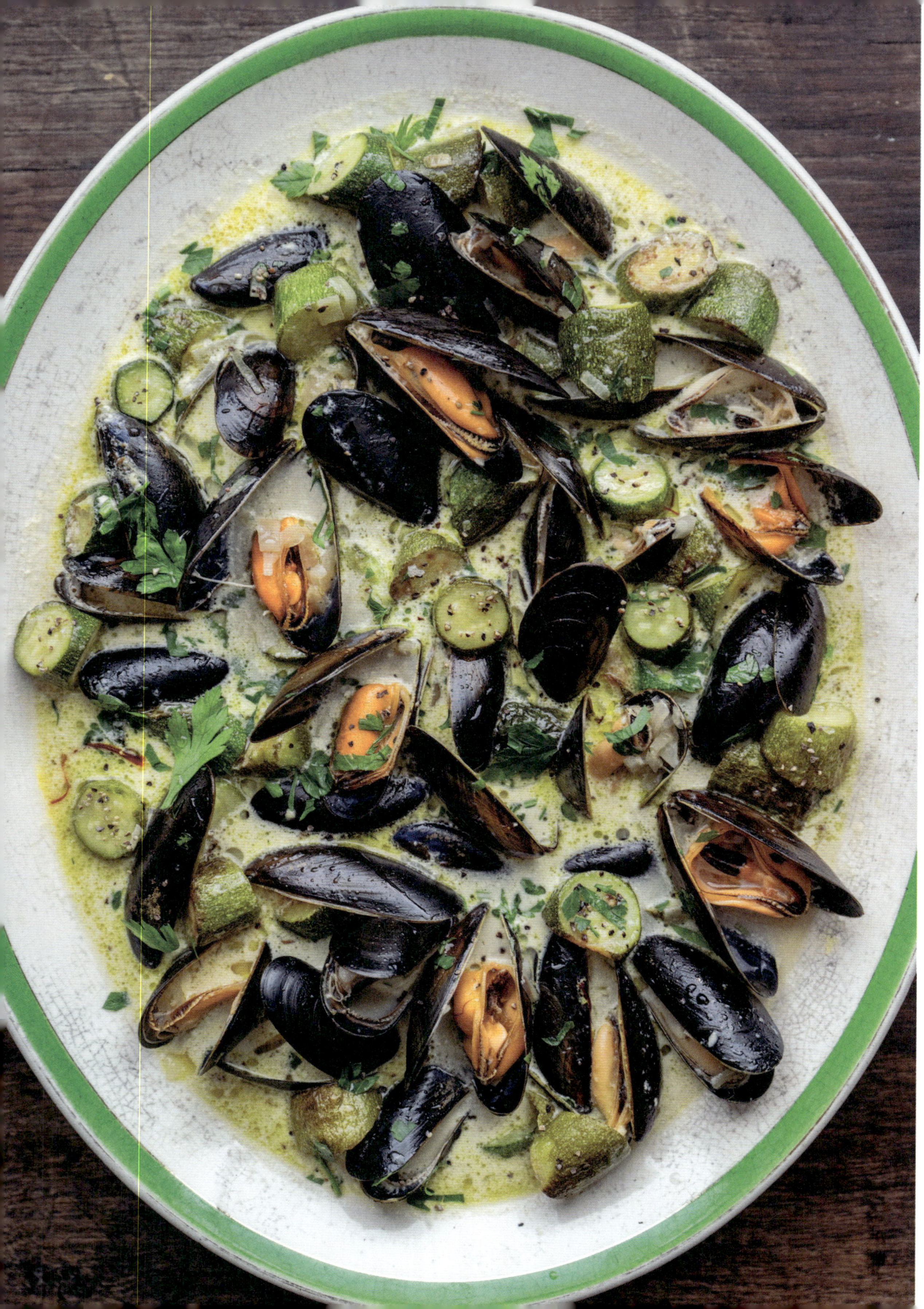

SERVES 4 — Spring

Mussels with Saffron, Cream & Courgettes

When you live very near the coast, you cannot help but notice how the seashore seems to encroach inland as soon as Easter marks the calendar. Tourists descend with their bright buckets and spades, and cars strapped with surfboards, taking over our sleepy villages. Alongside the holiday makers, the fishing community becomes busy making the most of the clement weather. There are great benefits to the shift in season. For me, spring marks the moment when some of the finest seafood is more frequently landed by dayboats. There are tantalizing ingredients on offer as 'catch of the day'. It is, however, the last hurrah for the mussel, whch will return to my plate only once the tourists have re-tied their surfboards and headed home.

1kg (2lb 4oz) rope-grown mussels, well scrubbed and cleaned
a drizzle of extra virgin olive oil
a knob of grass-fed butter
2 courgettes, roughly chopped
2 shallots, finely chopped
2 garlic cloves, finely chopped
1 teaspoon saffron
125ml (4fl oz) English white wine
3 tablespoons Tarquin's Cornish Pastis
200ml (7fl oz) double cream
a small bunch of flat-leaf parsley, roughly chopped
flaky sea salt and freshly ground black pepper

To prepare the mussels, tip them into a sink filled with cold water. Swish them around with your hands to wash them thoroughly. Use a small, sharp knife to scrape off any barnacles attached to the shells. Discard any mussels with broken shells. Pull off any beards, using the knife to help you. If any mussels are open, tap them sharply against the side of the sink, and discard them if they don't close: they are dead and therefore inedible. Rinse the mussels again in fresh, cold water to remove any bits of shell or barnacle. Drain in a colander, then set aside.

Place a cast-iron pan over a medium–high heat and add a drizzle of olive oil and a small knob of butter. Once the fat is sizzling, add the courgettes along with a pinch of salt, then fry for about 7–8 minutes, or until the courgettes have caramelized. Set to one side.

Add a little more butter and a drizzle of oil to a separate, large cast-iron pan. Add the shallots and garlic and sweat for around 5–6 minutes. Increase the heat and add the saffron, wine and pastis to the pan. Once bubbling, tip in the mussels and cover with a lid. Cook for around 2 minutes. Remove the lid and add the cream along with the courgettes. Cook for a further 2–3 minutes, shaking the pan from time to time to ensure the mussels cook evenly – they are ready when the shells have opened. Remove the pan from the heat to stop the mussels cooking any further.

Spoon the mussels and courgettes into warmed bowls, pour over the pan juices and scatter with chopped parsley.

Serve with some warm, buttered, crusty bread.

Hungry Gap Canned Seafood Pasta

The Hungry Gap is the hardest time of year for UK farmers: a few weeks, usually in April, May and early June, after the winter crops have ended but before the new season's plantings are ready to harvest. It all comes down to the UK's latitude. We sit right at the geographical limit for many spring crops, which would not survive our cold winter temperatures if grown any earlier. At the same time, as the days warm up into spring, many hardy winter crops such as sprouts, kale and cauli 'bolt'. The result is unproductive fields and fewer British-grown crops. During this time, in order to avoid fresh produce that has been shipped around the world, we cooks need to get creative, or at the very least utilize our store cupboards. Every single component of this recipe has been harvested, processed and preserved in season so that the produce can be enjoyed at a later date, truly making it the ultimate store-cupboard feast and perfect for when the Hungry Gap strikes.

120g (4¼oz) British stoneground casarecce pasta
125g (4½oz) canned Cornish sardines in olive oil
2 garlic cloves, sliced
200g (7oz) preserved cherry tomatoes (see page 77)
400g (14oz) passata
80g (2¾oz) olives, roughly chopped
a small handful of flat-leaf parsley, chopped
50g (1¾oz) Old Winchester cheese, grated
a splash of extra virgin olive oil
flaky sea salt and freshly ground black pepper

Fill a saucepan with boiling water, add a generous pinch of sea salt, then bring to a rolling boil over a high heat. Add the pasta and cook according to the instructions on the packet until al dente. Drain and set aside somewhere warm.

Place a frying pan over a low–medium heat. Add the sardines, including their oil, and fry gently. Add the garlic and cherry tomatoes and continue frying gently for a couple of minutes, stirring occasionally. Add the passata and bring to a simmer. Once the sauce has reduced by half (this should take around 5–8 minutes), add the chopped olives and cook for a further 3 minutes.

Add the drained pasta to the pan and stir through the fragrant sauce. Check the seasoning and adjust with a little salt and pepper.

Finish with a generous sprinkling of chopped parsley and a grating of Old Winchester cheese, the perfect British alternative to Parmesan. Generously drizzle the dish with a glug of extra virgin olive oil before serving.

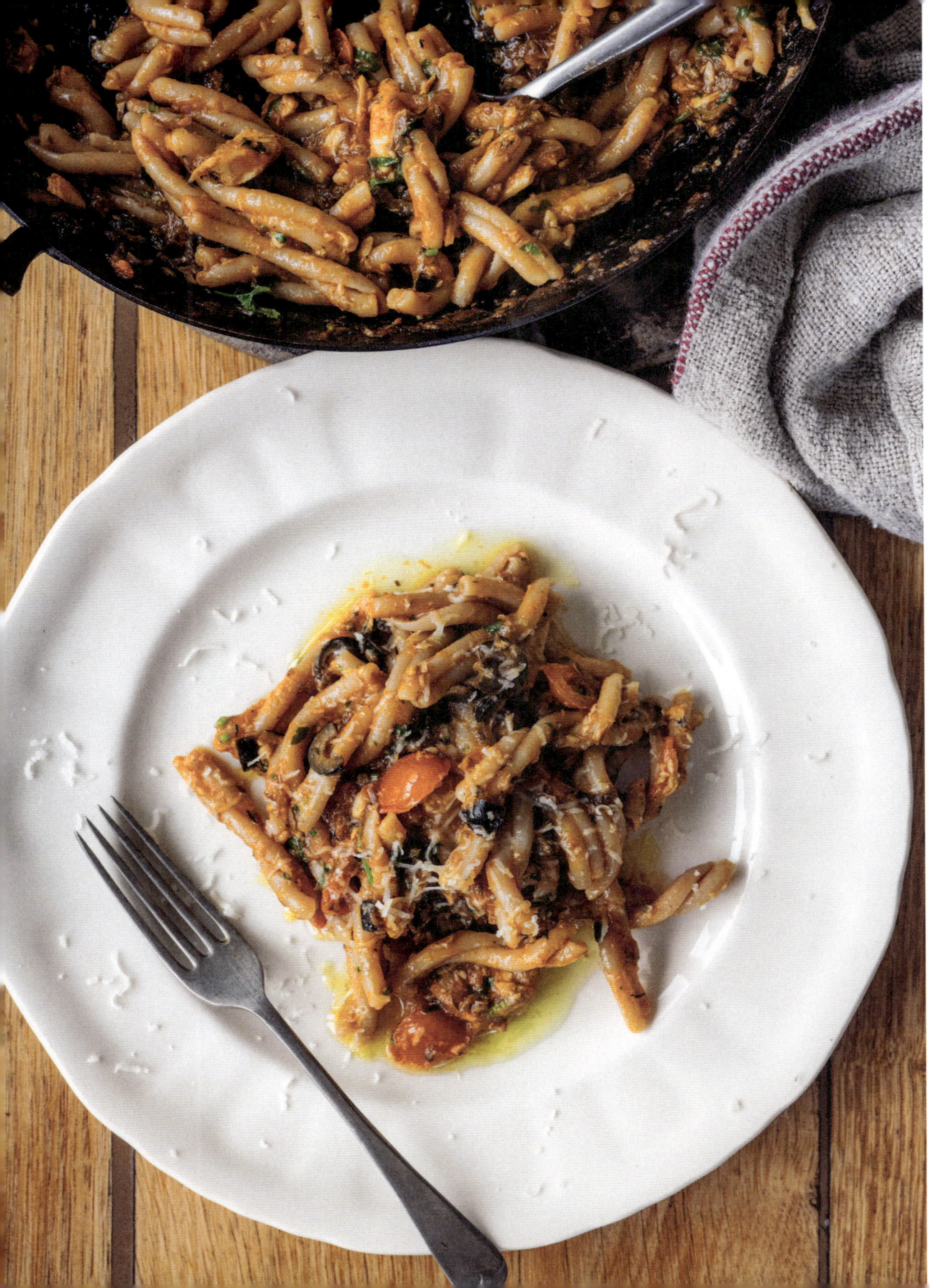

Speltotto Kedgeree with Purple Sprouting Broccoli & Kale

My former boss and founder of the famed TV smallholding River Cottage coined the rather wonderful term 'speltotto' when referring to risottos made with spelt in place of rice. Pearled spelt works in the same way as risotto rice, but offers a nutty flavour and a more robust texture. It works beautifully in this dish, absorbing the spices and providing a starchy base on which the sustainably caught pollack can rest.

4 organic and/or free-range eggs
100g (3½oz) kale
a large knob of grass-fed butter
a drizzle of extra virgin olive oil
1 onion, finely sliced
1 leek, finely sliced
2 garlic cloves, finely sliced
1 small dried red chilli
1 teaspoon ground turmeric
1½ tablespoons medium hot curry power
½ teaspoon ground ginger
200g (7oz) pearled spelt or pearl barley
750ml hot vegetable stock
500g (1lb 2oz) sustainably caught smoked pollack or haddock, skinned and cut into 2–3cm (¾–1¼in) chunks
100g (3½oz) purple sprouting broccoli
a small bunch of parsley, roughly chopped
a few spring onions, finely chopped
flaky sea salt and freshly ground black pepper

Bring a small saucepan of water to the boil, carefully lower the eggs into the pan and simmer for 7–8 minutes. Once cooked, lift the eggs out of the pan and run them under cold water to stop the cooking. Lightly crack and peel off the shells (under a gently running cool tap), then cut in half lengthways and set to one side.

Strip the leaves from the kale stalks and give them a rinse. Slice the stalks into 1cm (½in) pieces. Roughly shred the leaves and set them aside.

Set a large, heavy-based saucepan over a medium–high heat. Add a small knob of butter and a drizzle of olive oil. When the butter is bubbling away, add the kale stalks, onion, leek, garlic, dried chilli and a pinch of salt, and cook gently, stirring regularly, for 5–6 minutes. Don't let them colour. Once the veg have softened, add the ground spices and stir for around a minute.

Rinse the pearled spelt and add it to the pan, giving everything a good stir. Start adding the hot stock a couple of ladlefuls at a time, stirring regularly as you go. When you've used up half the stock, add the smoked fish, purple sprouting broccoli and the shredded kale leaves. Stir well and add more stock. Continue to cook the spelt, fish and vegetables for a few more minutes, until the fish and broccoli are cooked through.

Stir in another generous knob of butter, along with the parsley and spring onions.. Adjust the consistency with a splash more stock if necessary (it should be slightly loose) and season with salt and pepper to taste.

Spoon the kedgeree into bowls, arranging the sliced eggs on top, then dive in.

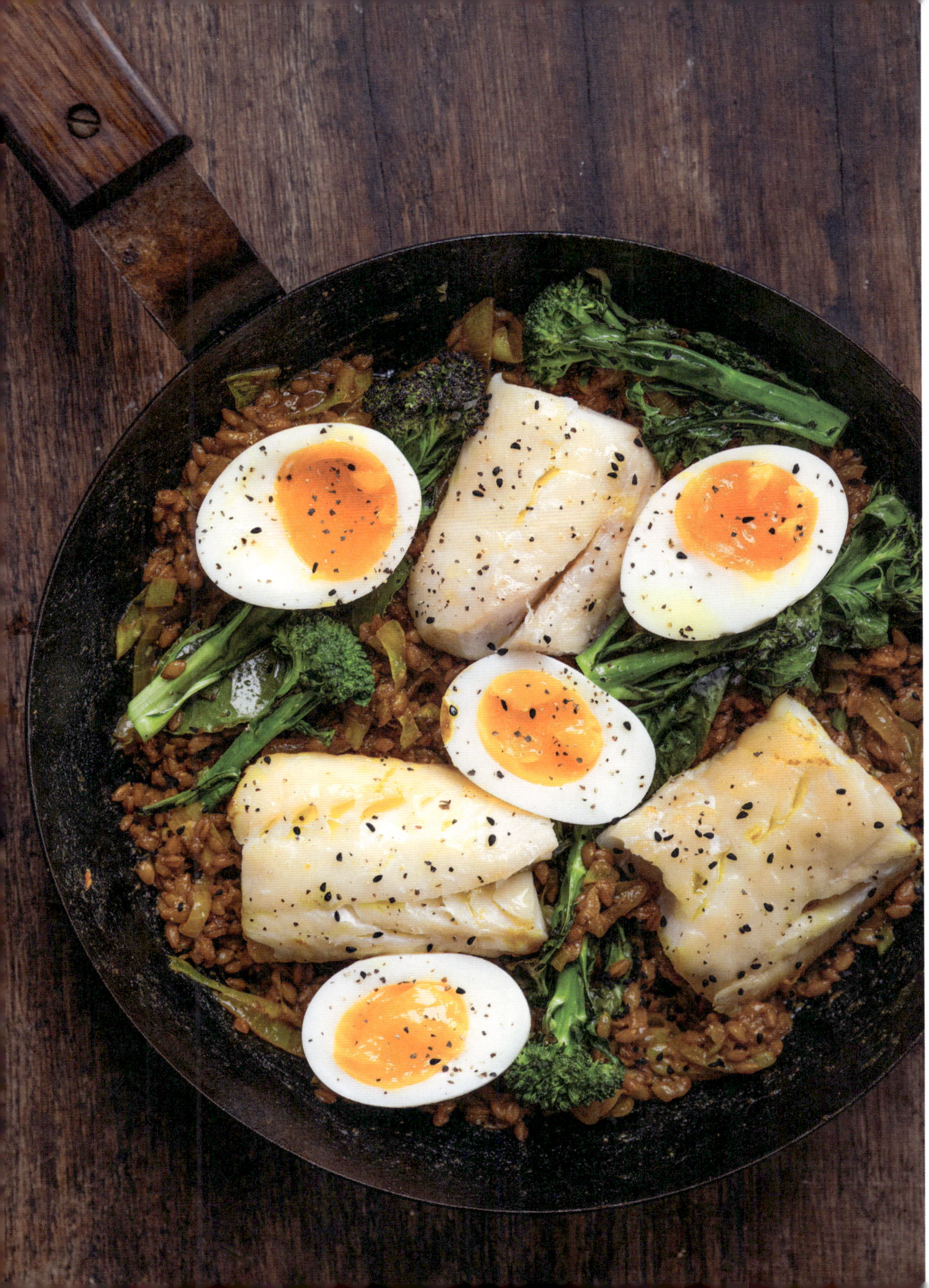

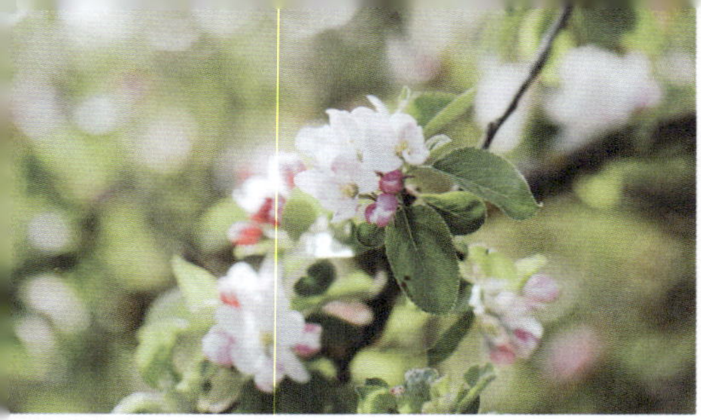
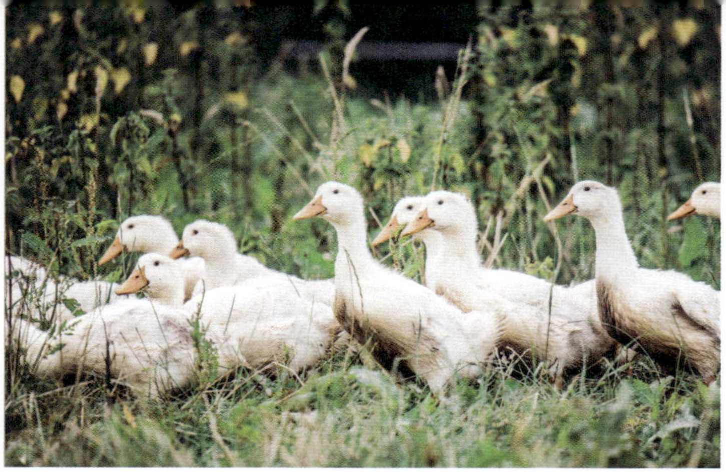
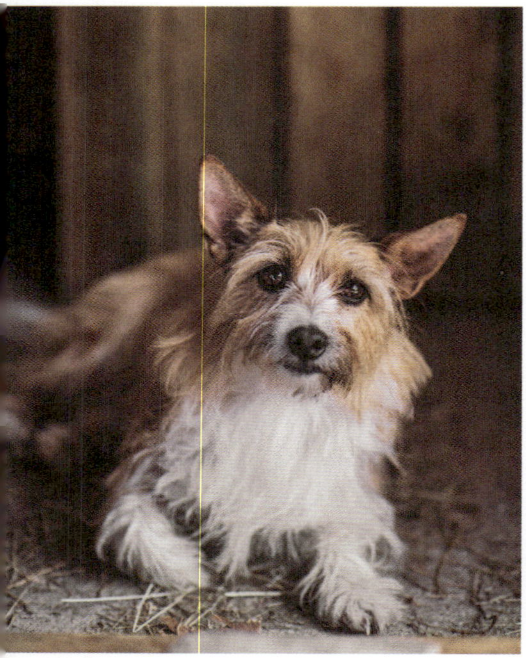
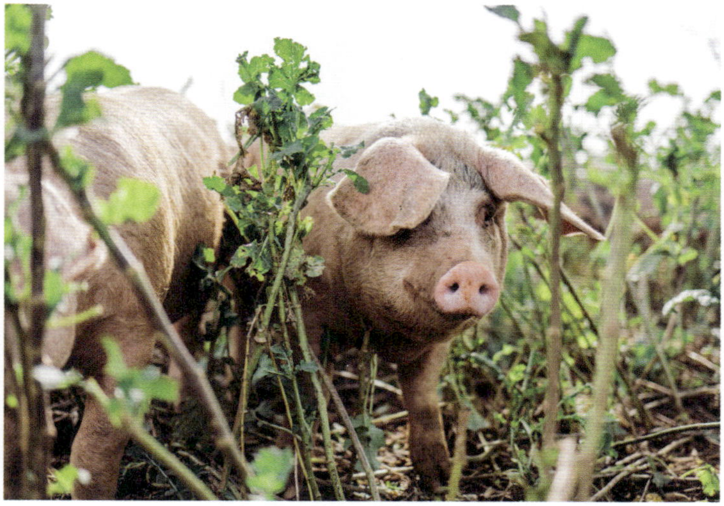
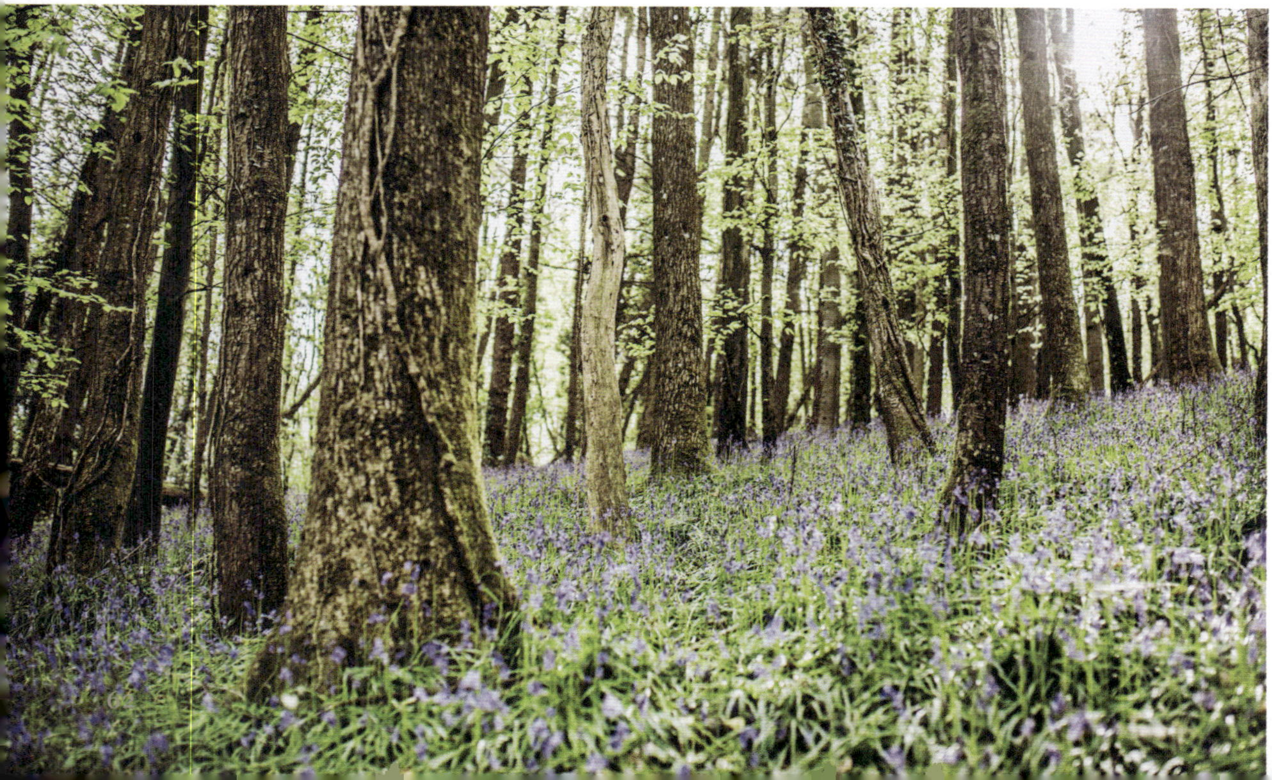

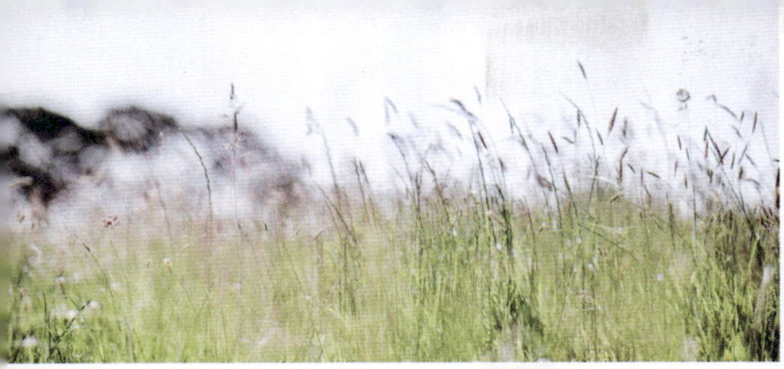

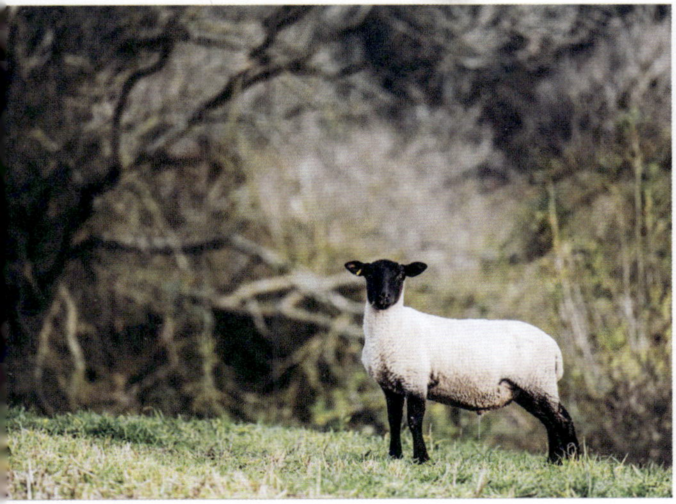

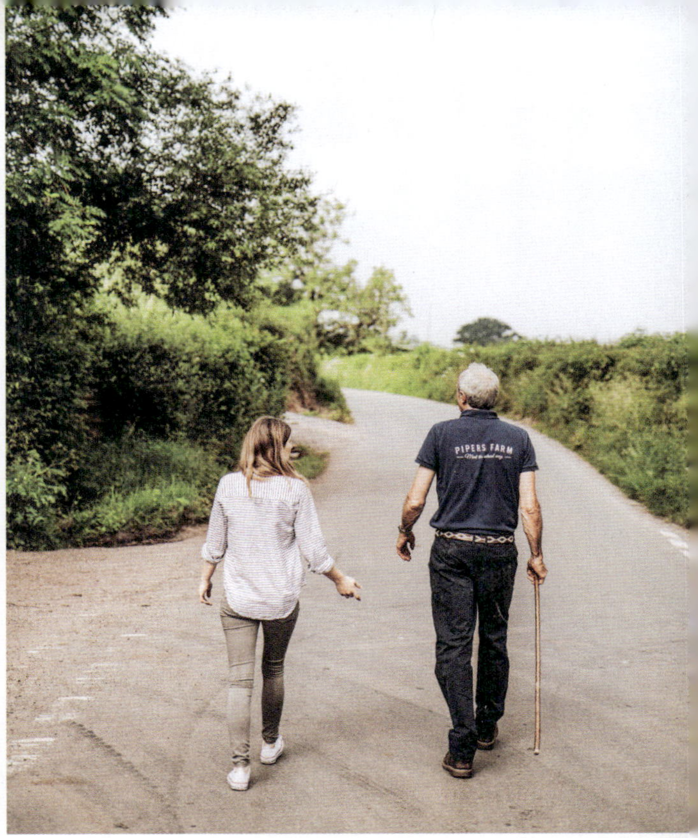
PIPERS FARM

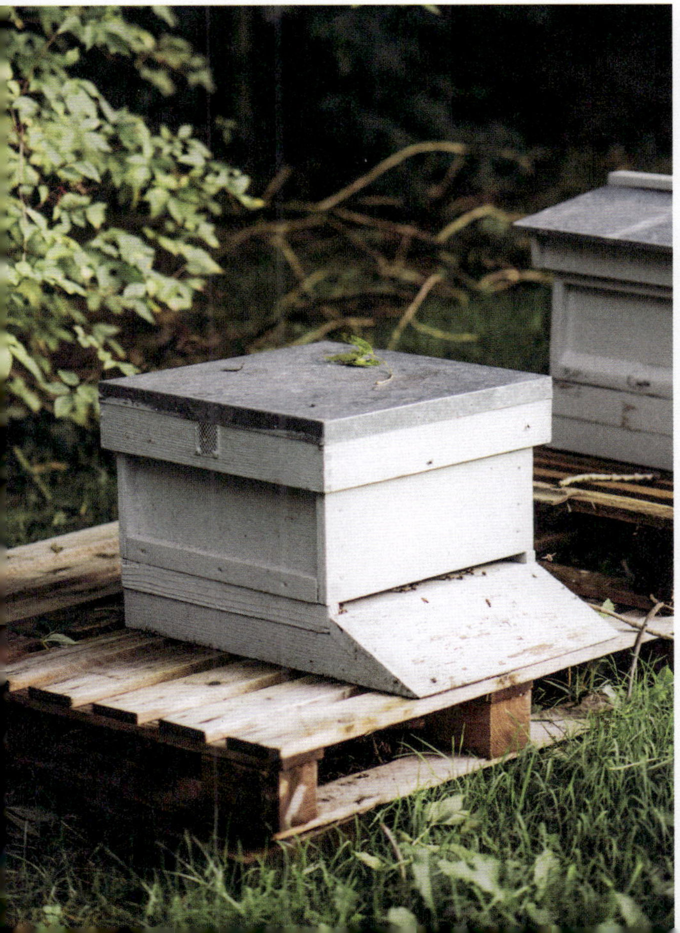

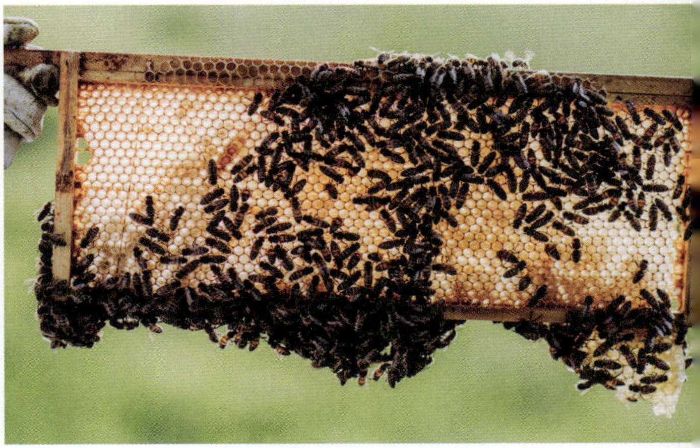

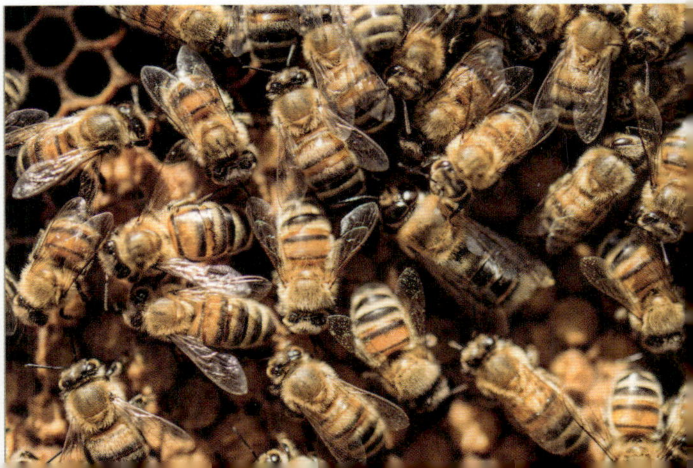

xx

Summer

SUMMER

The verdant fields of home, so lush and bountiful, will always stir my beating heart. They are flanked by thick hedgerows that are showing off with a riot of colour, where pale pink dog roses and lemon-yellow honeysuckle twist and interlace with spiky blackthorn, rich with a flourish of tiny, creamy flowers. Yet the most iconic plant has to be the cow parsley, dancing in the summer breeze. An English summer is a joy to behold. If it could be bottled and sold, you'd never want for much.

Taking shelter under an old oak tree as the midday sun bakes my freckled shoulders, I look on as my trusty friend the buzzard sits atop a telephone pole. Our native cattle are lowing, as they spy an even richer pasture cordoned off from their greedy grasp by a moveable electric fence. Our barn is filling with freshly cut and dried hay and sileage, providing that sweet scent of pickled and preserved pasture that once again makes my heart skip a beat. It is without a doubt the best fragrance money cannot buy. The neighbour's field is filled with freshly shorn lambs, who have moved on from their bouncing and leaping days in spring and are now contentedly heads down, chomping away.

A few dark grey clouds appear, threatening summer rain, which would give us all a little respite from the heat of the day. They soon drift off into the distance – a nice idea, but not today. It is a curious characteristic of farmers, always wanting for something else; the grass always greener. In winter and spring we lament the rain, yet a too-long and too-hot dry spell will find us praying for a downpour to kiss the hardening soil and feed the roots that provide both food and shelter.

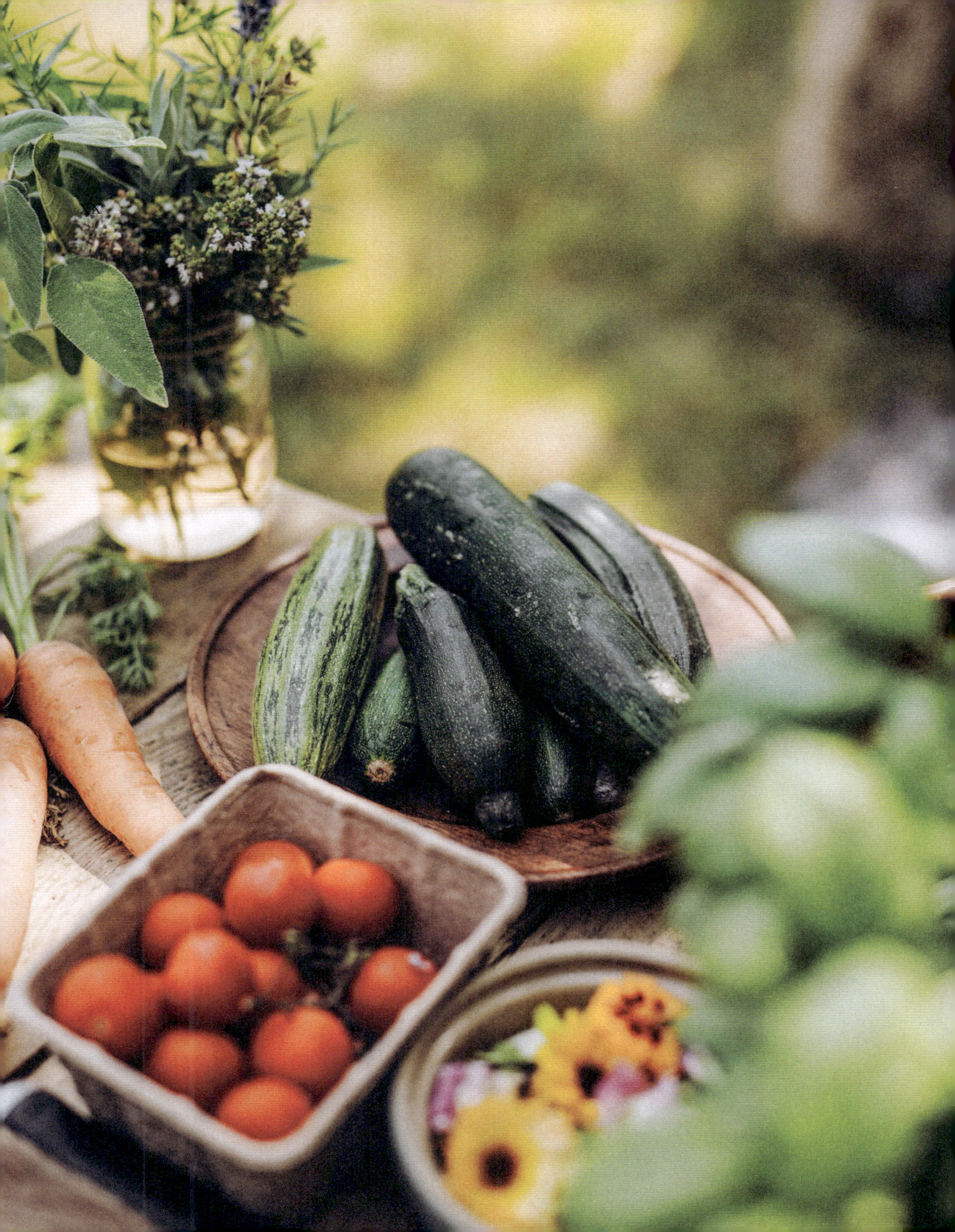

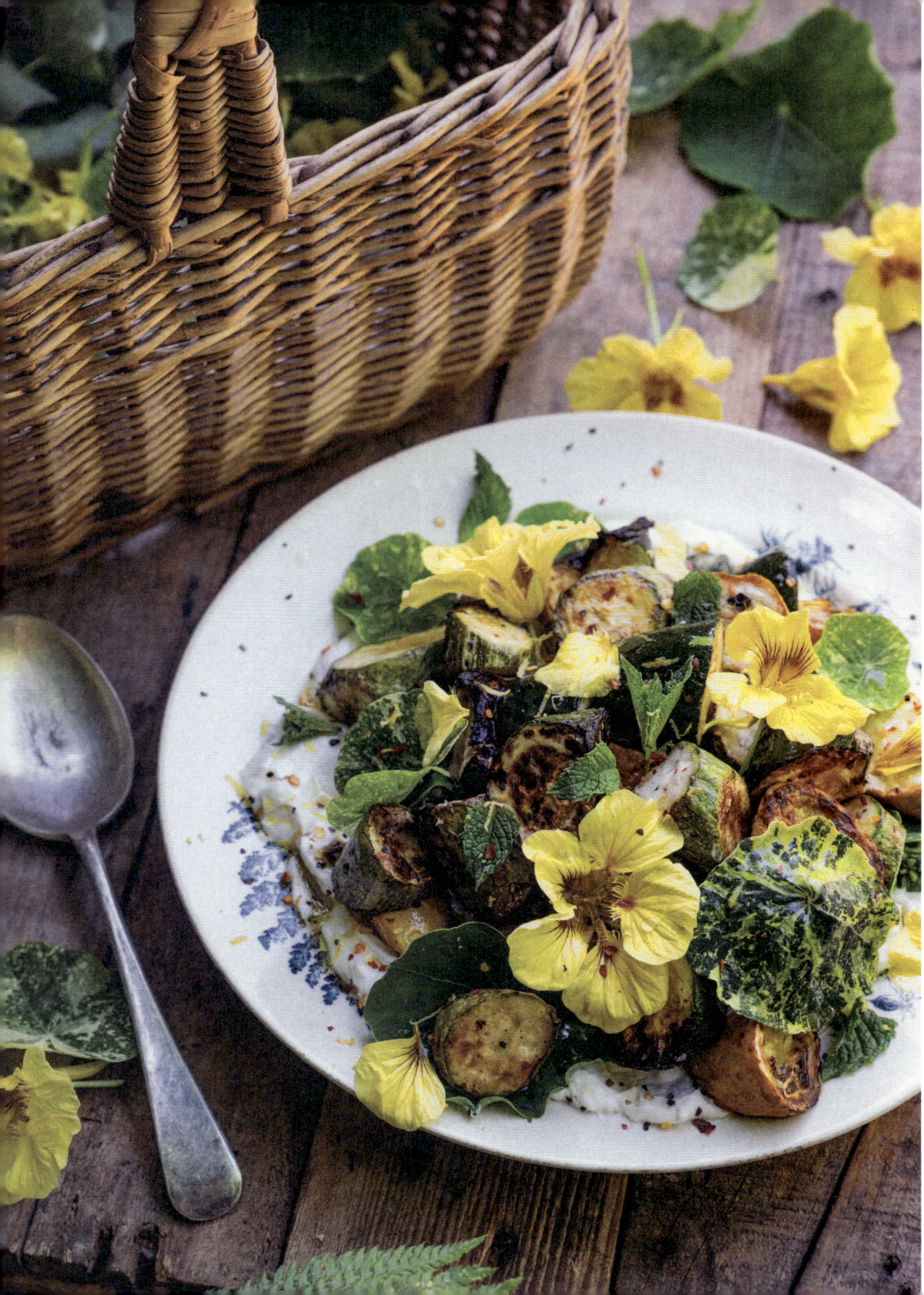

Charred Courgettes with Mint, Whipped Ricotta & Nasturtiums

One of our greatest joys is being able to share our farm with friends and family, and there's no better moment to gather loved ones together than the summertime. We throw down blankets or lay rustic tables in all sorts of picturesque corners of our land, sitting out in the evening light, watching the tall grass sway in the gentle breeze and marvelling as the sun sets with that ethereal orange glow you see only after solstice.

This is a favourite recipe for such occasions, as I can find almost all the ingredients by hunting around our vegetable garden. It's simply a case of making one component ahead of time, then throwing a few things together and letting the fire work its magic, giving me more time to savour these special moments.

4 courgettes
2 tablespoons extra virgin olive oil, plus extra to finish
grated zest and juice of 1 unwaxed lemon, plus extra juice to finish
½ teaspoon chilli flakes
200g (7oz) ricotta cheese
50g (1¾oz) pine nuts
a handful of nasturtium leaves and flowers
a handful of mint leaves, torn
flaky sea salt and freshly ground black pepper

Roughly chop the courgettes into 2.5cm (1in) chunks and tip into a mixing bowl. Add the olive oil, half the lemon zest and juice, the chilli flakes and a pinch of salt and pepper, giving everything a really good mix to ensure each piece of courgette is well coated. Leave to marinate for at least 30 minutes.

Tip the ricotta into a medium mixing bowl along with a good pinch of salt and pepper. Add the remaining lemon zest and juice. With a hand-whisk or an electric whisk, whip the ricotta until it becomes light and fluffy. Set to one side.

Fire up your barbecue ready for two-zone grilling so that you can cook both directly and indirectly. This means lighting charcoal on one side of your barbecue and leaving the other side of it fire-free. This gives you heat flexibility and instantly puts you more in control. Make sure your fire has settled down to glowing embers; a nice steady heat, nothing too fierce.

Add the courgettes to the charcoal side of the grill, leave them for around 2 minutes, then turn. Keep turning the courgettes, moving them around the heat, so they cook as evenly as possible until they are tender and beautifully charred. This should take around 8 minutes in total.

Place a dry frying pan over the fire. Add the pine nuts and toast for around 2–3 minutes, ensuring they don't catch. Set aside.

Spoon the whipped ricotta onto a large plate or platter, then scatter over the charred courgettes along with the nasturtium leaves and flowers. Scatter over the mint, then sprinkle with the toasted pine nuts. Drizzle a generous glug of olive oil over the dish and add another squeeze of lemon juice.

Serve straight away with some flatbreads on the side for scooping.

Smashed Cucumber with Halloumi & Tahini Dressing

It's been a stiflingly hot day. Even as the sun begins to set, there is still plenty of heat in the air. Lovely for those who can escape to the beach and bask in all the sun's glory, but more challenging for those of us who have vegetables, crops and livestock to look after. I am less concerned about the animals; our cattle are a resilient breed who take changes to weather in their stride. When it's too hot they simply gather under the canopy of our many trees, but often I find them sitting in the middle of the field, chewing the cud, unbothered by the unrelenting heat.

The fields that surround my vegetable garden, where my cucumbers are ripening in plentiful sunshine, are clinging on to their green hue, which tells you all you need to know about how we manage this land. As my gaze stretches further, it's a sad story, bare soil baking in the heat, and grasses burnt to a crisp brown. It's a stark reminder that as weather patterns become increasingly erratic and droughts more common, half the world's staple diet could be under threat. As extreme weather events become the norm, we are now caught in a race against time, and those who don't adapt may find themselves on the losing side.

2 cucumbers
2 tablespoons flaky sea salt
½ teaspoon chilli flakes
a squeeze of lemon juice
150g (5½oz) British halloumi-style cheese
flaky sea salt and freshly ground black pepper
edible flowers, to decorate (optional)

For the dressing
200g (7oz) grass-fed yogurt
zest and juice of ½ lemon
1 teaspoon tahini
a pinch of freshly ground black pepper
1 small bunch of mint, leaves picked and chopped, with a few reserved whole for garnish

Place the cucumbers on a chopping board and use a rolling pin to carefully bash them until they have broken up. Generously sprinkle the flesh with salt, a few chilli flakes, a twist or two of black pepper and a squeeze of lemon juice. Set aside to allow the cucumbers to macerate and tenderize.

To make the dressing, pour the yogurt into a mixing bowl and add the lemon juice, tahini, and a pinch of salt and pepper. Mix well to combine. Add the chopped mint leaves and stir through the tangy yogurt. Set aside.

Slice the halloumi into strips and pan-fry or grill on the barbecue for 1 minute on each side, or until lightly caramelized.

Drain the cucumbers and arrange on a platter. Pile the halloumi on top, then drizzle the mound with the luscious tahini yogurt dressing. Finish with the lemon zest, a few more mint leaves and some edible flowers if you like.

Serve as the main event or a light, fresh side dish at a summer gathering.

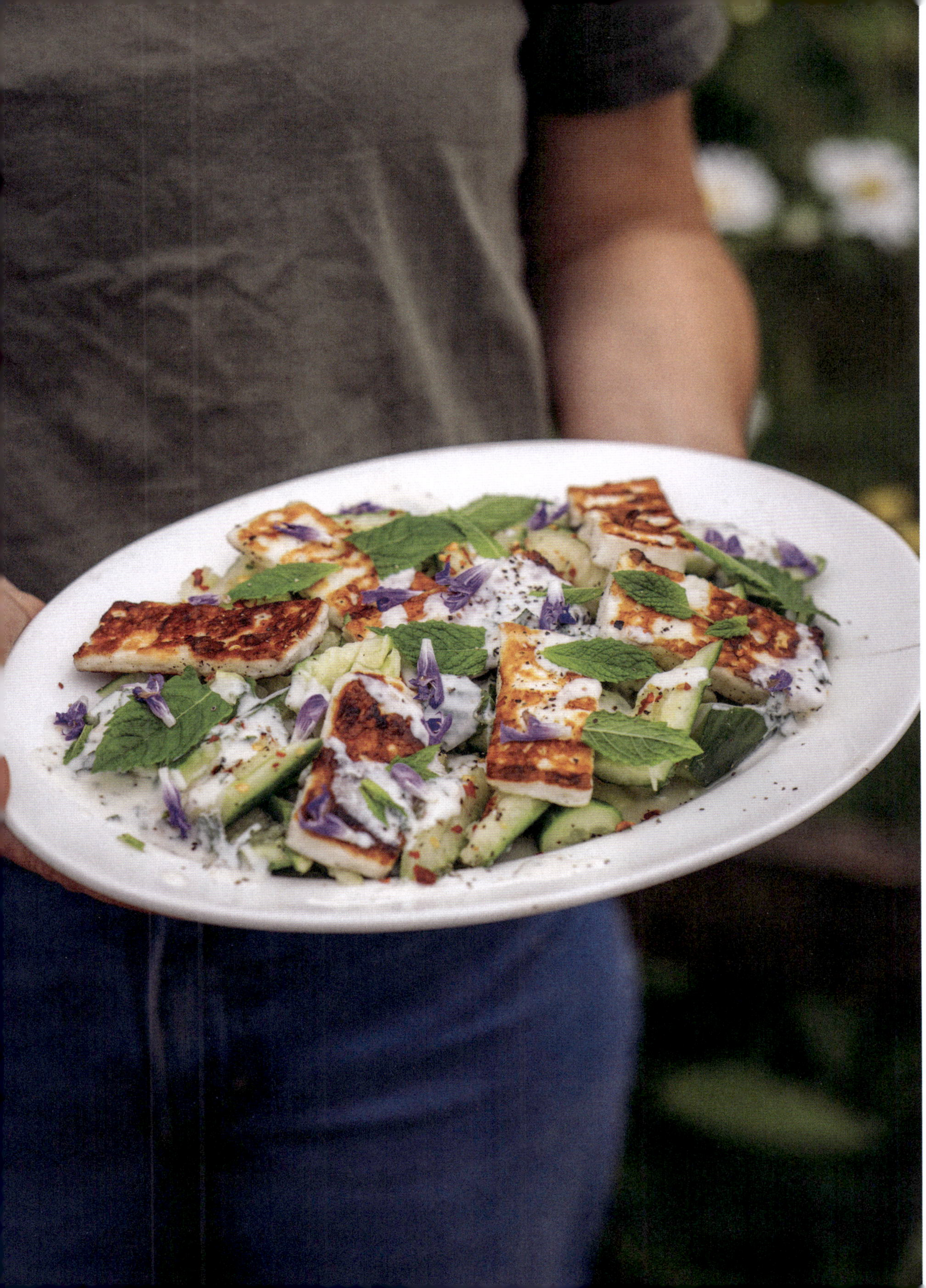

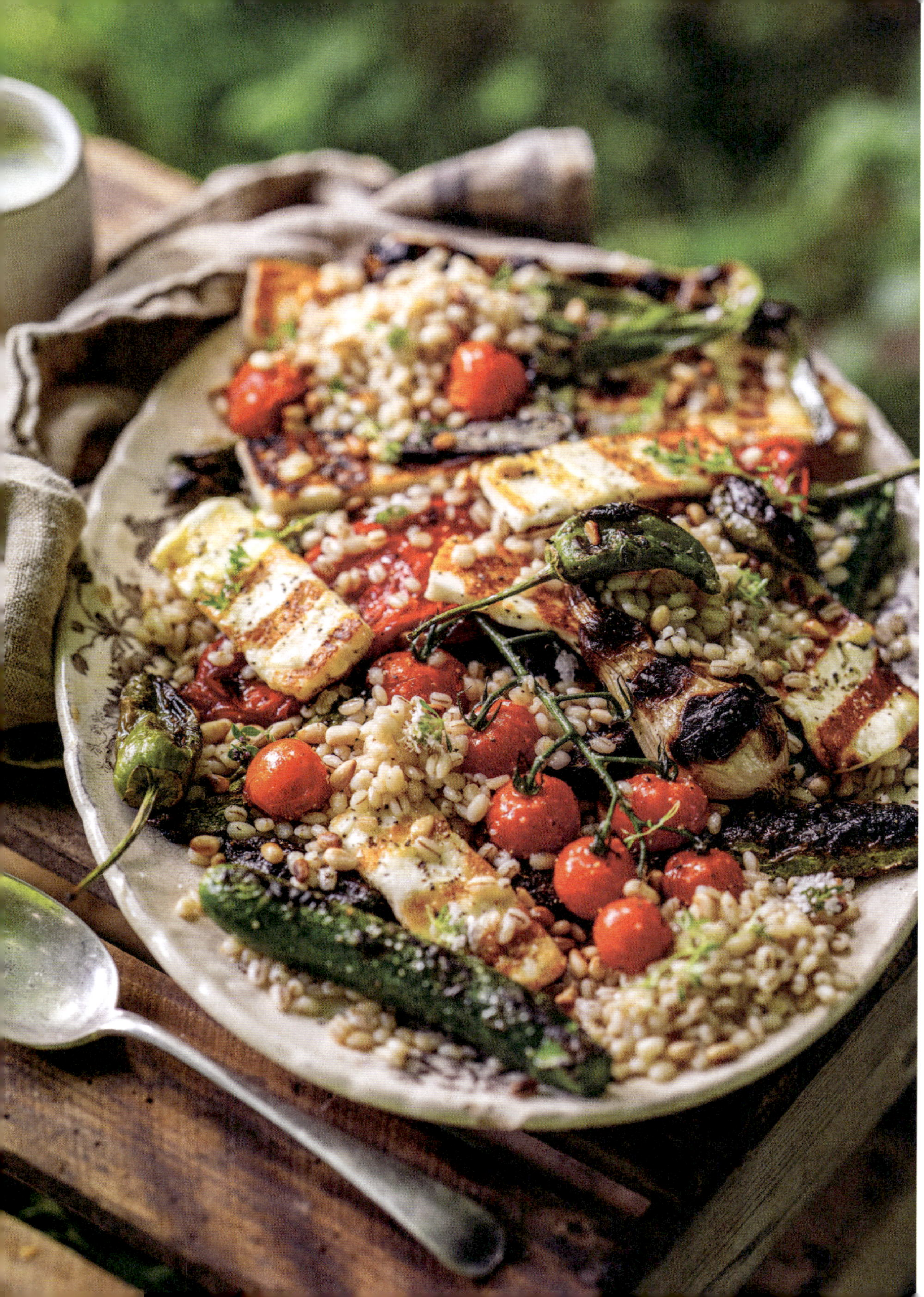

Spelt with Charred Summer Veg, Halloumi & Kefir Dressing

I really enjoy the ritualistic aspect of this recipe. There's something very calming about the grains simmering away, sending steam up into the atmosphere. There is mindfulness required in ensuring each bright vegetable strip turns perfectly charred instead of 'whoops that's burnt'. Then it's the final coming together of things, building a layered mountain of texture and flavour that your gut microbes will thank you for later. This recipe is good for you in so many ways.

2 litres (3½ pints) water
300g (10½oz) spelt
150g (5½oz) cherry tomatoes on the vine
4 garlic cloves
a drizzle of extra virgin olive oil
2 courgettes, sliced lengthways
1 red pepper, sliced lengthways
1 aubergine, sliced into strips
flaky sea salt and freshly ground black pepper

For the dressing
150ml (5fl oz) kefir
3 tablespoons extra virgin olive oil
zest and juice of 1 unwaxed lemon
1 small bunch of mint, leaves picked and chopped
1 small bunch of parsley, roughly chopped
1 small bunch of dill, roughly chopped
flaky sea salt and freshly ground black pepper

To serve
200g (7oz) British halloumi-style cheese
1 small bunch of mint, leaves picked and chopped
1 small bunch of parsley, roughly chopped

Light the barbecue and let it get to a nice steady heat.

Meanwhile, make the dressing. Combine the kefir, olive oil and lemon juice with a pinch of salt and pepper in a blender and give it a good blitz. Pour into a mixing bowl and add the chopped herbs and lemon zest. Give it a good stir and adjust the seasoning, adding more lemon, salt or pepper as needed. Set aside.

Place a saucepan on the barbecue, fill with the measured water and bring to the boil. Add the spelt and cook for 30 minutes. Once cooked, add a big pinch of salt and pepper and set aside.

Place a frying pan on the barbecue and add the tomatoes and garlic along with a drizzle of oil. Leave to sizzle away for about 8 minutes, or until the tomatoes have almost collapsed and the garlic has caramelized.

Generously drizzle the remaining veg with olive oil and season with a good pinch of sea salt. Place over the charcoal and char well for around 5 minutes, until the veg have become tender and beautifully caramelized. Once cooked, place in a large mixing bowl, tip in the tomatoes and garlic, then drizzle with more olive oil and set aside.

Slice the halloumi and place on the barbecue. Grill for around 3 minutes on each side. Remove and set aside.

Add the spelt to the vegetable bowl along with the rest of the chopped herbs. Give everything a really good mix to allow all the flavours to combine. Serve on a plate or platter, scattered with the grilled halloumi and generously drizzled with the kefir dressing.

Grilled Aubergines with Honey, Goat's Curd, Herbs & Seeds

I have only recently found affection for the aubergine. Perhaps it was because they were often rather bitter, although most growers now breed this out. More likely, it was because I had only ever eaten them in rather unimaginative ways, as a miscellaneous mush. Once you get your head around their anatomy, you can then truly get excited by their versatility. This recipe was inspired by a very special tapas bar we visited in Barcelona. The aubergines had been deep-fried and were crisped to perfection. They were doused in honey and sprinkled with herbs, one of the most joyous ways I have ever eaten them. We asked for thirds.

3 small/medium red onions
2–3 aubergines
4 tablespoons extra virgin olive oil
flaky sea salt

For the dressing
200ml (7fl oz) extra virgin olive oil
5 tablespoons balsamic vinegar
2 garlic cloves, crushed to a paste

To serve
2 tablespoons roughly chopped walnuts
2 tablespoons pumpkin seeds
2 tablespoons sunflower seeds
1 small bunch of parsley, roughly chopped
a few sprigs of thyme
4 tablespoons fresh goat's curd
2–3 tablespoons local runny honey
a drizzle of extra virgin olive oil

Fire up your barbecue ready for two-zone grilling so that you can cook directly and indirectly – simply light charcoal on one side of your barbecue and leave the other side of the grill fire-free. This gives you heat flexibility and instantly puts you more in control of the fire. Make sure your fire has settled down to glowing embers; a nice steady heat, nothing too fierce.

Wrap the onions tightly in foil and throw them into the coals of the fire. Leave to roast in the embers for around 30–40 minutes. Using tongs, remove the onions, peel off the foil and leave to cool slightly.

Slice the aubergines into strips, then lightly prick the flesh with a fork. Cover with a generous amount of olive oil and a good pinch of sea salt. Using tongs, carefully lay the aubergines over the grill and cook for about 2–3 minutes, or until they have become tender and lightly charred. Once cooked, move to the back of the barbecue where they can keep warm.

In a clean jam jar, combine the olive oil, vinegar and crushed garlic. Twist on the lid and give the dressing a good shake.

The red onions should now be cool enough to handle. Remove the tough outer skin, then slice the flesh into quarters.

Arrange the onion quarters on a platter. Drape the aubergines over them and drizzle with the dressing, allowing the flesh to really soak it up. Serve sprinkled with the nuts, seeds and herbs, then dollop on the goat's curd. Finish with a generous drizzle of runny honey and some really good olive oil.

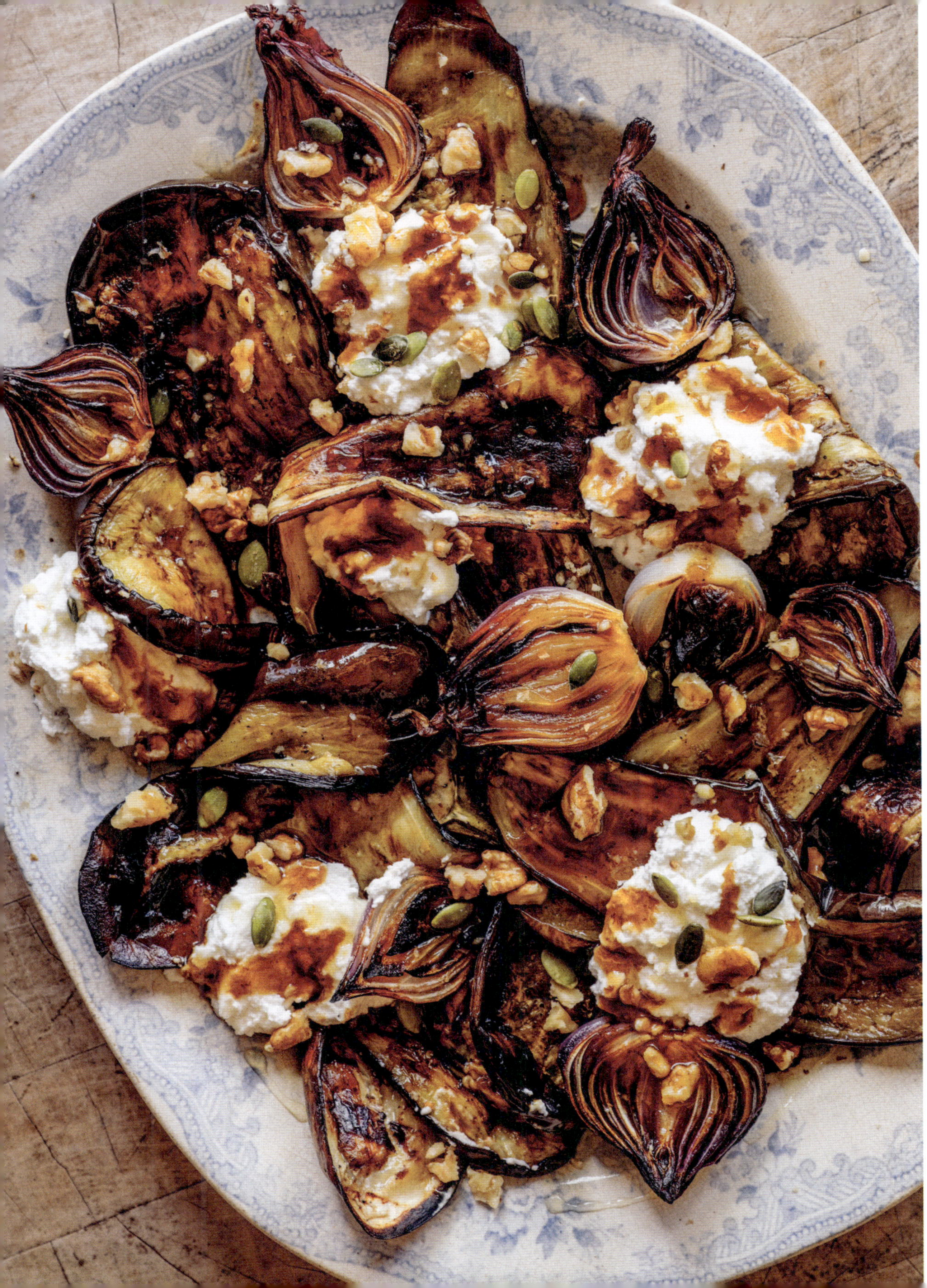

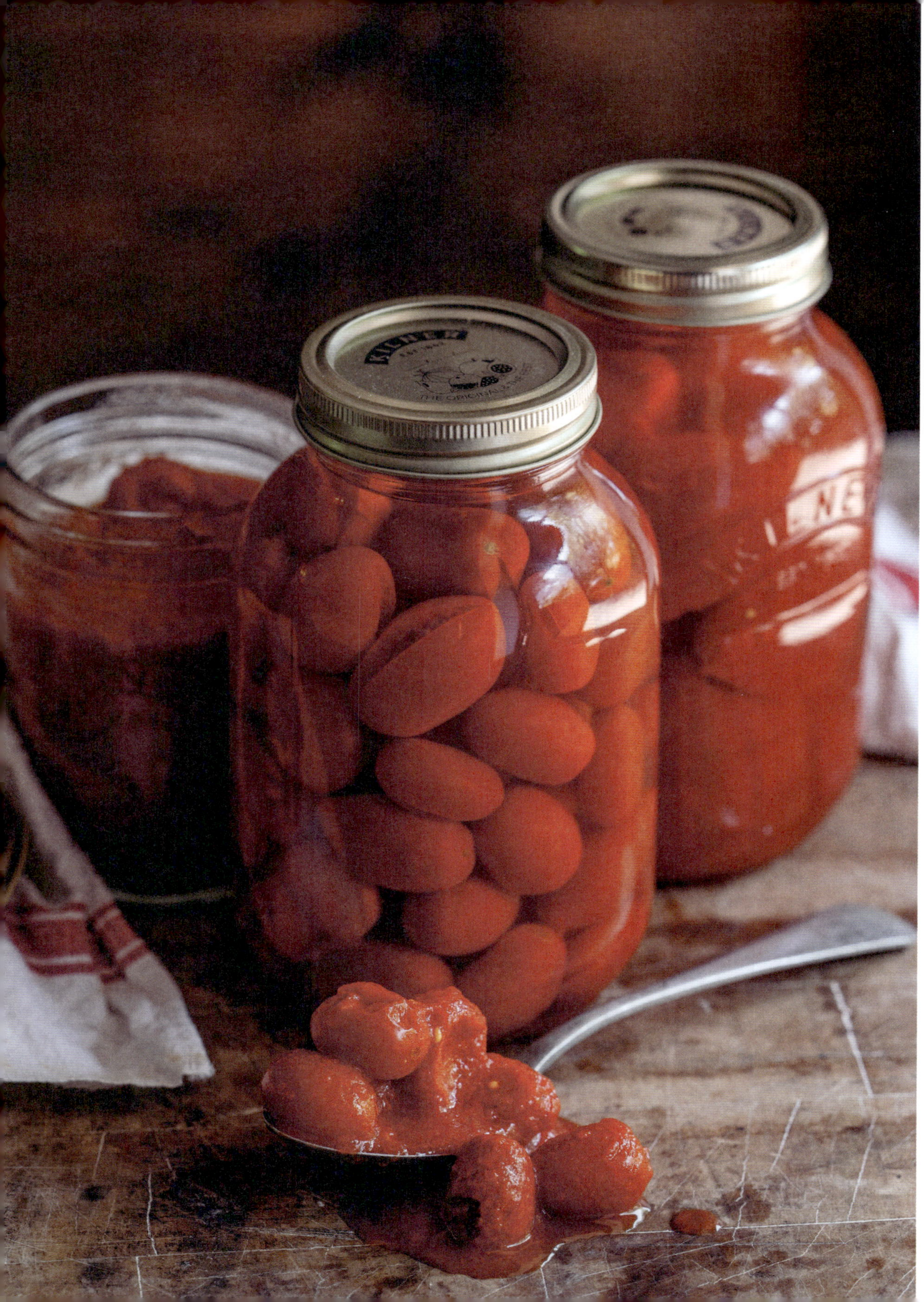

Preserved Tomatoes

It's not long ago that most rural households would have preserved the bounty of food grown in their gardens, or that of their neighbours. My granny was a keen preserver, using up all the gluts grown by both her and my Grampy's hard working hands. I grew up with the idea of preserving being the norm, even though it didn't happen much in our household; my mum's generation had already begun to loosen its grip on the waste-not culture with the advent of supermarkets and cheap imported food.

There's nothing much wrong with a good tin of tomatoes, canning is a wonderful preserving method. However, if like me you are a keen grower or live in the vicinity of one, there is something magical about capturing the summer in a jar and then reaching for it in the depths of winter.

2.75kg (6lb) tomatoes
7½ teaspoons lemon juice
10 teaspoons flaky sea salt
5 teaspoons caster sugar

You will also need
5 x 500ml (18fl oz) sterilized screw-top bottling jars (with a flat disc lid and a metal band to seal)

Note: The number of tomatoes it takes to fill a bottling jar can vary depending on their size. Generally, it takes about 550g (1lb 4oz) tomatoes to fill a 500ml (18fl oz) bottling jar.

Give the tomatoes a good rinse, then using a paring knife to score a cross on their bottoms (not the stalk end). Place them in a bowl (you may need to use a few bowls), then cover with boiling water. Allow the tomatoes to steep in the water for 1–2 minutes, then drain. Once cool enough to handle, carefully peel away the skins.

For chopped tomatoes, cut into halves or quarters, depending on the size of the tomato. Alternatively, keep them whole for the equivalent of plum tomatoes.

Into each sterilized jar, add 1½ teaspoons lemon juice, 2 teaspoons salt and 1 teaspoon caster sugar. Pack the tomatoes tightly into each jar, leaving about a 2.5cm (1in) gap at the top so the tomatoes can expand during the bottling process. Screw the lids on tightly and then loosen by about a quarter of a turn.

Sit a large pan that's taller than the jars on the hob and place a folded tea towel in the bottom. Stand the jars in the pan on top of the towel then add enough warm water to the pan to reach the shoulder of the jars. Bring to a simmer over a gentle heat (88°C/190°F). This should take around 40 minutes. Maintain this temperature for 2 minutes, then remove the pan from the heat.

Scoop out some of the water to make it easier to reach the lids of the jars. Use a tea towel to carefully remove the jars and stand them on a wooden surface or thick folded towel. Quickly twist the lids so they are all fully tight, then leave the jars undisturbed to cool.

Check the seals to make sure they have formed a vacuum by unscrewing the ring; if any jars are not sealed, process again. Store in a cool, dry spot and use within 12 months.

TIP: *To sterilize jars, wash them along with their lids in hot, soapy water and rinse well. Still wet, stand them upside down on a large baking tray with their lids separately alongside, and place in an oven preheated to 160°C/325°F/gas mark 3 for about 15 minutes. Ideally, fill them while still warm.*

Roasted Tomatoes with Za'atar Labneh & Oregano

You might look at this recipe and think it would make a lovely side dish for a summer party. Sometimes looks can be deceiving; it's so good and so filling, it deserves to be the main event. Or perhaps go mezze-style. If I could be so indulgent as to suggest you might serve it alongside one or two other recipes in this chapter, such as the Grilled Aubergines with Honey, Goat's Curd, Herbs & Seeds (page 74) and the Charred Courgettes with Mint, Whipped Ricotta & Nasturtiums (page 64). For the carnivores among you, some perfectly charred hogget chops would make a perfect addition to this feast.

400g (14oz) mixed cherry tomatoes on the vine
1 bulb of garlic, cloves separated and peeled
200ml (7fl oz) extra virgin olive oil
200g (7oz) Labneh (see page 94)
flaky sea salt
a few sprigs of fresh oregano

For the za'atar
1 tablespoon cumin seeds
1 tablespoon coriander seeds
1 tablespoon sesame seeds
1 tablespoon sumac
1 tablespoon dried oregano
¼ teaspoon chilli flakes
½ teaspoon flaky sea salt

First, make the za'atar spice mix. Take a small cast-iron frying pan and place over a medium heat. Once the pan is warm, add the cumin, coriander and sesame seeds and toast for a few minutes until they have become fragrant. Tip the seeds into a mortar and add the sumac, oregano, chilli flakes and salt. Grind with the pestle until you have a fine powder. This can be tipped into a sterilized jar (see page 77) and stored for 6 months.

Preheat the oven to 180°C/350°F/gas mark 4. Take a shallow cast-iron pan and tip in the tomatoes and garlic cloves. Generously pour in enough olive oil to cover the tomatoes and garlic, then place in the oven and roast for 35 minutes. Alternatively, set the pan over the grill of a barbecue and leave to sizzle away for around 35–40 minutes. Either way, you are looking for the skins to have just started to blister and the tomatoes should be on the verge of collapse.

Once cooked, you can either use the tomatoes straight away, or transfer them to a sterilized jar. As long they're stored under oil, they'll keep in the fridge for at least a month.

Mix 1 tablespoon of the za'atar into the labneh, strring it in well. Generously spoon the pillowy mixture onto a plate or platter, then pile the blistered tomatoes over the top, ensuring you include some softened garlic cloves and plenty of the fragrant oil. Finish with a pinch of sea salt, another scattering of za'atar and a few sprigs of fresh oregano.

Serve with crusty bread or homemade flatbreads to scoop up the tomatoes and labneh, and enjoy.

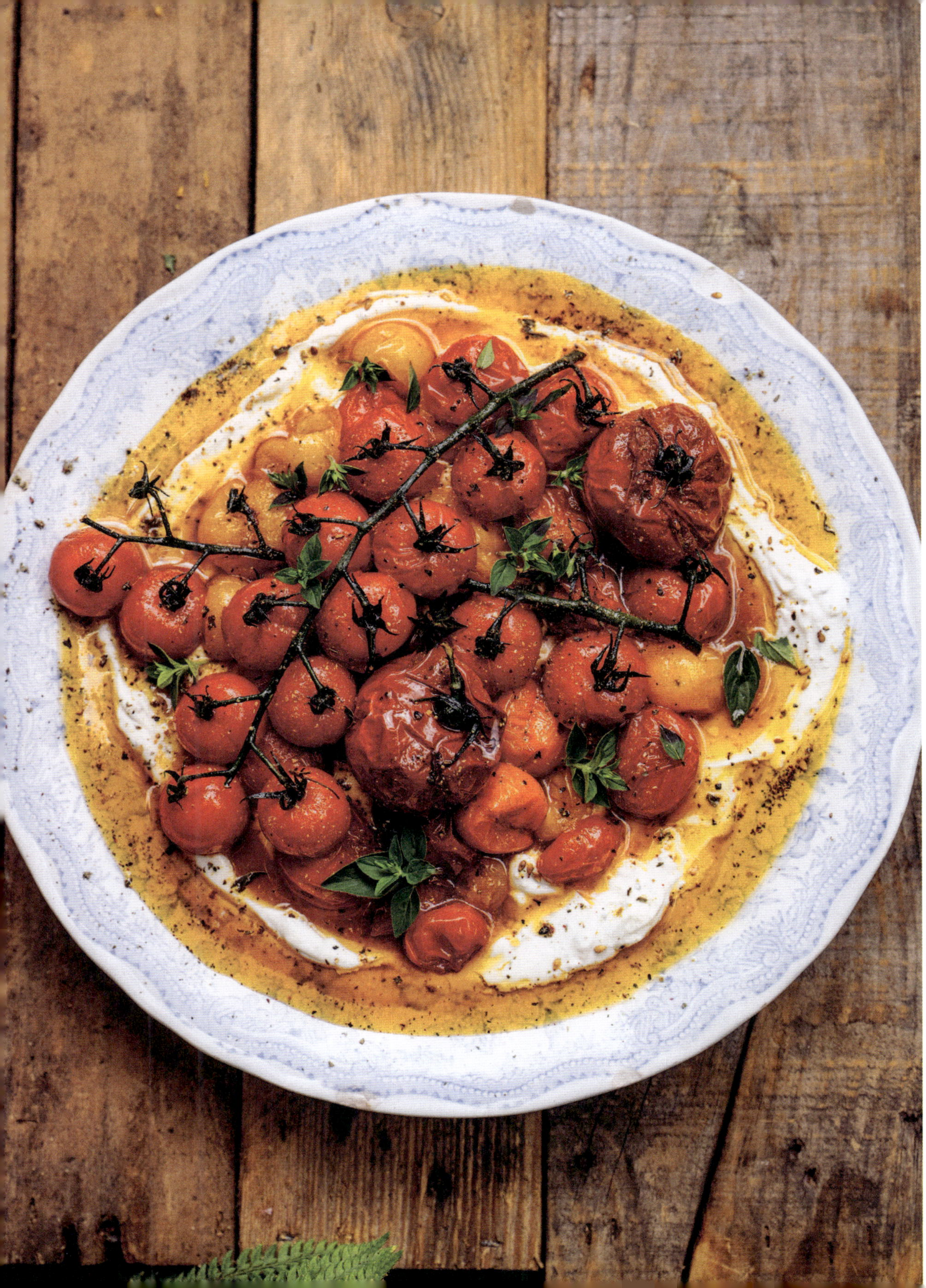

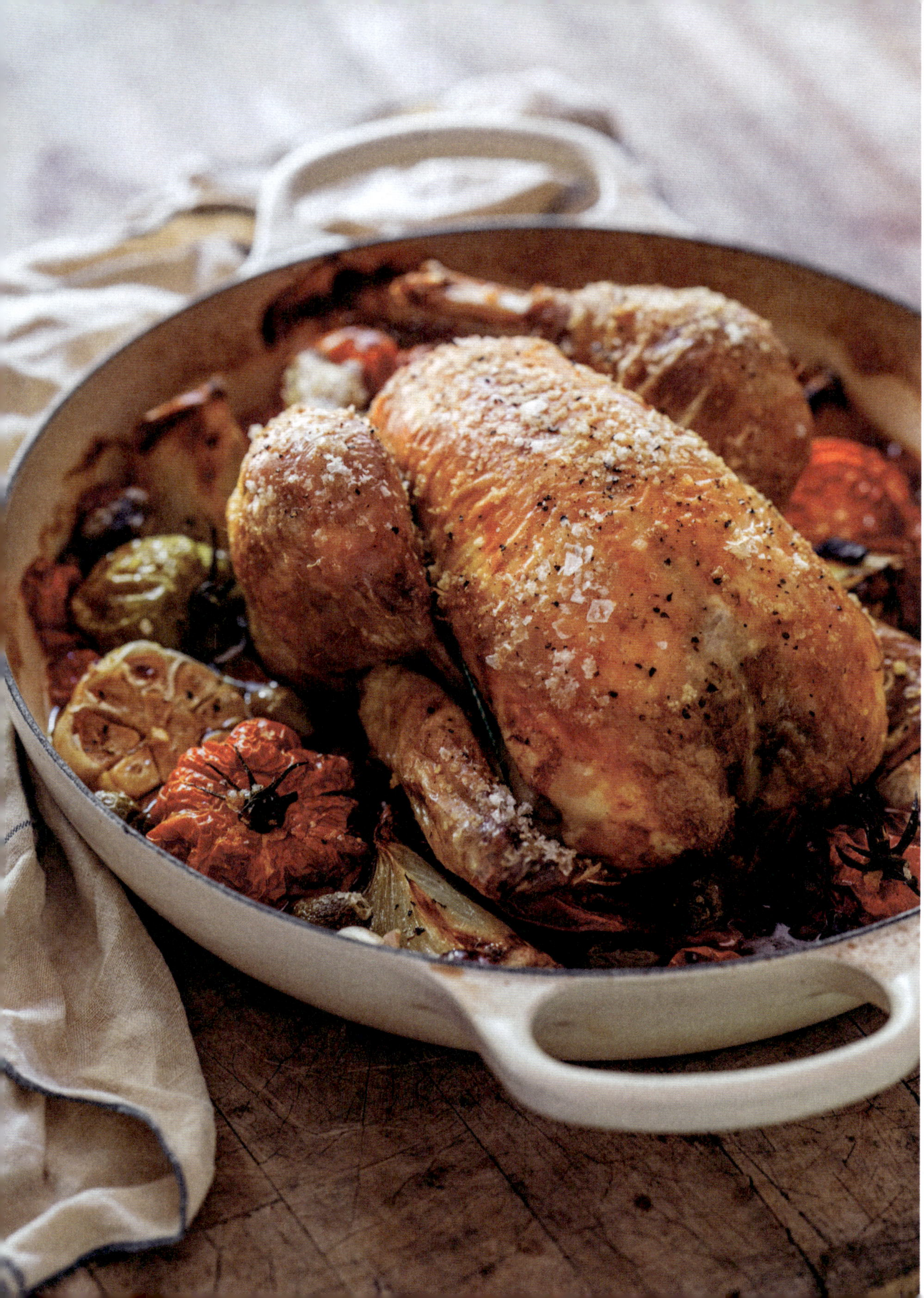

Summer Roast Chicken with Tomatoes, Olives & Lemon

Growing our own food was a central pillar of my life. I would spend hours watching both my grandparents and my mum carefully tend to the most spectacular gardens, absorbing every moment. Once I had apprenticed for long enough, I was given my own corner of the garden in which to sow seeds and watch them flourish. I became quite good at growing things from my little patch of earth. While my sunflowers, sweet peas and pumpkins were renowned, I never outstripped my Grampy in one area – tomatoes. Grampy was legendary when it came to producing a bumper crop. To this day, I have never tasted better. He was a true master. Between you and me, I have a suspicion he had an extra special ingredient. There is a wonderful Roald Dahl quote that will always make me think of my magnificent Grampy: 'If you have good thoughts, they will shine out of your face like sunbeams, and you will always look lovely.' His face was pure and kind, his hands worn and caring, he was sunshine and warmth. I think his tomatoes soaked up all his majesty, and that was his special ingredient.

Grampy, this one is for you. An ode to your beautiful tomatoes. A recipe to gather loved ones together, to soak up the summer sunshine, enjoy the good life and remember how lucky we are to bask in each others' light.

600g (1lb 5oz) mixed heritage tomatoes
2 whole bulbs of garlic
2 onions
50g (1¾oz) green olives
1 lemon, cut into wedges
5–6 tablespoons extra virgin olive oil
1 large organic or free-range chicken (1.7–2kg/ 3lb 13oz–4lb 8oz)
a few oregano sprigs or basil leaves
flaky sea salt and freshly ground black pepper

Preheat the oven to 190°C/375°F/gas mark 5.

Place the tomatoes in a large roasting tray, slicing any very large ones in half. Slice the garlic bulbs down the centre and nestle in with the tomatoes. Quarter the onions, leaving the skin on and add these to the tray. Scatter the olives around the other veg and then wedge in pieces of lemon, keeping one or two back. Give the veg a good drenching in good-quality olive oil and season well with salt and pepper. Place the chicken on top of the veg and stuff the remaining lemon wedges inside the cavity of the chicken. Season the skin generously with salt and pepper.

Place the roasting tray in the oven for 1 hour 15 minutes.

Remove the tray from the oven, lift the chicken out and leave to rest on a carving board. Keep the beautiful roasted veg warm while the chicken rests.

Once cooled, carve the chicken, giving everyone a little meat from the leg and breast. Spoon over heaps of the roasted veg, making sure you scoop up plenty of the gorgeous juices. Take the warm garlic bulbs and squeeze out a few cloves onto each plate. Finish with a few roughly torn leaves of fresh oregano or basil.

Serve with buttered potatoes, or – even better – crusty bread for mopping up the mouthwatering juices.

Chicken Legs with Lemon, Potatoes, Thyme & Oregano

After reading *My Family and Other Animals* by Gerald Durrell, I became enchanted by stories set on Greek islands. Through his captivating tale of life on Corfu, I found myself feeling the intense dry heat and smelling perfumed wafts of wild oregano. I simply had to go. This recipe is one that captures some of the magic of the Greek islands, and you can enjoy it wherever you are in the world. We have so much to thank Durrell for. He was a champion of all animals, especially those under threat and overlooked by others. Through his writing, he generated sufficient income to create his own zoo, with a clear mission of saving species from extinction. His pioneering work not only brought awareness of the wonders of nature, but it changed the way zoos displayed animals to the public, making them more humane and dramatically improving links with wider conservation efforts.

6 free-range chicken legs
1 bunch of lemon thyme
1 bunch of oregano
4–5 tablespoons extra virgin olive oil
800g (1lb 12oz) Marfona or other waxy potatoes
1 bulb of garlic, halved
1 large unwaxed lemon, sliced
small glass of white wine
flaky sea salt

The day before you plan to serve this dish, remove the chicken legs from the fridge and pat dry. Generously season with salt, scatter over some of the lemon thyme and oregano, then drizzle with a good glug of olive oil and massage the meat well. Place the dish back in the fridge and leave overnight to marinate.

The next day, set a pan of salted water over a high heat. Once boiling, add the potatoes and cook for around 8 minutes, or until just tender. Drain and leave to cool for a couple of minutes, then cut into slices 3cm (1in) thick.

Preheat the oven to 180°C/350°F/gas mark 4.

Drizzle a little oil into a large roasting tray, then add the chicken legs, potatoes, garlic bulb and lemon slices. Season well and scatter over a little more thyme and oregano. Place in the oven and roast for 1 hour, giving the tray a shake to toss the potatoes around halfway through the cooking time. Once the chicken skin is golden and the potatoes are crisp, remove from the oven.

Lift the chicken, potatoes, garlic bulb and lemon slices out of the tray and pile onto a platter. Set the roasting tray over a medium–high heat and tip in the wine, allowing it to bubble away for 5–6 minutes, while using a wooden spoon to scrape up all the delicious bits from the bottom. Pour this mixture over the platter.

Serve with a sharply dressed, fresh garden salad and a cold summer drink of your choice.

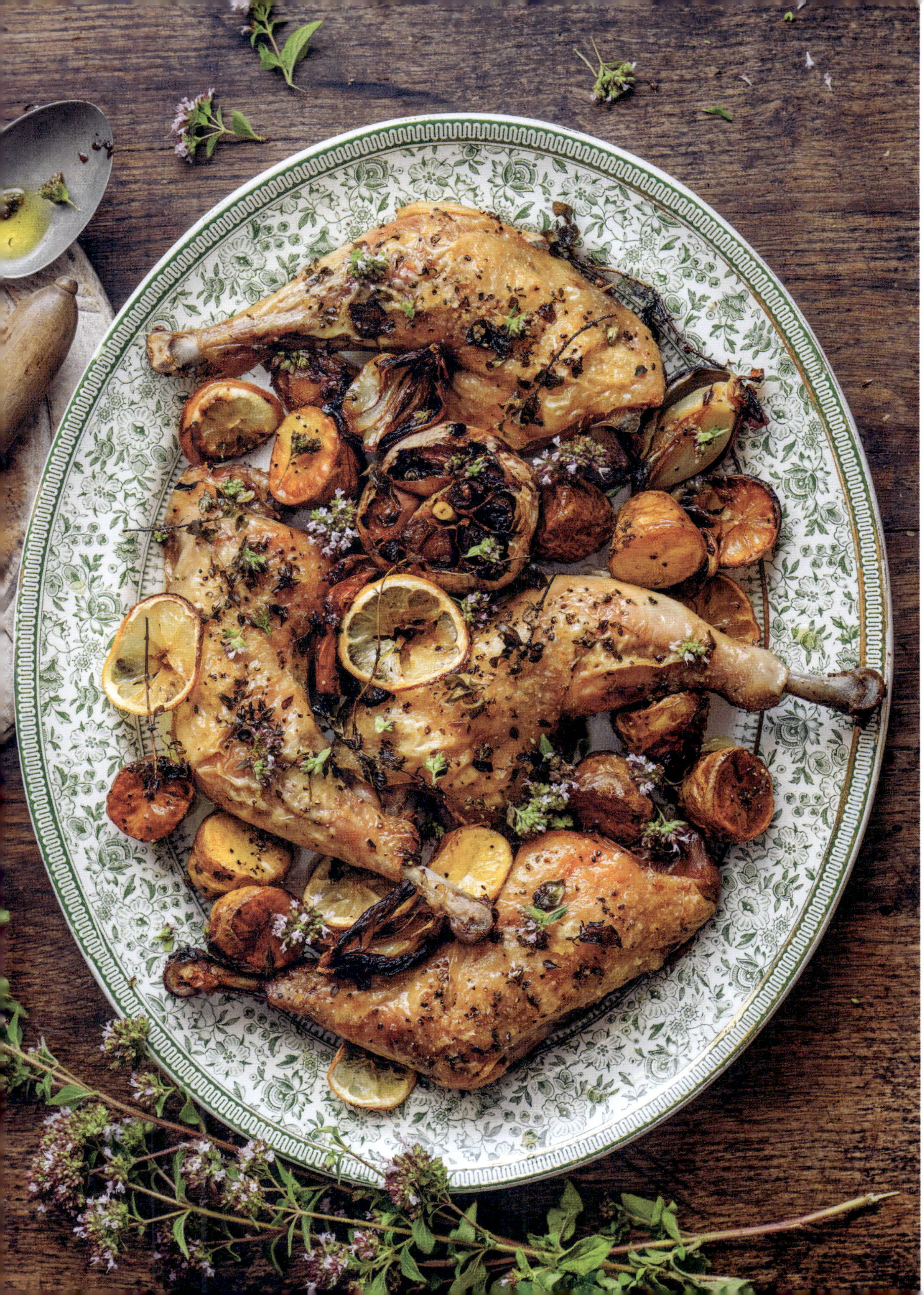

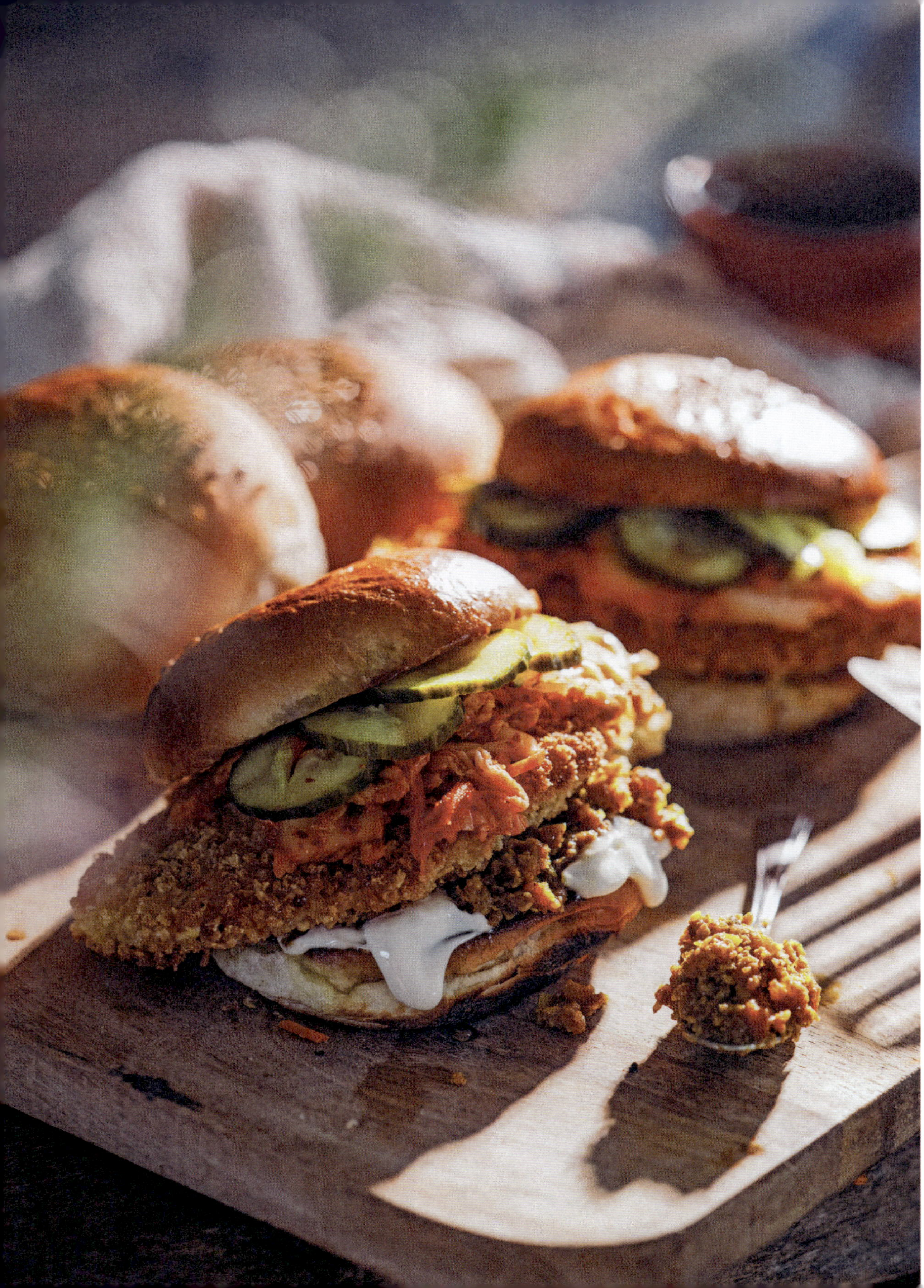

Chicken Schnitzel Burger with Cucumber Pickle

There has been an explosion of burger restaurants over the last decade, with wonderfully creative menus packed full of the most mouthwatering-sounding, American-influenced flavours. Smoky, spicy, cheesy – they all feature. Sadly, though, the fundamental element in most of these dishes – the meat – tends to lack provenance. This is understandable; it's never been harder for the restaurant industry to turn a profit. The advent of chains with their centralized kitchens drove down prices and pushed out independents. The cost of ingredients, labour and energy have all sky-rocketed, putting pressure on businesses to find savings, which usually target the protein element of a dish. I spent many years working with chefs, and I absolutely love going out to restaurants. I have a long list of favourites where I know the origins of the ingredients, I often know the owners and I am willing to pay well for the beautiful food they so carefully make. What I don't do these days is venture into the mass-market places where I know I will be left disappointed, so I created this recipe to satiate Will's craving for an indulgent burger!

5 tablespoons stoneground plain flour
2 organic and/or free-range egg yolks
175g (6oz) breadcrumbs
4 organic and/or free-range skinless chicken breasts
8 tablespoons organic rapeseed oil
flaky sea salt and freshly ground black pepper

For the cucumber pickle
3 cucumbers, total weight about 1kg/2lb 4oz
3 onions, halved and finely sliced, total weight approximately 250g/9oz
1 tablespoon flaky sea salt
100ml (3½fl oz) water
400ml (14fl oz) cider vinegar
175g (6oz) unbleached granulated sugar
½ teaspoon ground turmeric
2 teaspoons dill seeds
3 teaspoons yellow mustard seeds
a pinch of chilli flakes
3 cloves

To serve
4 burger buns
1 tablespoon mayonnaise per burger
1 tablespoon kimchi per burger

See overleaf for method.

Summer

First, make the cucumber pickle. Trim the ends of the cucumbers, then slice them in half lengthways. Running a spoon down the centre, scoop out the seeds (you could add them and the cucumber ends to a jug of water for a cooling summer drink).

Slice the cucumbers into 4mm (¼in) pieces and tip them into a large mixing bowl. Add the onions, then sprinkle over the salt and mix well. Cover the bowl with a clean tea towel and a plate and leave for at least 2 hours to allow the salt to draw out the liquid.

In a medium saucepan, combine the water, vinegar, sugar, turmeric, dill seeds, mustard seeds, chilli flakes and cloves. Bring to a simmer and stir until the sugar has fully dissolved.

Strain the cucumber and onion through a sieve, then add the slices to the simmering pan and cook for 3–4 minutes.

Spoon the cucumbers and onions into small sterilized jars (see page 77), pouring in enough liquid to make sure they are well covered. Seal the jars tightly and turn them upside down for 2 minutes, then leave them to cool the right way up. The pickle is ready to eat straight away, or it can be kept in a cool cupboard for up to 1 year. Once opened, eat within a week.

To make the chicken schnitzel, take three shallow bowls and place the flour in one, the whisked egg yolks in the second and the breadcrumbs in the third. Cover a chopping board with a sheet of greaseproof paper. Place the chicken breasts on it, and place another sheet of greaseproof paper on top. Using a rolling pin, carefully bash each breast to flatten. Remove the top sheet of greaseproof paper and discard. Generously season the chicken breasts, then dip them first into the bowl of flour, then the egg and finally the breadcrumbs, covering both sides.

Once each schnitzel has been prepared, place a cast-iron pan over a medium–high heat and pour in the oil for shallow frying. Once it is sizzling hot, add the schnitzels one at a time and cook for around 3 minutes on each side, or until they are beautifully golden. Drain on kitchen paper.

Place a clean and dry cast-iron pan over a medium heat. Add each burger bun, face-down, and leave to toast for 1–2 minutes. Generously slather them with the mayonnaise, then add a warm schnitzel. Dollop on a spoonful of kimchi and plenty of cucumber pickle. Put the bun lid on, then dive in.

Flat-Iron Steak with Romesco & Charred Spring Onions on Toast

Dusk has fallen on the farm. We have left it rather late to move the cattle, but better late than never, as they say. By the time we move electric fences and water, night has crept in. As the herd jovially plod through the yard, past the old bullock shed I am aware we are not alone. There is barely any daylight left, other than the moon, yet I can feel the night air is thick with bats, swooping and fluttering above us. They are following the cattle as they push on to new pastures.

There is a very special symbiotic relationship between bats and cattle. Our native breed cattle graze the hedgerows and pastures of the farm, chewing the cud and digesting forage, turning it into natural fertilizer. Often before their healthy, nutrient-rich pats have even landed, insects are in flight ready to feed. This is great news for our friend the bat, who must eat around 3,000 insects a night to survive. Like many other species, bats have seen significant decline through changes to land use and the intensification of farming practices.

Many of you will have heard and read stories telling you to cut out beef, that it is the key driver of climate change and species decline. Native breed cattle reared in harmony with nature, that are fed a totally natural diet and are part of a healthy ecosystem are, in fact, a vital tool in boosting biodiversity and mitigating climate impact. I encourage you to seek out beautiful pasture-reared meat and turn it into sensational recipes such as this. By doing so, you are supporting our farming community, and also a thriving, vibrant ecosystem.

500g (1lb 2oz) grass-fed flat-iron steak
extra virgin olive oil, for brushing
1 bunch of spring onions
4–6 slices of sourdough bread
1 garlic clove, peeled
a small handful of chives, chopped
flaky sea salt and freshly ground black pepper

For the romesco
extra virgin olive oil
2 large red peppers
50g (1¾oz) whole blanched almonds
1 slice of sourdough bread
3 garlic cloves, peeled and crushed
1 teaspoon smoked paprika
cold water, as needed
2 teaspoons sherry vinegar, to taste
flaky sea salt

See overleaf for method.

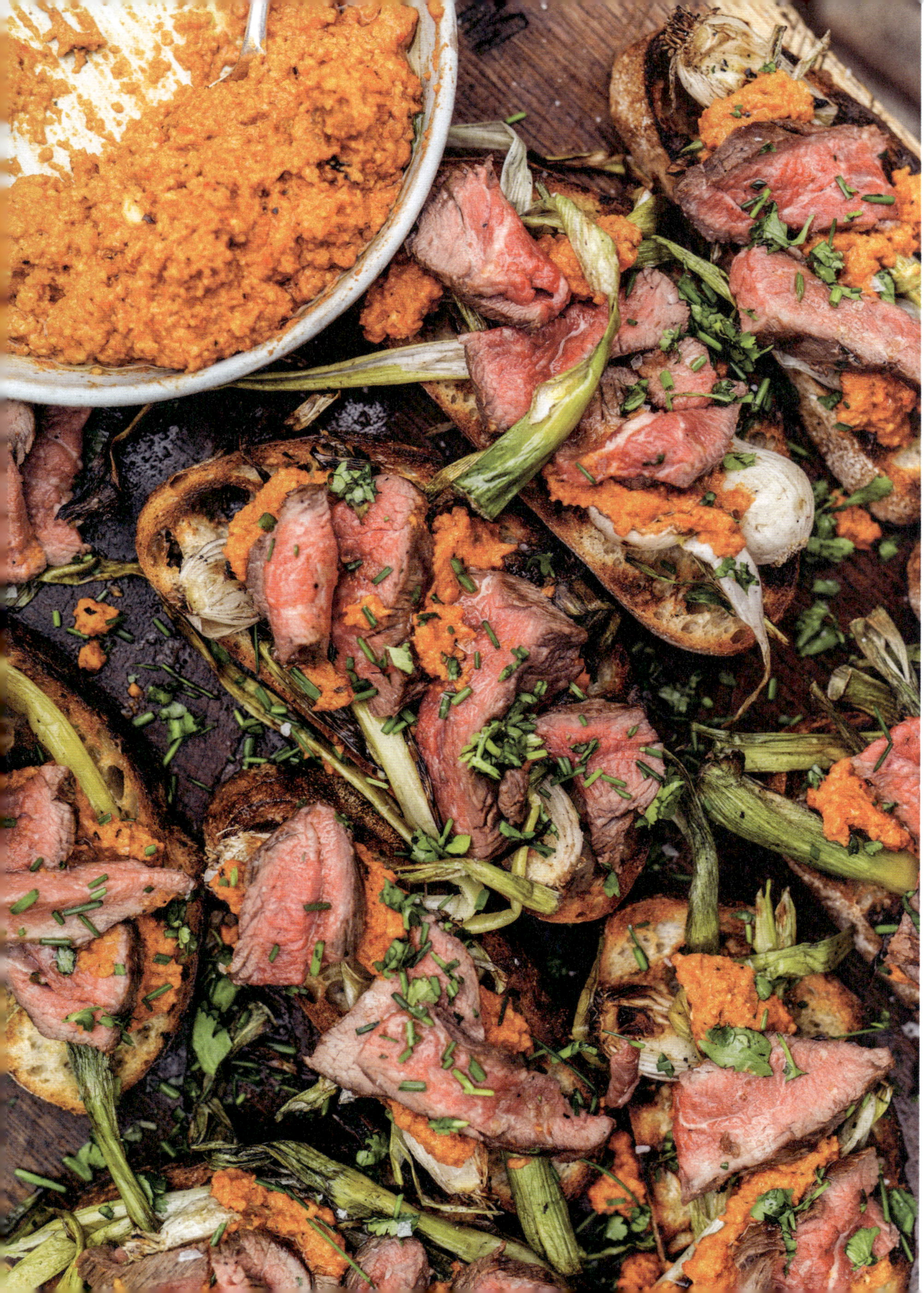

Fire up your barbecue ready for two-zone grilling so that you can cook both directly and indirectly. This means lighting charcoal on one side of your barbecue and leaving the other side of it fire-free. This gives you heat flexibility and instantly puts you more in control. Make sure your fire has settled down to glowing embers; a nice steady heat, nothing too fierce.

Begin with the romesco sauce. Brush a little oil over the red peppers and place them over the coals for around 15–20 minutes, rotating regularly, until the peppers are soft and lightly charred. Remove from the heat and allow to cool for a few minutes, then slice in half and remove the seeds and stem. Set to one side.

Meanwhile, toast the almonds in a dry frying pan over a medium heat for a few minutes, until they are golden. You can do this on the barbecue by setting the pan slightly off the fire. Tip into a food processor and pulse until ground.

Drizzle a little oil over the slice of bread and grill for a couple of minutes to toast it, then roughly chop and add to the almonds in the food processor, along with the cooked peppers, garlic and smoked paprika. Blitz until smooth, adding just enough cold water to make a smooth paste. Season with a little vinegar, to taste, and a pinch of salt, then set aside.

Make sure your barbecue grill is hot. Brush the steak all over with a little olive oil and season with plenty of salt. Place on the grill directly over the coals for around 5 minutes on one side, or until a beautiful char has just started to form. Flip over and cook on the other side for 4 minutes. Using a meat probe, check the temperature of the meat at the thickest point. For rare steak, you want to get it off the grill at 40°C (104°F), for medium-rare, take it off at 45–50°C (113–122°F). Set aside to rest. The temperature will continue to rise by 5–8°C (40–45°F) while resting, bringing it up to a perfect eating temperature.

Meanwhile, drizzle a little oil over the spring onions and season with salt and pepper. Cook over the hot barbecue for about 10 minutes, turning occasionally, until cooked and nicely charred in places, then set aside.

Brush the bread with olive oil, set over the coals and grill both sides until lightly toasted. Rub the garlic clove over each slice of toast.

To serve, pile the romesco on the toast to form a base. Arrange a few spring onions on the sauce, then slice the steak and lay it on top. Season with a pinch of salt and scatter over some chopped chives. Tuck in straight away.

Healing the Land

It's a myth that the countryside is slow and quiet. Perhaps it is, in comparison to the fast-paced excess of city life, but stop for a while and listen; you'll be amazed at what you might find.

It's late evening, the last hour before sunset – the golden hour. A veil of the sun's last rays catch between the treetops, shooting like outstretched arms. It's the time this land seems at its most enchanted. As I sit here among the long grasses that make up this farm, there's the low hum of crickets, the buzzing of bees, the sound of a buzzard calling as it hunts its prey, the melodic crunch and munch as the cattle cut through pasture with their incisors. Even as day slowly gives way to night, there is riot of activity going on; some I can see and hear, but much happens deep below my feet in the dark mass that we call soil. No wonder, when there are more microorganisms in three tablespoons of soil than the global population. The more fertile the soil, the more organisms live and thrive there.

The safe homes and habitats of billions of living creatures are under threat by the choices we make each day as we sit down for breakfast, lunch and dinner, because the food we choose to eat and the farming systems we choose to support directly impact the world we live in. It is the difference between a farm soundtrack of bees, birds, bats and butterflies, or one that is sterile and devoid of wildlife – instead you'll hear the loud boom of machinery reminiscent to that of city life.

Recently, we have begun to understand both the environmental and health implications of a globalized food system. As concerns change about climate, biodiversity loss and food-related illnesses grow.

More than half the habitable area of our planet is farmed, and many farming systems are intensive, driving up greenhouse gases, reducing biodiversity, degrading soils, worsening animal welfare, negatively impacting our health and producing eye-watering amounts of waste.

It is important to remember, we mustn't blame farmers for the situation we have found ourselves in, as they have simply been following directives set by governments around the world, who for the last 50 years have driven our food system towards commoditized, intensification to attract trade deals and feed ever-growing populations. As the climate changes and populations grow, there will be increased pressure on the efficient use of limited resources, so there has never been more urgency to replace our current extractive and exploitative farming system with one that is rehabilitative and regenerative.

Agroecological farming systems are a beacon of hope, offering us a clear pathway towards a more resilient and restorative food system. One of the cornerstones of a an agroecological or a 'regenerative' farming system is a focus on soil health, with pastoral farming playing a fundamental role in this.

I have seen first-hand nature's ability to heal, through implementing gentle ruminant animal grazing and long rest periods. By covering the soil with a cosy green blanket to protect the billions of microorganisms that call it home, by providing hooves to tread in native seeds to increase biodiversity of flora and attract symbiotic fauna, and by distributing nourishment in the form of natural manure – in all these ways,

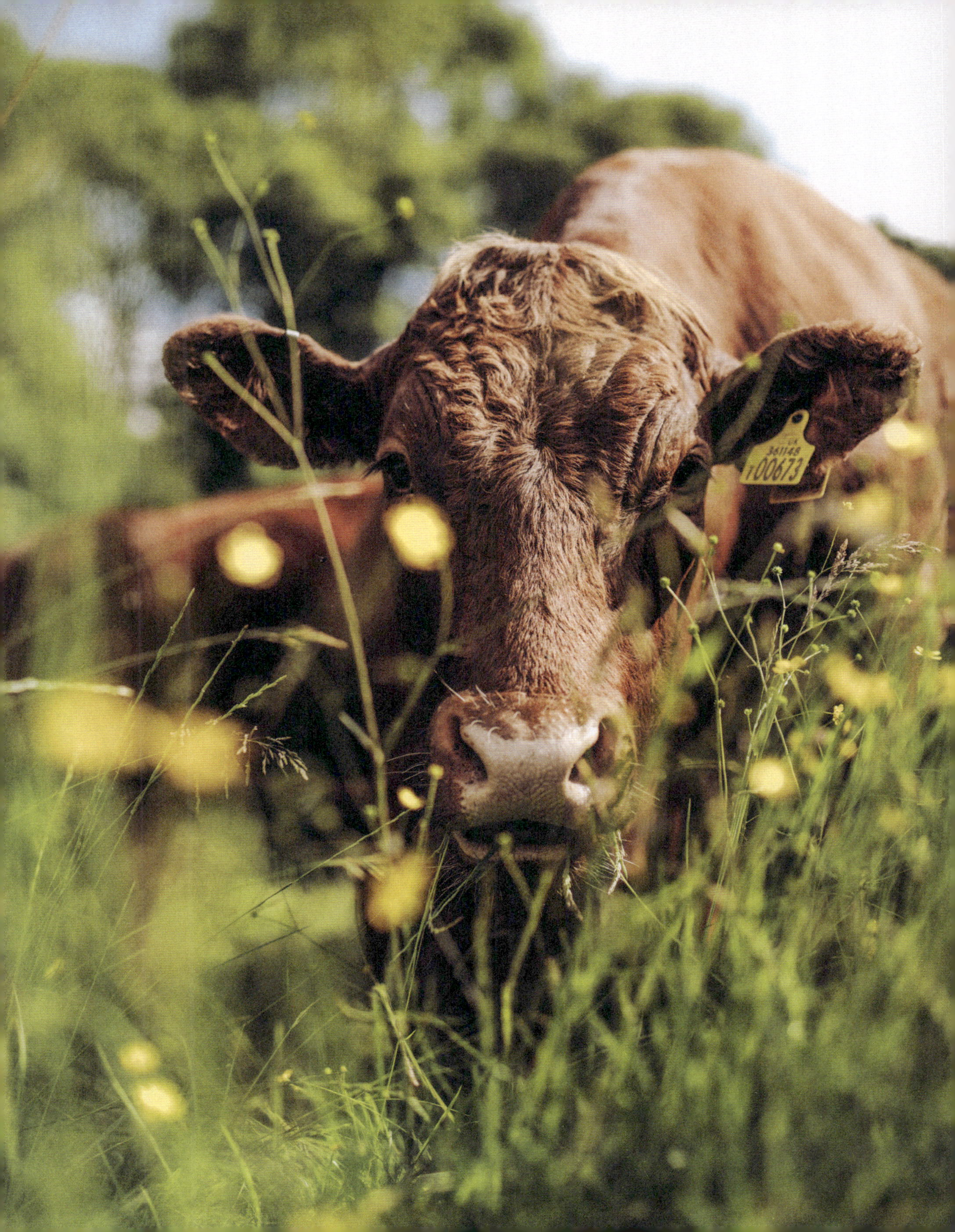

Mother Nature's cycle kicks into gear, and soon barren, degraded landscape becomes lush and thriving ecosystems.

Over 95% of all food comes from the soil. The quality of soil influences the quality of food, especially in relation to the trace elements required for a healthy diet. Soil still contains more carbon than the atmosphere and the world's forests combined, and is a key defence against climate change. The healthier the soil, the more carbon it holds – it is as simple as that.

It is almost impossible not to become bewitched by the beauty of the British countryside, its exquisite tapestry of rolling hills, green fields and dense woodland. Beneath this blanket of green, there are plains of soil that run like muscles around the body of our country. Clay, sand, flint and peat, each soil type requires a different approach to its management and as such is suited to specific farming enterprises. Not all the land in this country is suitable for growing fruit and vegetables, just as not all of it is suitable for raising livestock. However, with over 40% of the UK primarily pastured land, appropriate numbers of grazing livestock, suitable rest periods and a focus on encouraging other insects and animals to thrive alongside, are crucial elements in our ability to feed the nation a healthy, sustainable diet.

Pastoral farming, utilizing the value of ruminant animals, is a fundamental tool in managing our soil. However, for much of the last decade the cow, beef or dairy, has been blamed for the pace at which the climate is warming. Nature-friendly farmers, as well as a growing community of scientists, refer to this as 'It's the how, not the cow'. Wild herbivores have been shaping the evolution and diversity of species, habitats and ecosystems in Britain for millennia, alongside intervention by the hand of man, in order to sustain growing communities. Grazing by large herbivores, such as cows, remains the most natural and effective way of managing vegetation naturally, shaping the landscape in ways that human interventions and machinery simply cannot replicate.

While foraging in the landscape, cows and sheep make holes with their hooves and flatten areas, creating microhabitats, which are incredibly important for a whole host of species. This action also creates patches of barer ground where plants can set seed. Animal teeth act as grinding plates that start the difficult process of breaking down plants for digestion, but further bacterial processing requires fermentation within the gut. Cows have the most sophisticated digestive system which includes a stomach comprising four compartments. Tougher plants are regurgitated and munched again, a process known as 'chewing the cud'. Being browsers (feeding from trees and hedgerows) as well as grazers (munching on pasture) cows have the widest impact on the largest diversity of plant life.

Nature is intrinsically dynamic, and changes over time according to the interactions between the plants and animals present, so rearing livestock and incorporating rest periods for the land are vital in the careful balancing act of a healthy ecosystem.

Some argue that the answer is simply rewilding our countryside and passing our problems to other nations through importing more food. While there may be some short-term biodiversity benefits to an increase in wilded land, with the removal of almost all the UKs natural apex predators, species such as grey squirrels, rabbits, deer, foxes, badgers and rodents that are already dominant in our countryside, will continue to grow their populations, taking other species, such as hedgehogs, songbirds, farmland birds and red squirrels, further to the point of extinction. In many rewilded systems, the debate centres around whether humans are prioritising the survival of one species above another. For example, reintroducing wolves into Scotland would almost entirely eradicate the already dwindling numbers of mountain hares. Having urbanized so much of our landscape and already lost the natural order of things, simply letting nature run totally wild doesn't seem to me like the silver bullet solution its champions profess it to be.

Rewilding also leaves out one crucial element that, in the many years I have been engaged in agriculture, I believe is fundamental to the success or failure of any environmental or farming strategy – community. Like it or not, humanity has shaped landscapes as well as our interactions with the natural world for centuries. In order to live harmoniously, it is important that we understand the implications of the decisions we make, and in order to do this, we must have practitioners on the land whose role in society is to care, improve and protect the natural world for the benefit of us all. We need our rural communities to be able to thrive and earn a living from the land. By encouraging mixed farming systems that utilize crop rotations and livestock working in harmony, land can be productive, and small-scale family farms can not only be sustained, but empowered to carry out the actions that benefit us all, giving us clean air, clean water, increased biodiversity, healthy food and green spaces to enjoy.

It is my view that farming and ecology are bedfellows, neither more important than the other, so we should be creating food production systems that value nutrient-dense food sold at a fair price as highly as habitat restoration and carbon sequestration. Without healthy soils, diverse natural environments and an abundance of wild species – each a vital link in the chain – farmers are on borrowed time. Without farmers, paid fairly and given the opportunity to heal the land, nature will continue to suffer, making life on planet Earth ever more challenging.

We must strive for an end to factory farming and redistribute the land that had been housing cattle, as well as producing grain to feed them, to sustainable, mixed farming systems that replicate natural cycles. We know our current system isn't working for nature, for farmers and for our health, but it doesn't have to be this way. A transition to 'nature-friendly farming' or 'agroecological farming' is possible. However, we must align our diets as far as possible with what can be produced sustainably in the countries or regions in which we live. Here in the UK, pasture-fed beef and dairy cattle, sheep and mutton are some of the most nutritious foods we produce.

We must remember what is truly important and avoid siloed thinking and tribal arguments. Together, we have the ability to make change happen and, just as Lady Bird Johnson stated, hope will bloom.

Bavette Steak with Labneh & Radishes

At this time of year there is a symphony of blossoms and blooms, as spring makes way for summer. It can be difficult to keep up with sowing, planting out and tending. Gardeners know that a late frost can really spoil the party just as easily as a dry spell from an unexpected heatwave. During unpredictable weather, I cover as much bare soil as I can, sowing fast-growing plants in and among those slower to mature. This provides a canopy of protection as they shoot up, and means I have plenty to harvest and some to sacrifice. I use plants such as violas, spring onions and, one of my favourites, radishes for this purpose. It does mean, however, that I have radishes coming through thick and fast. One of the best ways to eat them is dunked into creamy labneh. There is something so wonderful about the freshness and pepperiness of these two ingredients and their opposing textures.

1 grass-fed bavette steak
extra virgin olive oil, for drizzling
a handful of radishes, fresh from the garden
flaky sea salt and freshly ground black pepper

For the labneh
475g (1lb 1oz) natural yogurt
1 teaspoon flaky sea salt

To make the labneh, drape a muslin cloth over a sieve and place it on top of a large mixing bowl. Pour the yogurt into the cloth and scatter over the salt. Leave it to thicken overnight (the longer you leave it, the thicker it will become).

The next day, you should find the whey has separated from the creamy cheese, leaving a pool of cloudy water in the mixing bowl. If, like me, you have two pet pigs, this makes a delicious treat for them, otherwise you can tip it into your garden to provide an extra boost of nutrients to the soil. Gather up the muslin cloth and give the labneh one final squeeze, then set to one side while you cook the steak.

Before cooking, remove the steak from the fridge, pat it dry and allow it to come up to room temperature. Preheat your barbecue (if using), or set a cast-iron pan over a high heat on the hob.

Generously season the steak with salt and pepper and drizzle it with a little olive oil.

Place the steak on the barbecue or in the hot pan and leave it there for around 5–6 minutes, until a caramelized crust has formed. Turn the heat down slightly and cook for another 5 minutes on the other side, then turn once again and cook for around 3–4 minutes. Remove from the heat and leave to rest in a warm place for at least 7 minutes before carving.

While your steak is resting, head to the veg garden and pull up a few fresh radishes. Give them a rinse.

On a platter, spoon out generous pillows of labneh and smooth to form a creamy base. Arrange the radishes on the plate, then slice the steak and place alongside. Give the dish a drizzle of some really good olive oil and then season with salt and pepper.

Serve with some warmed flatbreads for scooping and dunking.

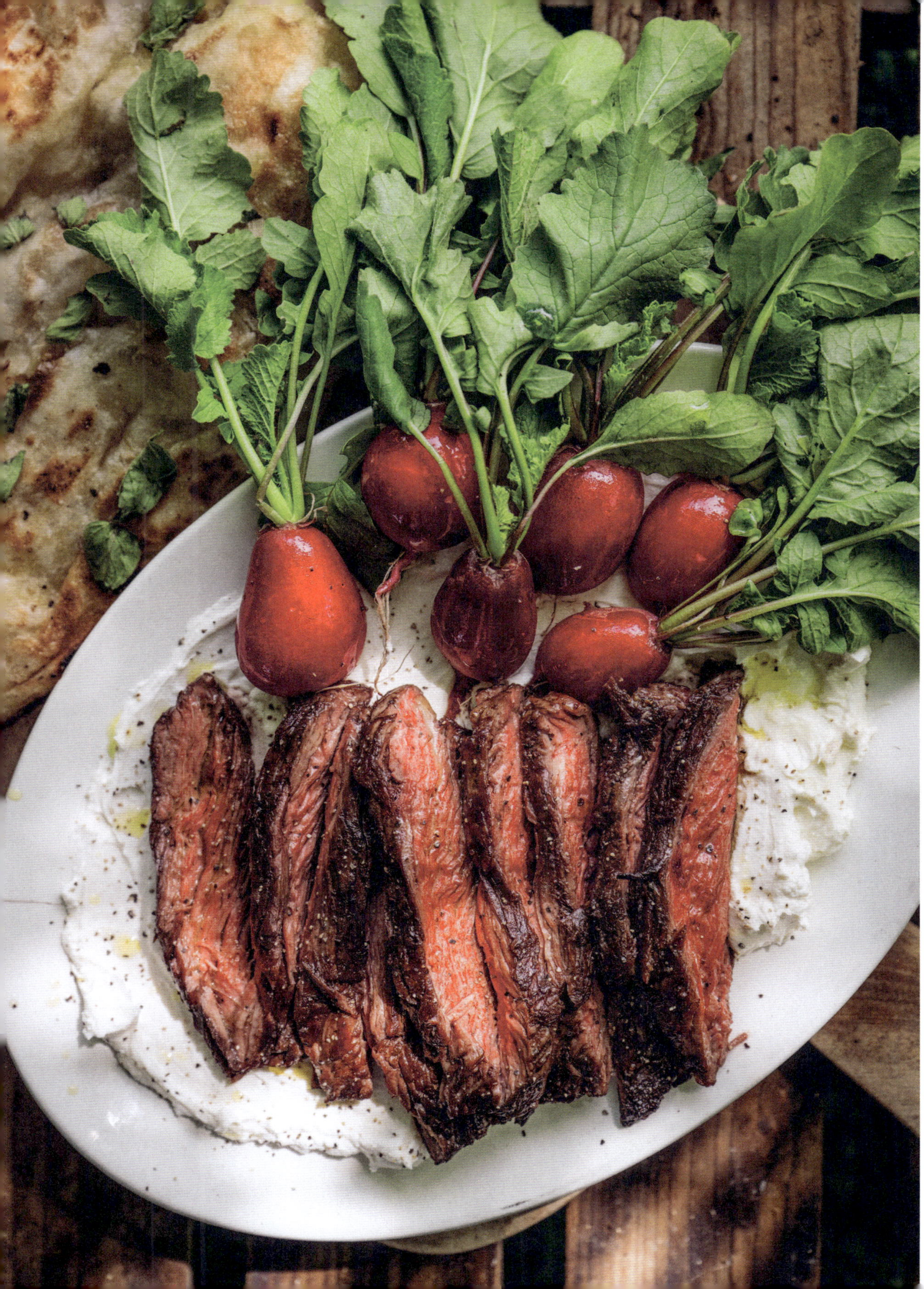

Summer

Picanha with Roasted Carrots & Harissa Carrot Hummus

SERVES 4–6

The season is merrily sliding into its swan song. The garden is so abundant I am spoilt for choice of what to eat. I settle on some beautiful carrots, pulling them from the soil and releasing the scent of warm earth. Everywhere I turn there are flowers filled with busy bees and flapping butterflies.

The sad truth is, my garden is rare. More and more land has become unsafe for species such as the magnificent butterfly. Our destructive behaviour has led to a terrifying 80% species decline of our winged friends since the 1970s. When butterflies are in trouble, we know the wider environment is in trouble too.

12–15 carrots, trimmed and scrubbed
extra virgin olive oil, for drizzling
2 red onions, finely sliced
4–5 garlic cloves, peeled and bashed
3 teaspoons fennel seeds, lightly crushed
2 teaspoons smoked paprika
½ teaspoon chilli flakes
2 tablespoons pumpkin seeds
2 tablespoons sunflower seeds
2 tablespoons honey
2 sprigs rosemary
flaky sea salt

For the carrot hummus
6–8 roasted carrots (see above)
1 garlic clove
2 teaspoons harissa paste
250g (9oz) canned or jarred chickpeas, drained
3 tablespoons olive oil

For the picanha
1kg (2lb 4oz) grass-fed beef picanha steak
a drizzle of organic rapeseed oil
flaky sea salt and freshly ground black pepper

To finish
4–6 flatbreads
200g (7oz) British feta-style cheese
a few sprigs of thyme, leaves picked
a large handful of nasturtium leaves and flowers

Preheat the oven to 180°C/350°F/gas mark 4 and light the barbecue.

Start with the roasted carrots. Halve any larger carrots lengthways. Place them in a large roasting tray and drizzle with extra virgin olive oil. Add the sliced onions, garlic, fennel seeds, paprika and chilli flakes. Roast for 30 minutes, shaking regularly. Remove the tray from the oven and add the seeds, honey, rosemary and a pinch of salt. Roast for a further 10–15 minutes, or until the carrots are tender and smelling wonderfully fragrant. Remove from the oven and set aside.

To make the hummus, take 6–8 of the roasted carrots and place them in a blender. Add the garlic, harissa paste, chickpeas, olive oil and a pinch of salt. Blitz to a smooth paste. You can adjust how loose you would like the hummus by adding a little more oil. Set aside.

Generously season the picanha steak with salt and pepper and drizzle it with some rapeseed oil. Lay the steak on the hot barbecue grill and cook for 8–10 minutes on each side. If using a meat thermometer, you are aiming for an internal temperature of 50°C (122°F). Leave to rest before slicing thinly.

To serve, take a flatbread and slather on a generous spoonful of hummus, pile on the roasted carrots and onions, then place strips of sliced beef over the top.

You could add some crumbled feta-style cheese, some picked thyme leaves and a few peppery nasturtium leaves and flowers.

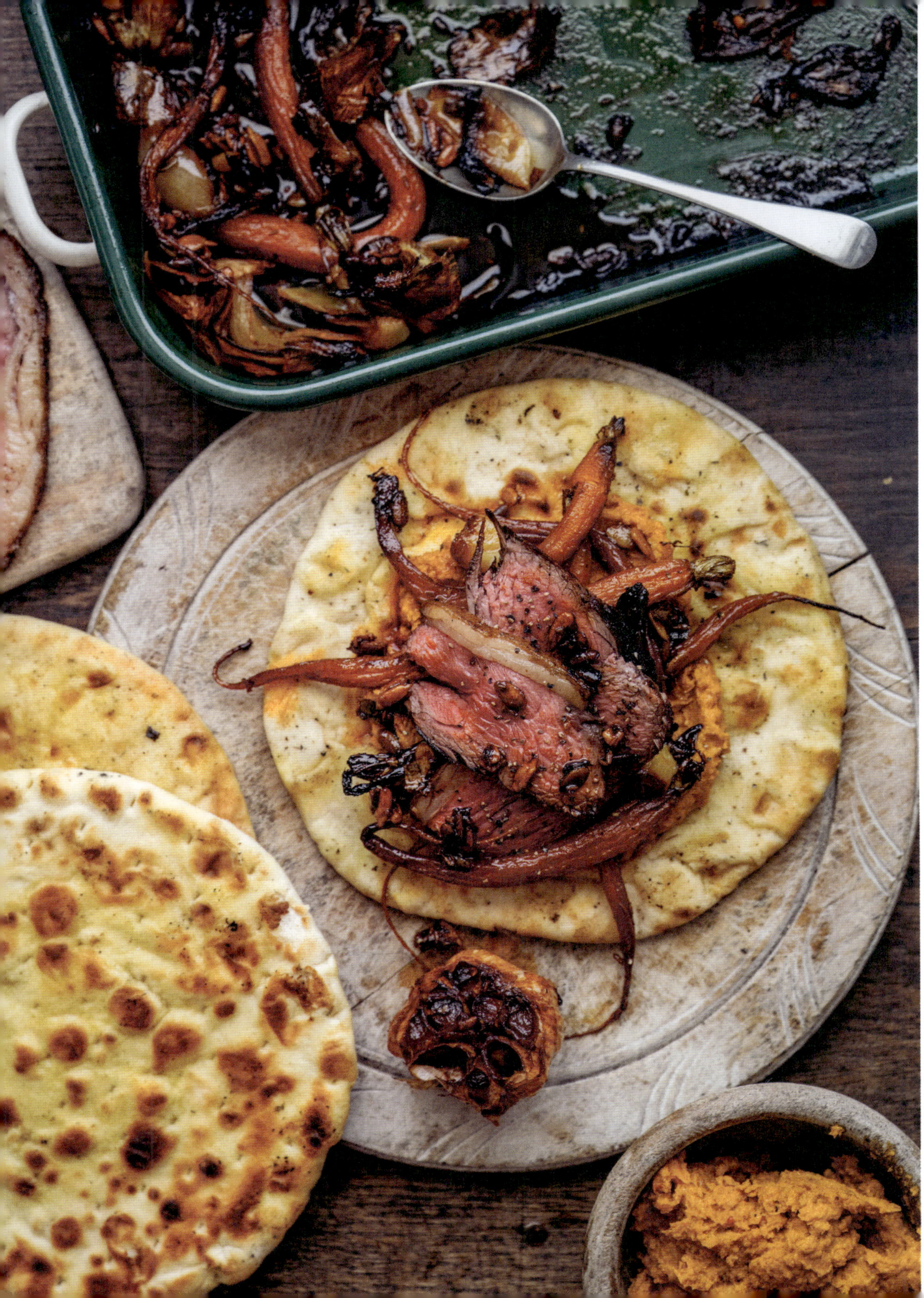

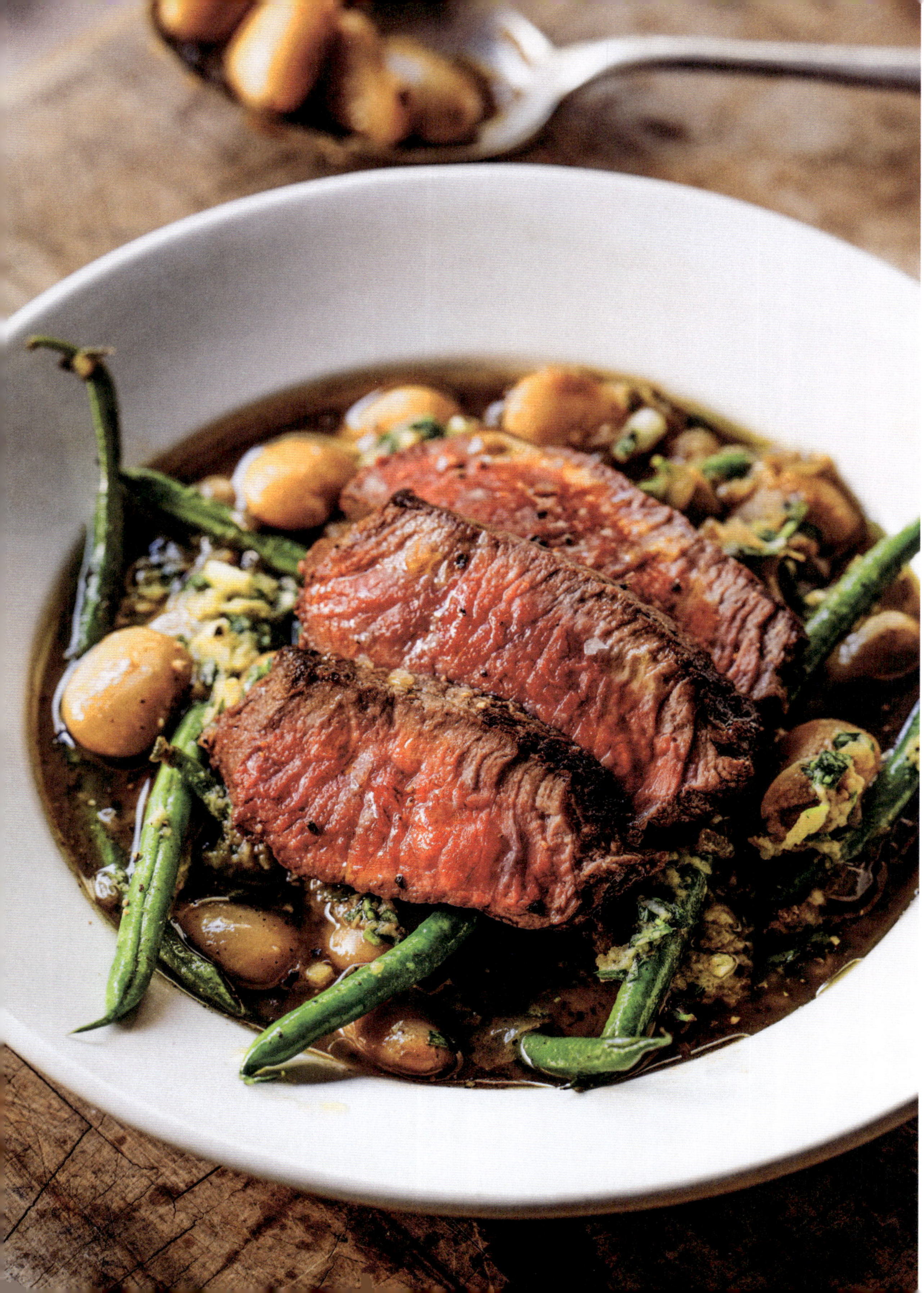

Rump Pavé with Green Beans & Salsa al Dragoncello

I first had a dish similar to this in a typical *osteria* in Bologna. Since then, I have tried to recreate it to transport me back to that magnificent moment.

Salsa al dragoncello hails from Tuscany, where tarragon was introduced by the Crusaders in the Middle Ages. The town of Siena has been known for its tarragon-flavoured dishes, none more famous than this sauce. It is utterly divine as an accompaniment to chargrilled chicken, lamb and all manner of delicious things. Here I have paired it with a perfectly butchered rump pavé, or 'heart of rump'. It is a lean, flavourful cut of beef; the muscle is seamed out, which means that any gristle is removed, leaving you with the perfect ingredient for cooking.

2 grass-fed rump pavé steaks
a drizzle of organic rapeseed oil
a knob of grass-fed butter
flaky sea salt and freshly ground black pepper

For the salsa al dragoncello
10g (¼oz) stale bread, crusts removed, torn into chunks
1 teaspoon red wine vinegar
1 large egg
30g (1oz) tarragon leaves
3 anchovies
1 teaspoon capers
½ garlic clove, peeled
70ml (2½fl oz) extra virgin olive oil

For the beans
a knob of grass-fed butter
2 shallots, finely chopped
2 garlic cloves, finely sliced
200ml (7fl oz) chicken stock
200g (7oz) butter beans
200g (7oz) green beans

Begin by making the salsa. Place the bread in a bowl and drizzle over the vinegar. Leave to soften while you cook the egg. Boil the egg for 9 minutes, until hard-boiled, then cool it under cold running water, then peel. Separate the white from the yolk – only the yolk is needed in this dish. Finely chop the tarragon, anchovies and capers and place in a bowl, then finely grate in the egg yolk and garlic into the bowl. Squeeze the excess vinegar out of the bread, chop it into small pieces and add to the bowl. Stir in the oil until you achieve a nice, loose consistency. Taste and season with salt and pepper. Set to one side.

Put the rump steaks dry. Rub with a little rapeseed oil and season generously. Place a cast-iron frying pan over a medium-high heat. Once hot, add the steaks to the centre of the pan and cook on one side for 4 minutes, then flip over and cook the other side for a further 4 minutes. Add a knob of butter to the pan and baste the steaks for around 1–2 minutes. Remove the steaks from the pan and leave to rest.

For the beans, place the pan you have just used to cook the steak back over a medium heat. Add a knob of butter, the shallots, garlic and a pinch of salt. Sweat the shallots for around 5 minutes, or until they have become translucent. Increase the heat a little and add the chicken stock, allowing it to simmer and reduce by a quarter. Add the green beans and butter beans and cook for around 2–3 minutes until the green beans have become tender but still with a good amount of bite. Check the seasoning and adjust with a little salt and pepper as necessary.

To serve, scoop the beans into two bowls. Slice the steak and place on top of the beans, before finishing with generous spoonfuls of the salsa.

Mutton Chops with Beetroot Hummus & Dukkah

There is a misconception that mutton has to be reserved for the slow cooker. A well-lived life combined with humane slaughter, dry ageing and meticulous butchery mean that this is some of the most delicious and ethical meat you can eat.

Laced with melting fat, packed with flavour and full of character, mutton is the perfect bedfellow to rich, earthy beetroot. I love to serve mutton with freshly pulled beetroot from the garden. There's something so harmonious to be enjoyed from the pairing of tender earthy beets with grassy herbal mutton. Seek out the good stuff and don't be afraid; once you've rendered the fat, cook it fast and keep it rare.

a drizzle of organic rapeseed oil
5 cull yaw mutton chops
2 large red onions
100g (3½oz) sheep's cheese

For the beetroot hummus
570g (1lb 4oz) jar chickpeas, including the liquid (I use Bold Bean Co Queen Chickpeas)
500g (1lb 2oz) beetroot, peeled and chopped
4 garlic cloves, peeled and chopped
5–6 tablespoons extra virgin olive oil
1 teaspoon tahini
2 tablespoons lemon juice
flaky sea salt and freshly ground black pepper

For the dukkah
2 tablespoons coriander seeds
1 tablespoon cumin seeds
3 tablespoons sesame seeds
75g (2½oz) hazelnuts
100g (3½oz) brazil nuts
1 teaspoon flaky sea salt
a pinch of freshly ground black pepper
a few sprigs of thyme, leaves picked

Preheat the oven to 200°C/400°F/gas mark 6.

To make the hummus, line a roasting tray with foil, leaving enough to fold over and seal the contents. Tip in the chickpeas along with their liquid, then add the chopped beetroot and garlic. Fold over the foil and seal by lightly scrunching the edges together. Bake for 1 hour.

Meanwhile, make the dukkah. In a dry frying pan, toast the coriander and cumin seeds until dark and fragrant, making sure you don't burn them, then transfer to a mortar. Toast the sesame seeds for a couple of minutes and tip them into the mortar. Crush to a coarse powder with a pestle. Finely chop the nuts and add to the mortar along with the salt, pepper and thyme leaves. Give it all a good bash to mix together, then set aside.

Check the beetroot are tender and remove from the oven. Once cooled, transfer the contents of the roasting tray to a food processor and blend to a smooth purée. Slowly add the olive oil to the blender along with the tahini and lemon juice, then check the seasoning, adding salt and pepper if required. Scrape into a serving bowl and set aside.

For the chops, place a cast-iron pan over a medium–high heat (or light your barbecue) and drizzle in the rapeseed oil. Season the chops and add to the pan, placing them on the fat side first, allowing the fat to render and caramelize. Cook for 2–3 minutes on each side, depending on the thickness of the chops, then remove from the heat and leave to rest for 5 minutes.

Slather the beetroot hummus over a platter, pile on the chops and roasted red onions, then scatter over the crumbled sheep's cheese and dukkah.

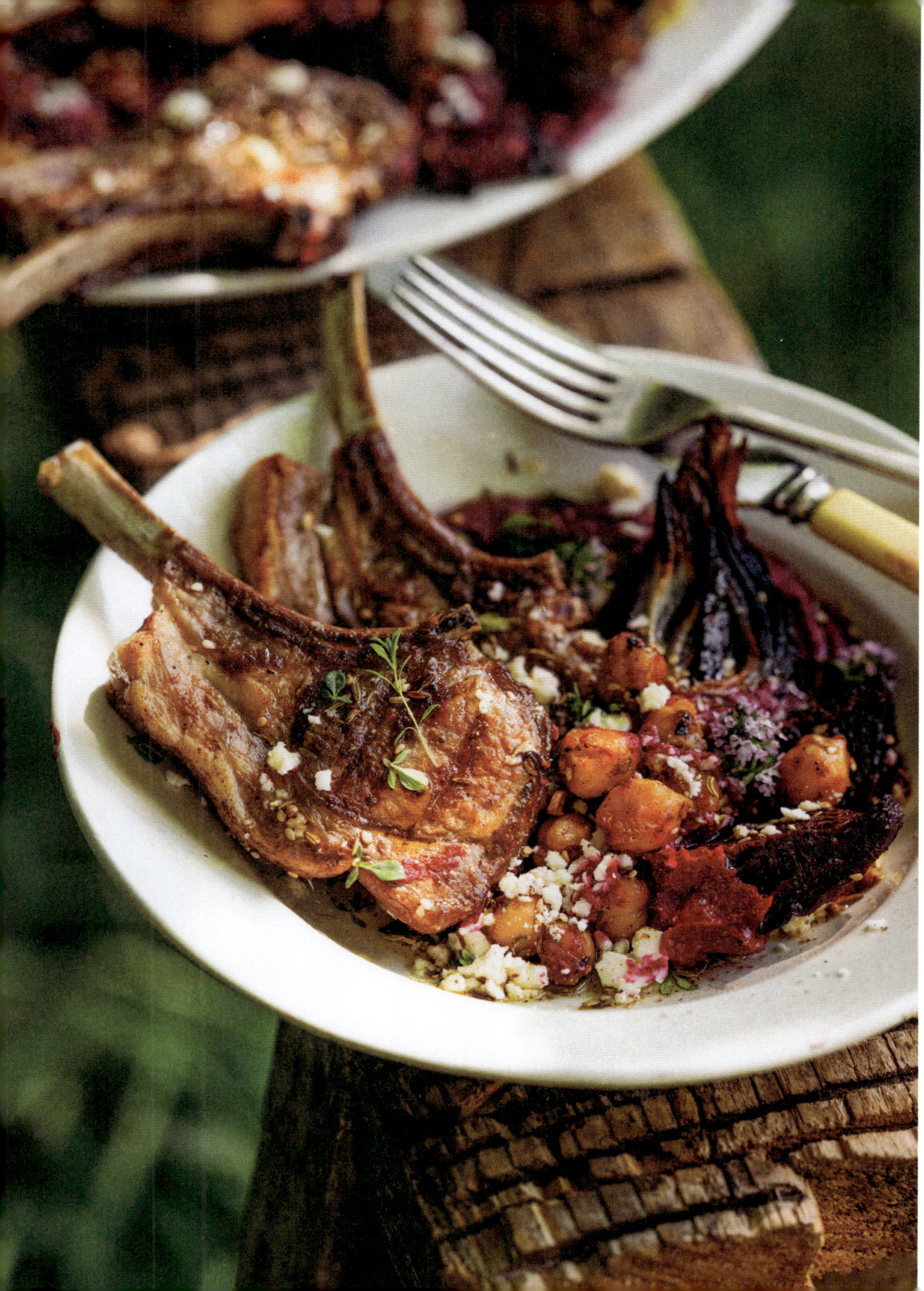

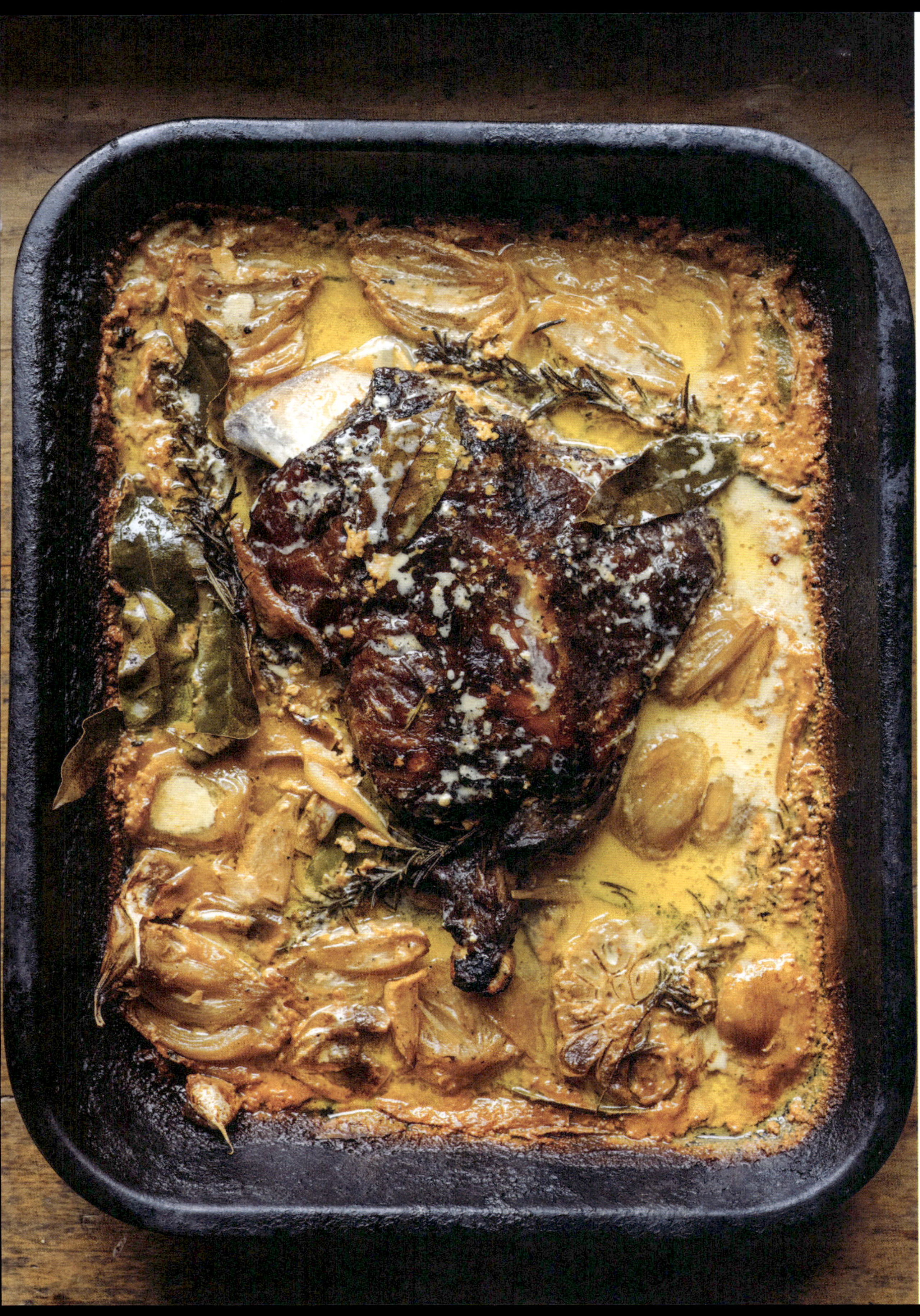

SERVES 8 Summer

Hogget Shoulder Cooked in Milk with Lemon & Herbs

Every now and again along the winding road that is life, someone crosses your path in a way that leaves a mark. It could be argued that Julius Roberts, a fellow farmer, gardener and chef, has done more to connect the everyday consumer with the majesty of life on a small farm than most others. The positive impact of sharing the trials and tribulations of growing your own food cannot be underestimated in helping shift the narrative towards farming systems that respect nature as well as the grower. Julius has kindly contributed this beautiful recipe for you all to enjoy.

If you've never cooked meat in milk before, it's a revelation. Just like a good stock, the milk is there to keep things juicy over the long cooking process. But, because of the fat in the milk, it also makes the most incredible sauce with fatty curds flavoured with garlic, bay and rosemary.

Preheat your oven grill as high as it will go.

Drizzle the hogget shoulder with oil on each side before seasoning generously with salt. Place it in a deep roasting tray and then under the grill to brown the top. Once properly caramelized, remove from the oven and set aside.

Turn the oven to 180°C/350°F/gas mark 4.

Pour 1 litre (1¾ pints) of the milk into a saucepan and warm gently until steaming but not scalded.

Meanwhile, add the onion quarters, garlic halves, bay leaves and rosemary to the roasting tray. Pare the zest from both lemons with a vegetable peeler and add to the tray along with the juice of 1 whole lemon. Pour the warmed milk over the top, so the tray is filled, but the hogget shoulder is still peeking through. As chef Fergus Henderson says, you're looking for 'alligators floating in a swamp'. Season with salt and lots of black pepper, then cover with a sheet of baking parchment and seal completely with foil before placing in the oven for about 5 hours, until the hogget is so tender you can pull it apart with a spoon. About halfway through, have a check and top up with the remaining milk, if needed.

When ready, pull the meat off the bone and mix through the molten veg and curdled gravy. Serve with buttery mash seasoned with nutmeg, ensuring everyone gets plenty of the sauce as well as some lemon zest.

2kg (4lb 8oz) grass-fed hogget shoulder
a drizzle of organic rapeseed oil
1.5 litres (generous 2½ pints) organic or grass-fed whole milk
4 onions, cut into quarters
1 bulb of garlic, cut in half horizontally
10 bay leaves
5 sprigs of rosemary
2 large unwaxed lemons
flaky sea salt and freshly ground black pepper

Summer

SERVES 2

Charred Cornish Sardines on Toast with Bean Mash & Gremolata

Sardines are pelagic fish, whch come and go in mass shoals as the water conditions and available food sources change. This makes them a frustrating or exciting catch for a fisherman, depending on which way you look at it! Here in the South West, sea temperatures are warming, which means the number – as well as species – of fish that gather around our shores is changing. With greater numbers of sardines, or pilchards as they are called locally, spending more time here, we've also seen the miraculous return of one of the most impressive fish in the sea, the blue fin tuna. I haven't gone as far as to create a tuna recipe in this book, as while numbers are good, it is still relatively early days of their return. We do tend to have a fascination with starting at the top of the food chain, which has led us to wipe out so many apex predators, changing the natural order of things perilously. Instead, I encourage you to enjoy my old mate the sardine, a fish that throughout British history has been a mainstay in our diet.

3 garlic cloves, peeled
350g (12oz) butter beans
1 teaspoon tahini
a pinch of chilli flakes, or to taste
2 tablespoons lemon juice
extra virgin olive oil, for drizzling
2 slices of sourdough
2–4 sustainably caught Cornish sardines
flaky sea salt and freshly ground black pepper

For the gremolata
30g (1oz) flat-leaf parsley, leaves and stalks
2 garlic cloves, peeled and grated
2 unwaxed lemons
1 tablespoon extra virgin olive oil, or as needed

Light the barbecue and let it get to a nice steady heat.

Start with the beans. Finely grate 2 of the garlic cloves into a mixing bowl and add the butter beans, tahini, chilli flakes, lemon juice and some salt and pepper. Mash the ingredients together using a fork – you want to keep some texture of the beans, so don't overmash. Stir in a drizzle of olive oil, then set aside.

To make the gremolata, finely chop the parsley and garlic cloves, then tip into a mixing bowl. Grate in the zest of both lemons and squeeze in the juice of one. Stir in a drizzle of olive oil to reach your desired consistency., then set aside.

Take the slices of sourdough and drizzle them with olive oil, using your hands to rub it in to ensure the bread is well covered. Place on the barbecue grill and toast for around 1–2 minutes on each side. While warm, rub the toasts with the remaining garlic clove and set aside.

Drizzle a little olive oil over the sardines and massage in a pinch of salt. Place over the barbecue grill and cook for around 2–4 minutes on each side, depending on their size.

Take the toasted sourdough and load with the creamy mash. Pile on the charred sardines, squeeze the remaining lemon over the fish and finish with a generous spoonful of gremolata and perhaps more chilli flakes, if you like a little heat.

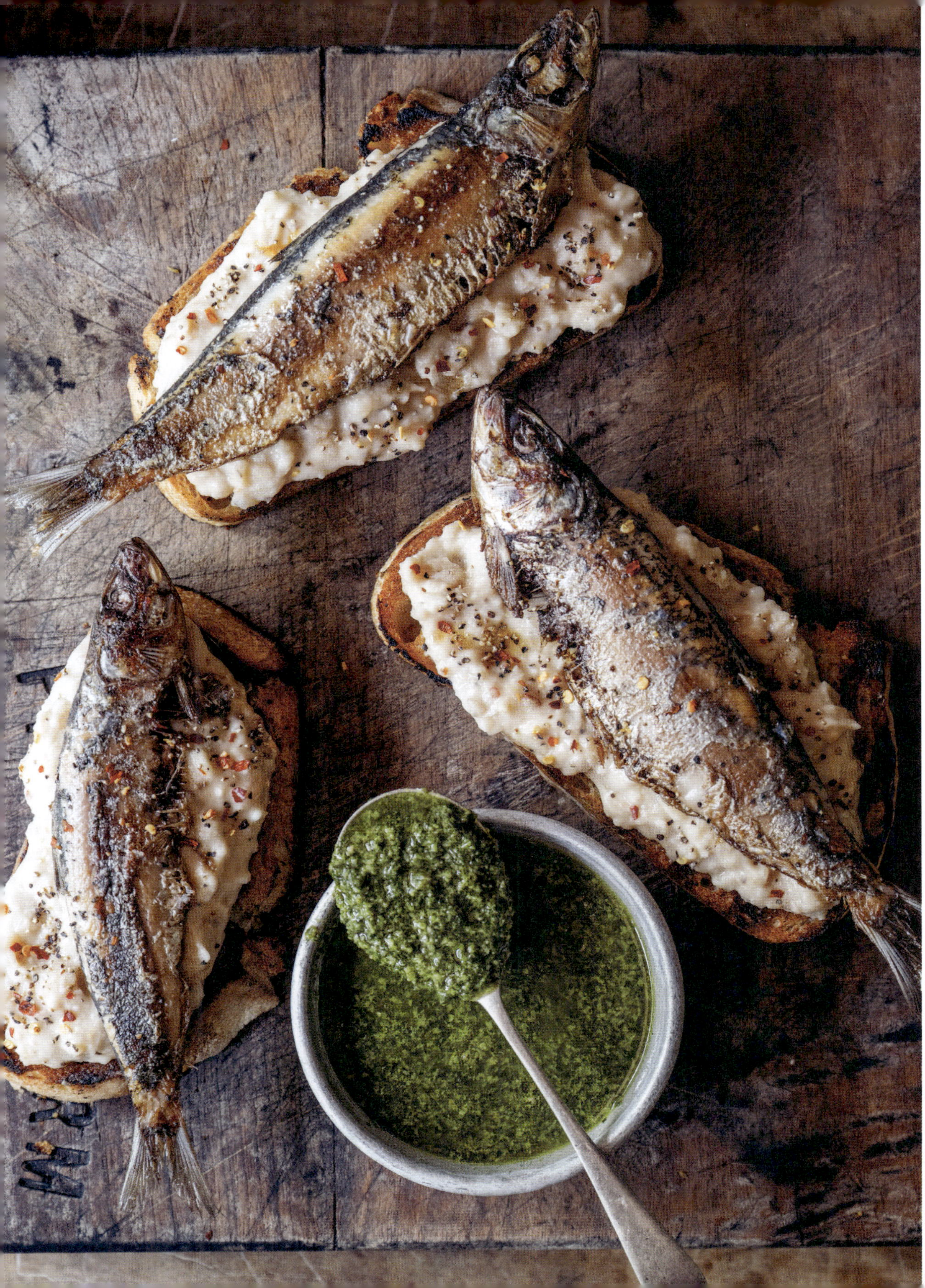

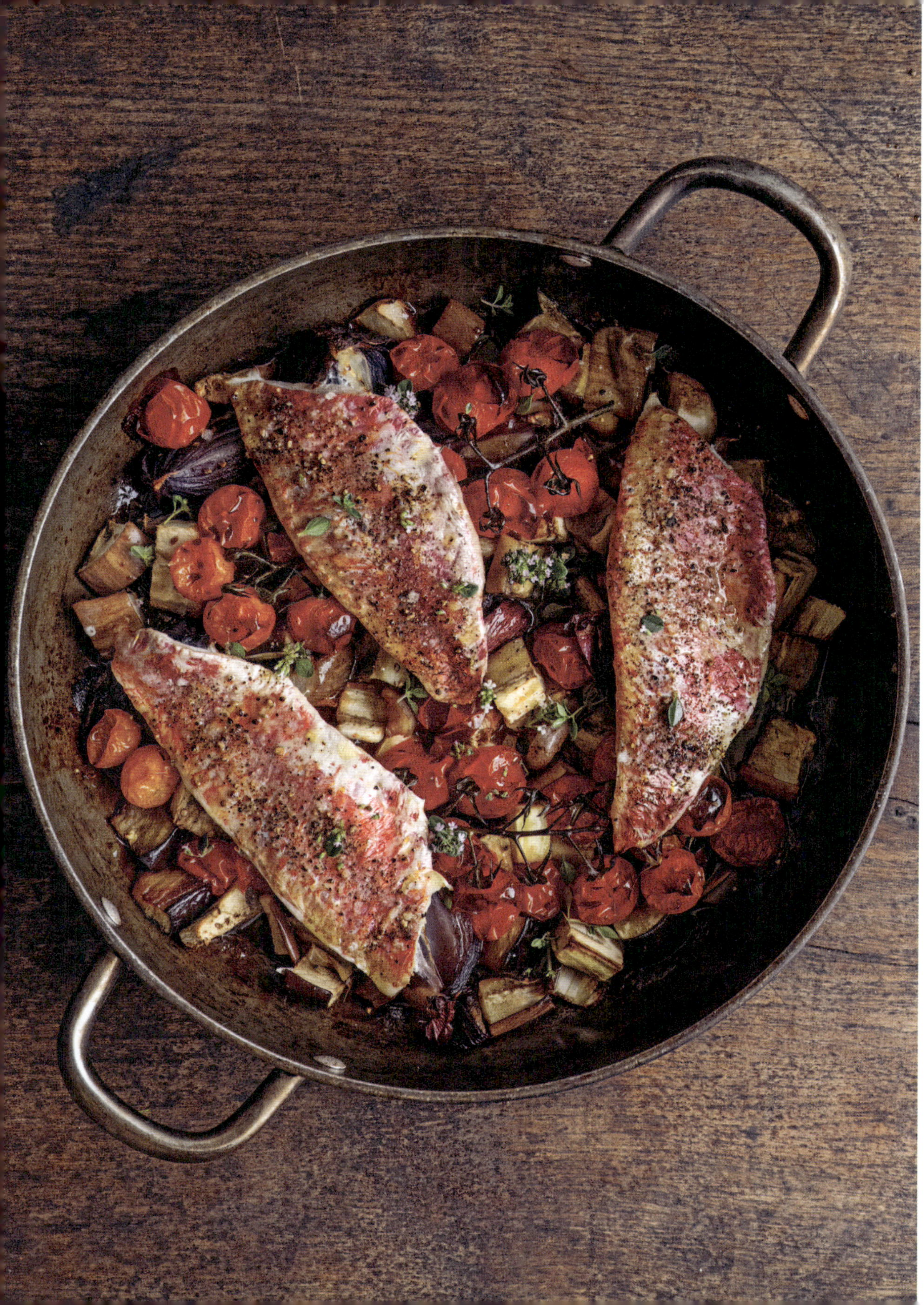

Roasted Red Mullet with Cherry Tomatoes, Aubergines & Thyme

Red mullet are in abundance when the water temperature is warmest, so we find them here in late summer and early autumn. They are easiest to catch at dawn or dusk, when the seas are calm and still. You'll find them more commonly off sandy beaches, so it's best to save our many pebbled shores for bass and mackerel fishing.

I adore red mullet. It perplexes me why this delightful fish hasn't taken off here in the UK. It looks beautiful with its glossy red, sparkling jacket on and tastes like a cross between lobster and mackerel. I know, a bizarre description, but once you have tried it, you'll see what I mean. It cooks beautifully, too. It's easy to create crispy skin and it is more forgiving than many other fish, making it incredibly versatile. I do hope you give it a try and fall head over heels in love. With sea temperatures rising, we will likely see more landed on our shores.

The concept of this recipe is a simple one: cook the tomatoes until they collapse and the fish until it is crispy – what a phenomenal combination. The sweetness of the tomatoes that burst in your mouth are such a perfect partner for the slightly oily fish. A little fresh thyme sets this dish off beautifully.

extra virgin olive oil
500g (1lb 2oz) cherry tomatoes
1 aubergine, diced
1 red onion, finely sliced
3 bay leaves
a few sprigs of thyme
4 sustainably caught red mullet fillets
a knob of grass-fed butter
a drizzle of good-quality balsamic vinegar
flaky sea salt and freshly ground black pepper

Preheat the oven to 220°C/425°F/gas mark 7.

Drizzle a good glug of olive oil into a roasting tray and shake to allow the oil to coat the surface. Season with a good pinch of salt and pepper, then add the tomatoes, aubergine, onion, bay leaves and thyme (reserving a few fresh thyme leaves for garnish). Give everything a good shake to ensure the vegetables are coated in oil and are well seasoned.

Season the fish and lay it over the top of the vegetables, skin-side up. Drizzle over a bit more oil and add the butter in small chunks around the pan. Place in the hot oven and roast for 20 minutes.

Remove from the oven, scatter over the reserved thyme leaves and drizzle the dish with some balsamic vinegar and a little more olive oil. Serve straight away with some crusty bread on the side.

Summer

SERVES 4

Scallops, Chorizo & Padron Pepper Rosemary Skewers

This recipe is simply a bit of fun. After all, cooking should be fun, it should draw out the creative side of you and remind you to touch, smell and taste the world! I should also say it is really rather delicious, too. Bold and beautiful, buttery diver-caught scallops are paired with spicy, piquant chunks of chorizo and finished with the Russian roulette of fruit, the Padrón pepper. Those of you lucky enough to have a greenhouse or even a polytunnel can grow their own Padrons and play the game of hot or bitter all summer long. Padrón peppers are growing in popularity here, so you are increasingly likely to find them in good veg box schemes, farmers' markets and independent retailers. If you fail on your hunt, simply swap them for mild chillies or peppers – whatever tickles your pickle, so to speak!

To create your skewers, select a few long, thick stems of rosemary from the garden. Strip off almost all the leaves, setting some of them aside for later. Place the stems in a bowl of water and leave them to soak for between 30 minutes and 1 hour.

Light the barbecue and let it get to a nice steady heat.

Set a small saucepan over the grill and add the butter, garlic, chilli and some of the rosemary leaves. Gently caramelize the garlic and release the oil from the rosemary. Move the pan to the coolest part of the barbecue, then add the chopped parsley and keep warm while you make the skewers.

Slice the chorizo into discs, similar in size to the scallops. Carefully thread the scallops, chorizo and peppers onto the rosemary skewers, then season with salt and drizzle with a little oil. Using a pair of tongs, carefully place the skewers on the barbecue, keeping the leafy end away from too much flame. Cook the skewers for 2–3 minutes on each side.

Once the skewers are wonderfully charred, remove them from the heat and pile onto a platter. Dress with the warm garlic butter and serve immediately.

6–8 thick spears of rosemary
75g (2¾oz) grass-fed butter
2 garlic cloves, finely chopped
½ red chilli, seeds removed and finely chopped
a handful of parsley, chopped
200g (7oz) British cooking chorizo
12 sustainably caught British scallops
200g (7oz) Padrón peppers
a drizzle of extra virgin olive oil
flaky sea salt

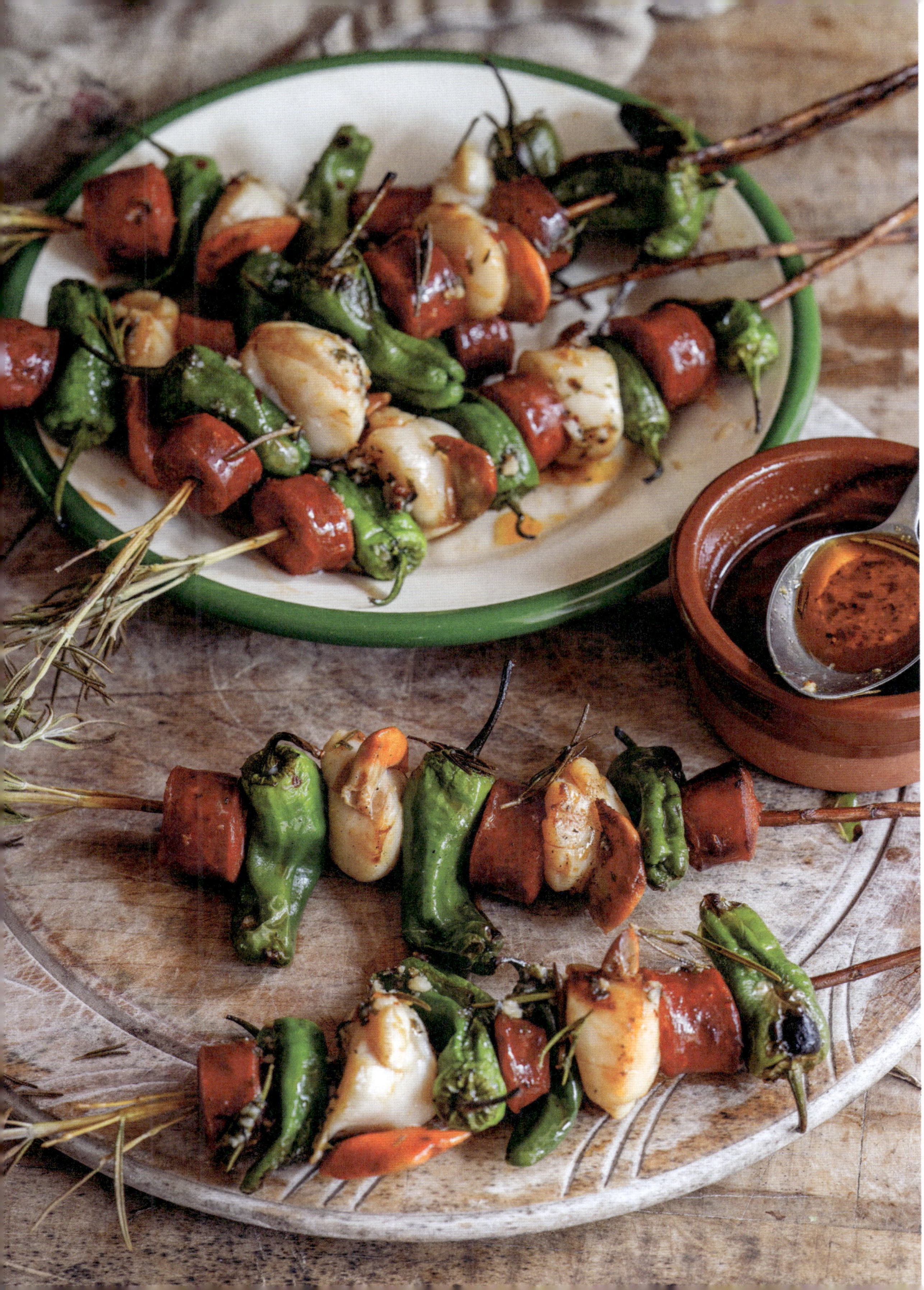

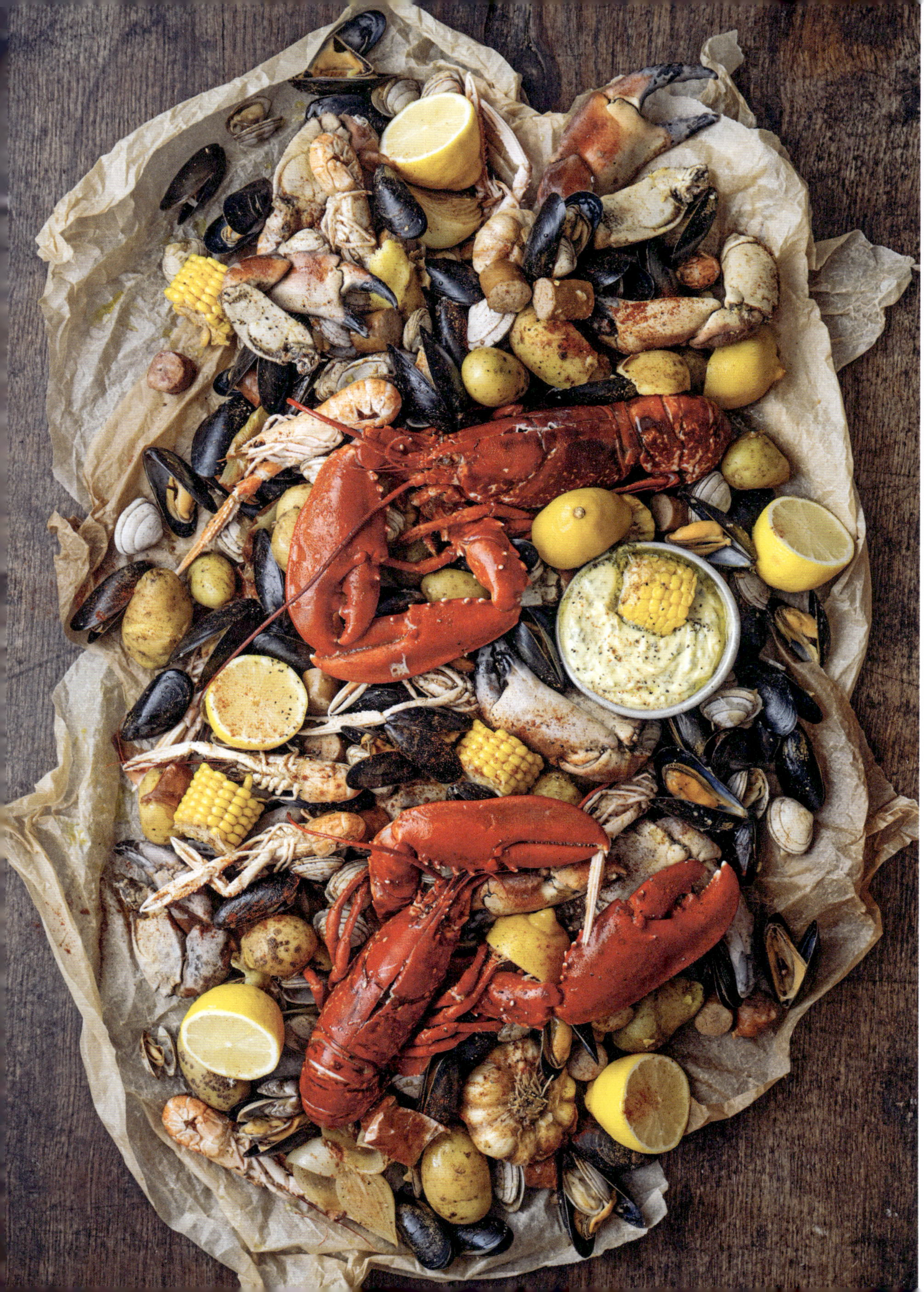

A British Take on a Southern-style Seafood Boil

The reason I adore this recipe so much is the sense of community that a seafood boil brings. It's the ultimate sociable food that you can create with minimal fuss while enjoying the magic that cooking outside brings. Each summer, we gather together a group of our friends, lay down some newspaper on the garden table and tip a mountain of spicy seafood all over it. Everyone dives in with reckless abandon, fishing out their favourites and scooping up garlic butter with exuberance. It's such a great way to celebrate some of the best and most sustainable seafood landed on our shores.

1 orange
3 lemons
2 onions, skin on, sliced in half horizontally
2 bulbs of garlic, sliced in half horizontally
8 first early or maincrop waxy potatoes (I like to use Charlotte potatoes)
4 corn on the cob, cut in half
4 British free-range frankfurter-style or spicy sausages, cut into chunks
2 whole British native lobsters, humanely killed (see page 112)
6–8 British native crab claws
1kg (2lb 4oz) rope-grown mussels, cleaned
1kg (2lb 4oz) Dorset clams, cleaned
6–8 Scottish langoustines
hot sauce, to serve

For the garlic butter
200g (7oz) grass-fed butter, at room temperature
2 bulbs of roasted garlic
a pinch of flaky sea salt

For the seasoning
6 tablespoons smoked paprika
3 tablespoons flaky sea salt
2 tablespoons onion powder
2 tablespoons garlic powder
2 tablespoons dried oregano
2 tablespoon dried thyme
1 tablespoon dried basil
1 tablespoon freshly ground black pepper
1 tablespoon white pepper
1 tablespoon cayenne pepper

First, make the garlic butter. Add the butter to a mixing bowl. Squeeze in the roasted garlic and scatter over a pinch of sea salt. Use the back of a fork to mash the garlic through the butter and mix thoroughly to combine. Set aside.

Mix together all the ingredients for the seasoning.

Bring 2 litres (3½ pints) of water to the boil in a large stockpot. Make sure you have chosen a pot large enough to fit in all the ingredients. Once the water is consistently boiling, tip in the seasoning mix; this may bubble up, so just be careful. Slice the orange in half, squeeze the juice into the pot, then throw the spent halves in. Slice two of the lemons in half and squeeze in the juice, throwing the spent halves into the pot too. Follow this with the onions and garlic. Finally, tip in the potatoes and boil for 6 minutes.

Now add the corn on the cob and sausages to the pot and boil for 2 minutes.

Add the lobsters and crab claws and boil for 2 minutes, then add the mussels and clams and boil for 3 minutes. Finally, throw in the langoustines and boil for 5 minutes.

Carefully pour the boil through a colander, discarding the liquid.

Tip the boil onto the table and serve with wedges of the remaining lemon, the garlic butter, and hot sauce for the brave among you.

Lobster Roll with Lemon & Herb Mayonnaise

To my mind, there is no way to buy lobsters other than live. This involves heading down to my local coast, and parting with an extraordinary amount of cash for a very small item. I once had an unfortunate incident travelling back home, when a particularly lively lobster managed to lift the flap of the box it was in, freeing itself and came face to face with my belligerent Jack Russell. I have never been more thankful for the elastic bands placed on its claws.

The less you do to a lobster the better. However, there's something about sweet, tender lobster meat nestled in a warm, buttered roll that gets me every time. It's the perfect dish to serve on a late summer's evening and, what's more, it's guaranteed to make you the most popular host.

2 live British lobsters
4 tablespoons grass-fed butter
1 celery stick, finely chopped
4–6 brioche rolls
juice of 1 lemon
flaky sea salt and freshly ground black pepper

For the mayonnaise
2 large organic and/or free-range egg yolks
½ garlic clove, grated
½ teaspoon Dijon mustard
finely grated zest and juice of 1 unwaxed lemon
a pinch of flaky sea salt
175ml (6fl oz) extra virgin olive oil
175ml (6fl oz) organic sunflower oil
50g (1¾oz) chives, chopped, plus extra to serve
50g (1¾oz) dill, chopped, plus extra to serve

Prepare your lobsters for cooking by putting them in the freezer for about 35–40 minutes, which puts them to sleep. Place a tea towel over the tail and hold on to it. Using a sharp knife, push the tip through the lobster's body shell, about 2cm (¾in) back from the eyes. Push down and then back firmly so the knife penetrates the shell and cuts through the head. This will kill the lobster immediately. It is far more humane to do this than drop them straight into boiling water.

Bring a large pan of salted water to a rolling boil. Drop the lobsters into the water and cook for 1 minute for every 100g (3½oz) of weight. Once cooked, carefully remove the lobsters from the pan and allow them to cool.

Once cool enough to handle, slice the lobsters in half with a sharp knife and pull out the meat. Crack the claws and remove the meat from each one. Set the meat to one side while you make the mayonnaise.

Place the egg yolks, garlic, mustard, lemon zest and juice into a food processor. Season with a small pinch of salt and whizz for about 30 seconds. Mix the two oils in a jug. With the food processor running, slowly dribble in the oil. Once you have added it all, you should have a thick, glossy mayonnaise. Stir in the chopped herbs, taste and add more salt, mustard or lemon, if required.

Melt the butter in a small saucepan over a medium heat.

In a mixing bowl, combine the lobster meat along with the mayonnaise, celery, a pinch of salt and pepper and the melted butter, stirring to combine.

Take the brioche rolls and fill generously with the lobster mayo. Squeeze a little more lemon over the rolls and scatter with some more chopped herbs.

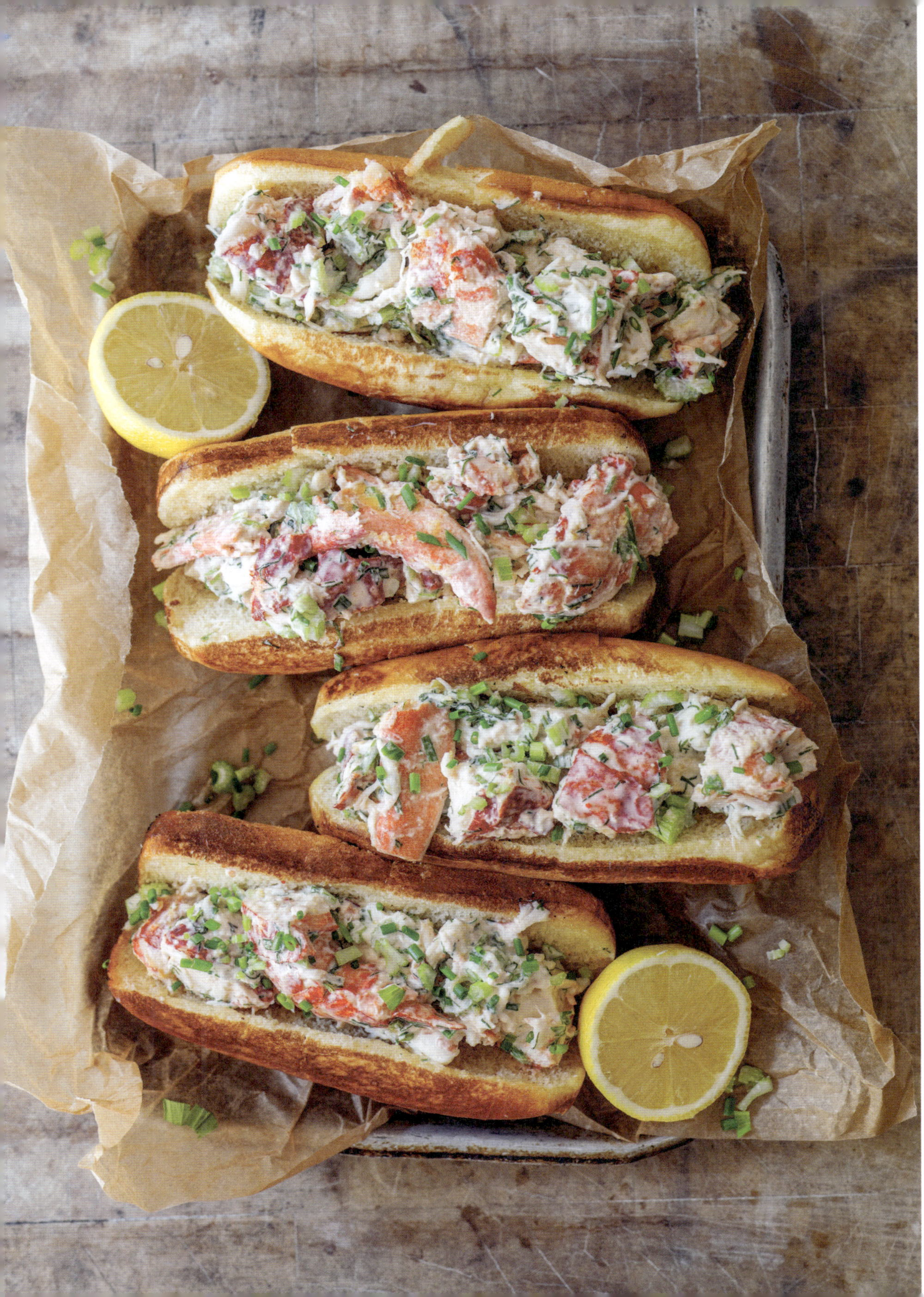

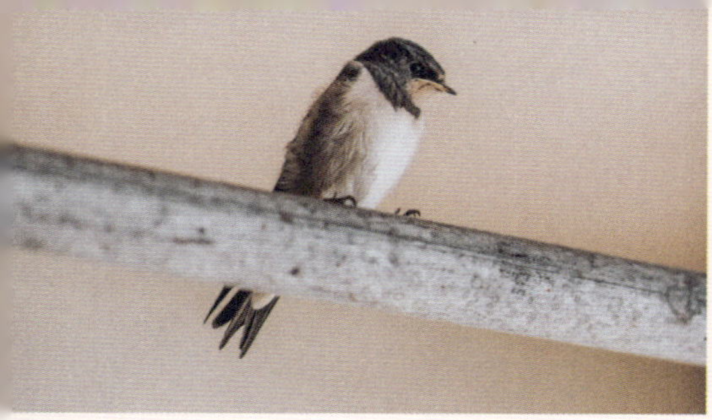
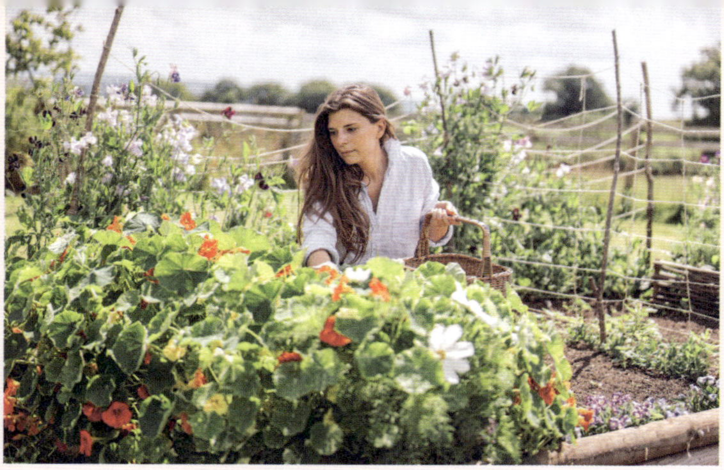
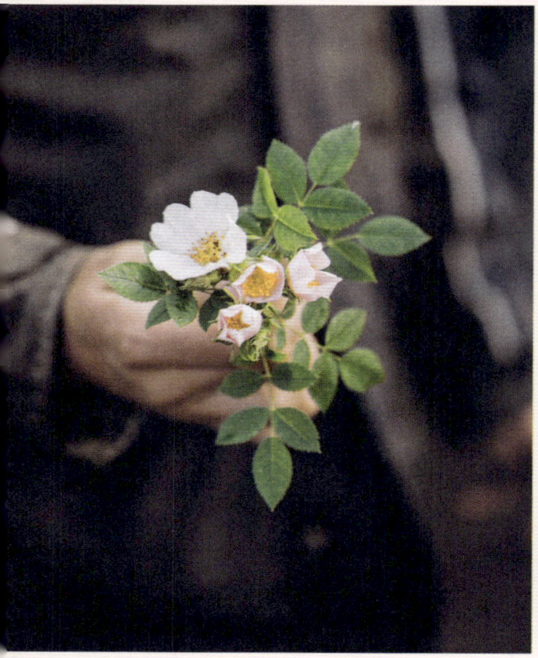
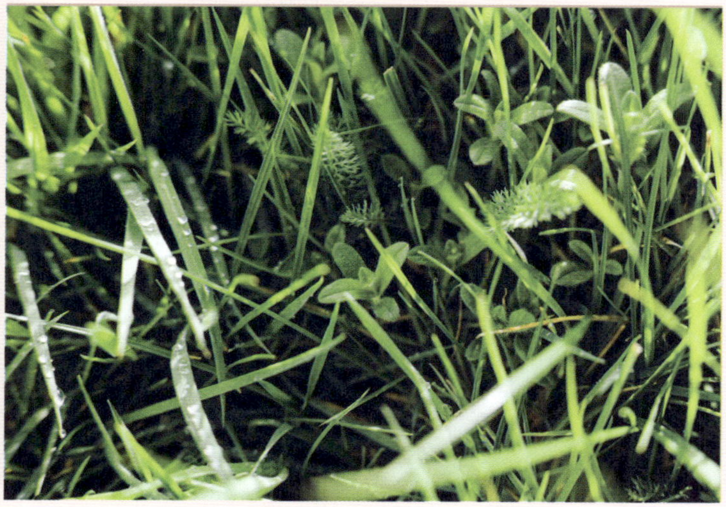
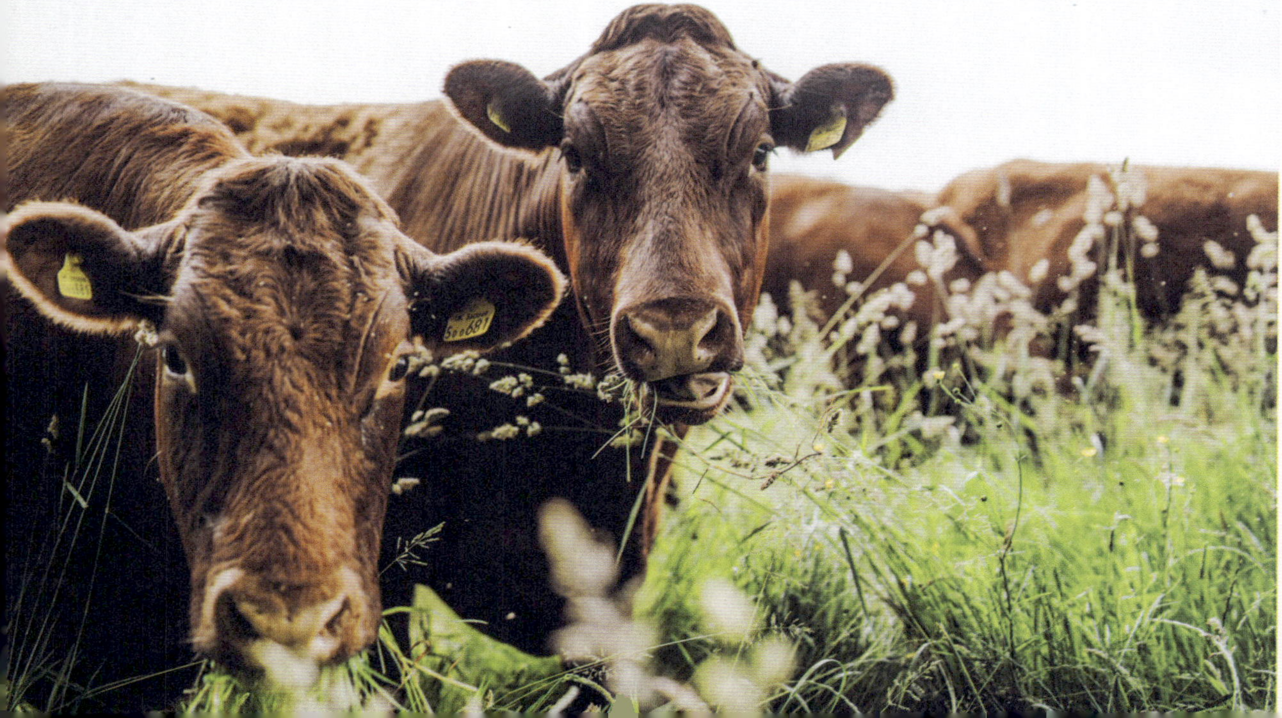

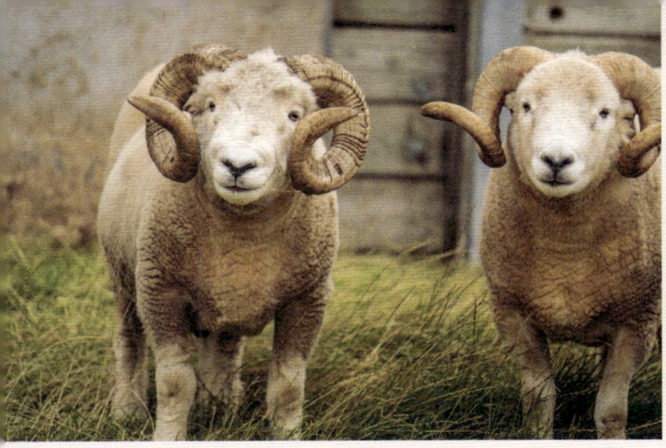
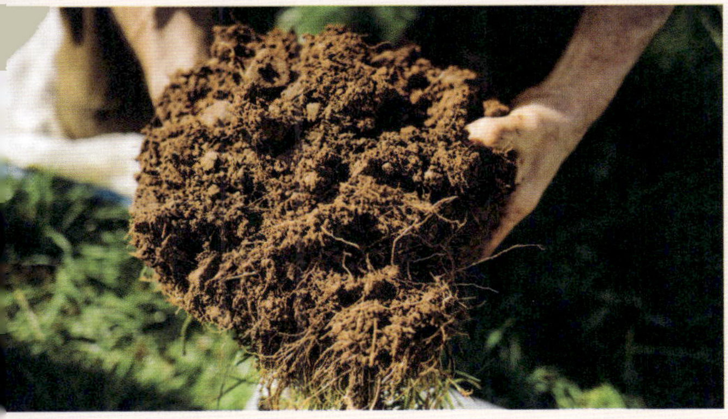
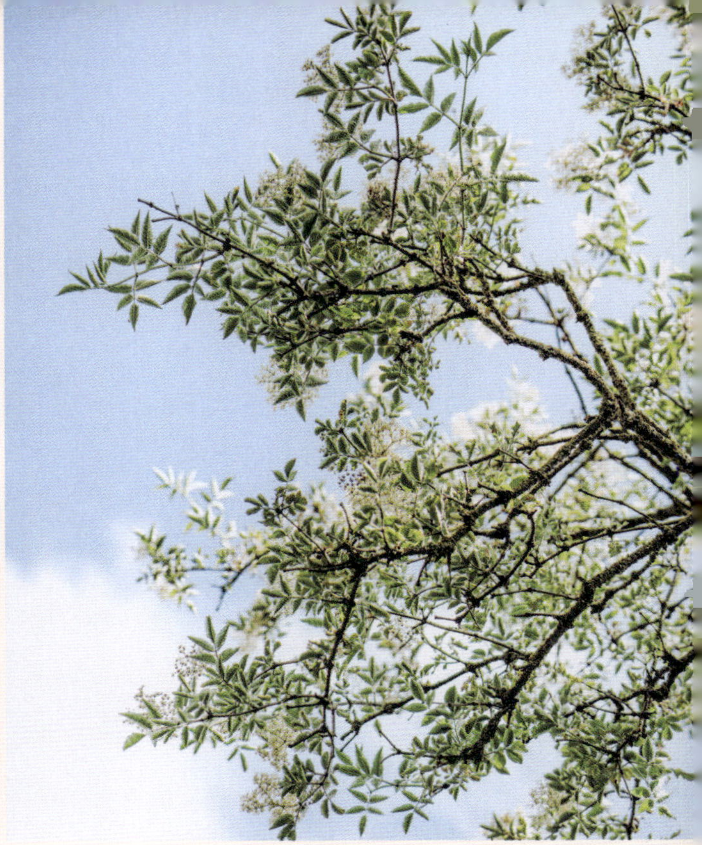
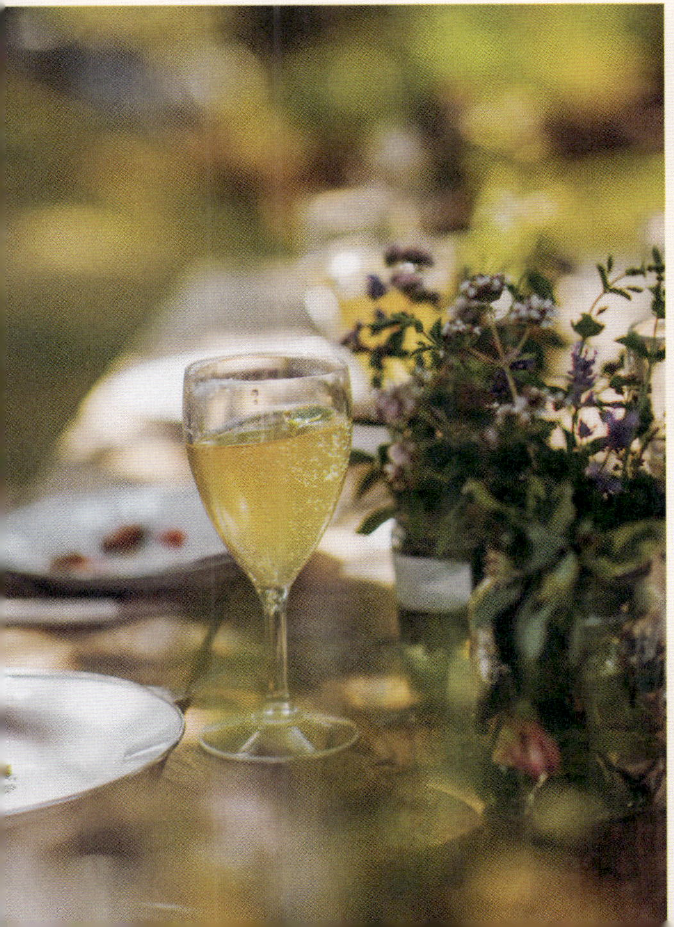
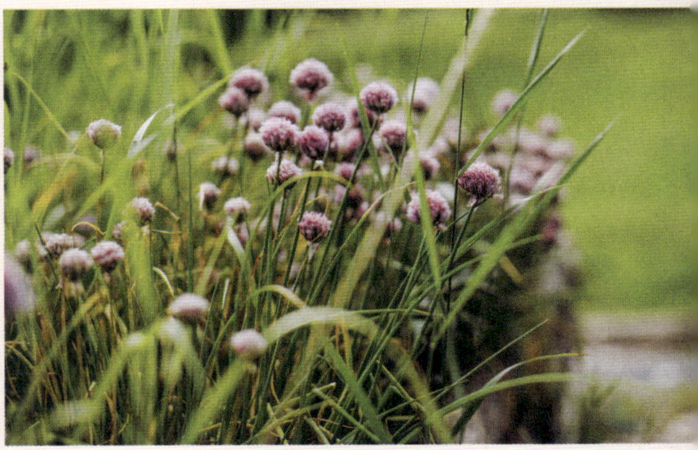
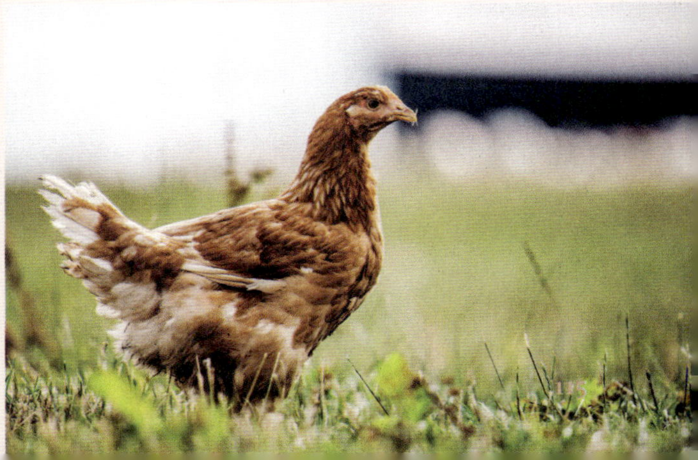

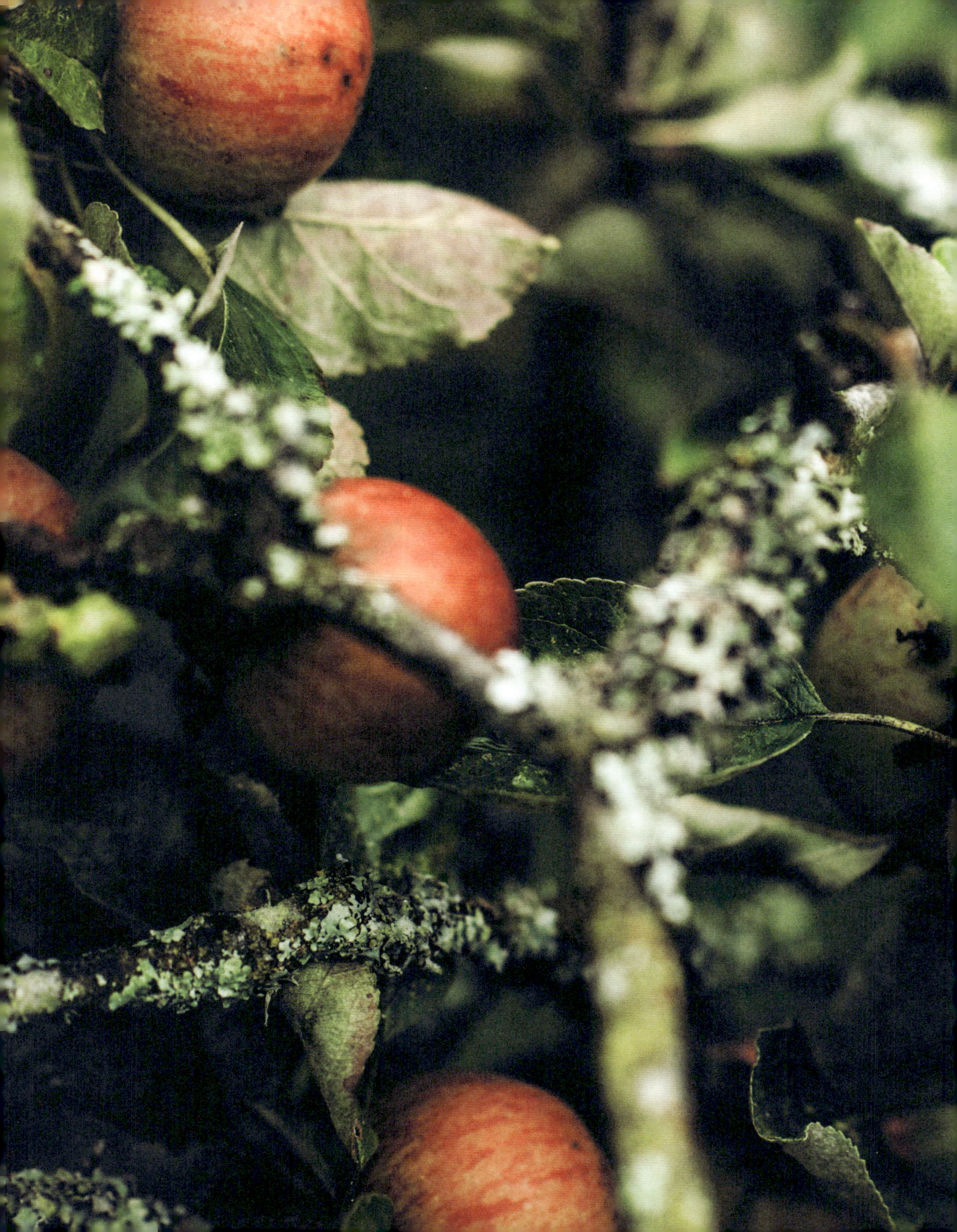

Autumn

AUTUMN

The season has once again shape-shifted. Plaited strings of onions are hung up to dry, the last hopeful sunflowers sit in a stoneware vase on my windowsill and the earthy perfume of freshly pulled beetroot hangs in the air. But there is one fragrance, above all others, that to me cements the arrival of autumn – the sweet, honeyed scent of apples piled high in wooden crates, lying in wait.

Autumn is always heavy with apples. You can rely on this fact the same way you can rely on the arrival of dawn and dusk. There are always more apples than one can use or even give away.

It's the sheer abundance of autumn that makes it my favourite season. As the days turn, the list grows longer of what is ripe for the picking, not just in my cultivated garden, but out in the wilds of nature, too.

Autumn is the time when Mother Nature dances with us. She hides her treasures in the landscape, where only those in the know, or perhaps careful enough to notice, will be able to locate her hidden jewels. We must be cautious, though, as not all her shiny gifts are edible.

For me, the romance of autumn is simply about noticing what is right in front of you.

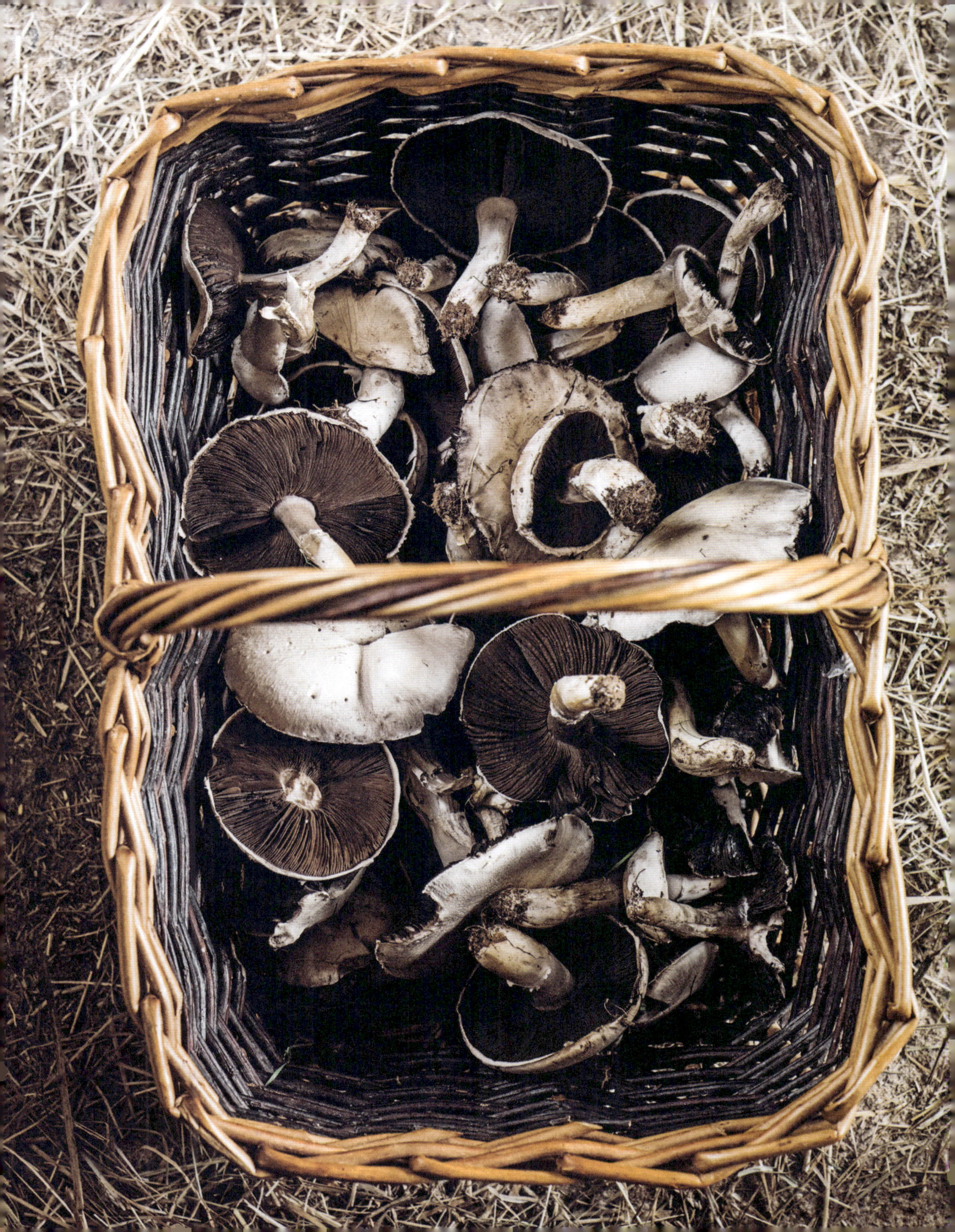

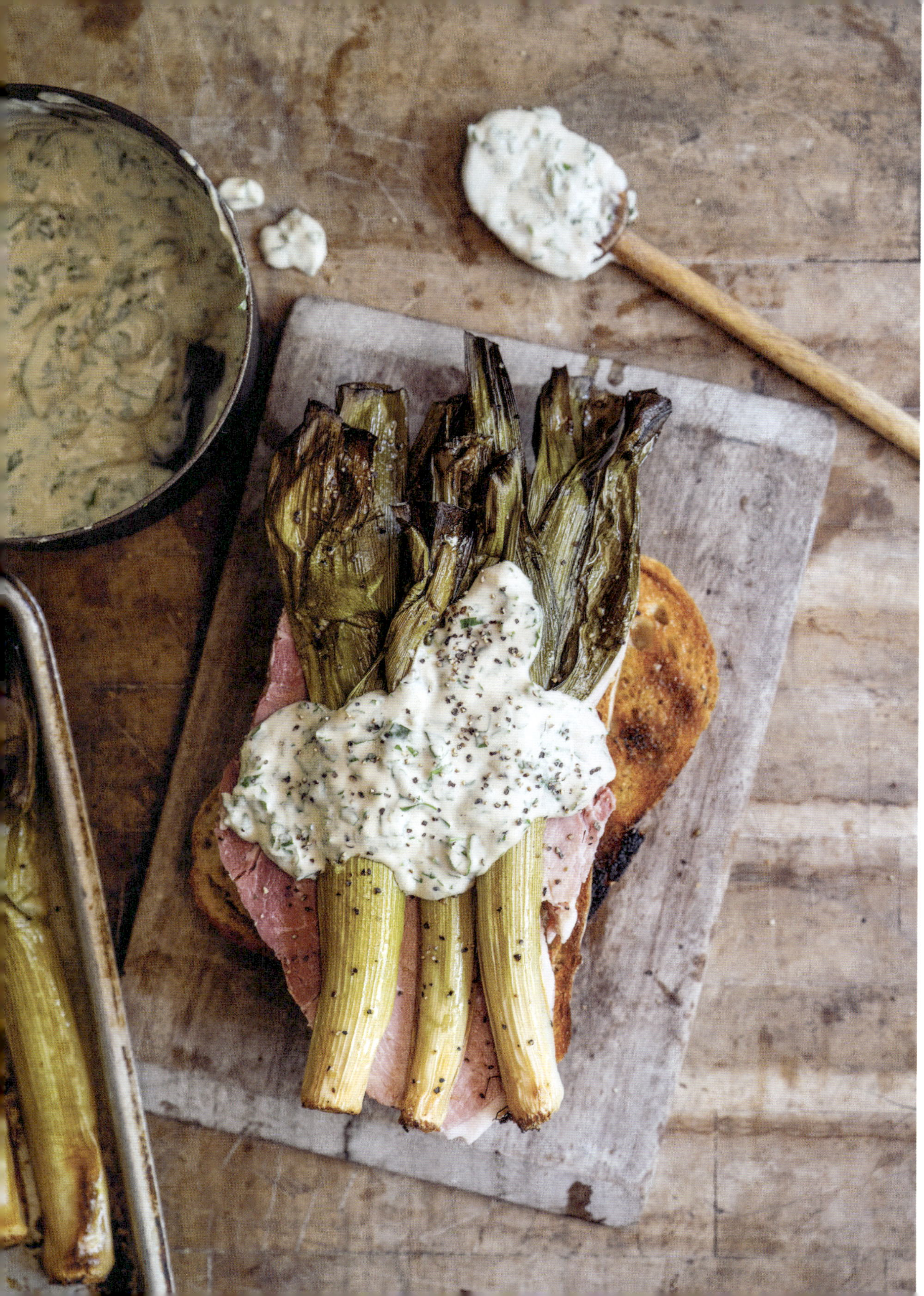

Baby Leeks & Ham on Toast with Ricotta Parsley Sauce

I find this recipe useful to make as the seasons slowly melt into one another.

At this time of year the leeks are fattening up, ready for harvesting during winter. I can't help but greedily pinch a few young, pungent stalks. Once the leeks are roasted in lashings of butter, smothered with parsley sauce and stacked on top of pink ham and crunchy soughdough, any guilt I may harbour from pulling them up in their half-grown state is assuaged.

2.5kg (5lb 8oz) free-range unsmoked gammon
2 onions, halved
4 celery sticks, halved widthways
4 carrots, halved lengthways
1 whole garlic bulb, halved horizontally
4 bay leaves
1 tablespoon black peppercorns
8 baby leeks
35g (1¼oz) grass-fed butter
flaky sea salt and freshly ground black pepper
4 pieces of sourdough bread, to serve

For the parsley sauce
50g (1¾oz) grass-fed butter
40g (1½oz) stoneground plain flour
300ml (10fl oz) whole grass-fed milk
a pinch of ground nutmeg
2 tablespoons ricotta cheese
1 large handful of flat leaf parsley, finely chopped
grated zest and juice of ½ unwaxed lemon
flaky sea salt and freshly ground black pepper

Remove the gammon from the fridge and take off any packaging a couple of hours before you intend to cook it; this allows the gammon to breathe and come to room temperature, which means it will cook more evenly.

Take a pan large enough to hold the gammon and fill it with cold water. Place the gammon in the pan and leave to soak for about 1 hour.

After the soaking time, tip away the water, then refill the pan with fresh, cold water and nestle the onions, celery, carrots, garlic, bay leaves and peppercorns around the gammon. Set the pan over a medium–high heat, bring to a low simmer and cook gently for 1 hour 40 minutes (20 minutes per 500g/1lb 2oz meat). Once cooked, carefully lift the ham out of the hot stock and leave to cool slightly before slicing.

While the gammon is cooking you can prepare the leeks. Preheat the oven to 190°C fan/375°F/gas mark 5.

Clean and trim the leeks, then lay them in a baking tray. Season with salt and pepper and dot the butter around the tray. Add a splash of water – about 1 tablespoon – then cover the tray with foil and roast in the oven for 40 minutes, or until completely soft. It's helpful to check the leeks occasionally to see how they are softening, as the cooking time will depend on their size. Once cooked, remove from the oven, keep the foil on and leave somewhere warm.

To make the parsley sauce, melt the butter in a large saucepan over a medium heat, then stir in the flour to make a roux. Cook out the flour and stir for about 2 minutes, then slowly add a splash of the milk, stirring constantly to thicken. Add another generous splash of milk and keep stirring. Repeat until you have used all the milk and have a smooth, glossy sauce. Whisk in the nutmeg, ricotta, parsley, lemon zest and juice, then season generously and take the pan off the heat.

To serve, toast the bread, then pile with slices of ham, the softened leeks and a generous spoonful of parsley sauce.

Harvest Minestrone Soup

One of the many reasons I adore autumn is the requirement at this time of year, more than at any other, to engage your senses. It begins with an ancestral perception that lets me know when rain is coming, or if perhaps frost is heading our way. Scanning the fields, my eyes inform me whether the barley is ready to cut. My nose signals what's ripe in the vegetable patch, rich with its sweet and earthy scent. My hands feel whether my eyes and nose are correct. Harvest is all about making a judgement, connecting to and understanding the land to reap the benefits. If all goes to plan and my senses are correct, there's no greater season for gluts. Onions, leeks, kale, carrots, pumpkins, peas, corn, oats, barley and even a few stubborn tomatoes, the list goes on and on for what needs to be used, stored or saved.

This soup makes utilizing a diverse list of ingredients a breeze. It stores well, too – frozen for winter, to be pulled out on a frosty day and eaten hot with chunks of buttered bread.

4 tablespoons pearl barley
3 tablespoons British green lentils
3 tablespoons British split fava beans
3 tablespoons British split green peas
3 tablespoons British carlin peas
1.2 litres (2 pints) chicken stock
a drizzle of extra virgin olive oil
2 onions, finely diced
1 large leek, finely sliced
1 carrot, chopped
1 celery stick, chopped
2 garlic cloves, finely diced
½ red chilli, deseeded and finely sliced
½ small swede, chopped into small cubes
100g (3½oz) pumpkin, chopped into small cubes
a small bunch of kale, leaves stripped and sliced, stalks chopped
1 tablespoon tomato purée
½ teaspoon smoked paprika
1 tablespoon stoneground flour
400g (14oz) Preserved Tomatoes (see page 77) or canned plum tomatoes
2 bay leaves
a few sprigs of thyme
2 sprigs of rosemary
¼ Savoy cabbage, finely sliced
flaky sea salt and freshly ground black pepper

Take a large mixing bowl and add the dried grains, pulses and peas. Add cold water to cover – you'll need double the volume of dried ingredients, about 240ml (8½fl oz) – and leave to soak for 6 hours.

Once soaked, drain away the water and tip the grains, pulses and peas into a medium saucepan. Pour in the chicken stock, then set the pan over a medium heat and cook for 30–40 minutes, or until everything is tender. Set the pan to one side, keeping everything warm.

Drizzle a little oil into a cast-iron casserole dish and add the onions, leek, carrot and celery, as well as a generous pinch of salt. Sweat the vegetables for around 8–10 minutes, until softened.

Add the garlic, chilli, swede, pumpkin, kale stalks (keeping the leaves back for later), tomato purée, paprika and flour, and cook for around 5 minutes, or until the veg have just started to brown lightly.

Add the tomatoes and herbs along with the chicken stock mixture, increase the heat and bring to a simmer. Cook for around 5–10 minutes.

Finally, add the reserved kale leaves and cabbage and cook for a final 5 minutes, until all the veg are soft and the flavours have intensified. Check the seasoning and adjust with more salt or pepper as necessary. Ladle into generous bowls and serve as it is or with warm crusty bread on the side.

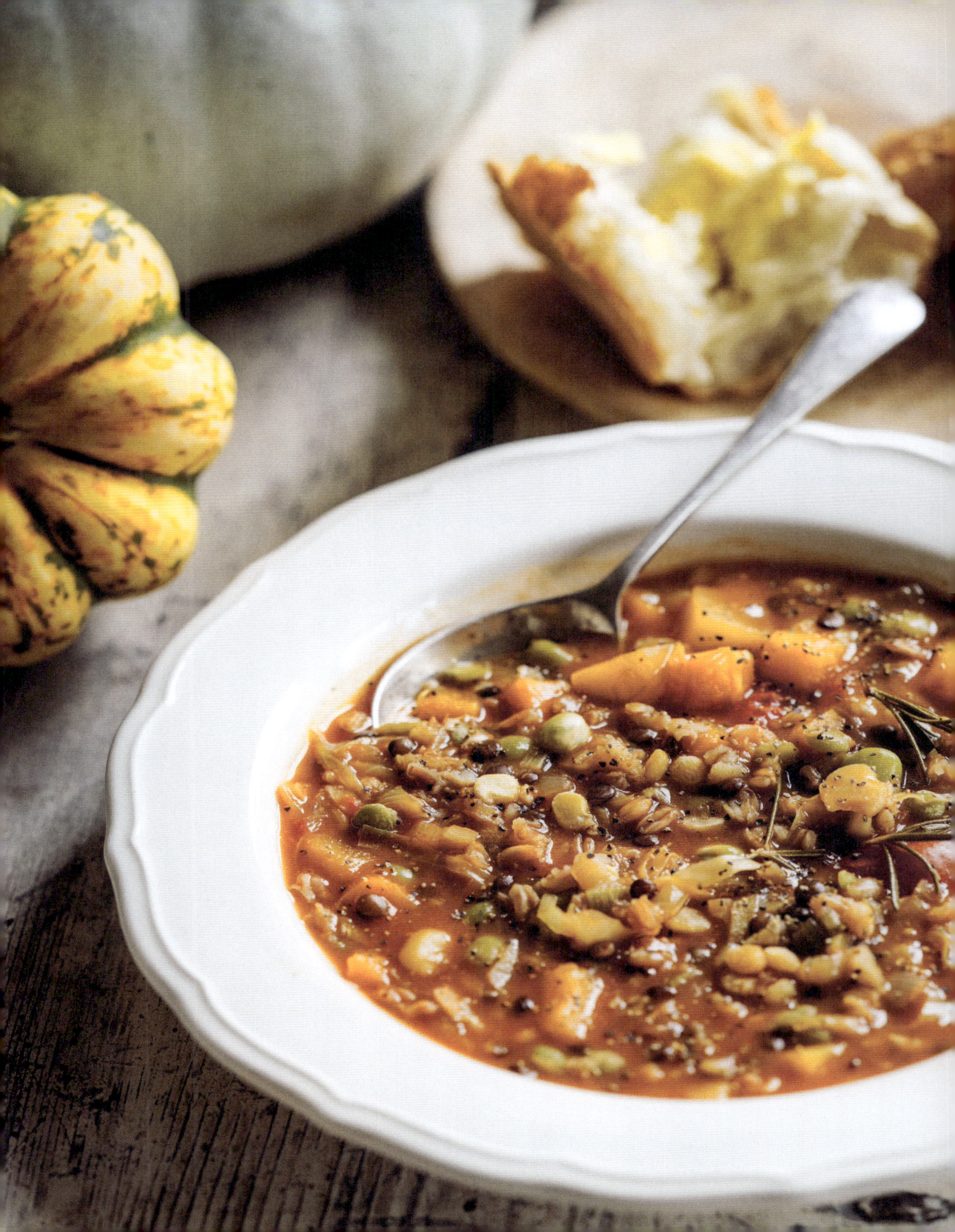

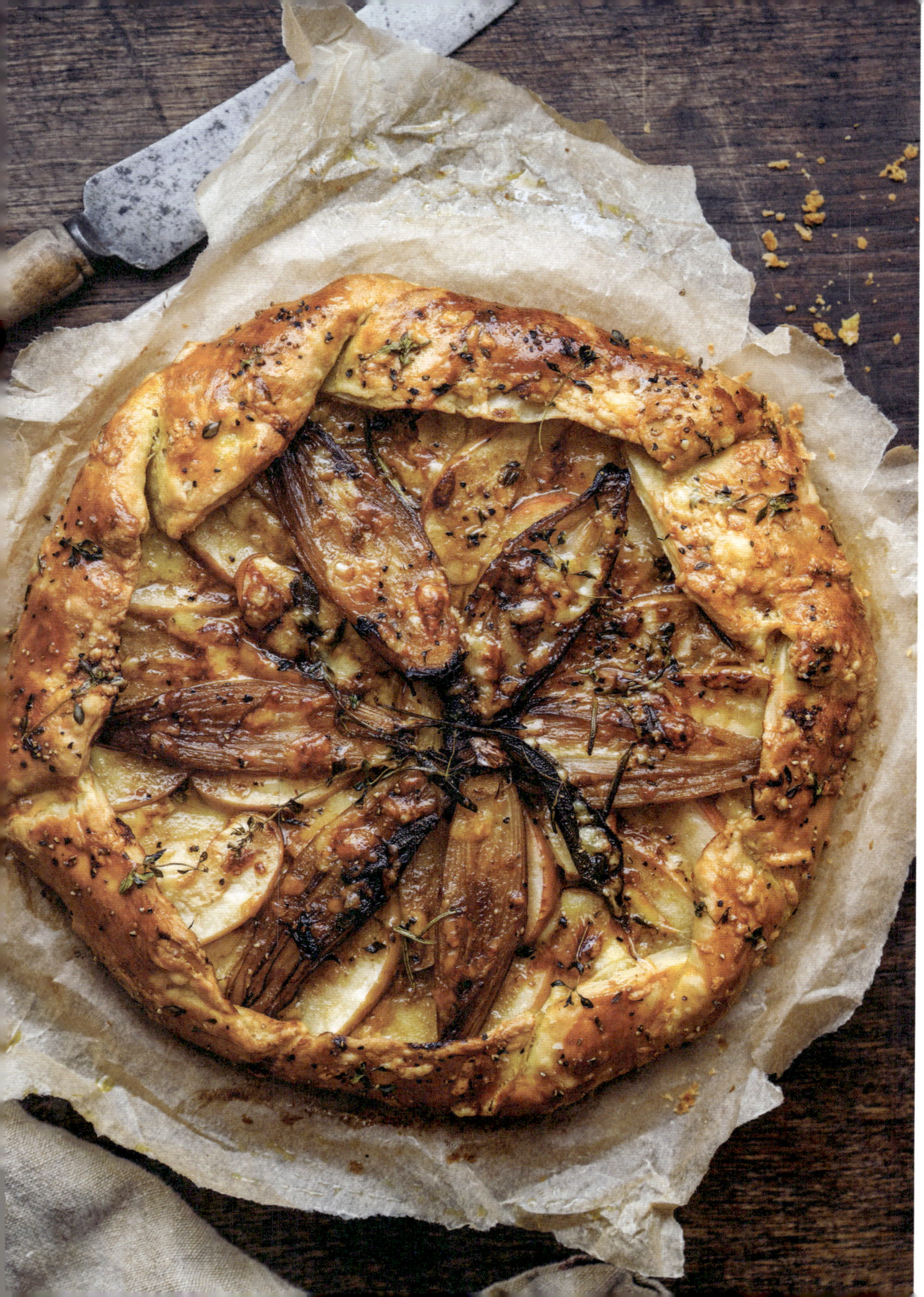

Apple, Shallot, Cheddar & Thyme Galette

At this time of year in the countryside, there are apples everywhere. You'll see them framing cottage gardens and in orchards throughout South West England. Sadly, many of the apples produced are wasted – if not picked and consumed, they will slowly be broken down by wasps, moths, aphids and caterpillars.

This recipe is a real celebration of autumn. It's a sweet–savoury combo that I find incredibly moreish, and works equally well hot from the oven as it does cold as leftovers, giving you plenty of flexibility for how and when you want to serve it.

50g (1¾oz) grass-fed butter
3–4 small shallots, quartered
250ml (9fl oz) dry cider
1 teaspoon English mustard
200g (7oz) mature clothbound Cheddar cheese, grated
3 eating apples, cored and finely sliced
1 organic and/or free-range egg yolk, beaten
a few sprigs of thyme, leaves picked
flaky sea salt and freshly ground black pepper

For the pastry
250g (9oz) stoneground spelt flour
175g (6oz) grass-fed butter, cold and sliced into cubes
a large pinch of flaky sea salt
50g (1¾oz) unbleached granulated sugar
½ teaspoon thyme leaves
cold water, as needed

First, make the pastry. Blitz the flour, butter, salt, sugar and thyme in a food processor, then carefully add a little cold water until everything comes together into a dough. Wrap the dough in muslin cloth or beeswax wrap and leave to chill in the fridge for an hour.

For the filling, melt the butter in a cast-iron pan over a medium–high heat. Season the shallots with salt and pepper, and place them face-down in the pan. Fry for 4–5 minutes, until they have caramelized on one side. Turn the heat up and pour in the cider, allowing it to bubble up, simmer and reduce by half, then turn the heat right down and cover with a lid. Leave the shallots to steep and cook gently in the buttery cider for a further 5–6 minutes.

Once the shallots are tender, gently lift them out of the pan and set to one side. Add the mustard to the pan and simmer until you have a thick, glossy reduction.

Preheat the oven to 200°C/400°F/gas mark 6. Line a baking sheet with parchment paper.

Unwrap the pastry dough, roll it out into a large circle and place on the prepared baking sheet. Leaving a border roughly 3cm (1¼in), scatter most of the cheese over the pastry. Add the apple slices, arranging them evenly around the galette, then arrange the shallots on top, fanning them out from the centre. Pour over the cider sauce.

Fold the edges of the pastry up around the filling to partially cover, then brush the exposed pastry with the beaten egg yolk. Scatter over the thyme leaves and remaining cheese, then bake for 30–35 minutes.

Let the galette cool on the baking sheet for 5 minutes, then carefully transfer it to a wire rack. Season with salt and pepper, then slice and serve with a sharply dressed salad.

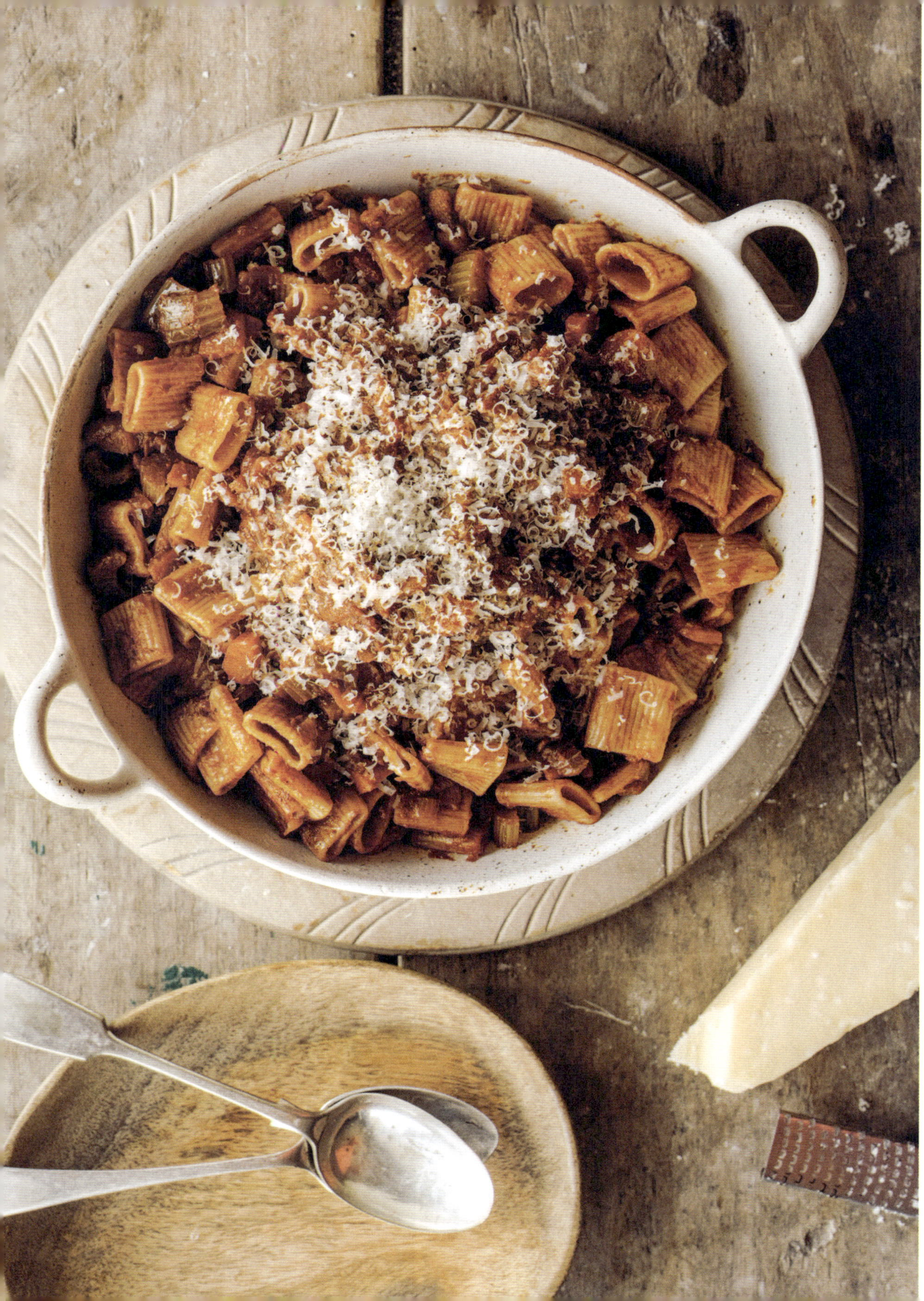

SERVES 4   Autumn

Gardener's Bolognese

As the season begins and shiny produce is shared, there are excited, gleeful and thankful faces queuing up to reap the rewards of my sowing and digging. However, as the season rolls on and courgettes become marrows through weariness of picking, the tomatoes are less ripe than the earlier jewels, and what's left in the ground is a little wonkier or woodier, I realize I have given away all that I can.

This is the perfect recipe to use up harvest gluts. Any weird or wonky veg, tomatoes that are yet to ripen, and even the last of the courgettes that you have run out of ideas for, can all be thrown in and cooked down to make a generous, filling sauce. No one needs to know that it isn't the first flush of the season – all cooked together with love, this provides so much more than the sum of its parts.

a drizzle of organic rapeseed oil
2 onions, finely chopped
3 carrots, grated
2 courgettes, grated
2 celery sticks, finely chopped
4 garlic cloves, finely sliced
400g (14oz) chestnut mushrooms
100g (3½oz) British green lentils, cooked and drained
a handful of cherry tomatoes
175ml (6fl oz) red wine
800g (1lb 12oz) Preserved Tomatoes (see page 77)
2 tablespoons Worcestershire sauce
a few sprigs of rosemary
a few sprigs of thyme
2 bay leaves
400g (14oz) rigatoni pasta
50g (1¾oz) hard cheese (Pecorino or Old Winchester work well), finely grated
flaky sea salt and freshly ground black pepper

Add the oil to a cast-iron pan and place over a medium heat. Tip in the onions, carrots, courgettes, celery and garlic along with a good pinch of sea salt. Sweat the veg down for around 10 minutes, or until everything has softened.

Turn up the heat and add the mushrooms, lentils and cherry tomatoes. Once the pan is nice and hot, add the red wine and allow it to bubble. Pour in the preserved tomatoes and Worcestershire sauce, stirring everything together. Throw in the herbs and check the sauce for seasoning; you may want to add a little more salt or some pepper here. Reduce the heat and let the sauce simmer gently for around 30 minutes until everything has thickened and the flavours have intensified. If the sauce looks a bit too thick for your liking, simply add a little water.

Bring a large pan of salted water to the boil and add the pasta. Cook for about 8–9 minutes, ensuring the pasta still retains a little bite. Drain, then toss the pasta through the sauce. Finish with a hefty shower of black pepper and a generous grating of hard cheese.

Creamy Baked Eggs with Wild Mushrooms & Spinach

In a fast-paced world, we often miss the small adjustments nature makes as each season turns. The constant change that morphs around us, as we go about our lives unaware and unnoticing.

The sheer abundance of nature makes me so happy. With the dawn of each day there's always something new to discover. It's about acknowledging what's right in front of you. A patch of gold beneath beech trees, that starts off small and before you know it becomes a forest of splendid chanterelles. These small gifts given each day are a reminder that we are only here for a time and to use that time wisely. So let's start the day with a celebratory breakfast!

200g (7oz) spinach
grass-fed butter, for frying
2 shallots, finely sliced
4 garlic cloves, peeled, bashed and finely chopped
150g (5½oz) chestnut mushrooms, chopped
a small handful of dried mushrooms, soaked for 20 minutes, then drained and chopped
a few sprigs of thyme
100ml (3½fl oz) Somerset cider brandy
250ml (9fl oz) double cream
50g (1¾oz) hard cheese (I like to use Old Winchester, but you could use Parmesan, Pecorino or even Gruyère here)
200g (7oz) wild mushrooms, cleaned, trimmed and cut into equal sizes
a pinch of ground nutmeg
4–6 organic and/or free-range eggs
flaky sea salt and freshly ground black pepper

Preheat the oven to 190°C/375°F/gas mark 5.

Bring a small saucepan of water to the boil, then add the spinach and cook for around 2 minutes. Use a slotted spoon to remove the spinach from the pan and plunge it immediately into cold water. Drain, then place the spinach in a dry tea towel, roll it up and set aside.

Heat a cast-iron, ovenproof frying pan over a medium heat, then add a knob of butter along with the shallots and a pinch of salt. Allow the shallots to soften gently for around 5–6 minutes, then add a little more butter, along with the garlic, chestnut and drained mushrooms and thyme. Fry for a few minutes.

Roughly chop the cooked spinach and add it to the pan, then turn up the heat and add the cider brandy, allowing it to bubble away for about 5 minutes.

Add the cream, cheese and wild mushrooms, then give everything a good stir. Season with a little salt, pepper and nutmeg, then crack the eggs over the top. Slide the pan into the oven and bake for 6–10 minutes, or until the eggs are just set.

Serve immediately with some really good sourdough toast to scoop up the creamy eggs.

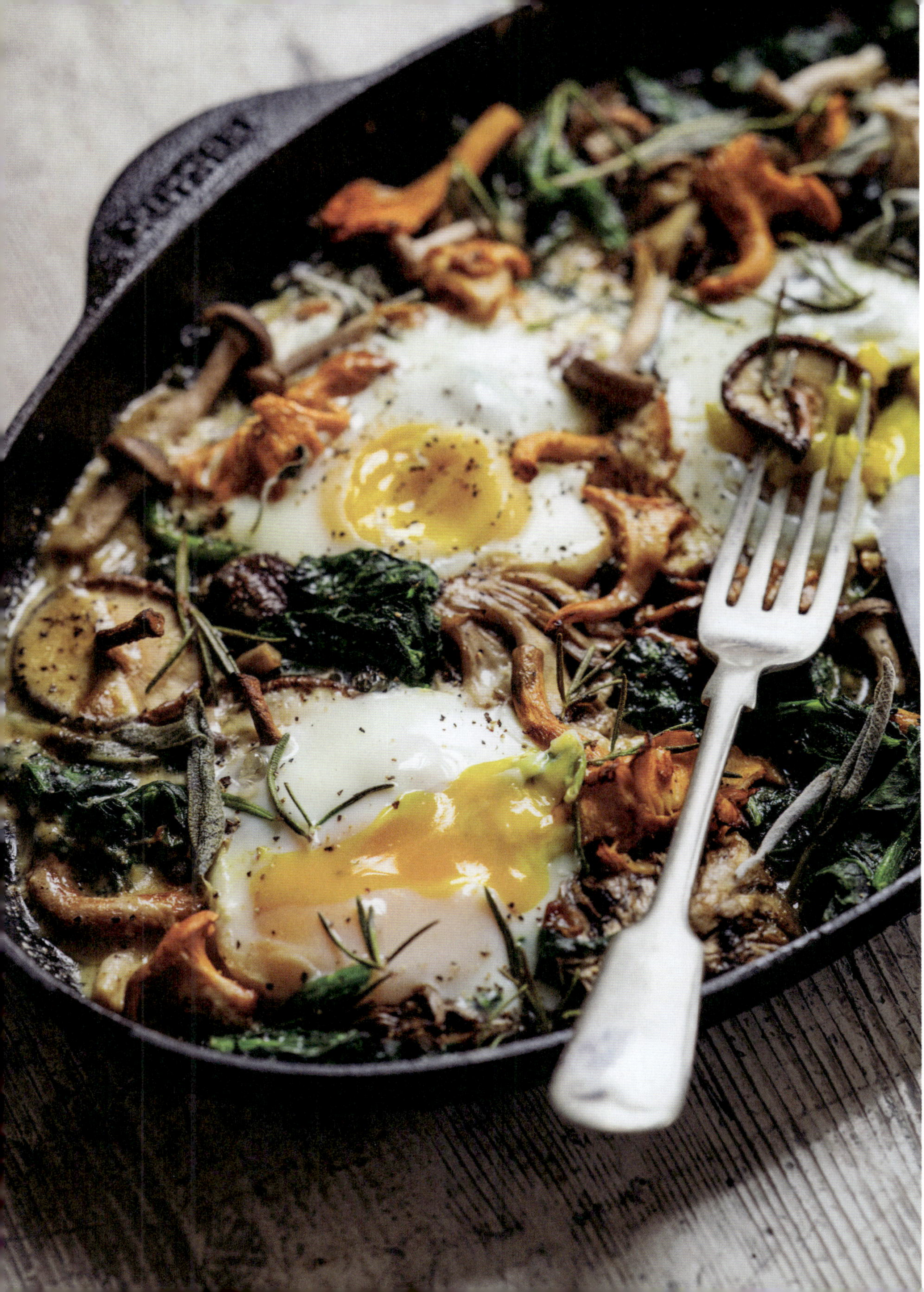

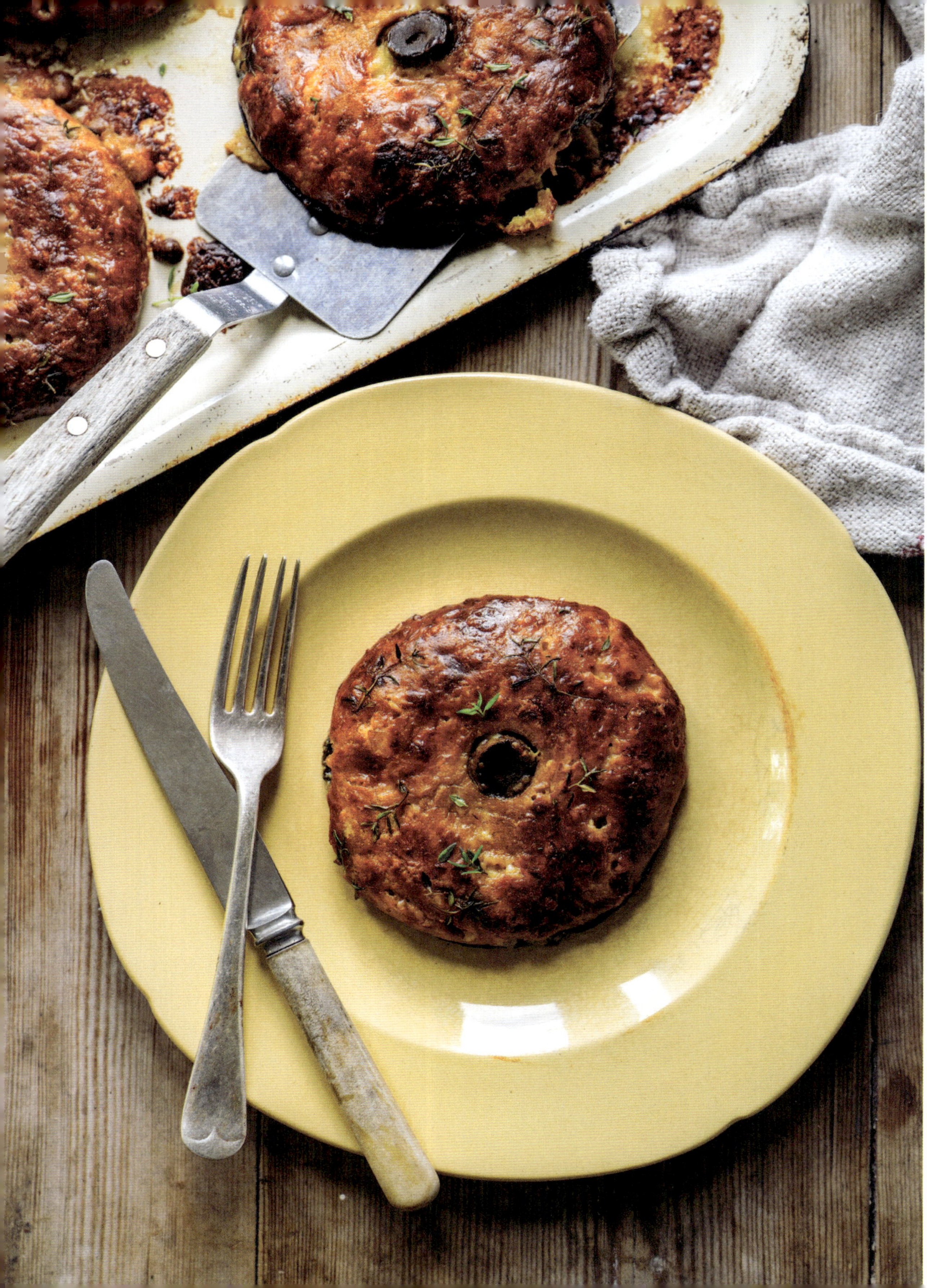

Field Mushroom Rarebit

When I start to see mushrooms pepper our pastures, my heart fills with joy. You see, bountiful mycelium is a sign of very good soil health; it's one of nature's key indicators that the way we are managing our land is healthy and functional. Warmth, as well as a good long shower of rain, really make our fields pop in the autumn with an abundance of species, but none more delicious than the humble field mushroom. *Agaricus campestris*, to use its fancy name, used to be commonplace in the countryside. However, due to the increased use of chemical sprays and the loss of permanent pasture and species-rich meadow habitats, it has become harder to track them down. If you are not lucky enough to find them in your area, portobello mushrooms can easily be used instead.

Do remember, when foraging, to make sure you know exactly what you are picking. This is particularly important for mushrooms. If you are in any doubt, just leave it be and head to your local farm shop for safe supplies.

6–8 field mushrooms or portobello mushrooms
a drizzle of extra virgin olive oil
2 organic and/or free-range egg yolks
150g (5½oz) clothbound Cheddar cheese, grated
10g (¼oz) stoneground plain flour
50ml (2fl oz) white wine
1 tablespoon Worcestershire sauce
1½ teaspoons Dijon mustard
½ teaspoon paprika
a pinch of chopped fresh herbs, such as thyme
flaky sea salt and freshly ground black pepper

Preheat the oven to 190°C/375°F/gas mark 5.

Carefully trim and clean the mushrooms and pat dry. Place the mushrooms onto a baking sheet, drizzle with a little olive oil, making sure they are evenly coated, then season well with sea salt.

In a mixing bowl, combine the egg yolks, cheese, flour, wine, Worcestershire sauce, mustard, a pinch of pepper and a little of the paprika, then mix everything together well.

Spoon the cheesy mixture into the cavity of each mushroom. Sprinkle the top with the remaining paprika, the fresh herbs and a couple more drops of Worcestershire sauce.

Bake in the hot oven for around 20 minutes, or until the filling has puffed up and is beautifully golden.

Scatter the mushrooms with a few fresh herbs, then serve with a smear of mustard and a sharp salad, either on toast or as an indulgent side dish.

Reconnecting with Nature

It's easy to forget that we are all part of nature. Most of us live in insulated homes. We wake up with the blinds down, shutting out the first glimmers of what the day has to offer us. We get ready for the day with a dozen products that come out of tubes and tins made in factories, using a long list of artificial ingredients you would need to be a chemist or have a scientific degree to understand. We breathe fresh air for less than a minute on our way from the front door to the car, or hurrying from the car to the office. Many of us can spend our entire day not giving nature a second thought.

Not to recognize that the choices we make in our daily lives have a direct influence on the natural world, is to gravely misunderstand the order of things. From the chemicals we pour down the sink in the morning, to the type of food we feed ourselves over breakfast, and even the fuel we use to get ourselves from A to B, every single choice we make is interlinked with an action that can either deplete or regenerate our environment.

The natural world is our most precious resource, yet most people today could recall more brand names than could recognize the different species of tree. It's not surprising when we live life at such a pace, never worrying what we are leaving in our wake. Nature has become a blur of green, whizzing past us from the car window. Yet many of us are beginning to realize the impact of our actions, that we as citizens have the ability to shape the world around us by the choices we make, whether governments or corporations like it or not.

I live in an island nation, a floating mass of earth that over 450,000 years ago detached itself from mainland Europe due to rising sea levels caused by a shift in climate. You see, climates changing and species evolving is not a new phenomenon. What is worrisome today, though, is the pace of this change, the speed at which we are asking the natural world to adapt, the pressure we are putting on our precarious resources and the dominance we are inflicting as the apex species. To my mind, there is no question that if we carry on in a similar vein, we will become the architects of our own destruction.

Each year, the UK alone wastes around 95 million tonnes of food, which is about one-third of what it produces. This is enough food to feed more than 30 million people. Globally, one-fifth of food produced for human consumption is wasted, which amounts to a billion meals a day, and 60% of all food wasted happens in our homes.

Not only are we wasting eye-watering amounts of food, putting resources to produce vast quantities under extreme pressure, but most food that comes through our kitchens these days is protected in packaging, with the ironic aim of keeping us safe from food-related illnessness and makng the ingredients last longer. But the trouble with food packaging begins at its creation. Each form of packaging requires a lot of resources – energy, water, chemicals, petroleum, minerals, wood and fibres – to produce. Its manufacture generates significant emissions, including greenhouse gases. After it is used, most packaging is discarded and is either buried in landfill or becomes litter that is carried along by wind and water into the environment.

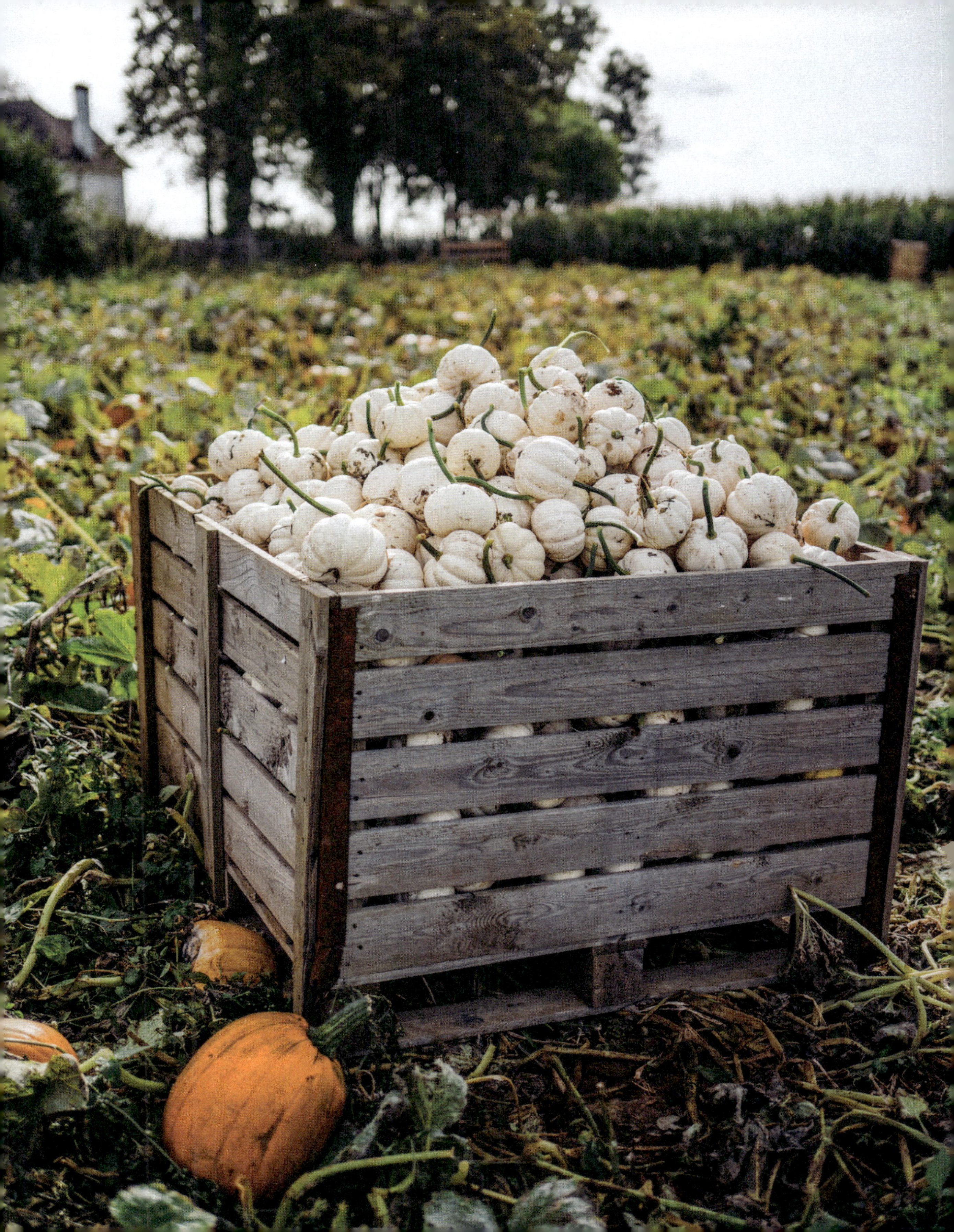

One study estimated that one-third of all discarded plastic ends up in soil or in fresh water. Some scientists believe that microplastic pollution in soils around the world is an even more severe problem than microplastic pollution in our oceans. An estimated 4 to 23 times more severe, depending on the environment. Once in the soil and waterways, degrading plastics leach out toxic chemicals, the contaminated pieces can make their way through the food chain and into humans through ingestion. Some food packaging materials degrade relatively quickly; others will take hundreds to even a million years to degrade, leaving us with a mounting problem that won't be going anywhere fast.

Before the industrial revolution, food would stay relatively local. Some items, such as pineapples and tea, would travel a great distance to reach our shores, but they would come to us via slow methods of transport – ships, carthorses and trains. These prized ingredients would have been greatly valued for their intrepid journey and, as such, would have been eaten rarely and only by those willing to pay the high price.

Suddenly, we found ourselves in a world where every corner of the globe was accessible, and more food was accessible to more people. Food could be brought in at a moment's notice, extending our seasons and introducing new flavours. Sadly, today we have taken this to the extreme and have lost sight of the joy of winter citrus landing on our shores, as we expect to see fresh oranges, lemons and limes on our shelves 365 days per year, simply switching from European production to far-flung countries as the sunshine moves around the globe – and all at a bargain price, as (unbelievably) these items are deemed 'an everyday staple' by multi-national retailers. The result of this is hefty, fuel-hungry supply chains using every method from air to road freight to get us our food 'just in time'. Transporting food from where it is produced to our dinner plates creates at least triple the amount of greenhouse gas emissions as previously estimated. 'Food miles' are likely responsible for about 6% of the world's greenhouse gas emissions.

Living in a modern world, where choice and opportunity are not always present due to the weight of corporations who have stifled smaller, independent businesses, it is impossible to be a perfect citizen, but there are things we can all do. First, we must spend more than just a few minutes communing with nature. There are many hectares of green space on offer to us completely free of charge, from local parks to national parks, a network of interlacing footpaths running like veins around the country. There are beaches, woodland, moorland and pastureland waiting for us to explore. By regularly connecting with our natural world, we form a deeper bond and a respect for all that it offers us. We begin to realize that perhaps we shouldn't place ourselves at the top of the pyramid and instead should be part of a circle, a holistic cycle that values all living things. Green spaces are not just an important reminder of the natural order of things, but they are invaluable to our mental and physical health, too, vastly reducing stress and anxiety, as well as, in some cases, increasing our rate of physical healing.

We must begin to take back control of what we eat and how our food reaches our plates. For those of us in a position to make choices, it is imperative that we prioritize the food we eat and the system it is produced from over other material goods. Many of us wouldn't bat an eyelid at spending multiple pounds on a small jar of face cream that insists it will stop us ageing, but we balk at the price of organic fruit and veg grown and distributed locally. We must remember what is truly more important and, while I can't officially attest to this, my gut tells me which one will make you feel younger for longer.

The food we choose to eat and the system it is harvested from have more impact on this planet than almost any other decision we make. We must reconnect with seasonal eating, buy locally, freeze, preserve, pickle and waste less, buy from people who care about our land, and eat a diverse diet, never taking more than we should. The more we make considered, positive decisions, the more we can make change within our own communities, as well as in marginalized communities around the world, and provide opportunities to support those that have less choice, removing pressure and exploitation from supply chains.

We must begin to see ourselves as active, free-range, free-thinking humans and remove the cages that have been placed around us like factory-farmed animals. We each have the power to shape the world we live in, and the sooner we grasp that power, the greater benefits there will be for us all.

Chicken, Chorizo & Butter Bean Soup

I almost wonder if I can get away with calling this recipe a soup. It's somewhere between a soup and a stew – somewhere very delicious.

Truly, the best time to make this recipe is following a roast chicken. Once the table has been cleared, the last scraps of meat can be shredded from the bone and reserved to use in place of the chicken thighs listed below. The carcass can then be popped into a pot and left to bubble away, perhaps while you stomp off some of the calories from lunch on a brisk walk, crunching leaves underfoot. This recipe makes wonderful leftover lunch fodder, preparing you for the week ahead. If you haven't managed to roast a whole bird, simply follow the recipe below to make this hearty meal from scratch.

3–4 organic or free-range skin-on chicken thighs
a drizzle of organic rapeseed oil
185g (6½oz) cooking chorizo, sliced or cubed
1 large onion, finely chopped
4 garlic cloves, finely chopped
2 sprigs of rosemary, leaves picked and chopped
2 sprigs of thyme, leaves picked and chopped
3 bay leaves
1 teaspoon smoked paprika
1 litre (1¾ pints) chicken stock, warmed
1 tablespoon stoneground plain flour
a knob of grass-fed butter
200g (7oz) canned butter beans, drained
100ml (3½fl oz) double cream
flaky sea salt and freshly ground black pepper

Preheat the oven to 190°C/375°F/gas mark 5.

Place the chicken thighs in a roasting tray, season generously with salt, then roast in the oven for 25 minutes, until golden. Remove from the oven and leave to cool. Once cooled roughly chop the chicken, skin and all.

Set a cast-iron pan over a medium–high heat and drizzle in a little oil. Once sizzling, add the chorizo and stir for a few minutes until it has crisped and caramelised. Reduce the heat, then add the onion, garlic, herbs and a pinch of salt. Once the onions have softened and the herbs have become fragrant, add the paprika and allow it to toast for a minute. Add the chicken thigh meat along with half the stock. Bring to the boil, then reduce to a simmer and leave it to bubble away for around 15 minutes.

Make a roux by combining the flour and butter in a small bowl until a smooth paste has formed. Mix the roux into the pan, then stir in the remaining stock and simmer for a further 10 minutes.

Tip the butter beans into the pan and simmer for around 5–6 minutes, then add the cream and adjust the seasoning to taste.

Serve in warmed bowls with a generous twist of black pepper over the top and some crusty bread on the side.

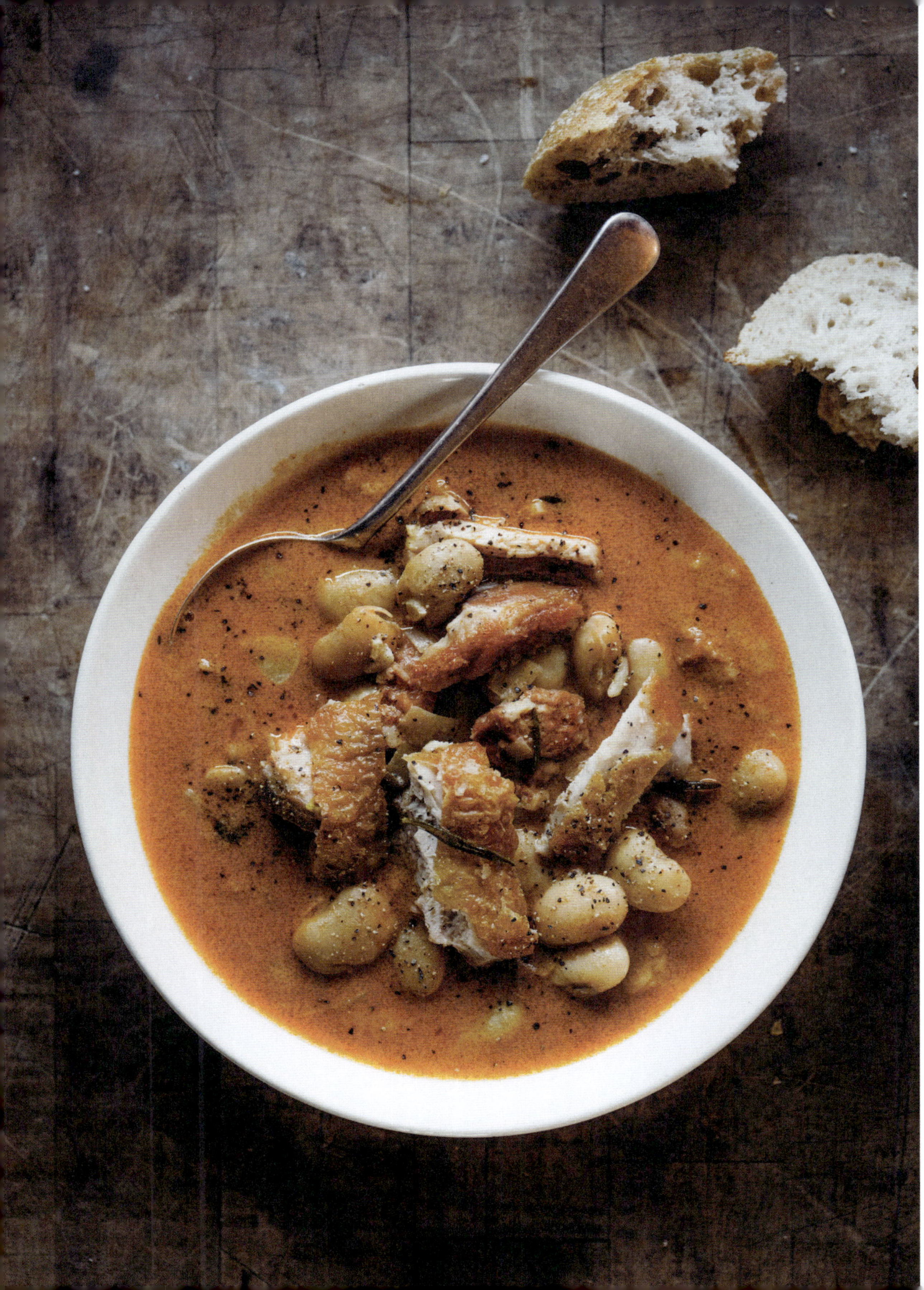

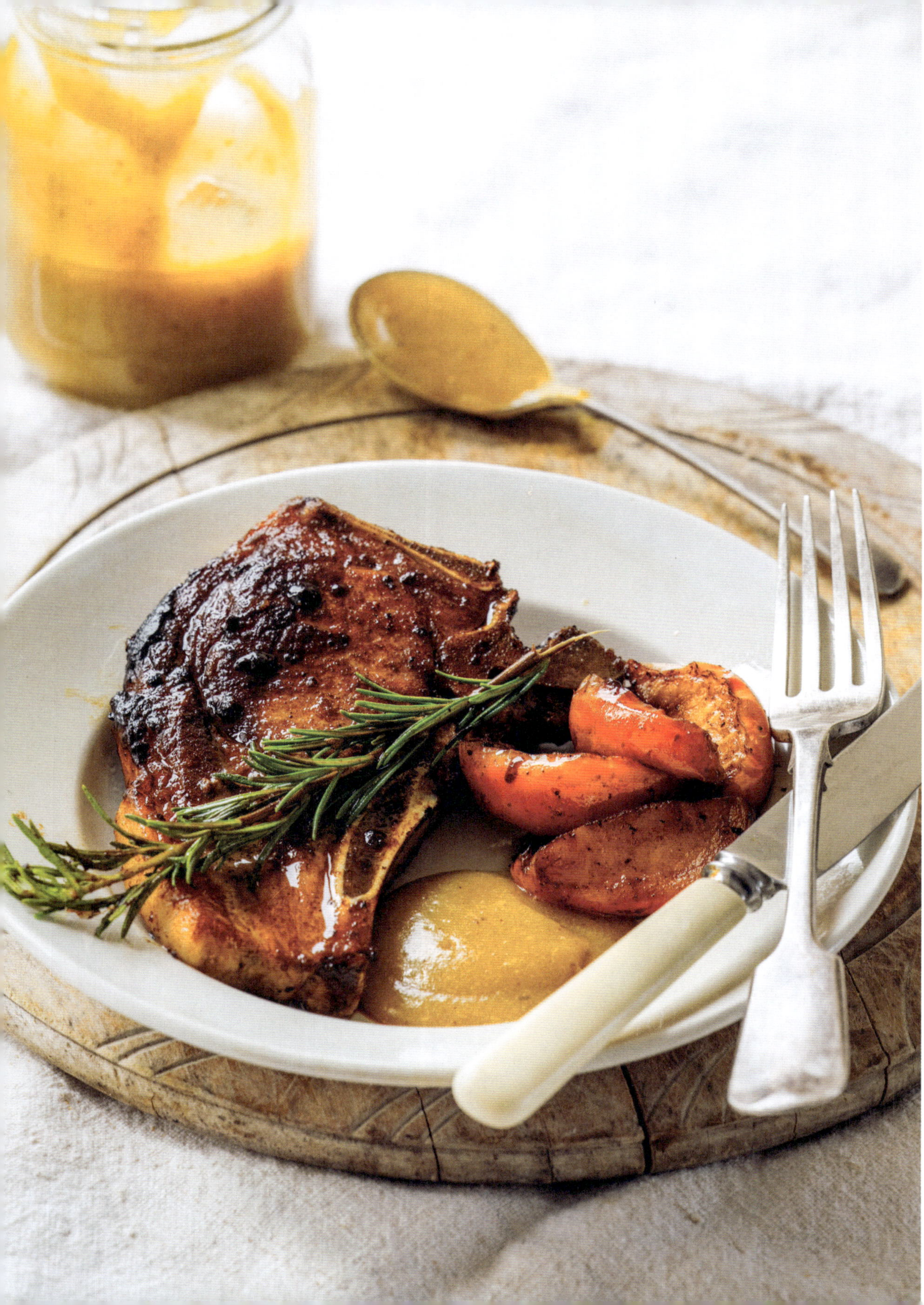

SERVES 4 Autumn

Pork Chops with Apple Ketchup

Before the advent of refrigeration, there was careful consideration of how to keep meat at its best for the longest time, so much so that our farming calendar dictated the best month in the year for a fat pig to be slaughtered.

Traditionally, hogs were fattened over the spring and summer months and slaughtered in the autumn or winter. The pairing of pork and apple is entwined throughout history, as both were ready for curing or fermentation at the same time of year. They would have been consumed together for weeks to follow. As luck would have it, they are the most delicious bedfellows. The tartness of the apple has the ability to cut through rich pork fat and enhance the sweet flavour of the meat. Here I have celebrated these two wonderful components of autumn's harvest, in time-honoured fashion.

4 organic or free-range pork chops
1 tablespoon Dijon mustard
1 tablespoon wholegrain mustard
½ teaspoon fennel seeds
a drizzle of organic rapeseed oil
a knob of grass-fed butter
3–4 garlic cloves, peeled and bashed
a few sprigs of rosemary
flaky sea salt and freshly ground black pepper

For the apple ketchup
5 large cooking apples
150ml (5fl oz) cider vinegar
2½ tablespoons honey
2–3 sprigs of thyme
1 bay leaf

Remove the pork chops from the fridge, pat dry with kitchen paper and season well with sea salt. Allow the chops to marinate in the salt and come to room temperature. If you can, do this an hour or two before you intend to cook them.

Preheat the oven to 190°C/375°F/gas mark 5.

For the apple ketchup, place 4 of the apples in a baking dish and bake in the oven for 35 minutes, or until soft and yielding. Set aside to cool.

In a small saucepan, combine the cider vinegar, honey and herbs and set over a medium–high heat. Bring to the boil, then reduce to a simmer and cook until the liquid has reduced by two-thirds. Discard the herbs, then pour the liquid into a blender along with the baked apples and blitz to a purée. You could leave the purée like this; for a more refined ketchup, use the back of a wooden spoon to push the apples through a sieve to remove the tough skins and pips. Adjust the seasoning with a little salt and pepper and set aside.

In a small mixing bowl, combine both mustards with the fennel seeds and set aside.

Set a cast-iron frying pan over a medium–high heat, drizzle in the oil and add the chops. You may want to do this in batches to ensure you do not overcrowd the pan. Fry for 2–3 minutes, then use a pair of tongs to turn and fry the other side for a further 2 minutes. Using the tongs, pick the chops up and press the fat side into the pan, holding it there for a couple of minutes, or until the fat crisps and renders.

With all the chops now in the pan, take the mustard mixture and slather it over the chops, then add a generous knob of butter along with the garlic and rosemary. Baste the chops with the cooking liquor for a further 2–3 minutes.

Remove from the pan and leave the chops to rest for 5–6 minutes. Meanwhile, cut the remaining apple into 8 segments, then caramelize them in the pan until golden on all sides.

Plate each chop with a spoonful of the cooking liquor, a dollop of apple ketchup and some caramelized apple. I like to serve these with roasted or mashed potatoes and seasonal greens.

Autumn

SERVES 4–6

Apple, Leek, Thyme & Cheddar Toad-in-the-Hole

There is no doubt, books have shaped my life. The stories I gravitated to as a child were those of great adventure, nature, kindness and bravery: my beloved Beatrix Potter, Enid Blyton and Colin Dann's *The Animals of Farthing Wood*. But one book, perhaps above all others, has lived long in my heart: *The Wind in The Willows*. Moles, rats and toads have long been maligned by us as unwanted creatures in nature, but this story taught me at a young age to view the world differently, that each soul in the natural world has a place on this earth and complex relationships that we will never truly understand. I like to think of Toad perched in his armchair at Toad Hall, hunkering down by the fire with an especially large slice of toad-in-the-hole, smothered in glorious gravy, and perhaps tail-ended with a rather decadent trifle. What a good life, indeed!

a drizzle of olive oil
6 pork sausages
2–3 tablespoons beef dripping
2 apples, cored and thinly sliced
1 leek, trimmed, cleaned and cut into batons
a few sprigs of fresh thyme, leaves picked
100g (3½oz) clothbound Cheddar cheese, grated

For the batter
140g (5oz) stoneground unbleached white flour
a few fresh thyme leaves
4 organic and/or free-range eggs, lightly beaten
200ml (7fl oz) whole grass-fed milk
flaky sea salt and freshly ground black pepper

Preheat the oven to 200°C/400°F/gas mark 6.

To make the batter, add the flour to a mixing bowl with a good pinch of salt, pepper and some thyme leaves. Add the eggs, then gently whisk in the milk to form a smooth batter. Set aside to rest for 30 minutes.

Set a frying pan over a medium heat, drizzle in a little oil and lightly fry the sausages until brown. Remove from the heat and set aside.

Dollop the beef dripping into a large roasting tray and place in the hot oven for a few minutes.

Once the beef dripping is sizzling hot, carefully remove the tin from the oven and quickly add the sausages, apples and leeks. Pour over the batter and finish with a scattering of Cheddar and thyme leaves. Carefully place back in the oven and bake for 30 minutes, or until puffed up and golden.

Serve the toad-in-the-hole with red onion gravy and some seasonal greens.

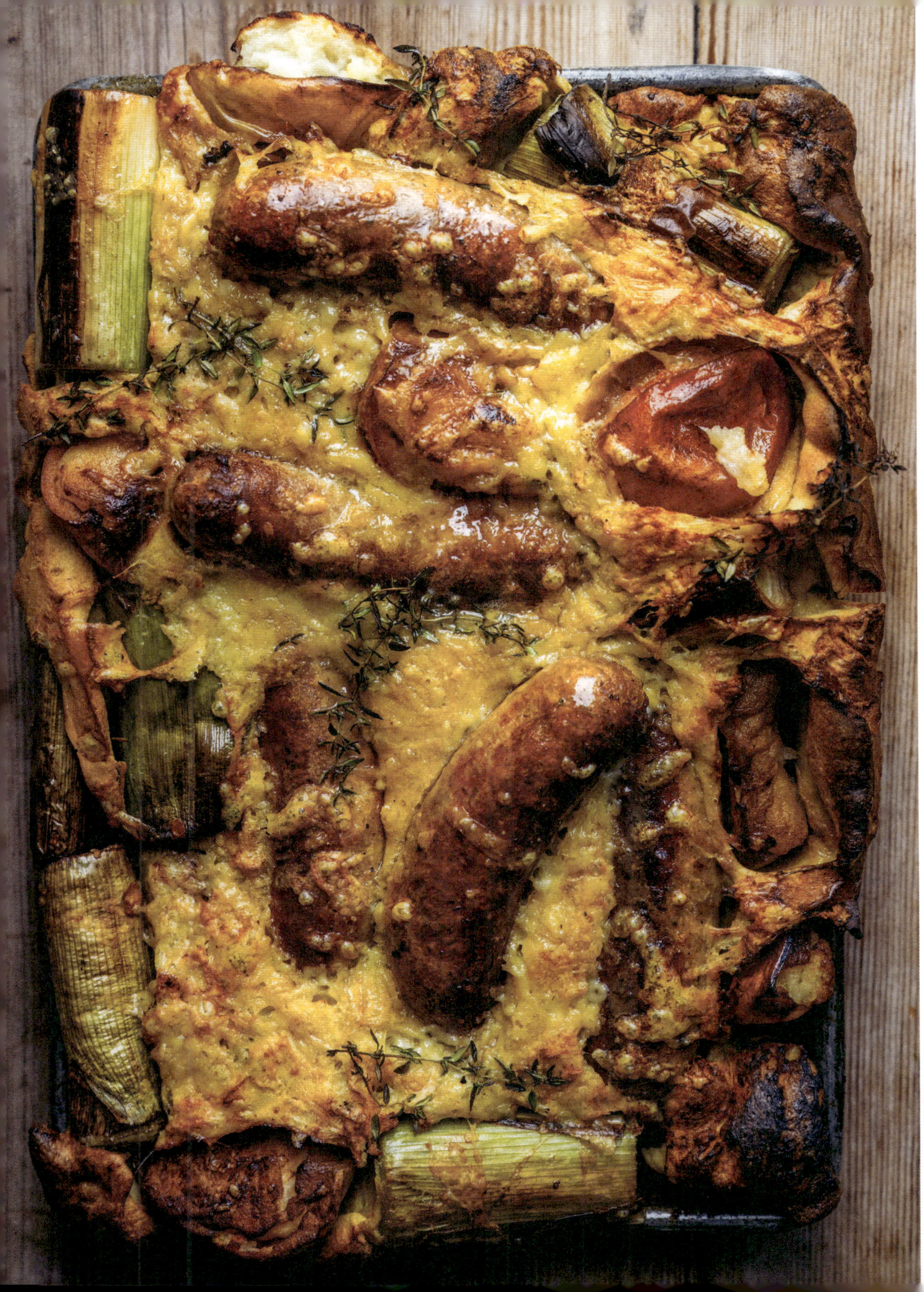

Sausages with Pearl Barley, Squash & Mustard

Light streams profusely through my kitchen window. It's that spectacular time of day: the golden hour. As sausages sizzle in hot fat, flecks of gold lift into the air and sparkle like glitter. Steam rises from the nutty pearl barley and wafts like mist hanging in the valley. The bright orange of squash is reminiscent of so much in nature at this time of year. Not only is my kitchen filled with the most comforting scent of cooking, but autumn is dancing here, filling the space with magic. This recipe is a reminder to delight in the seasons, in the small, quiet moments that are given to us as each day passes.

a drizzle of organic rapeseed oil or 1 teaspoon pork lard
6 organic or free-range pork sausages
a small knob of grass-fed butter
1 onion, chopped
2 garlic cloves, finely chopped
2 bay leaves
2 sprigs of rosemary
1 small squash (I like to use butternut or Crown Prince), peeled and sliced about 1cm (½in) thick
250g (9oz) kale, leaves stripped and stalks roughly chopped
240g (8½oz) pearl barley, rinsed under cold running water
100ml (3½fl oz) cider
750ml–1 litre (1⅓–1¾ pints) chicken stock, warmed
1 teaspoon English mustard
1 tablespoon wholegrain mustard
flaky sea salt and freshly ground black pepper

Set a large cast-iron casserole dish over a medium–high heat and add the fat (rapeseed oil or lard – you need to use a fat that can withstand a high heat). Once the fat is sizzling, carefully add the sausages to the pan. Use tongs to turn them gently to ensure they are beautifully caramelized all over. Once nicely browned, lift them from the pan and set aside.

Reduce the heat to low and add a knob of butter. Allow it to sizzle slightly, then add the onion, garlic, bay leaves, rosemary and a pinch of salt. Stir and allow to soften for around 7–8 minutes.

Increase the heat to medium–high and add the squash along with the kale stalks (keeping the kale leaves back for later). Every so often, move the squash around the pan, giving it a chance to caramelize – this should take around 5–6 minutes. Once the squash is just starting to colour, add the pearl barley and cider. Allow the cider to bubble up and the alcohol to evaporate, then pour in around half of the chicken stock. Reduce the heat and simmer for around 15 minutes, stirring every now and then.

Add more of the stock to the pan along with the mustards and give everything a good stir, then nestle the sausages back into the pan. Leave to cook gently for a further 15 minutes.

Add the remaining stock along with the reserved kale leaves. Check the seasoning and make any adjustments, then leave to cook for a final 5–6 minutes, or until all the stock has been absorbed and the barley is tender. Serve in warmed bowls.

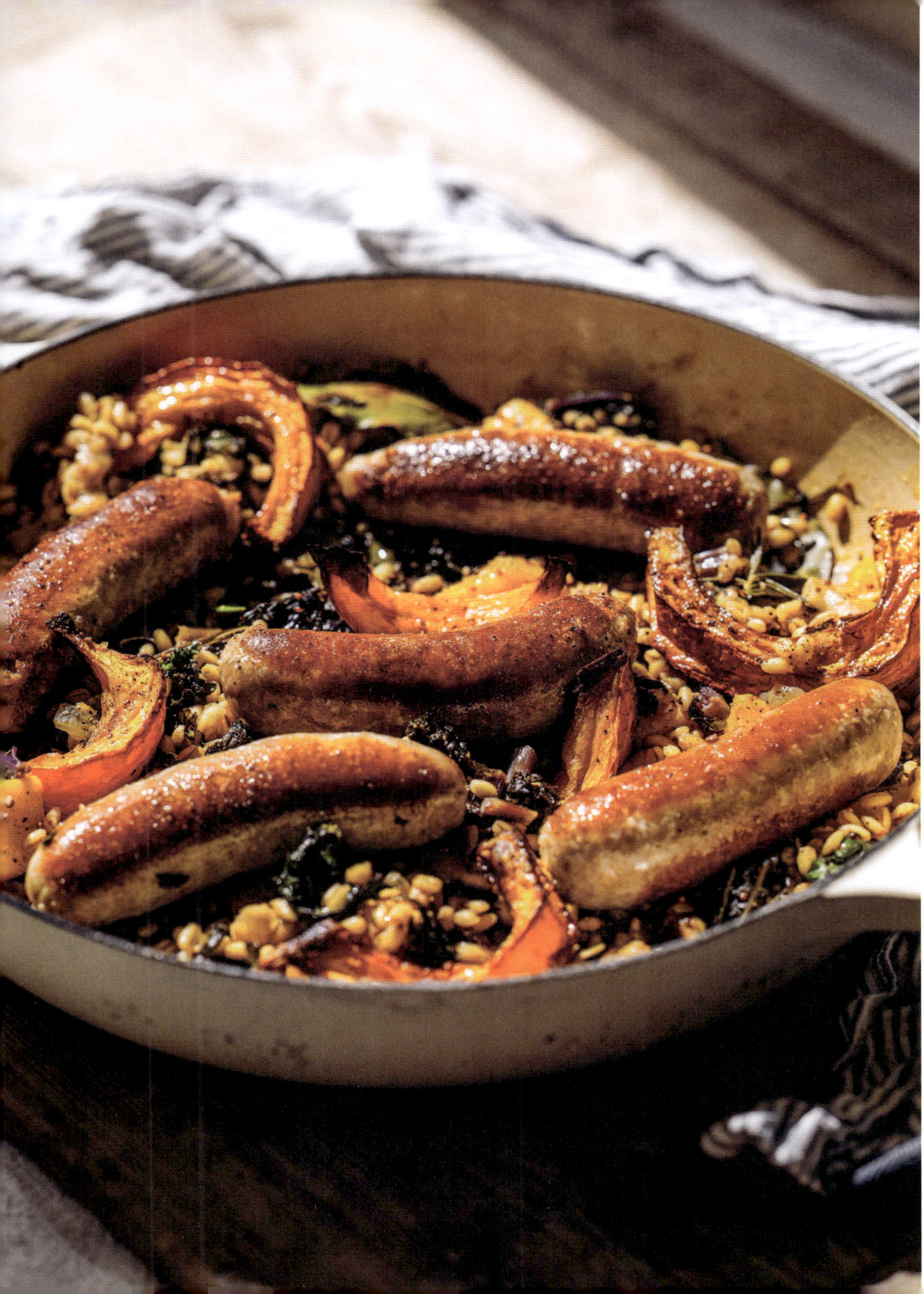

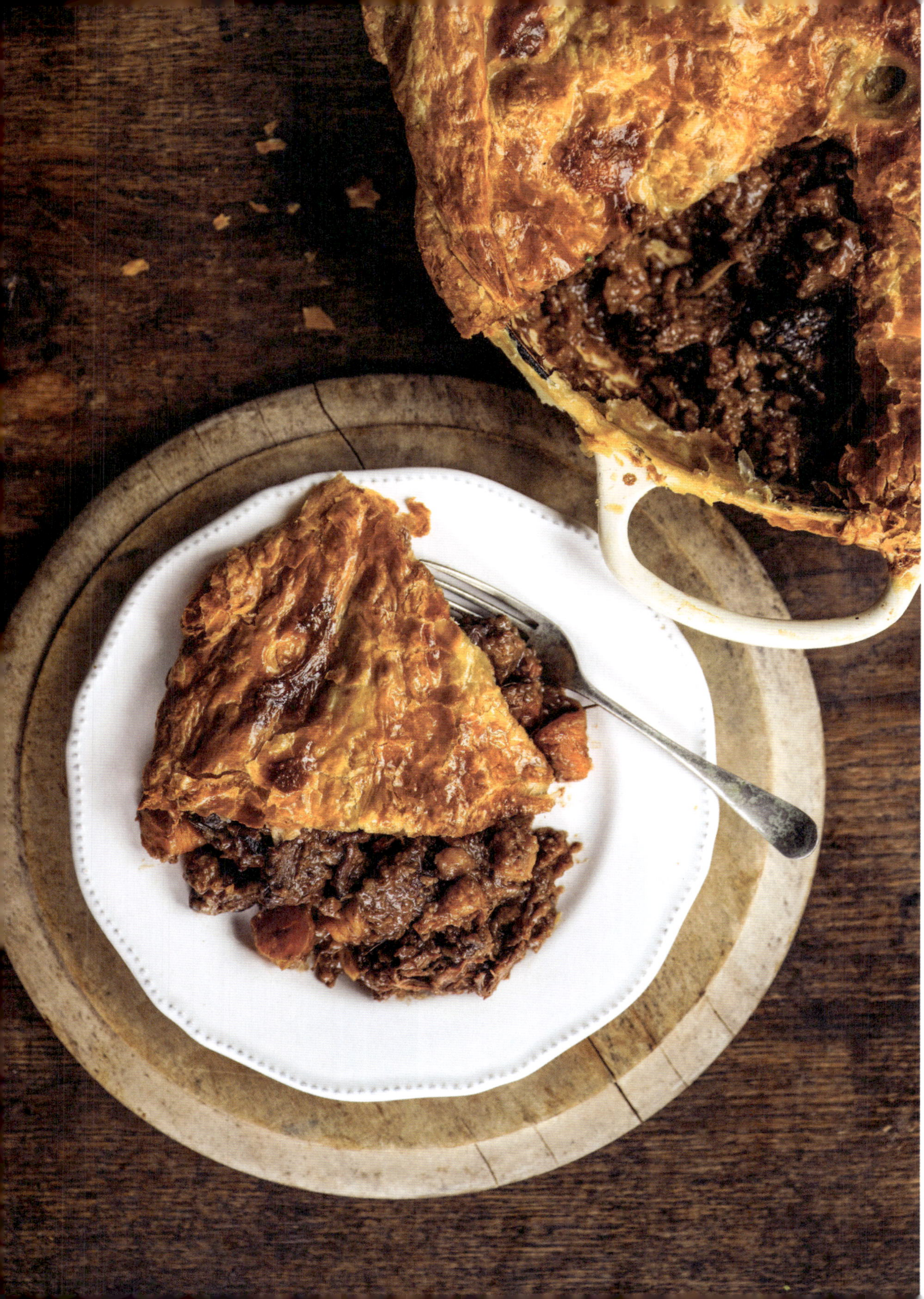

SERVES 6–8　　　　　　　　　　　　　　　　　　　　　　　　　　Autumn

Gamekeeper's Pie

As golden leaves begin to fall away, leaving skeletal frames in their wake, now is the time for the evergreen to shine. There are only five native Evergreen species left in the UK. Much of what you see in our landscape are intensive monocrop conifer plantations used for the logging industry.

Traditionally, much of the food we ate was hunted from tree-covered landscapes. Wild furred and feathered creatures, which had fattened naturally from the land and were rich with vitamins and minerals, would have been cooked alongside herbs, berries and mushrooms foraged from woodland fringes. There was no questioning where your food had come from, how far it had travelled or what additives might be hidden inside. There is a lot we can learn from the simplicity of our ancestors and their ability to survive and evolve.

750g (1lb 10oz) potatoes, peeled and diced
1 small celeriac, peeled and diced
a large knob of grass-fed butter
250g (9oz) wild-caught venison shoulder, cut into 2.5cm (1in) cubes
150g (5½oz) wild-caught mallard, meat removed from the carcass and diced into 3cm (1¼in) cubes
150g (5½oz) wild-caught wood pigeon, meat removed from the carcass and diced into 3cm cubes
4–5 tablespoons stoneground unbleached flour
organic rapeseed oil, for frying
1 onion, finely chopped
3 garlic cloves, chopped
1 celery stick, finely chopped
1 carrot, finely chopped
2 bay leaves
2 sprigs of rosemary
50g (1¾oz) smoked bacon lardons
1 small turnip, diced into 2.5cm (1in) cubes
3 field mushrooms (or use portobello mushrooms)
20g (¾oz) porcini mushrooms, soaked in warm water for 20 minutes, then drained and chopped
400ml (14fl oz) red wine
1 tablespoon Worcestershire sauce
500ml (18fl oz) warm chicken stock
flaky sea salt and freshly ground black pepper

Place a pan of boiling, salted water over a medium–high heat. Tip in the potatoes and celeriac and cook until soft, then drain. Return them to the pan, add a generous amount of butter along with a pinch each of salt and pepper, then mash. Set aside to cool.

Place all the game meat in a bowl, season with salt and pepper, then toss it all together with the flour, shaking off any excess.

Set a large, cast-iron casserole dish over a medium heat and add a drizzle of oil. Once hot, add the game pieces (you will need to do this in batches) and brown well on all sides. Use a slotted spoon to transfer the meat to a plate and set aside.

Preheat the oven to 180°C/350°F/gas mark 4.

Reduce the heat under the casserole dish and add a little more oil. Tip in the onion, garlic, celery, carrot, herbs and a pinch of salt and sweat for around 10–11 minutes, or until the veg have softened. Increase the heat and add the lardons, turnip and mushrooms (you may also need to add a little more oil at this point). Fry for 5–6 minutes, or until the turnip and bacon have started to colour. Pour in the wine and allow it to bubble up. Simmer for around 6 minutes, then add the Worcestershire sauce along with the warm stock. Stir and check the seasoning.

Remove the casserole dish from the heat and pile generous spoonfuls of the cooled mash on top of the stew. Once the surface is completely covered, take a fork and fluff up some jagged edges that will crisp in the oven. Bake for 45–50 minutes.

Leave to cool for 15 minutes, then serve with seasonal greens and English mustard.

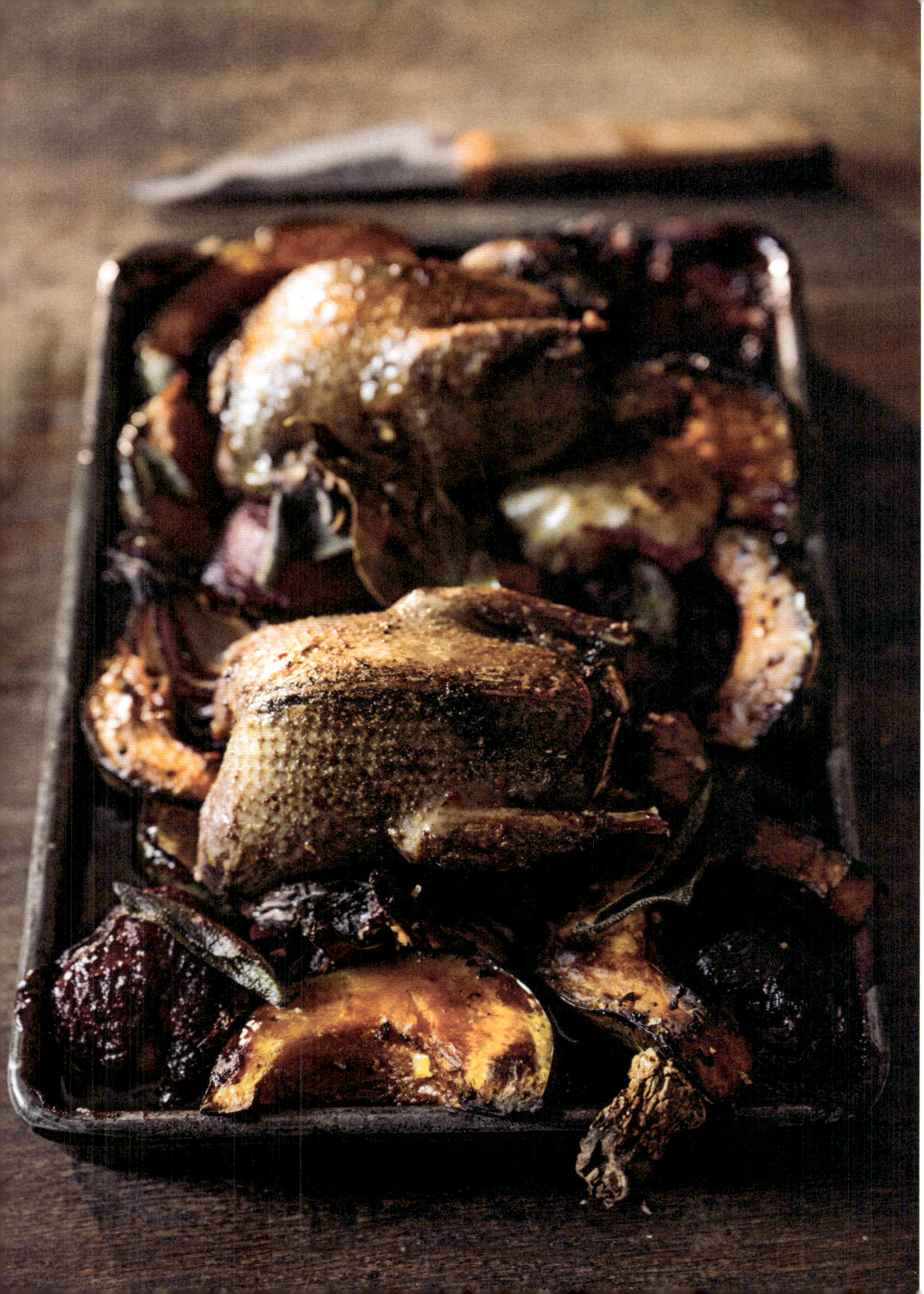

SERVES 4   Autumn

Pigeon with Roasted Plums, Red Onion & Crispy Sage Leaves

There's an old adage: 'What grows together, goes together'.

As the first of the season's pumpkins expand their flesh after autumn rains, plums ripen on branches soaking up the last of the late-summer sun and pigeons run amok in the countryside. It's time to harvest all three crops.

It might be odd to think about pigeons as a crop, as they whirl around freely in the sky. We do, however, need to see them as such, and one that needs to be harvested when in abundance. Pigeons can do untold damage to a farmer's field. It takes only a small handful of birds to blitz a field at harvest time; they are greedy and rather lazy in finding suitable food sources. Like everything in nature, balance must be maintained so that there is enough for us all to share. Pigeons have never really understood the sharing aspect of the land, so I'm never sentimental when a feathered bird lands in my larder. In fact, I delight in what delicious feast I can turn this rich, earthy bird into, to celebrate the harvest.

1 pumpkin, sliced into wedges
2 red onions, quartered
1 bulb of garlic, halved horizointally
a drizzle of rapeseed oil
1 teaspoon chilli flakes
4–5 plums
3–4 bay leaves
2 wild-caught wood pigeons
a knob of grass-fed butter
a small handful of sage leaves
flaky sea salt and freshly ground black pepper

Preheat the oven to 200°C/400°F/gas mark 6.

Place the pumpkin wedges, onion quarters and garlic bulb in a large roasting tray and drizzle with oil, then season the veg with chilli flakes, a pinch of sea salt and freshly ground black pepper. Place the roasting tray in the hot oven and roast for about 20 minutes, or until the pumpkin and onions have started to crisp at the edges.

Remove the roasting tray from the oven, add the plums and bay leaves, then return to the oven and roast for a further 20 minutes.

Season the pigeons all over with salt and pepper, and generously smother the birds in butter.

Remove the roasting tray from the oven and nestle the pigeons in among the fruit and veg. Dot some more butter around the tray, then add the sage leaves and return the tray to the oven to roast for a further 7–8 minutes.

Once the pigeons are beautifully brown, remove the tray from the oven. Lift out the pigeons and leave to rest for around 5 minutes, before carving and serving the beautiful, blushing pink meat alongside the roasted vegetables.

Autumn   SERVES 2–3

Pigeon Schnitzel with Pickled Pears, Hazelnuts & Lemon Mayo

The lush green of summer has turned to yellow, orange and brown. Much like the natural world around me, the colour palette in my kitchen has changed too. Out go vibrant green and bright red and in come more muted tones of gold, leaning into 'beige food' as different seasonal stars begin to shine.

One such ingredient is the humble wood pigeon, the scourge of farmers and gardeners alike. There is no doubt that the best cut of meat on this notoriously lean bird is the breast. As it carries little fat, you must be careful not to cook it in a way in which it can become dry. The answer is to cook the breasts briefly and off the bone, in a shallow-sided pan with plenty of butter.

Here, I have showcased one of my favourite ways to cook wood pigeon, which I hope will leave you asking why on earth we don't eat it more often? Crunchy, salty, sharp and earthy, this dish has all bases covered.

For the pickled pears
(makes enough to fill a 1–1.5 litre kilner jar)
1 unwaxed lemon
8–10 cloves
1–2 bay leaves
2 teaspoons black peppercorns
5cm (2in) piece of fresh root ginger, finely sliced
1 litre (1¾ pints) cider vinegar
1kg (2lb 4oz) unbleached caster sugar
2kg (4lb 8oz) small pears

You will also need
1.5-litre (2¾-pint) sterilized kilner jar (see page 77)

For the lemon mayo
2 large free-range or organic egg yolks
1 heaped teaspoon Dijon or English mustard
½ small garlic clove, peeled and grated
zest and juice of ½ unwaxed lemon
a pinch of sugar
200ml (7fl oz) sunflower oil
50ml (2fl oz) extra virgin olive oil
flaky sea salt and freshly ground black pepper

For the pigeon schnitzel
4 pigeon breasts
100g (3½oz) plain flour
1 organic or free-range egg, whisked
150g (5½oz) panko breadcrumbs
a few sprigs of thyme, leaves picked
2–3 sage leaves, finely chopped
50g (1¾oz) grass-fed butter
flaky sea salt and freshly ground black pepper

To finish
6 sage leaves
1–2 pickled pears (see above), sliced
50g (1¾oz) hazelnuts, toasted

See overleaf for method.

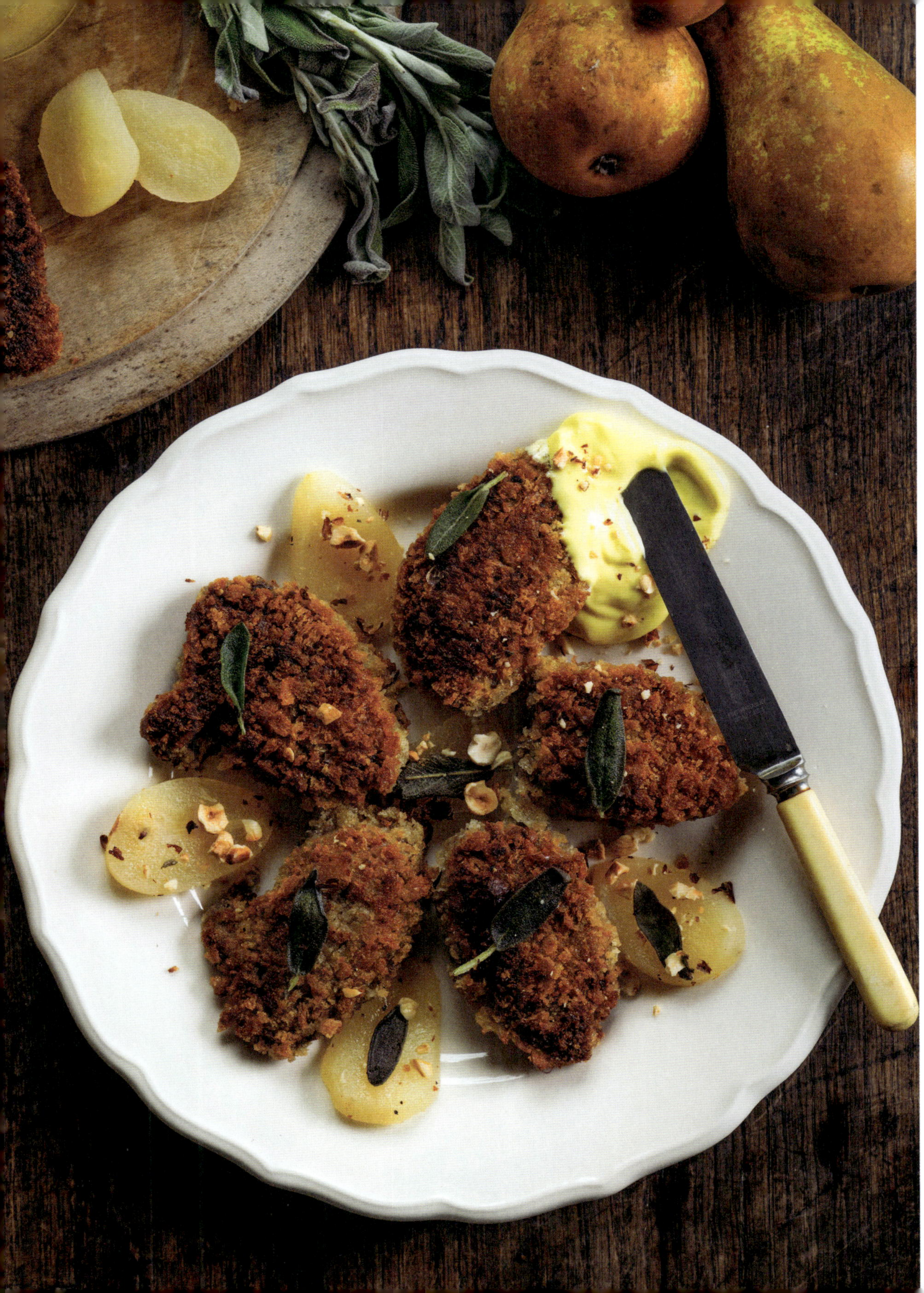

To make the pickled pears, zest the lemon and squeeze the juice into a saucepan. Add the cloves, bay leaves, peppercorns, ginger, vinegar and sugar, then set over a low heat and allow the sugar to dissolve gently and the aromatics to infuse.

Peel, core and halve the pears, then add to the pan and simmer for 15 minutes, until tender. Using a slotted spoon, remove the pears from the liquor and place in a colander to drain.

Meanwhile, increase the heat and boil the liquor rapidly for 15 minutes until the syrup has reduced by about a third and thickened slightly.

Pack the fruit into the warm sterilized jar and pour over the hot syrup to fully cover. Seal and store in a cool, dry place for a month before using.

To make the lemon mayo, place the egg yolks in a food processor with the mustard, garlic, lemon juice, sugar and some salt and pepper. Blitz for 30 seconds, until everything is thoroughly mixed. Combine the oils in a jug, then, with your food processor running, start pouring the oil into the eggs a few drops at a time at first. Once all the oil is in, you should have a thick mayonnaise. If it seems too thick, stir in 1–2 tablespoons of warm water. Add the lemon zest and a little more seasoning, to taste.

To make the schnitzel, place the pigeon breasts on a chopping board and carefully give them a little bash with a rolling pin to flatten them out. Season the breasts with salt and pepper.

Place the whisked egg, flour and breadcrumbs in three separate bowls. Add the thyme and chopped sage to the breadcrumbs. Dip the seasoned pigeon first into the flour, then into the egg and finally the herby breadcrumbs, just enough to coat them lightly.

Place a cast-iron frying pan over a medium heat. Give it a minute or two to heat up, then add the butter. Lay the pigeon breasts in the pan and leave them to cook until you can see the meat change colour, around 1–2 minutes. Gently turn them over and cook for about the same time again. If the pan starts to smoke, turn the heat down a touch. Once beautifully golden, remove the pigeon from the pan and leave to rest.

Meanwhile, add the sage leaves to the same hot pan and allow them to sizzle and crisp in a matter of seconds. Remove from the pan and set aside.

On a large plate or platter, arrange the sliced pears, pigeon schnitzels and crispy sage. Spoon on a generous dollop of lemony mayo, then finish with a sprinkling of toasted hazelnuts and a pinch of salt.

SERVES 2–4   Autumn

Chuck Steak Sandwich with Smoky Beetroot Ketchup

While it's true that you could enjoy this recipe at any time of year, I always enjoy it best in autumn. Perhaps it's the joyful claret colour of the beetroot ketchup that reflects the bountiful berries hanging from the hedgerows. Or maybe it's the earthy, slightly smoky flavour that is reminiscent of bonfires. Needless to say, for me this recipe is an ode to autumn.

For those of you reading this who may not be familiar with preserving – fear not! This is one of the easiest preserves to make. The most complex part of the process is correctly sterilizing your jars; once that is behind you, you are off to the races. Beetroot ketchup also happens to make a rather nice Christmas gift, helping you get ahead before the season of goodwill is upon us.

2 grass-fed chuck steaks
a drizzle of organic rapeseed oil
grass-fed butter, for frying and spreading
2 garlic cloves, peeled and bashed
2 sprigs of thyme
2–4 slices of sourdough bread
flaky sea salt and freshly ground black pepper

For the beetroot ketchup
3–4 large beetroots, peeled and cut into roughly 2cm (¾in) chunks
2 small onions, finely sliced
1 celery stick, finely sliced
1 fennel bulb, finely sliced
3 large Bramley apples (or any other cooking variety), peeled, cored and chopped
220ml (8fl oz) cider vinegar
200ml (7fl oz) boiling water
110g (4oz) soft light brown sugar
2 teaspoons ground cumin
2 teaspoons ground fennel
4 tablespoons smoked paprika
½ teaspoon flaky sea salt
1 teaspoon freshly ground black pepper

For the crispy onions
4 onions, thinly sliced
4 tablespoons cornflour
organic rapeseed oil, for frying
flaky sea salt

You will also need
3 x 300-ml (½-pint) sterilized jam jars with lids (see page 77)
an airtight container

See overleaf for method.

Autumn

SERVES 2

First, make the ketchup. Tip the beetroots into a large pan and cover with water. Bring to a simmer, then cook for 40 minutes, or until tender. Drain and set the beetroot to one side.

Drizzle a little oil into the same pan, then cook the onions, celery and fennel over a medium heat until soft. Return the beetroot to the pan along with the apples, vinegar and measured boiling water, then simmer for around 12 minutes, or until the apples have completely collapsed. Remove the pan from the heat, then pour the mixture into a blender and blitz until smooth.

Give the pan a quick rinse and dry, then return the beetroot mixture to the pan and stir in the sugar, cumin, fennel, paprika, salt and pepper. Bring to a simmer for 15 minutes, regularly stirring the mixture until the ketchup has thickened.

Meanwhile, boil two full kettles of water. Pour the boiling water into a saucepan large enough to fit the jam jars and place over a medium heat so the water simmers gently.

Off the heat, pour the ketchup into the jars and seal immediately. Carefully place the filled jars in the simmering water and leave for 5 minutes, then remove the jars from the water and leave to cool. The ketchup is ready to eat straight away, or it can be stored in a cool, dark place for up to a year. Once opened, store in the fridge and use within 2 months.

To make the crispy onions, combine the sliced onions and cornflour in a small mixing bowl and toss to make sure the onions are evenly coated. Place a deep, cast-iron frying pan over a medium heat and pour in a generous amount of oil to a depth of around 2–3cm (¾–1in). Wait for the oil to heat – you want it to be sizzling hot. Carefully fry the onions in batches for around 5–6 minutes, or until crispy and golden. Use a slotted spoon to transfer them to a plate lined with kitchen paper. While still warm, season with salt. Once cooled, you can store the onions in an airtight container, where they will keep well for 3–4 days.

Remove the steaks from the fridge and allow them to come to room temperature. Pat dry and season generously all over with salt.

Heat a drizzle of oil in a cast-iron pan over a medium–high heat. Once hot, add the steaks and cook for 2 minutes on each side, until the juices start to appear on the surface. Add a knob of butter to the pan along with the garlic and thyme. Allow the butter to foam up, then flip the steaks again and cook for a further minute. You are looking to cook the steaks for around 6 minutes in total. Remove from the pan, season with pepper and leave to rest somewhere warm for around 8 minutes.

While the steak is resting, toast the bread, then slather it generously with butter and dollop on the beetroot ketchup. Slice the steak and load it on, then finish with piles of crispy onions. Dive in immediately.

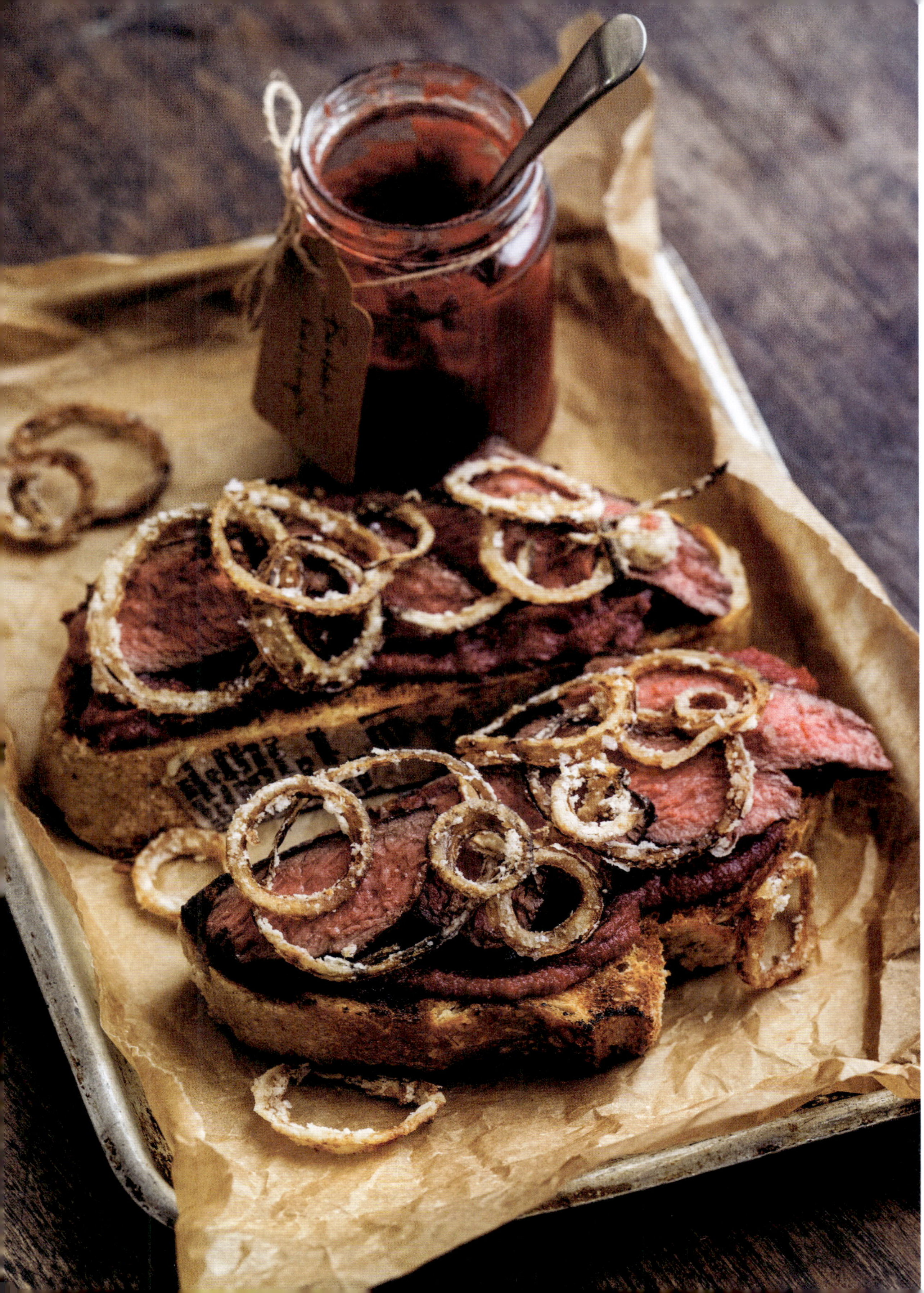

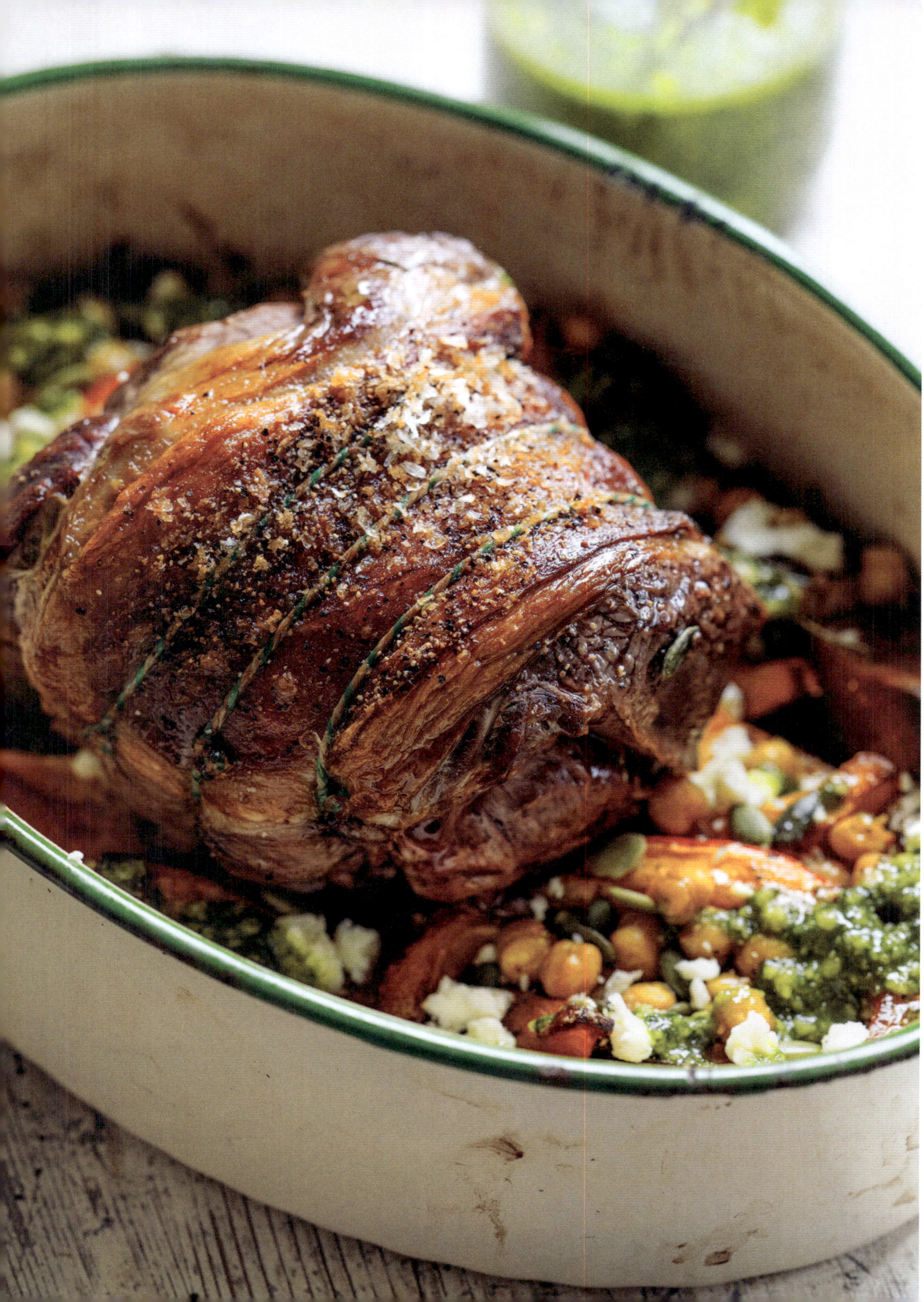

SERVES 4–6

Autumn

Mutton Rump with Roasted Squash, Sheep's Cheese & Pesto

In late summer, the ewes are gathered down from the high hills where they had been left to merrily graze away post-lambing. Once in the lowlands, their condition is checked. First teeth – can they still eat well? Then the udder – are both teats functioning? Finally, feet – can they move about freely? All of this will determine whether the ewe can carry another lamb. If she fails on any of these fronts, her time has come, and such is life.

A good piece of mutton cooks and eats like any good beef or lamb, it doesn't have to be reserved for the slow cooker. Here I'm roasting a rump, a little as I would a beef topside, and serving it with another seasonal treat in abundance at the very same time as mutton.

1 small squash (I like to use Red Kuri or Crown Prince, but butternut works equally well)
extra virgin olive oil
a pinch of chilli flakes
a few sprigs of rosemary
2–3 bay leaves
750g (1lb 10oz) mutton rump
200g (7oz) chickpeas, cooked and drained
100g (3½oz) sheep's cheese
flaky sea salt and freshly ground black pepper

For the pesto
100g (3½oz) pumpkin seeds
1 garlic clove, peeled
50g (1¾oz) flat-leaf parsley, chopped
50g (1¾oz) basil, chopped
50g (1¾oz) pecorino cheese, grated
100ml (3½fl oz) extra virgin olive oil
flaky sea salt and freshly ground black pepper

Preheat the oven to 200°C/400°F/gas mark 6.

Cut the squash in half and scoop out the seeds (these can be saved to dry on a low setting in the oven and used for future recipes). Slice the squash into thick crescent moons and place in a roasting tray. Drizzle over a generous glug of olive oil, then scatter over the chilli flakes and herbs. Slide into the oven and roast for 15 minutes.

Generously season the mutton rump all over with salt and pepper, remove the tray of squash from the oven and nestle the rump in the centre. Slide the tray back into the oven and roast for a further 20–25 minutes.

Remove the tray from the oven one final time. Lift the meat and toss the squash about, then scatter in the chickpeas and nestle the mutton back in place. Back into the oven it goes for a final 5–6 minutes.

Remove the roasting tray from the oven and leave to rest while you make the pesto.

Put a dry pan over a medium heat, then add the pumpkin seeds and toast them, shaking the pan occasionally, until they begin to brown and pop. Transfer the pumpkin seeds to a mortar and add the garlic and a small pinch of salt. Bash with a pestle until you have a rough paste. Add half the chopped herbs to the mortar and bash until crushed, then add the rest of the herbs and continue to bash until a paste forms. Stir in the cheese and the oil, then check and adjust the seasoning to your liking.

Crumble the fresh sheep's cheese over the squash and chickpeas in the roasting tray, then spoon over plenty of pesto. Finish with a final drizzle of good olive oil and another pinch of black pepper. Serve to the table in the tray, then lift out the meat and carve slices for each person. Serve the blushing pink meat with a generous helping of veg.

Hake & Carrot Dhal

Hake, the great flavour carrier of the sea. The wonderful thing about hake is that you can cook it simply – a little butter, a pinch of salt, perhaps a small handful of soft herbs – and it will still be a showstopper. You can, however, pile on the flavours, as I have done here. Hake can take it. Not just take it, but thrive on it, losing none of its own flavour or wonderful flaky texture in the process.

A fine ingredient like freshly caught hake requires a starchy pillow to rest upon for a balanced meal at this time of year. There is something about dhal that I find so healing. Perhaps it's the slow ritual of making it – watching the lentils collapse and become rich and creamy with each swirl of my wooden spoon – that is rather satisfying. Or maybe it's the act of spooning the gloriously gloopy texture into one's mouth that is so enjoyable. I wonder, though, whether it might just be some ancestral instinct that it is just really good food for our bodies?

This is healthy, nourishing comfort food that can be enjoyed, bowl and spoon in hand, curled up on the sofa while the rain lashes outside.

extra virgin olive oil
2 onions, sliced
3 garlic cloves, finely chopped
1 chilli, deseeded and finely chopped
1 tablespoon curry leaves
2 tablespoons medium curry powder
150g (5½oz) coral or red lentils, rinsed well
400ml (14fl oz) coconut milk
2 tomatoes, chopped
1 teaspoon nigella seeds
2 sustainably caught British hake fillets
a drizzle of olive oil
flaky sea salt and freshly ground black pepper

Add a drizzle of oil to a saucepan and place over a medium heat. Add the onions, garlic, chilli and curry leaves and fry together for a few minutes until the onions have collapsed and the curry leaves have become fragrant. Add the curry powder along with the lentils, coconut milk and tomatoes. Cook for about 25 minutes, until the lentils are tender. You may need to top up with water if the lentils start drying out; you are aiming for a consistency like porridge. Remove from the heat and sprinkle with the nigella seeds. You could also add some fresh coriander and parsley to finish the lentils.

To cook the hake, season the fish all over with salt and pepper. Set a large cast-iron frying pan over a medium–high heat and add a drizzle of oil. Once hot, add the fish, skin-side down. Cook for 3–5 minutes, depending on thickness, then turn the fillets over and fry for 1–2 minute, until the flakes separate when pressed lightly with a fork.

Serve the beautiful, flaky hake on top of the dhal and dig in for the ultimate comfort food.

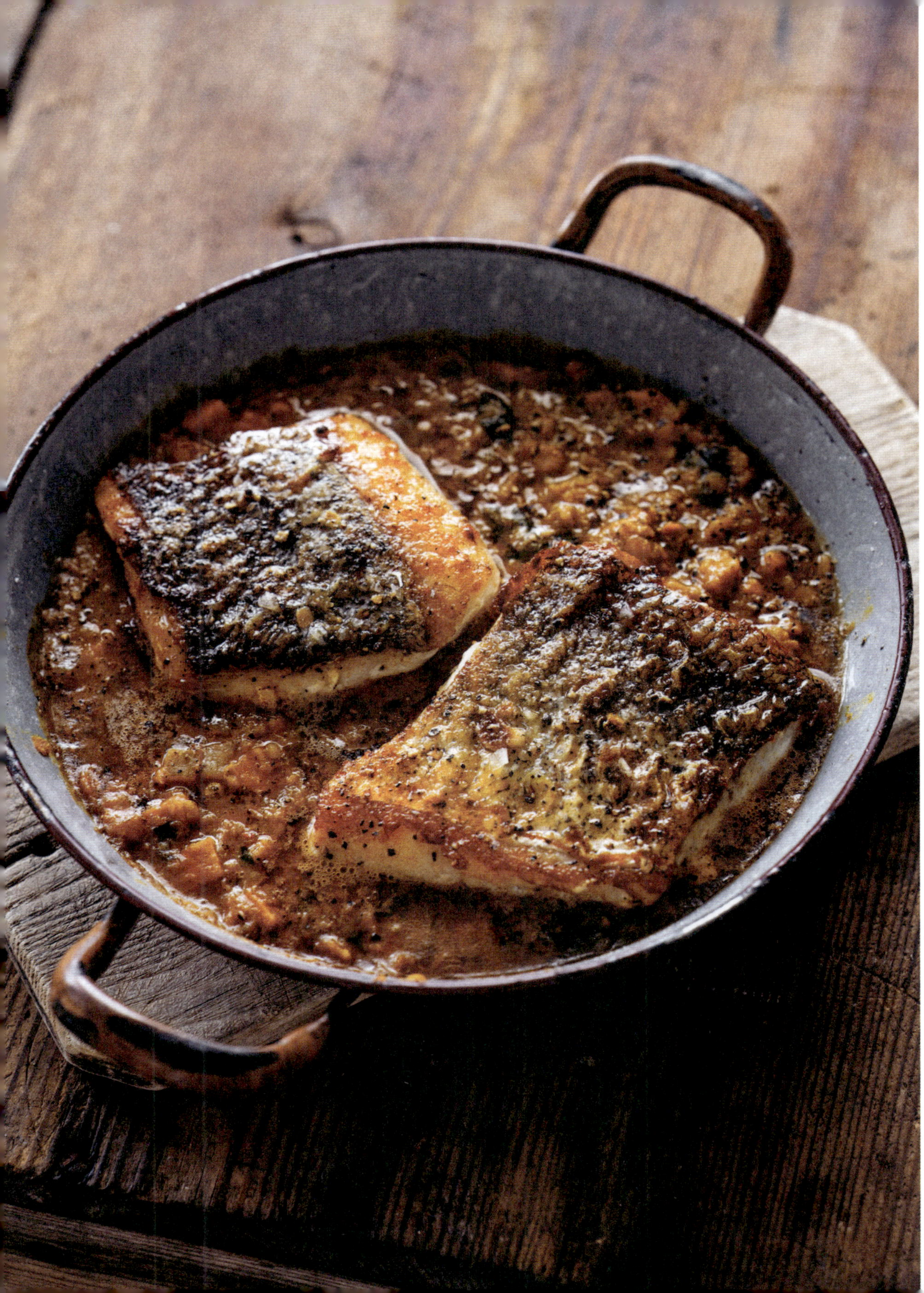

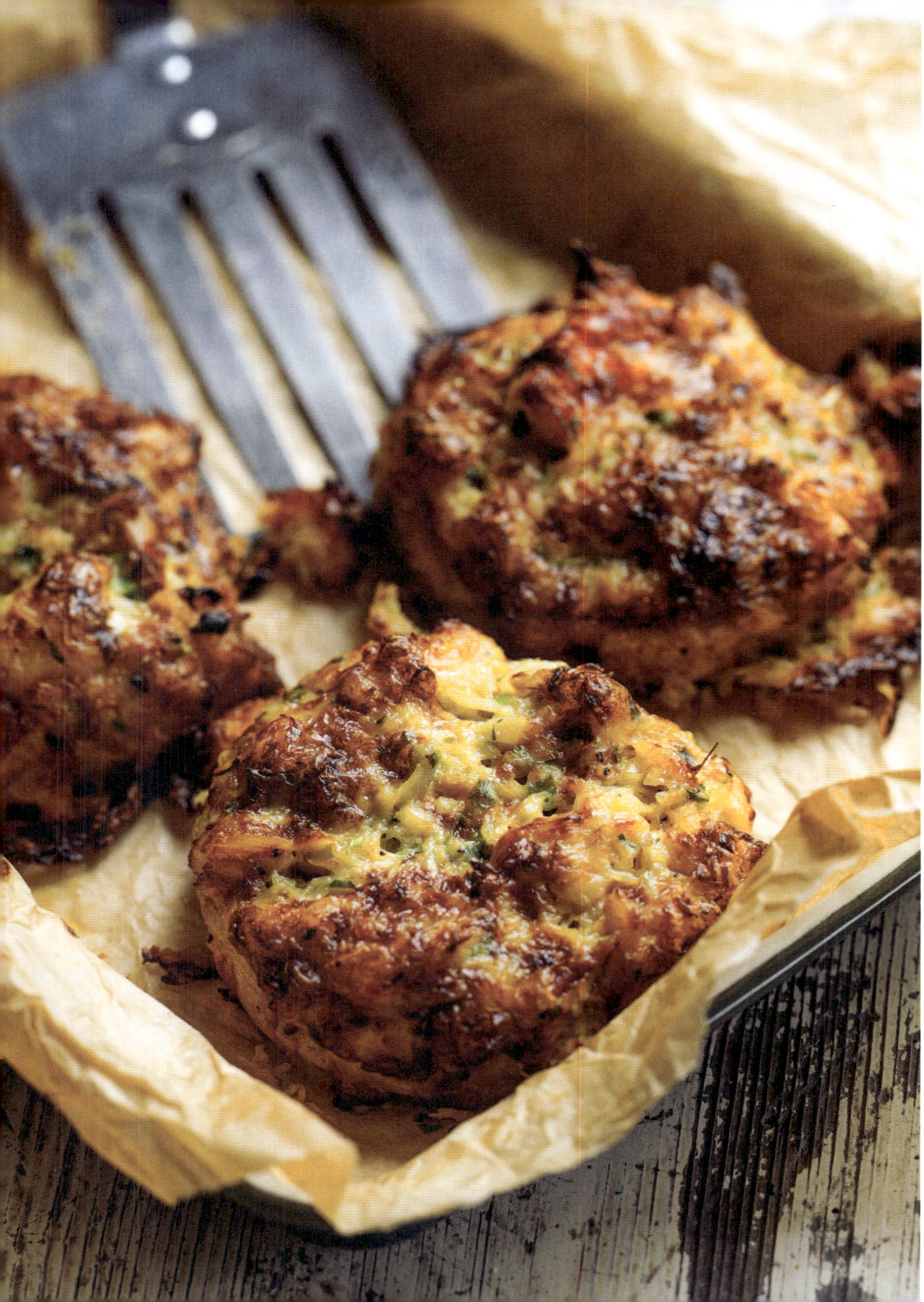

Crab Thermidor Crumpets

It was my Granny who taught me to love cooking and all things creative. She made the best scones, Christmas cake and Easter biscuits, and many other celebratory recipes. I will be forever grateful, not only for what Granny taught me in the kitchen, but also for what she instilled in me as a person.

For a time, my grandparents lived near the sea – at Brixham in Devon – so trips out fishing and crabbing were commonplace. This lovely recipe is an embodiment of those special times. I do hope when you make it, that you can create memories to cherish too.

25g (1oz) grass-fed butter
2 large shallots, finely chopped
400ml (14fl oz) fish stock
2 tablespoons Somerset cider brandy
75ml (2½fl oz) double cream
½ teaspoon English mustard
a small bunch of soft herbs (chives, parsley and tarragon), chopped
juice of ½ lemon
100g (3½oz) brown crab meat
200g (7oz) white crab meat
50g (1¾oz) hard cheese, grated (I like to use Old Winchester or pecorino)
flaky sea salt and freshly ground black pepper

For the crumpets
400ml (14fl oz) whole grass fed milk
1 tablespoon fast-action dried yeast
1 teaspoon unbleached caster sugar
100ml (3½fl oz) warm water
300g (10½ oz) unbleached white flour
½ teaspoon bicarbonate of soda
½ teaspoon flaky sea salt
grass-fed butter, for greasing and frying

First, make the crumpets. Gently warm the milk and pour it into a large jug. Add the yeast and sugar, stir to dissolve, then add the warm water. Leave in a warm place for 15–20 minutes, or until the yeast has activated and become frothy.

Sift the flour and bicarbonate of soda into a large bowl. Add the salt, then make a well in the centre and pour in the yeast mixture. Whisk to combine until a batter has formed and any lumps have been removed. Cover with a damp tea towel and set aside for 50 minutes, or until bubbles form on the surface.

Generously butter your crumpet rings (I use a set that measure around 9cm (3½in) in diameter). Place a cast-iron frying pan over a low–medium heat, then place the rings into the pan to warm slightly.

Spoon the batter into the rings until they are just over half full, then fry until cooked nearly all the way through and the tops have just started to harden slightly. Over a low heat this will take around 14 minutes. Patience is key – you don't want to rush them or you won't create that lovely, airy texture. Do keep a close eye on the heat, making sure it is warm but not hot, to avoid catching the bottoms. You can now remove the rings, flip the crumpets over and continue to cook the other sides for around 2–3 minutes, until lovely and golden.

Leave to cool. You can store the crumpets in the fridge for up to a week, or pop them in the freezer, or enjoy straight away with my delicious topping.

To make the thermidor, melt the butter in a small pan. Add the shallots and cook gently for around 4 minutes, until soft, but not browned. Add the fish stock, cider brandy and half the double cream, then boil until reduced by three-quarters. Add the rest of the cream and simmer until it has reduced to a luscious sauce consistency. Whisk in the mustard, herbs and lemon juice. Season to taste, then add the crab meat and stir through.

Preheat the grill to high. Carefully spoon the sauce over the crumpets and sprinkle with the cheese. Grill for 2–3 minutes, until golden and bubbling. Serve warm.

A South-West Bouillabaisse

A huge moon, shaped like a clothbound cheese, hung over our dining table, doing as much to light the scene as the tea light fervently twinkling away. We were in Cassis, a small fishing village on the French Riviera Côte d'Azur, and home of the famed dish, bouillabaisse. In typical French flair, the traditional fish soup was brought out in a huge stoneware terrine and presented ceremoniously to the table.

Like any good recipe I have enjoyed from another's hand, as soon as I'm home I try to recreate it. It's my way of trying to capture the experience and to remind myself of those special times. This is my take on that classic French dish, celebrating what lands abundantly on these shores.

a drizzle of extra virgin olive oil
2 medium shallots, finely sliced
4 garlic cloves, crushed
1 small fennel bulb, finely sliced
100ml (3½fl oz) dry white wine
600ml (20fl oz) fish stock
400g (14oz) Preserved Tomatoes (see page 77)
1 tablespoon tomato purée
grated zest and juice of 1 orange
a pinch of saffron, steeped in 1 tablespoon of warm water
a pinch of cayenne pepper
1 sustainably caught hake fillet, diced
4 sustainably caught red mullet fillets, skin on, halved
200g (7oz) squid rings
250g (9oz) shell-on prawns
500g (1lb 2oz) live mussels, cleaned (discard any that are still open)
500g (1lb 2oz) live Dorset clams, cleaned (discard any that are still open)
flaky sea salt and freshly ground black pepper
parsley leaves, to garnish

For the rouille
3 organic and/or free-range egg yolks
2 garlic cloves, sliced
1 teaspoon Dijon mustard, or to taste
juice of ½ lemon, or to taste
a pinch of flaky sea salt, or to taste
200ml (7fl oz) organic sunflower oil
2 pinches of saffron, steeped in 1 tablespoon hot water

To make the rouille, place the egg yolks, garlic, mustard and lemon juice in a food processor. Season with a small pinch of salt and blitz for around 30 seconds. With the food processor running, slowly dribble the oil into the mixture. Once you have added all the oil, you should have a thick, glossy mayonnaise. Stir the steeped saffron and water into the rouille. Check the seasoning and adjust with more salt, mustard or lemon, if required. Set aside.

Set a large, cast-iron casserole dish over a medium heat and drizzle in the olive oil. Once warm, add the shallots, garlic and fennel along with a pinch of salt and fry until the veg have softened. Add the white wine and allow it to bubble up, then add the fish stock, preserved tomatoes, tomato purée, orange zest and juice, the steeped saffron and water, and cayenne pepper. Bring to the boil, then reduce to a simmer and cook for 25 minutes.

Pour the mixture into a fine sieve with a bowl placed underneath to catch the liquid. Using the back of a spoon, squish the vegetables to extract as much flavour as possible. Discard the veg in the sieve, then pour the liquid into a clean pan and place over a medium heat.

Once the soup is simmering gently, add the hake, mullet fillets, squid and prawns and cook for 2 minutes. Add the mussels and clams, cover with a lid and cook for a further 2–3 minutes, until they have opened. Discard any mussels or clams that haven't opened by this point.

Ladle the soup, along with generous chunks of the fish and seafood, into bowls. Top with the rouille, season with black pepper and add parsley leaves to garnish, then serve immediately with crusty bread.

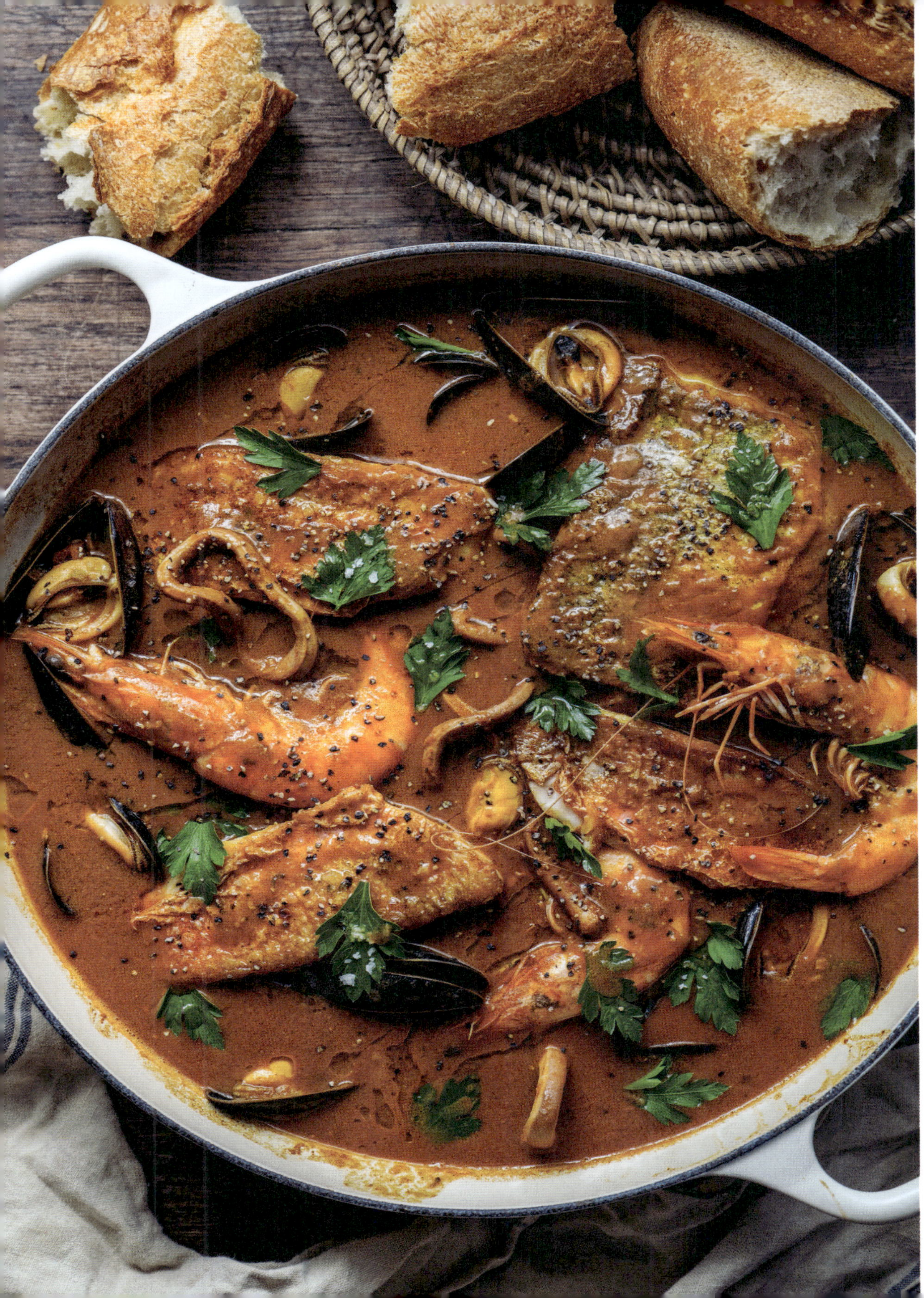

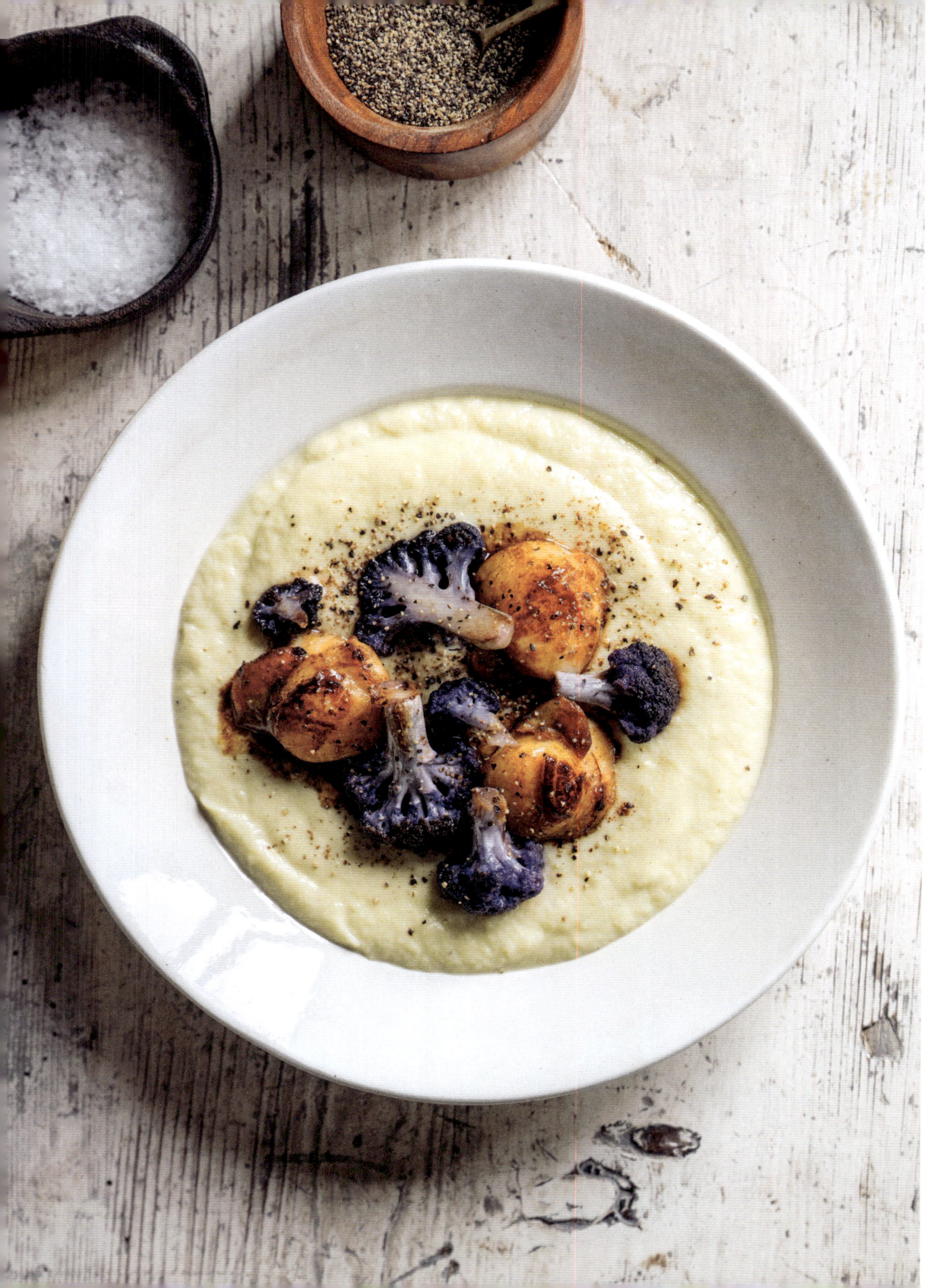

SERVES 4 Autumn

Cauliflower Soup with Seared Scallops

The UK's South West makes a very good spot for growing the humble cauliflower, as its mild climate and warm air from the sea keep frosts in check. Cauliflowers grow well during mild winters;, at anything below 5°C they will simply stop growing, but above this they will grow thick and fast. The farmer has to be quick to harvest them from the field, as once they start to open and show their curds, they are vulnerable to hail, frost and even vermin. This means that great gluts of cauliflowers are commonplace. We need to be on our toes to get the very best out of this humble ingredient.

1 large or 2 small heads of cauliflower (any type)
1 knob of grass-fed butter
a drizzle of extra virgin olive oil
1 onion, chopped
1 leek, finely chopped
2 small celery sticks, chopped
600ml (20fl oz) whole grass-fed milk
350ml (12fl oz) water
150ml (5fl oz) double cream
½ nutmeg, grated
flaky sea salt and freshly ground black pepper

For the toppings
extra virgin olive oil
grass-fed butter
8 prepared scallops
2 tablespoons lemon juice
a small handful of chopped chives

Trim the cauliflower, removing the leaves, which can be saved for another dish or to nourish your compost. Cut off a few of the smaller florets (around 8 will be fine) and set them aside. Continue slicing the rest of the cauliflower into small chunks.

Take a cast-iron pan and place over a medium heat. Add the butter to the pan along with a drizzle of olive oil and allow to sizzle slightly. Tip in the chopped onion, leek and celery along with a pinch of salt, and sweat gently for around 8 minutes, or until the veg have softened. Add the chunks of cauliflower, then pour in the milk along with the water and bring to the boil. Keep boiling for around 5 minutes, then reduce to a simmer for a further 5 minutes. Check the cauliflower is tender; then remove from the heat.

Transfer the pan's contents to a blender and give everything a good blitz until velvety smooth. It should be reasonably thick at this point, but remember, you will loosen it with the cream shortly. Check the seasoning and adjust as necessary.

Preheat the oven to 180°C/350°F/gas mark 4.

Pour the blended soup back into a saucepan and place over a low heat. Add the double cream and grate over the nutmeg to taste. Check the seasoning again and make any final adjustments. Keep the pan warm while you make the toppings.

Place the reserved cauliflower florets in a roasting tray, drizzle them with olive oil and season well. Dot a few knobs of butter around the tray, then place in the hot oven. Roast the florets for around 15–20 minutes, or until they are beautifully golden and caramelized. Remove from the oven and set aside.

Season the scallops all over with sea salt. Take a cast-iron frying pan and place it over a medium–high heat. Add a drizzle of oil and a knob of butter. Once sizzling , place the scallops in the pan and cook for 1 minute on each side. Remove from the heat and squeeze a little lemon juice over the top.

Ladle the creamy soup into bowls and top each with pieces of crispy cauliflower and seared scallops. Crack some black pepper over the top and finish with a scattering of chopped chives if you like. Serve with some warm, crusty bread.

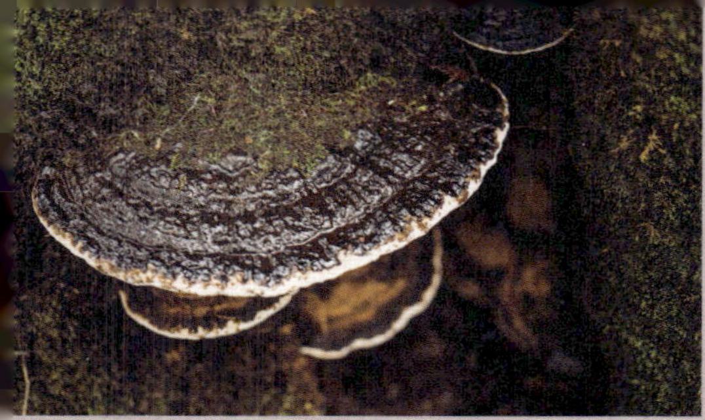
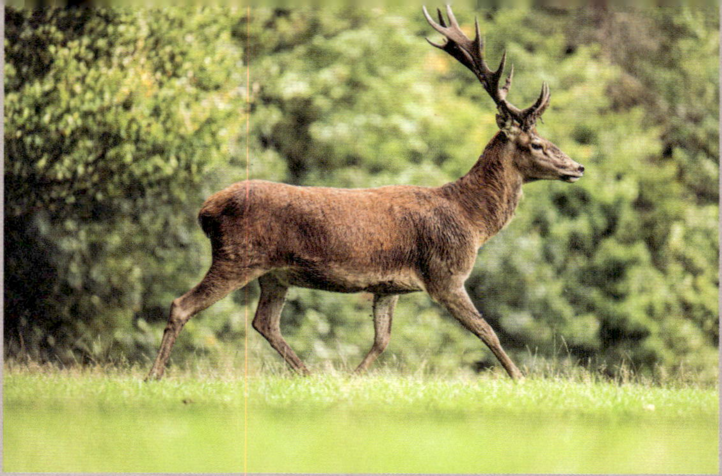
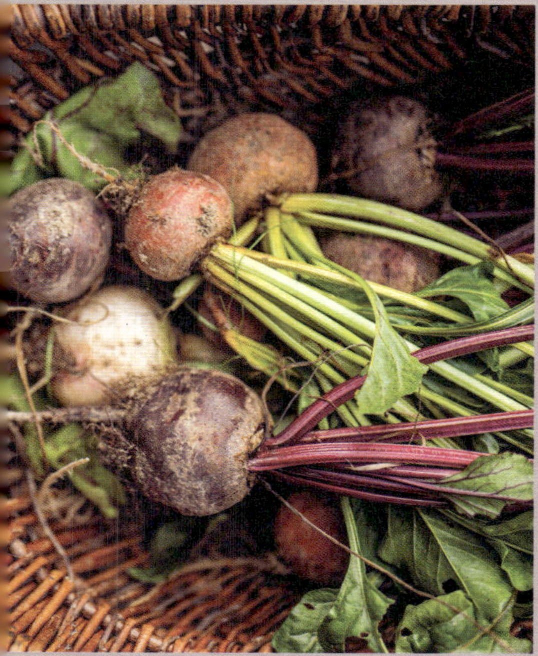
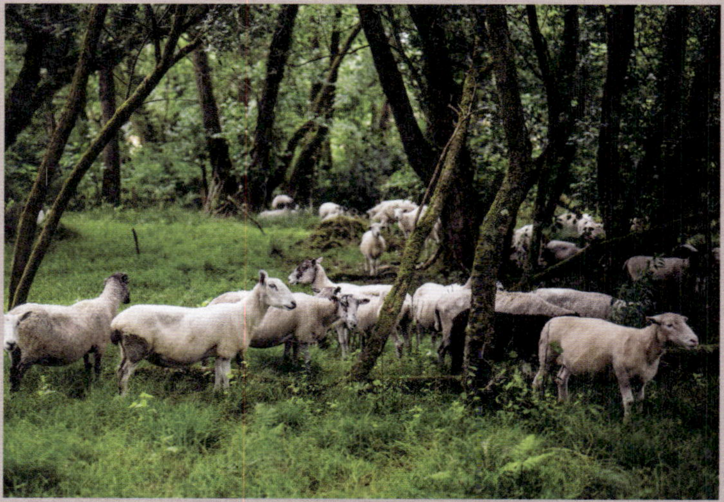
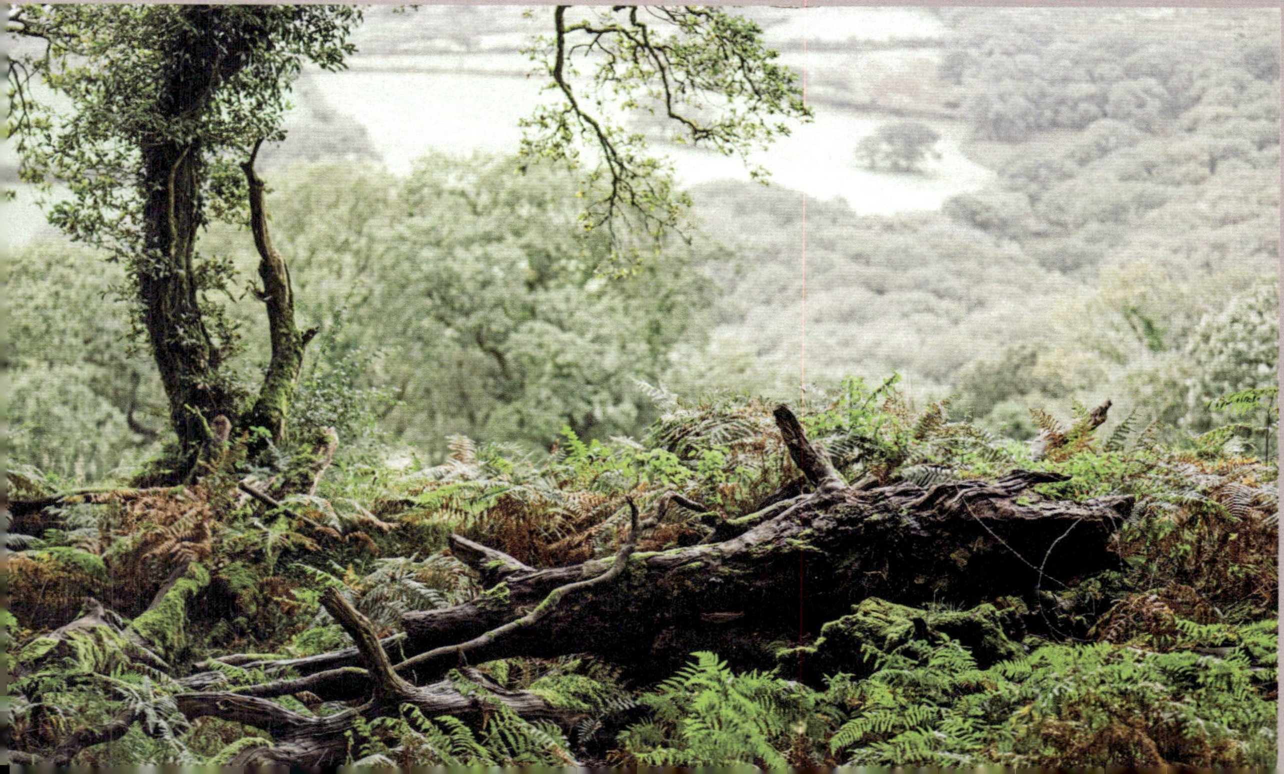

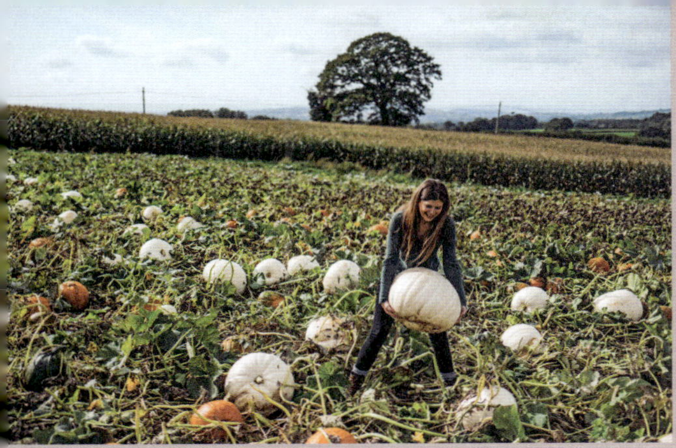
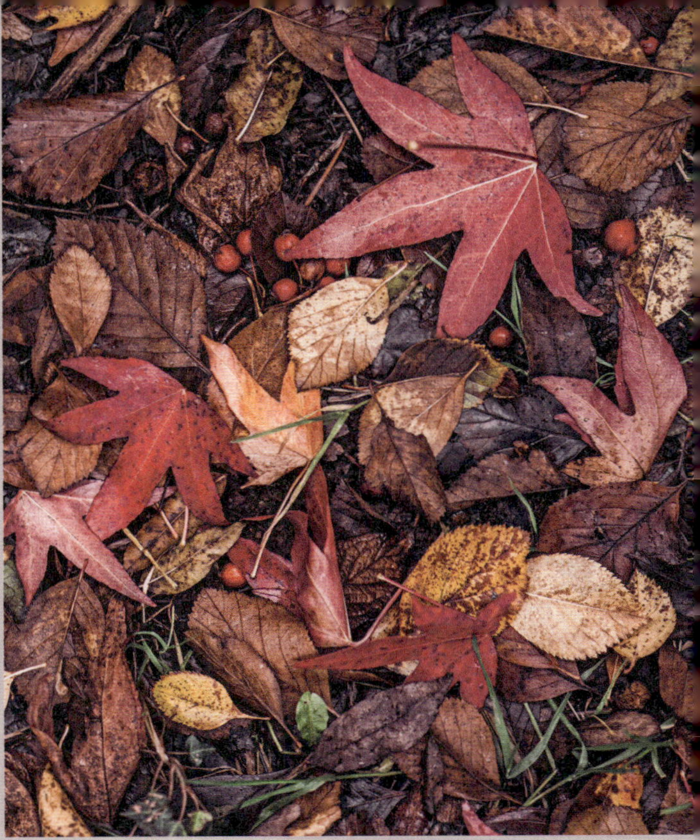
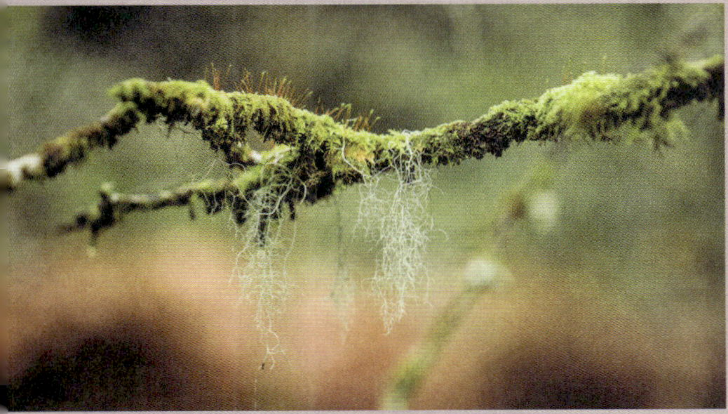
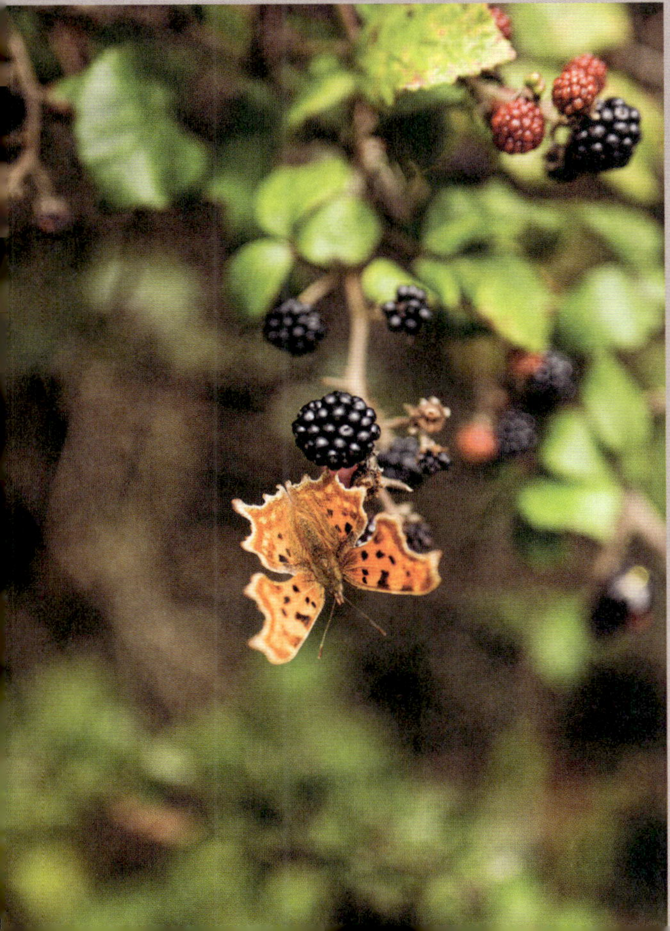
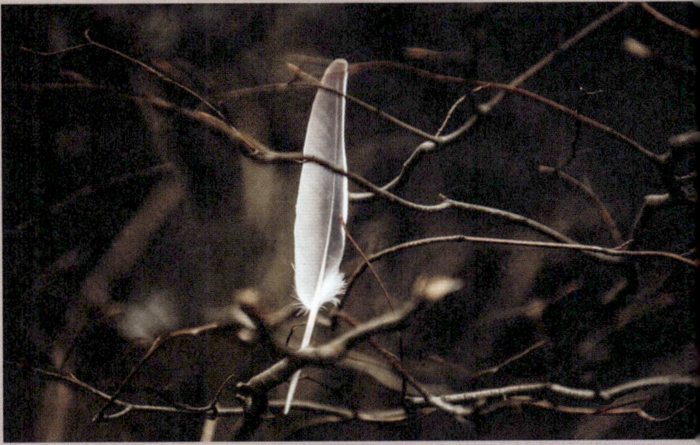
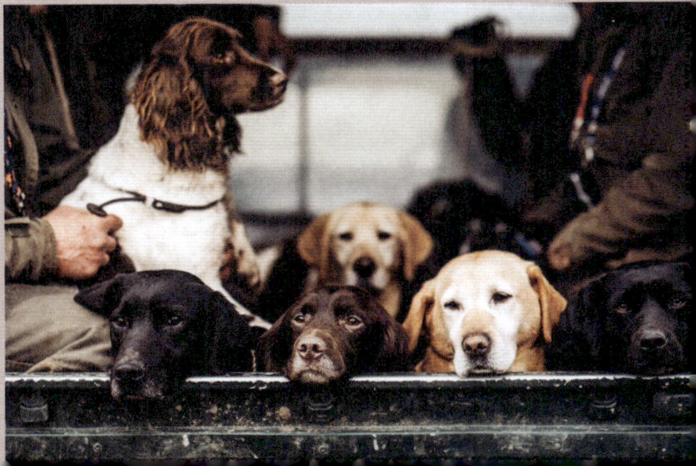

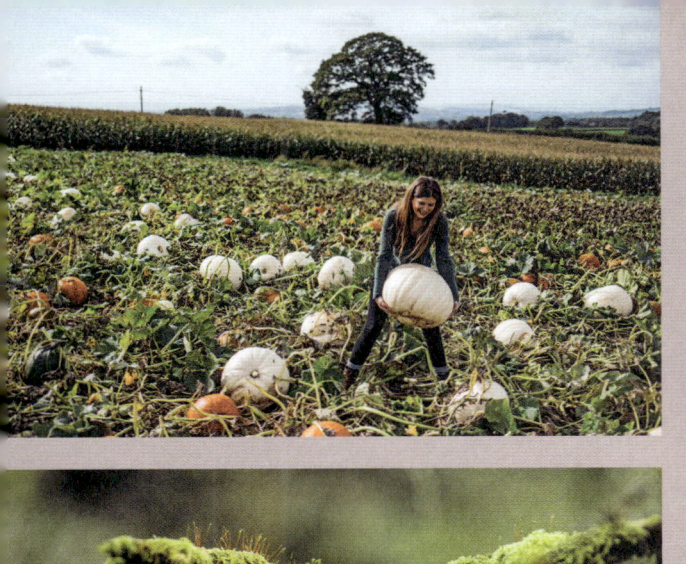

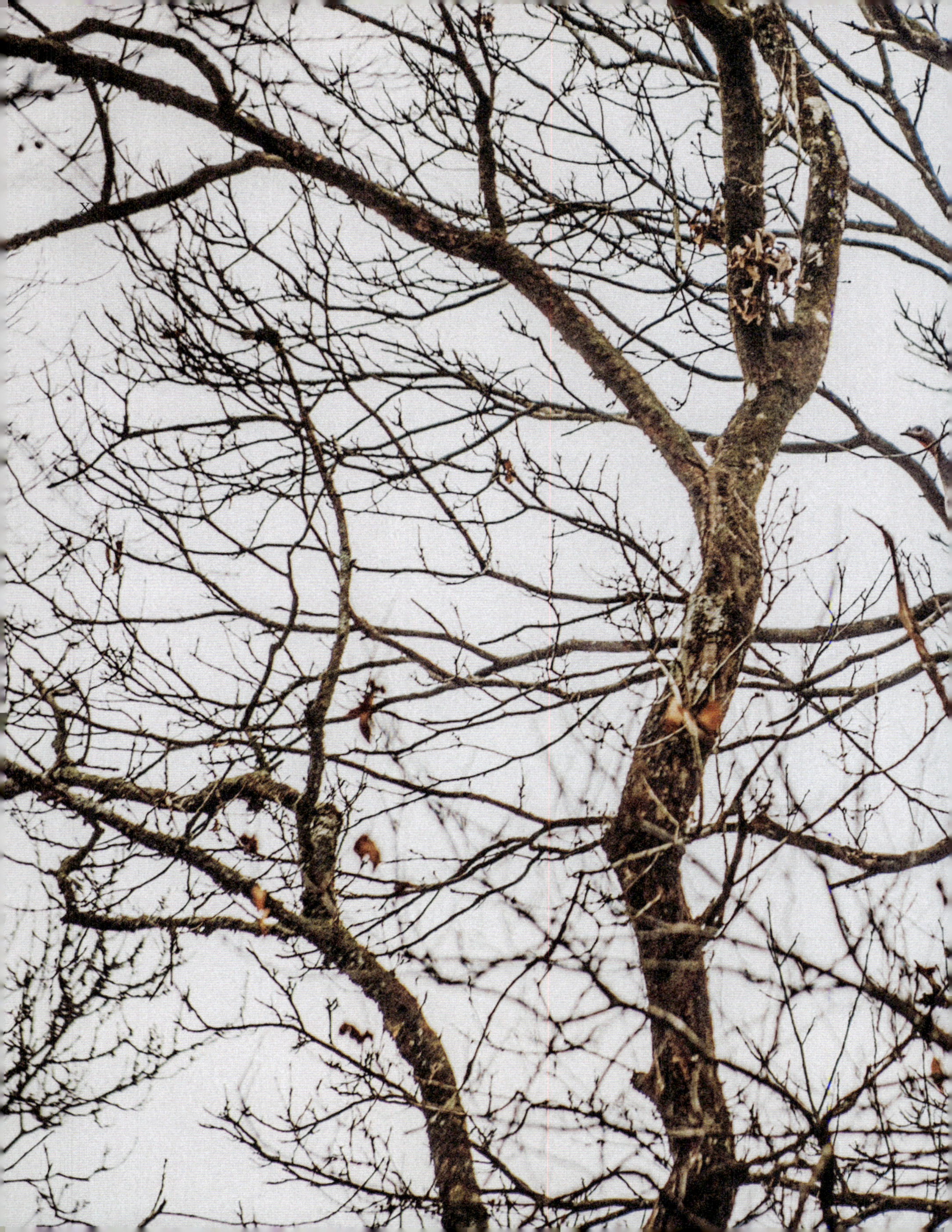

Winter

WINTER

There is a stillness to winter. The garden birds who once filled our skies with raucous chorus, now seem silent, quietly feeding on drying seedheads and, if they are lucky, tables bejewelled with hanging trinkets of fat balls and a smorgasbord of nuts and seeds. The hum of the busy tractors, working around the clock to bring in the harvest has faded, as they are now tucked up in creaking barns while the soil is too wet or too cold for much life. Sightings of wildlife seem few, as most animals with any common sense are hunkering down, storing their energy and their dwindling reserves.

While all may seem quiet in the wild, life in the countryside never stands still. There are always jobs to be done and, as the year draws to a close, farmers up and down the country prepare for the largest of all our festivals, Christmas.

Much of what we savour during the season of goodwill started its journey months ago. Tiny, fluffy geese and turkeys burst through porcelain-like shells back in the spring and have spent the summer and autumn gleefully fattening on the land. Potatoes that will be basted in fat, turned crisp and golden, were chitted at the end of the last winter and spent many months absorbing nutrients from the soil until swollen and bulbous, ready to be forked from the earth. Brassicas that survived the onslaught of summer's white butterflies have been gathered from under their nets and are now ready to be sliced, diced and prepared for the feast.

Whatever your religious affinity, this time of year marks a significant moment to take pause and celebrate the great joys in our lives and the generosity that the land provides. For me, there is no greater tribute to our farming community than a table laden with homegrown produce, where I can tell my loved ones the story behind each mouthwatering morsel of food. It is a time of shared goodwill, a moment to rejoice in uncomplicated pleasures, but some of the richest that life has to offer.

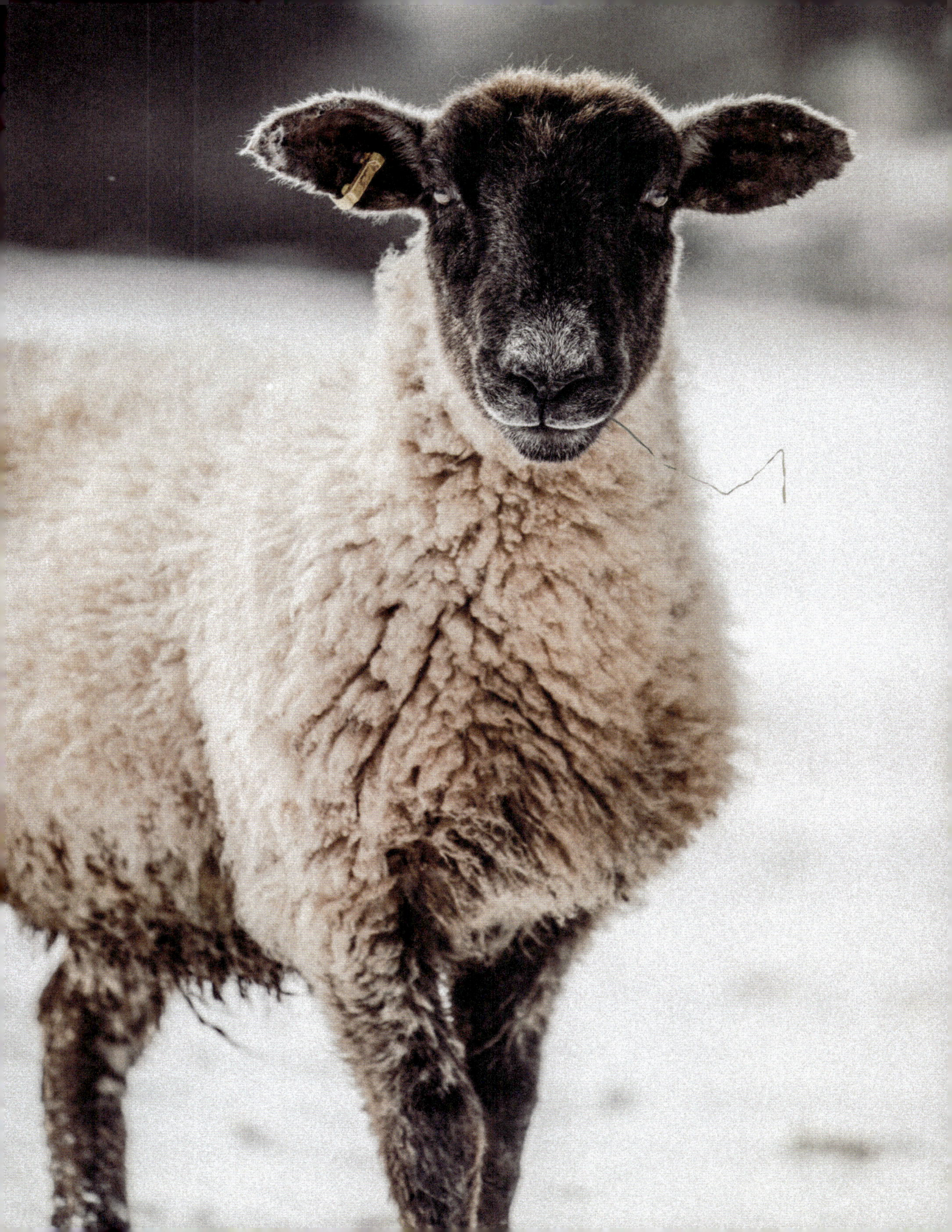

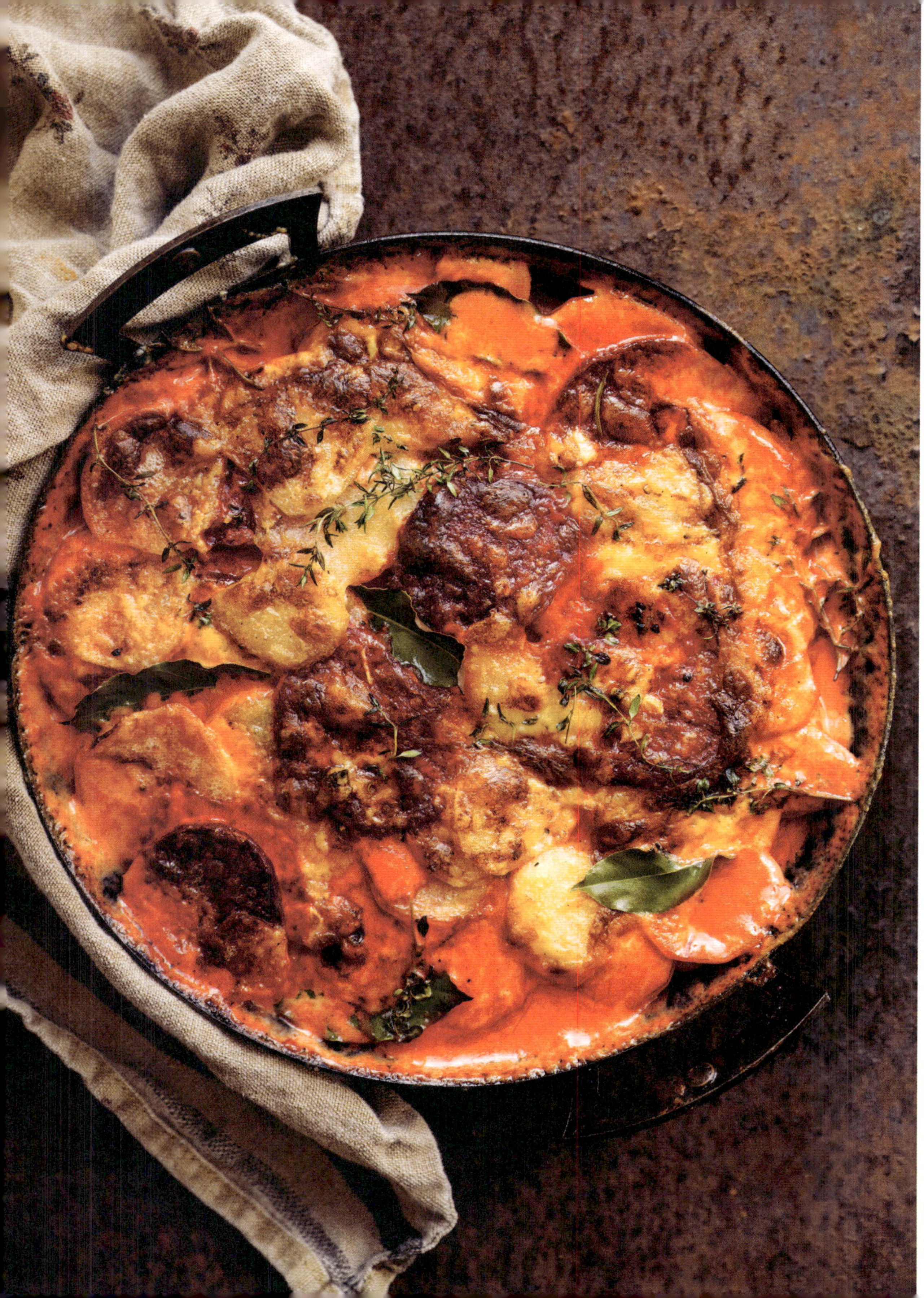

SERVES 4																			Winter

Beetroot, Celeriac, Potato & Thyme Gratin

I first made this recipe in celebration of Will's birthday. He's a shy, retiring type and not one to ever want a fuss, so I organized a big surprise party with all our family and friends! I cooked this dish along with everything else over fire on a bitterly cold day. It was the perfect molten comfort food that could be scooped and piled high, and made a superb partner for the rest of the spread. I'm not sure who turned pinker – the gratin or Will's blushing cheeks!

500ml (18fl oz) double cream
1 tablespoon Dijon mustard
200g (7oz) clothbound Cheddar cheese, grated
½ teaspoon grated nutmeg
1 onion, peeled and quartered
1 garlic head, cloves peeled and finely sliced
grass-fed butter, for frying and greasing
1kg (2lb 4oz) Maris Piper potatoes, finely sliced
300g (10½oz) beetroot, peeled and finely sliced
300g (10½oz) celeriac, peeled and finely sliced
a handful of thyme sprigs
a few sprigs of rosemary
3–4 bay leaves
flaky sea salt and freshly ground black pepper

Preheat the oven to 180°C/350°F/gas mark 4.

Mix together the cream, mustard, cheese, nutmeg, ½ teaspoon of black pepper and a pinch of salt in a jug, then set aside.

Heat a little butter in a frying pan, then add the onion and garlic and cook for 5–6 minutes, or until soft, then set aside.

Grease a 2-litre (3½-pint) ovenproof dish with butter, then cover the base with a quarter of the potato slices. Sprinkle over a quarter of the cooked onions and garlic, then layer on a quarter of the beetroot and celeriac slices. Scatter over a few thyme and rosemary leaves, ad a bay leaf and season lightly with salt and pepper. Repeat the process, building up the layers until you have used all the vegetables and herbs. Pour over the cream mixture, then place the dish into the oven and bake for 1 hour 20 minutes, or until the top is golden and the layers are tender.

Roast Cockerel with Cider Brandy & Mushroom Gravy

If you want to be the most popular person in the room, make this recipe. It has never failed me and always results in plates wiped clean. You see, that's what you get when you combine a few really good ingredients and let the alchemy of heat and time work their magic. I like to think this recipe is good enough to replace a beloved Christmas turkey and hold the central spot in your winter feast. However, if you cannot bear to break from tradition, try this recipe for a special Sunday lunch instead when you are out to impress, yet want little hassle.

4kg (8lb 13oz) whole free-range cockerel, giblets (neck, heart and gizzard) reserved and liver removed
2 onions, unpeeled and quartered
1 head of garlic, sliced crossways
2 celery sticks, chopped into 3 pieces
2 medium carrots, chopped into 3 pieces
4 bay leaves
a sprig of rosemary
a drizzle of extra virgin olive oil
flaky sea salt and freshly ground black pepper

For the gravy
4 tablespoons stoneground plain flour
500ml (18fl oz) chicken stock, warmed
a knob of grass-fed butter
1 shallot, finely chopped
200g (7oz) wild mushrooms, small ones left whole, large ones roughly chopped
100ml (3½fl oz) Somerset cider brandy
100ml (3½fl oz) double cream
flaky sea salt and freshly ground black pepper

Preheat the oven to 190°C/375°F/gas mark 5.

Take a large roasting tin and fill the base with the giblets, onions, garlic, celery, carrots and herbs. Season the veg with sea salt and drizzle with oil. Place the cockerel on top of the trivet of veg and drizzle with more oil. Season the bird well, including inside the cavity. Roast in the oven for 15 minutes per 400g (14oz) (approximately 2½ hours total), basting every 45 minutes or so. If the cockerel is browning more than desired, loosely cover it with foil. Once cooked, lift the bird from the roasting tin and leave to rest on a wooden board.

To make the gravy, set the roasting tin of veg and giblets over a medium–high heat. Sprinkle the flour over the veg and scrape up all the pan juices with a wooden spoon. After a couple of minutes of scraping up the juices and toasting the flour, pour in the warmed stock, allow it to bubble and cook for 6–7 minutes.

Place a sieve over a lipped bowl and pour the contents of the pan through. Using the wooden spoon, push down the veg so you are able to extract as much flavour as possible. Discard the pulverized veg and giblets and set the bowl of gravy to one side.

Take a large cast-iron frying pan and set over a low–medium heat. Add a little butter along with the shallot and a pinch of salt and sweat until soft. Increase the heat and add a little more butter along with the wild mushrooms. Fry for a couple of minutes, being careful not to move them about too much in the pan. Pour in the cider brandy and allow it to bubble up and reduce by two-thirds. Pour in the gravy and stir, then finish with the cream. Check the seasoning and adjust with salt or pepper to taste.

Carve the cockerel into thick slices, giving each person a little of the dark and white meat, then serve with lashings of mushroom gravy, with goose fat roast potatoes and seasonal veg on the side.

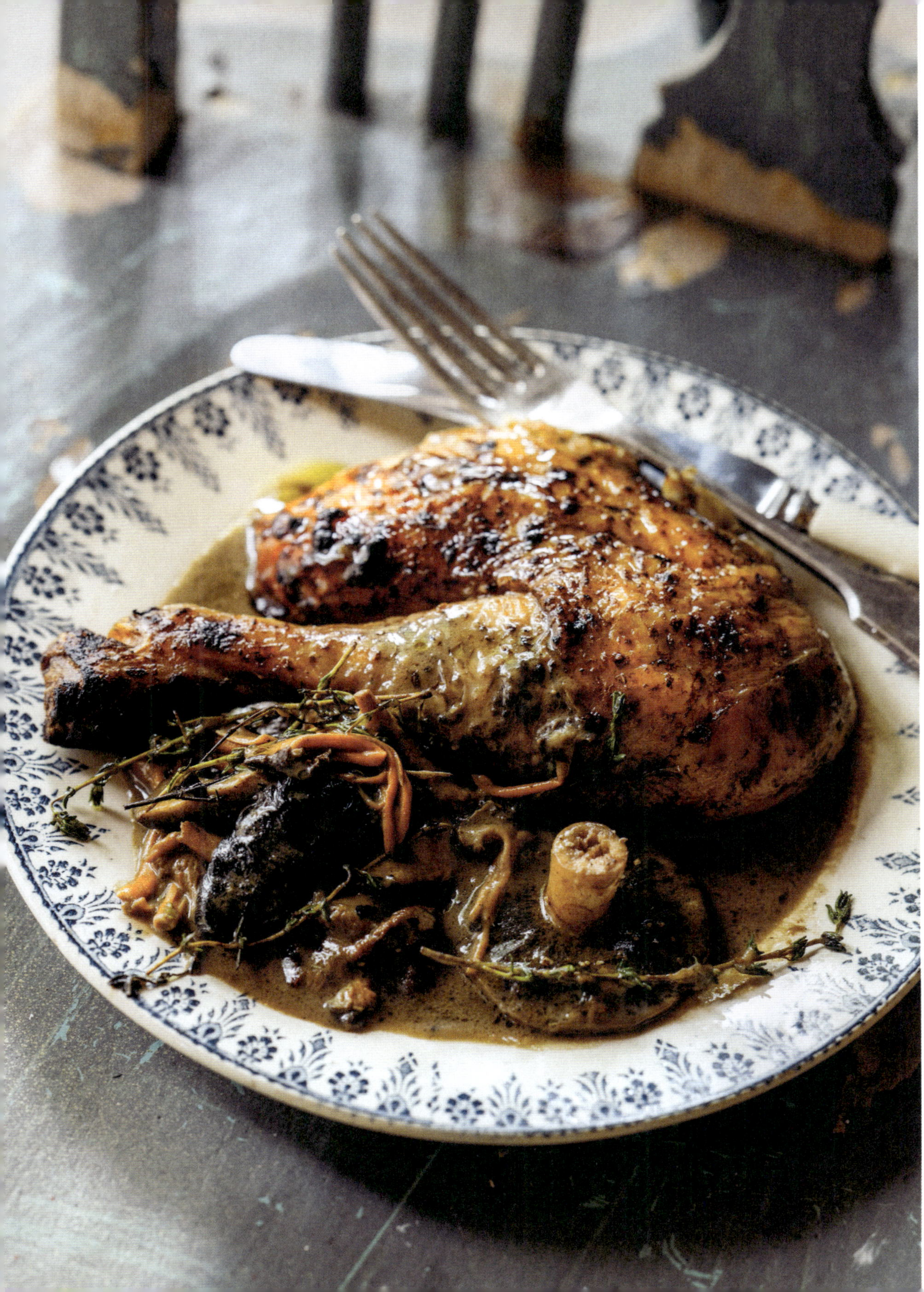

Roast Goose with Sage & Onion Sausagemeat Stuffing & Crispy Goose Fat Potatoes

The glorious goose; for me, it simply wouldn't be Christmas without a plump bird. As geese take up a significant amount of space in an oven, a little planning is required to juggle things about, which is why I like to make many of the side dishes ahead of the big feast. Don't forget, your goose will require resting, this is valuable oven time for warming dishes through, ready to sit alongside the main event.

For the roast goose
5–6kg (11lb–13lb 3oz) free-range whole goose
2 onions, finely chopped
1 garlic bulb, halved
4 celery sticks
2 carrots, halved
flaky sea salt and freshly ground black pepper

For the stuffing
50g (1¾oz) stale bread
2 large onions, finely chopped
200g (7oz) cooked chestnuts, roughly chopped
500g (1lb 2oz) free-range or organic sausagemeat
1 bunch of fresh sage (30g/1oz)
zest of 1 lemon
1 fresh whole nutmeg, for grating
a pinch of flaky sea salt

For the goose fat potatoes
2.5kg (5lb 8oz) Maris Piper potatoes, peeled and chopped into 8-cm (3¼-in) chunks
2 bay leaves
3 sprigs of rosemary
2 tablespoons goose fat
1 garlic bulb, cloves peeled
3–4 sprigs of thyme
flaky sea salt and freshly ground black pepper

See overleaf for method.

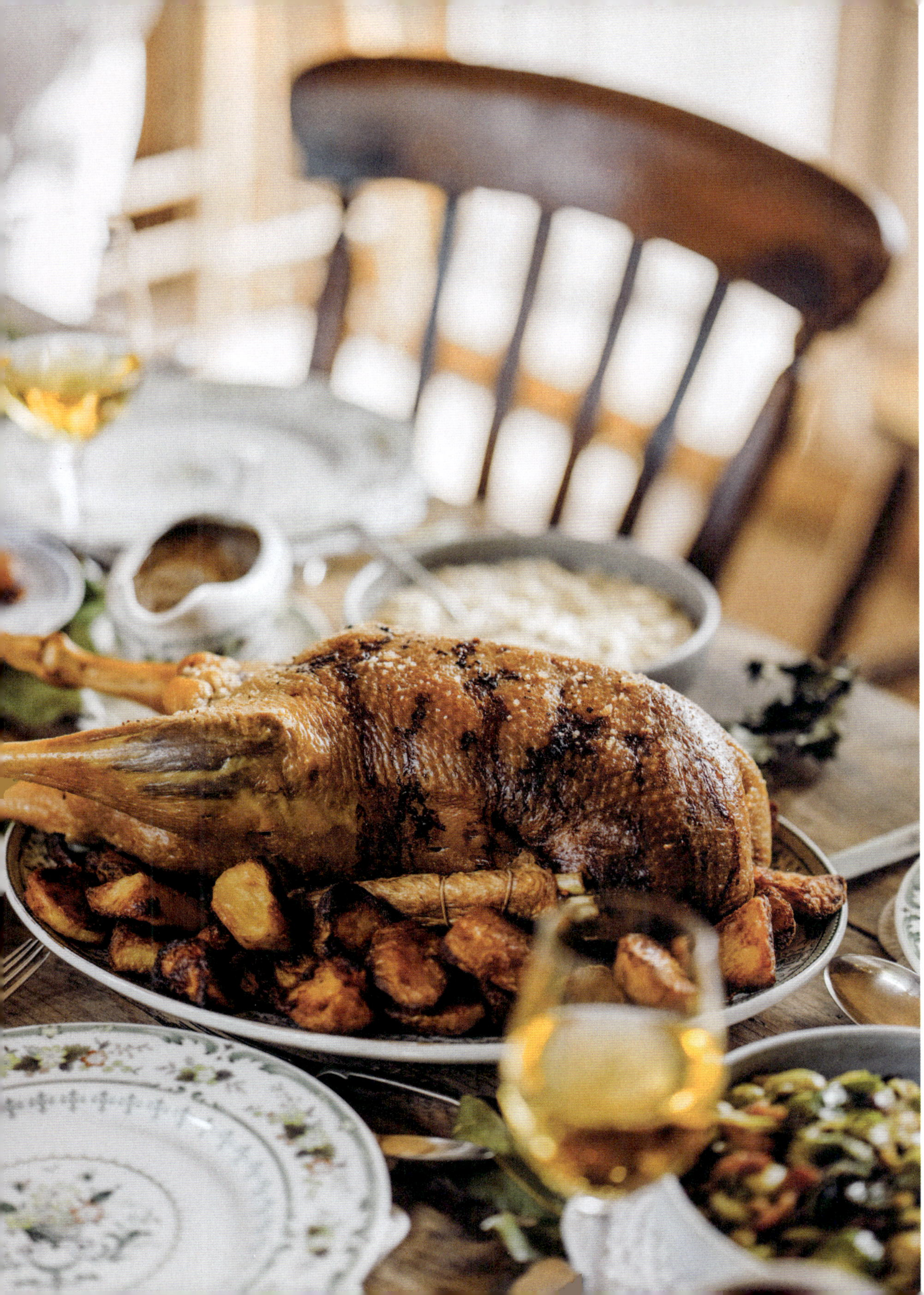

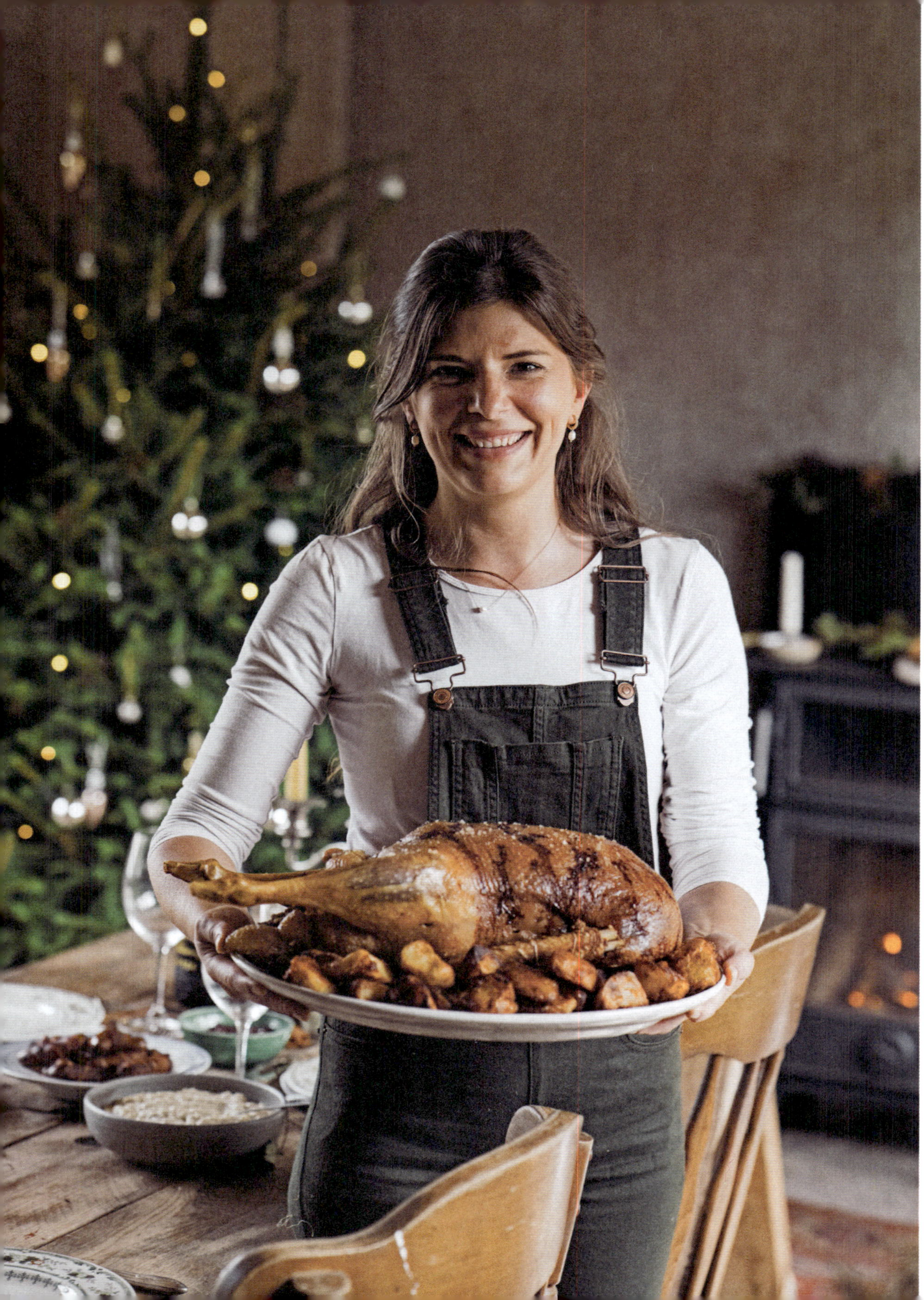

Remove the goose from the fridge the night before you intend to cook it and leave it to come up to room temperature overnight. This also gives the skin time to dry off. If you want to create crispy skin with yielding meat, it is imperative that the bird is dry.

To make the stuffing, blitz the stale bread in a food processor until smooth breadcrumbs have formed, then tip them into a large mixing bowl. Add the onions, chestnuts, sausagemeat, sage leaves, lemon zest, a generous grating of nutmeg and a large pinch of salt. Get your hands into the bowl and thoroughly mix all the ingredients until everything is really well combined. Set to one side and turn your attention to the potatoes.

Preheat the oven to 190°C/375°F/gas mark 5.

Set a large pan of boiling salted water over a high heat. Drop in the potatoes along with the bay leaves and a sprig of rosemary and boil for 10 minutes – this will ensure that the insides become fluffy. Drain in a colander and leave to steam dry for 5 minutes, this will enable the fat to coat the potatoes. Give the colander a few light shakes to bash up the edges of the potatoes, giving you maximum surface area for crispiness.

Take the bag of fat from the goose giblets and spoon out two generous tablespoons into a roasting tray. Place the tray into the oven for around 5 minutes, or until the fat is smoking hot. Being very careful, remove the tray filled with sizzling fat from the oven and tip in the par-boiled potatoes, shaking the tray to coat them in the fat. Generously season with salt and pepper and sprinkle in the garlic cloves. Set to one side.

Pierce the fattiest parts of the bird. You are aiming to pierce just the skin and fat, without puncturing the flesh. Give the parsons nose a thorough pierce. Season the cavity, then fill it generously with stuffing, being careful not to over-pack it, as you want the hot air to be able to freely circulate around. Season the legs and breast with salt and pepper.

Arrange the chunky veg in a large roasting tray, laying them out to form a trivet. Place the stuffed and seasoned goose on top of the veg, then slide the tray into the centre of the oven. Place the tray of potatoes into the oven on the shelf above. Roast the goose for 20 minutes at 200°C/400°F/gas mark 6 to crisp the skin.

Turn the oven temperature down to 180°C/350°F/gas mark 4. While you are at the oven, give the potatoes a good shake to ensure they are not sticking and roast for a further 40 minutes. Cook the goose for approximately 20 minutes per kilo (remember to take the weight of the stuffing into account). During the cooking, if the skin starts to brown too much, lightly cover the goose with kitchen foil, making sure you then remove the foil for the last 10 minutes of cooking, to re-crisp the skin.

Once the potatoes have been roasting for an hour, remove them from the oven and use the back of a fork to press down on each potato so they break up slightly. Give them a further shake in the pan, then add in the rest of the rosemary and some thyme. Roast for another 15–20 minutes until they are perfectly crisp, then remove from the oven and leave somewhere warm while the goose continues to roast.

Remove the goose from the oven and allow it to rest uncovered somewhere warm for around 30 minutes.

Carve the goose and serve generous slices of meat, stuffing and crispy potatoes along with lashings of gravy and seasonal veg.

Turkey & Ham Christmas Crumble

SERVES 6

Much merriment has been had over the preceding few days. Debris signaling good times is strewn about the house, and I can almost hear the dishwasher groan 'not again' with each load of crockery. Some of the best meals are enjoyed after 'the big feast' – that epic turkey sandwich, or the buffet of leftover cheese and pickle scoffed late into the evening while snuggled up on the sofa with the ones I love.

This recipe was a happy accident. I had planned to make a classic pie to use up all the leftover scraps in one lazy trough. However, with all the festive baking, I had run out of flour, so there would be no pastry lid for my pie. Searching the kitchen I noticed stale bread, nuts aplenty and a large jar of oats that we had been using for porridge. The rest is history and forevermore Christmas Crumble is part of folklore.

a knob of grass-fed butter
2 shallots, finely chopped
3 garlic cloves, finely sliced
a pinch of flaky sea salt
2 bay leaves
1 leek, finely sliced
2 tablespoons stoneground plain flour
125ml (4fl oz) dry white wine
300ml (10fl oz) turkey or chicken stock
200ml (7fl oz) crème fraîche
300g (10½oz) leftover Christmas cheese (a mixture of creamy brie and Cheddar works well)
2 teaspoons wholegrain mustard
a sprig of rosemary
100g (3½oz) leftover cooked Christmas turkey
100g (3½oz) leftover cooked Christmas gammon

For the crumble topping
200g (7oz) breadcrumbs
150g (5½oz) hazelnuts, chopped
100g (3½oz) sunflower seeds
150g (5½oz) rolled oats
100g (3½oz) clothbound Cheddar cheese, grated
small handful of flat-leaf parsley, roughly chopped
flaky sea salt and freshly ground black pepper

Preheat the oven to 180°C/350°F/gas mark 4.

Place a cast-iron casserole dish over a medium heat. Add a knob of butter along with the shallots, garlic and a pinch of salt and gently cook until the onions have become translucent, around 5–6 minutes. Add the bay leaves and leek and cook until the leeks have just begun to caramelise, this should only take a few minutes. Sprinkle a little flour over the veg and stir to mix well. Increase the heat and pour in the wine. Allow the wine to bubble and reduce, then add the stock and crème fraîche, stirring until the sauce has thickened. Crumble or grate in your leftover cheese and continue to stir until it has completely melted. Add the mustard and mix it through the sauce. Once the sauce is thick, glossy and full of flavour, add a few picked rosemary leaves and the leftover turkey and gammon. Keep the pan gently bubbling away over the heat while you make the crumble topping.

In a mixing bowl, combine the breadcrumbs, nuts, seeds, oats, cheese, parsley and a pinch each of salt and pepper. Sprinkle the mixture over the top of the creamy filling, place the dish into the oven and bake for 20–25 minutes, or until the top is beautifully golden.

Serve in generous bowls and enjoy while sat by a roaring fire.

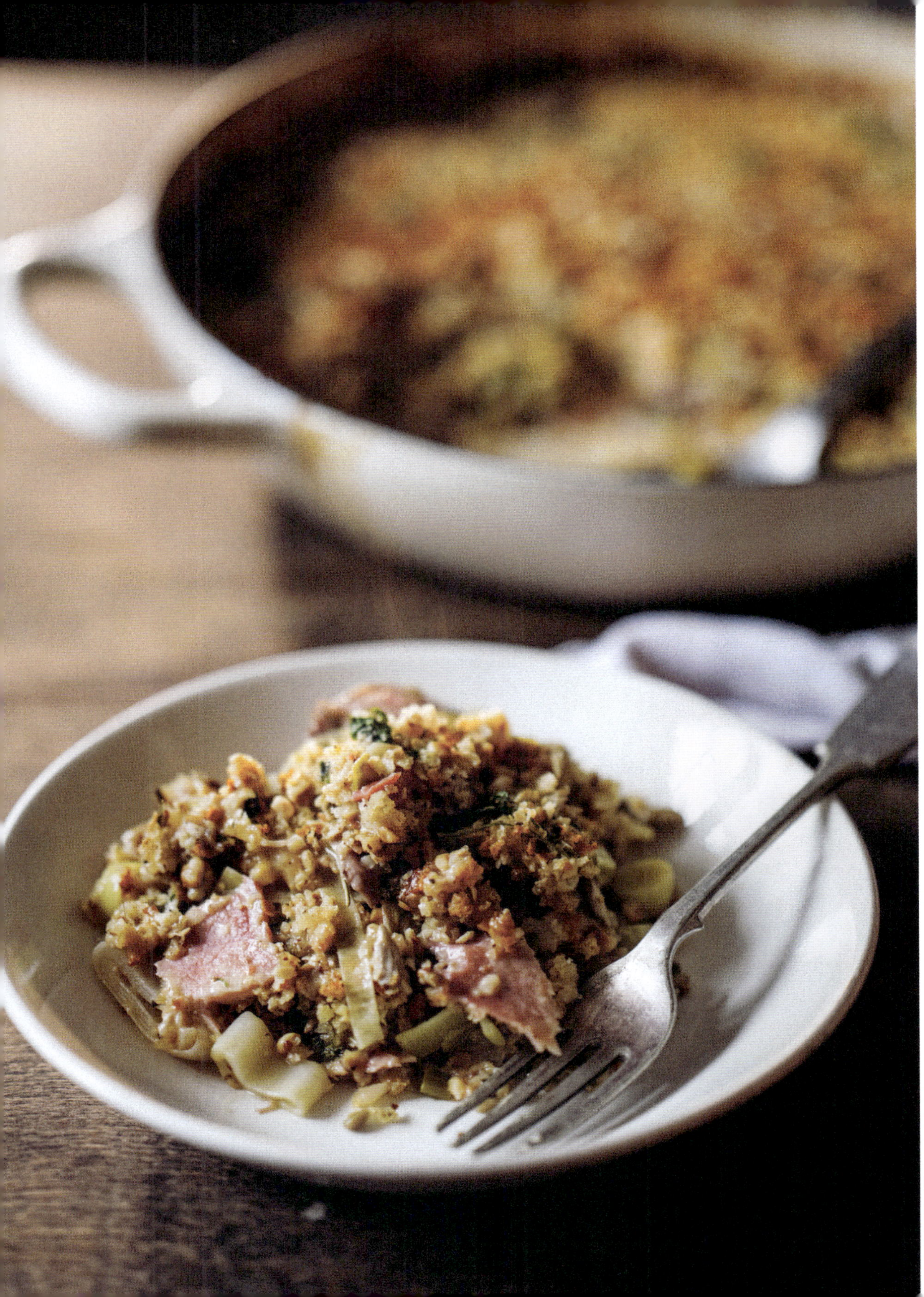

Community

People are as much a part of the countryside as nature itself. I'm reminded of this fact every time I gaze upon a stone wall dutifully protecting a flock of sheep. Each stone has been dug out from the earth and painstakingly placed by hand to create a fortress, signifying who owns which parcel of ground. Over generations, as the walls have become weary and collapsed with age, new hands replace the stones as the next generation takes on the responsibility. Memories become entwined with the landscape as generations leave their mark.

Field, road and farm names tell us much about the history of our countryside, indicating what came before. On our home farm, 'Pump Field' indicates where the old well was once situated. 'River Field' indicates a marshy, wet field that was once home to a meandering river, where today sits a much smaller stream.

It's easy to understand why many want to preserve the idea of the countryside in aspic, to hold on to a romantic idea of a rural idyll. However, the idea that things shouldn't change is foolish. Landscapes have changed for centuries, and they will go on changing. What we must strive for is balance. There is much to be lost in forgetting a well-trodden path we have walked before, but as much to be missed out on if we too tightly preserve an idea that perhaps no longer fits.

I have visited hundreds of farms around the country, each on their own unique journey. However, I have found one common thread that connects them all – they want to make farming work. North, south, east or west, I have never been far from encountering people who fill my heart with hope for our future. The privilege of coaxing a landscape this way or that, echoing previous ages or striving for new ideas is not lost upon those who carry the heavy burden of what to do and how to do it. In recent years, that burden has become too much for some, reluctantly giving up their dream and in many cases their homes too, when faced with financial uncertainty, coupled with the external pressures of negative media coverage surrounding farming that is ever-present.

'I wouldn't say we are thriving, but we are managing well enough,' says one of the more optimistic of my clan when I talk to him about the idea of thriving, not just surviving. Ensuring my farmers wellbeing is a responsibility I feel deeply.

The farming community, or 'landworkers', have filled our village pubs, post offices, churches, village halls and sports teams. Wives, girlfriends, grandmothers and daughters baked cakes and biscuits for raffles, coffee mornings and ubiquitous cricket teas, while sons, brothers and fathers filled sports teams, attended race nights and put a couple of quid behind the bar once or twice a week. When hedgerows became too unwieldy for dog walkers, it was the local farmer with his strimmer who, often without being asked, would give footpaths a tidy. When food was spare it would be gleefully shared, marked out by handwritten signs: 'Cider', 'Eggs', 'Free Apples'. A jam jar with a rusted lid placed on a creaking table or upturned crate, there to collect a small fee. Often, the couple of pounds and pennies that made their way into the jars would be donated to the local church or primary school fundraiser.

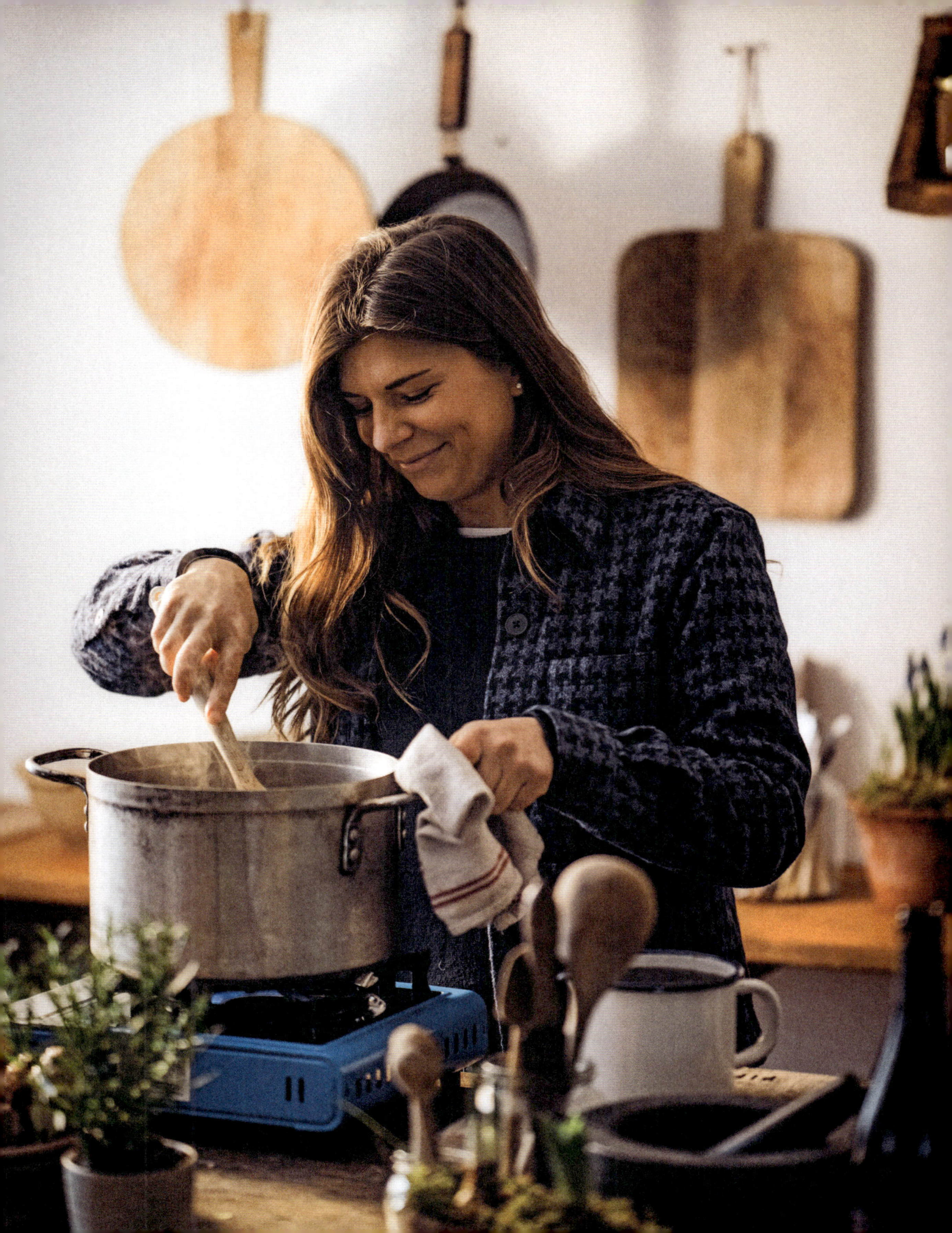

There is an overwhelming sense of community within agriculture. Unlike many professions, you cannot simply farm in isolation. When times are tough and nature has given you a kicking, relying on neighbours is not just important, it can be vital for survival. Machinery might be kindly leant to a neighbour, silage and hay cut in partnership and shared, and gossip – such as who's bull is doing the business – bestowed at the local livestock market. The farming community can often be one of the greatest examples of how acting together can make a positive difference. However, in equal measure, farming can be incredibly isolating.

The majority of farming takes place on private land. This presents a tension between widely held virtues of individual freedom and growing public and governmental concerns over how to produce food in a way that fosters positive benefits to the planet – as well as whether that land should be used for growing food at all. The tug of war between the climate crisis, food and energy security, and passionate cries about habitat and species loss have mounted increasing pressure on the shoulders of farmers, leaving many no alternative but to scale up, swallowing up a neighbour's farm and intensifying by the use of machinery – not manpower – in order to survive. Or giving way to new money looking to offset or acquire an increasingly valuable asset. We are losing the lifeblood of our rural communities at a rate of knots.

It isn't just the perennial discussion around the price and availability of land that is killing our farming communities. In many cases, there simply are not the jobs available to sustain those who want to work the land. Nor the 'workers' cottages' that would have been filled with families. Instead, these homes have to play a crucial role in the landowner's diversification, bringing in an important revenue stream as a holiday let, often funding the losses from producing food. Many of what governments like to describe as 'low-skilled jobs' pay so little in comparison to the inflated cost of living, a mortgage on a cottage near a farm would be unthinkable anyway. This means that most workers live outside the hamlet and face commuting costs, which need to be factored into their low wage. No wonder there is little left for the village pub, the post office or the donation pot. And for the landowner, with fewer hands to help, there is less time to cut hedges, clear pathways and help out at charity fundraisers.

Stripping our farming community back to the bare bones, continually asking them to do more with less, while pitting them against corporate giants and unfair trade deals is destroying our countryside and what do we have to show for all of this? The U.N.'s State of Food Security and Nutrition report led with a depressing summary: 'the world is moving backwards in efforts to eliminate hunger and malnutrition.' Close to one-third of the world's population is food insecure and, after falling for decades, the number of people affected by hunger has risen to well over 800-million people, nearly 10% of the global population.

Food security is a much greater concern in the UK than some might realize, too. Some 10% of UK households are food insecure. The UK's self-sufficiency has declined considerably over recent decades, something that should be of serious concern given the dire warnings around the impacts of climate change on many of the world's major food exporting regions. At the same time, thousands of hectares of productive agricultural land have been developed for housing, as well as many that have been converted from small-scale farms into intensive factory farms.

While the social fabric of rural life is becoming fragmented, it is my view that the mountain is not yet too steep to climb and grass roots revolutions around the world, as well as in our very own backyard, can hold us back from the tipping point.

In the verdant fields of the UK, a stark reality unfolds amid the bustling aisles of supermarkets. With 94% of food sourced from just eight retailers, the landscape resembles a tightly woven tapestry, where fierce competition dictates the rhythm of commerce. Should one of these giants dare to raise prices to support their suppliers, they are likely to be undercut by their rivals, losing customers at a rapid rate. This precarious system offers little resilience against external shocks, like devastating crop failures more frequent than ever due to our climate changing. The already strained supply chain hangs by a thread, vulnerable to collapse, while consumers watch in dismay as inflation soars, pushing prices beyond their reach.

For farmers, by sharing the rich narratives of their produce – its provenance, quality and sustainability – they can shorten the supply chain, removing the 'middle man' and the barriers that separate them from their customers. This enables them to gain fairer prices for their produce and build more resilient links to their marketplace.

This approach does, however, require farmers to have the resources to either sell direct or to maintain traceability from their farm gate direct to the retailer, where the consumer ultimately buys. In this system, farmers and short supply chains should be supported for sustaining traditional practices, along with the required infrastructure for local production and innovation to flourish. It calls upon consumers to embrace the story behind their food, and be willing to pay a fair price for supporting their local stewards of the land. Where the wealth of public goods a healthy farming system provides are clearly visible (improved human health, a reduction in waste, boosting the local economy, reduced habitat loss and climate-friendly production), farmers must be positively supported, not just by the customer, but by governments too, as the wider benefits the farmer creates affect us all.

Yet, for communities striving to improve access to food for those most in need, the challenge lies in finding innovative pathways. Facilitating improved access to food for the poorest groups requires the ability to source produce cheaply, competing with the mainstream marketplace, without engaging in its destructive practices. There has been significant success with concepts like buying clubs, where groups of people can gather together to buy in bulk, as well as surplus food hubs, which rescue waste food from fragile supermarket and wholesale supply chains and redistribute it to those in need. Enabling individuals to cultivate their own food in community gardens supported by local charities or councils has some of the most significant benefits. These initiatives not only address food insecurity but also weave a rich tapestry of community, where skills and knowledge are shared, isolation is diminished, and wellbeing flourishes.

By re-localizing our supply chains, putting people and communities at the heart of food production systems, the benefits are vast. We have the power to create thriving rural communities once more, erasing the tension of the urban and rural divide, and creating a healthier, nourished landscape around us, for the benefit of us all.

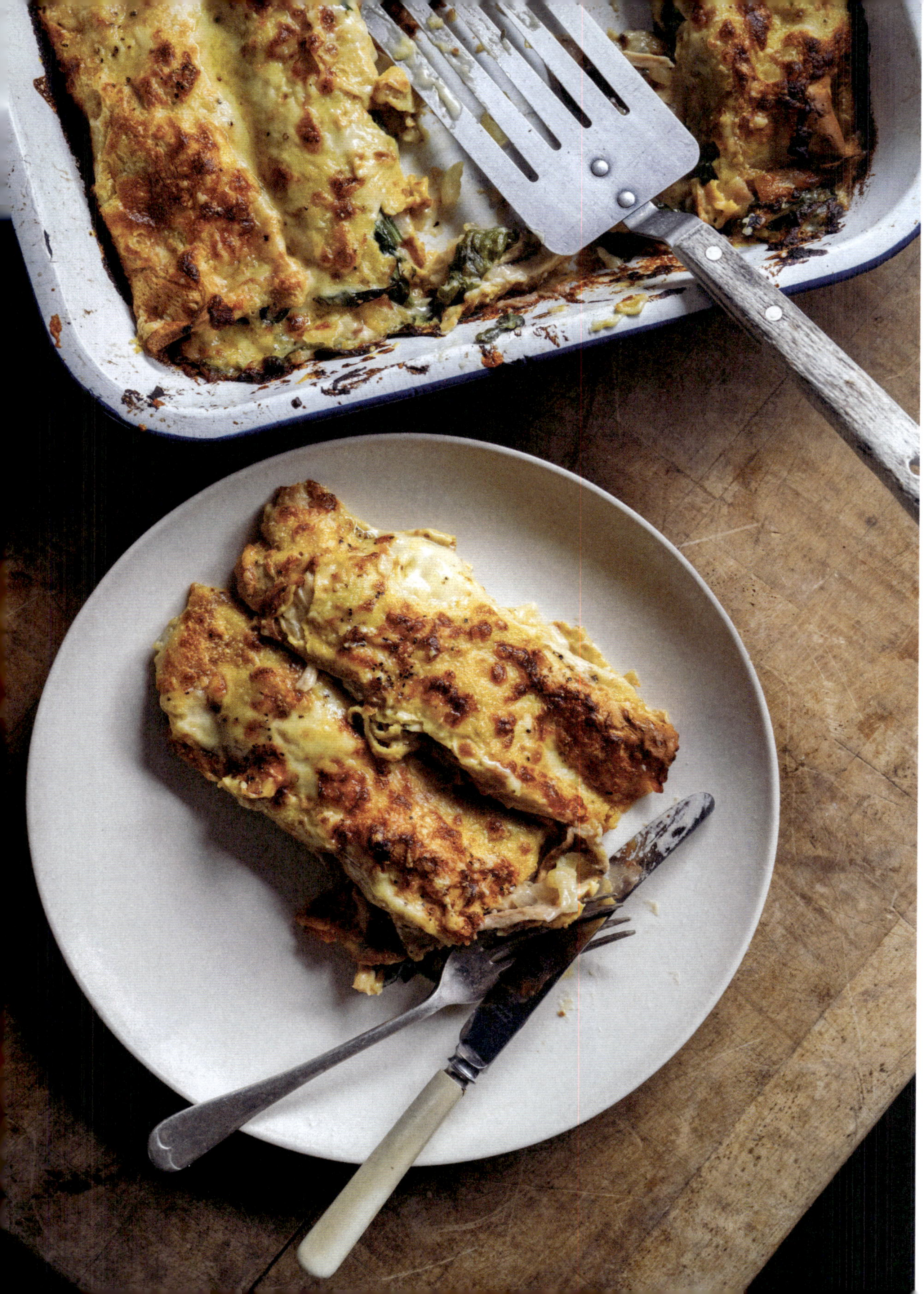

SERVES 4–6   Winter

Rabbit, Bacon, Wild Mushroom & Spinach Stuffed Pancakes

For many years I rarely made pancakes outside of Pancake Day, convinced the only way to eat them was in classic French style with a squeeze of lemon and a sprinkle of sugar. I eventually came to realise that I had been depriving myself of such a wonderfully versatile ingredient, equally as good as a savoury dish as it is sweet. Savoury pancakes work incredibly well in place of store-bought wraps that are packed full of preservatives and seem to last years in the pantry.

This recipe works brilliantly throughout the year – you can simply swap the filling for what's in season. Perhaps chicken and chard in spring, ham and peas in summer and slow-cooked beef and blue cheese in the autumn. I encourage you to get creative and ditch those store-bought wraps.

a drizzle of organic rapeseed oil
1 whole wild rabbit, prepared for the pot
500ml (18fl oz) chicken stock
3 bay leaves
a few sprigs of fresh thyme
50g (1¾oz) grass-fed butter
1 onion, finely chopped
2 garlic cloves, finely sliced
a pinch of flaky sea salt
100g (3½oz) smoked streaky bacon, sliced into lardons
200g (7oz) wild mushrooms
100g (3½oz) spinach leaves

For the pancakes
100g (3½oz) stoneground plain flour
2 organic and/or free-range eggs
300ml (10fl oz) whole grass-fed milk
a knob of grass-fed butter

For the béchamel
a knob of grass-fed butter
2 tablespoons stoneground plain flour
300ml (10fl oz) whole grass-fed milk
250g (9oz) clothbound mature Cheddar cheese, grated
½ teaspoon grated nutmeg
1 tablespoon crème fraîche
flaky sea salt and freshly ground black pepper

See overleaf for method.

First, make the pancakes. Sift the flour into a large mixing bowl. Make a well in the middle, break in the eggs and start whisking slowly. Add the milk in a steady stream, whisking constantly until the batter is smooth and all the flour has been incorporated. Set aside to rest for at least 30 minutes.

Place a cast-iron pancake pan over a medium heat and very lightly grease the pan with butter. Spoon a ladleful of batter into the pan and swirl it around so the bottom of the pan is evenly coated. You want to use just enough batter to make a delicate, lacy pancake. Cook the pancake for about 30–45 seconds on one side until golden and then use a fish slice to flip the pancake over and cook the other side until nicely golden and freckled. Remove from the pan and set aside. Repeat to make 4–5 more pancakes or until all the batter is used up.

Preheat the oven to 170°C/325°F/gas mark 3½.

To cook the rabbit, heat a drizzle of rapeseed oil in a cast-iron frying pan over a medium–high heat. Once hot, add the rabbit and brown it on all sides, around 10 minutes. Transfer the rabbit from the pan to an ovenproof dish, pour in the stock and throw in the herbs. Place the dish into the preheated oven and gently cook for 2½ hours.

Once cooked, remove it from the dish and leave to cool. When cool enough to touch, shred the rabbit meat from the bones and set aside.

To make the béchamel, set a saucepan over a medium heat and add the butter. Once it has melted, add the flour and mix well, allowing the flour to toast slightly. Begin to whisk in the milk, a quarter at a time, until incorporated. Add most of the cheese, reserving a little to finish the dish later. Once the cheese has melted into the béchamel, season generously with salt, pepper and nutmeg – you want to slightly over season, as this sauce will act as a seasoning for the whole dish. Spoon out around 4 large tablespoons of the béchamel and set to one side. Reduce the heat under the pan and leave to keep warm.

Increase the oven to 180°C/350°F/gas mark 4.

Set a cast-iron frying pan over a medium heat and add most of the butter. Once it is gently bubbling, add the onion, garlic and salt and soften for 7–8 minutes. Add the bacon lardons and gently cook until starting to caramelise. Increase the heat and add the mushrooms and thyme along with the remaining butter. Fry until caramelised, being careful not to move the mushrooms too often around the pan.

Tip the contents of the frying pan into the béchamel sauce. Add the shredded rabbit meat along with the spinach and stir to combine.

Take the stack of pancakes from earlier and add heaped spoonfuls of the filling into the middle of each pancake, before rolling and placing side-by-side in an ovenproof dish. Loosen the remaining béchamel sauce with the crème fraîche until you have a runnier consistency. Pour over the pancakes and top with the remaining grated cheese. Bake in the oven for 20 minutes, or until golden brown on top and bubbling.

SERVES 6 — Winter

Wild Rabbit Pie

We have a dysfunctional relationship with rabbits. What was once a wildly popular meat is now barely consumed. Crazy really, when the estimated rabbit population is around 40 million. This huge number of wild creatures causes havoc in both our ecosystems and food systems, not to mention the hundreds of thousands of pounds spent each year on fencing to keep rabbits at bay. You see, rabbits breed like rabbits, so with fine weather, warm summers and mild winters, populations explode. The imbalance of this species not only impacts hobbyist gardeners but large-scale growers, too. If a rabbit population is sickly, they are excellent carriers of all manner of diseases to other wild creatures, so it is crucially important we maintain suitable numbers to keep the colonies and our countryside healthy.

In a world demanding more and more protein, which is leading to further intensification of our farming system, I believe the answer may lie right under our noses – or perhaps in the corner of my veg garden munching on a cabbage leaf ... For those fearful of eating rabbit, this, my friends, is the best entry way to get to know this remarkable ingredient. I often refer to this recipe as my 'Not Chicken Pie'. Everyone who eats it loves it and is always amazed to hear it isn't made with chicken.

a drizzle of organic rapeseed oil
1 whole wild rabbit, prepared for the pot
250g (9oz) smoked bacon lardons (unsmoked can be used too)
a knob or two of grass-fed butter
2 onions, sliced
4 garlic cloves, sliced
1 celery stick, sliced
a handful of bay leaves
450ml (16fl oz) cider
500ml (18fl oz) chicken stock, warmed
1 tablespoon stoneground plain flour
200ml (7fl oz) double cream
1 teaspoon English mustard
a few fresh herbs, such as tarragon, rosemary or sage
300g (10½oz) rough puff pastry or puff pastry
1 organic and/or free-range egg, whisked
flaky sea salt and freshly ground black pepper

See overleaf for method.

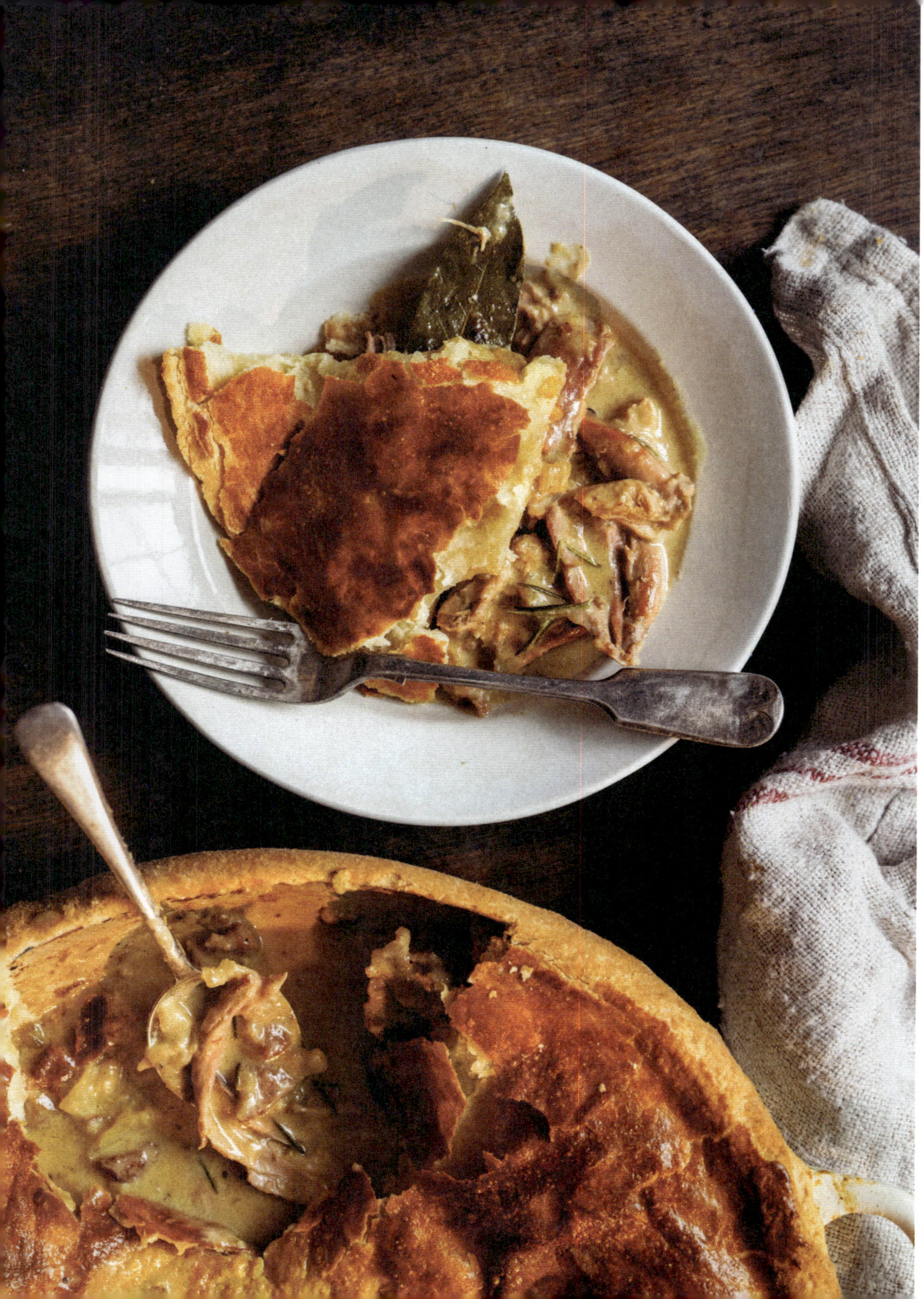

Place a large heavy-bottomed ovenproof pan or shallow casserole dish over a high heat and add a little rapeseed oil. Once the fat is smoking hot, season the rabbit and carefully place it into the pan. Leave it for around 2–3 minutes before turning. Once the rabbit is beautifully caramelised, remove it from the pan and set it to one side.

Add the bacon lardons to the pan and allow them to render down until they are crisp and golden. This will take just a few minutes. Once crisp, remove from the pan and set to one side.

Turn down the heat and add a little butter to the pan. Allow it to foam, then add the onions, garlic, celery and bay leaves, cooking everything down until soft and ranslucent. This will take about 6–7 minutes.

Turn the heat back up and then add the cider, letting it bubble up and rapidly boil. Allow this to cook off for a few minutes until the liquid has reduced by half and started to become sticky. Turn the heat down a touch and pour in the warm stock. Add the rabbit and bacon lardons back to the pan. Turn the heat down so the pan is gently bubbling away and not boiling or simmering. Place the lid on and leave to cook for about 1½ hours, checking from time to time that the liquid doesn't need a top up.

Once the rabbit is tender, carefully lift it from the pan and leave it to cool enough to handle.

In a small bowl, combine another knob of butter with the flour and mix to create a paste or a 'roux'. Dollop the roux into the sauce, a little at a time, whisking as you go to encourage the sauce to thicken.

Once the rabbit meat has cooled, carefully strip it from the bone and add the shredded meat back to the pan. Pour in the cream and add the mustard and fresh garden herbs – I like to use tarragon, rosemary or sage, but you could use chives or parsley too. Check the seasoning and make any adjustments.

Preheat the oven to 190°C/375°F/gas mark 5.

Roll out the rough puff pastry 2–3mm (⅛in) thick. Pace it over the pan, and trim away the excess edges. Generously douse the pastry in egg wash and poke two air holes, so the steam can escape from the pie.

Place the pie into the oven and bake for around 20 minutes, or until the pastry is crispy and golden.

Remove from the oven and serve with seasonal greens and buttered mash.

Oxtail Soup

It will take a few days to carefully craft this feast. Cooking to me has never been just about the end result. Apart from the pleasure of preparing food to be shared, there are also many moments throughout the process to enjoy. The rhythmic chopping of my old friend the onion, the satisfying crunch as you slice through celery, the pulling apart of tender, collapsing meat from bones, and the feel of the spoon as it seamlessly divides creamy set fat from gelatinous liquor. This is a recipe to relish, to take your time over and enjoy each and every step.

1 whole grass-fed oxtail, about 1kg (2lb 4oz), cut into manageable pieces
1 tablespoon beef dripping
a knob of grass-fed butter
2 onions, roughly chopped
2 celery sticks, roughly chopped
2 carrots, diced
3 garlic cloves, roughly chopped
3 bay leaves
a sprig of rosemary, leaves picked
a few sprigs of thyme, leaves picked
3 tablespoons tomato purée
½ teaspoon miso paste (or Marmite)
a few drops of Worcestershire sauce
300ml (10fl oz) red wine
1.5 litres (2½ pints) beef stock
½ teaspoon freshly ground black pepper
1 tablespoon stoneground plain flour
flaky sea salt

The day before you plan to serve this, remove the oxtail from the fridge and allow it to come to room temperature. Untie it, pat it dry and generously season with salt.

Place a large cast-iron casserole dish over a high heat and add the beef dripping. Once smoking hot and sizzling, add the oxtail. You may need to cook it in batches depending on the size of your pan. Brown the oxtail all over until beautifully caramelised, then remove from the pan and set aside.

Reduce the heat and add a knob of butter along to the pan along with the onions, celery, carrots, garlic, herbs and a small pinch of salt. Cook until the onions are translucent and the carrots and celery have softened, around 7–8 minutes. Add the tomato purée, miso paste and Worcestershire sauce and give everything a good stir. Increase the heat slightly and pour in the wine, allowing it to bubble for a few minutes.

Return the oxtail to the pan and pour in the stock. Bring to the boil, then reduce to a gentle simmer. Cover and cook for 3 hours until the oxtail is tender and falling off the bone.

Add the black pepper and check the seasoning. Using a slotted spoon, remove the oxtail from the pan and transfer it to a plate to cool.

Once the oxtail has cooled, shred the meat into a bowl, discarding the bones (or give them to the dog) and place the meat into the fridge. Strain the cooking liquor through a sieve into a large bowl and place in the fridge overnight.

The next day, scrape away and discard the layer of fat that has formed on top of the liquor. Spoon the jellified soup into a large pan and heat through until simmering.

In a small bowl, mix the flour with a couple of tablespoons of the hot soup until a smooth paste is formed. Whisk the paste into the soup and simmer for 2 minutes. Add the shredded oxtail meat to the pan and heat through for a minute or two before serving.

Ladle the rich liquor into bowls, making sure you evenly distribute the shredded meat. Serve alongside some buttered bread.

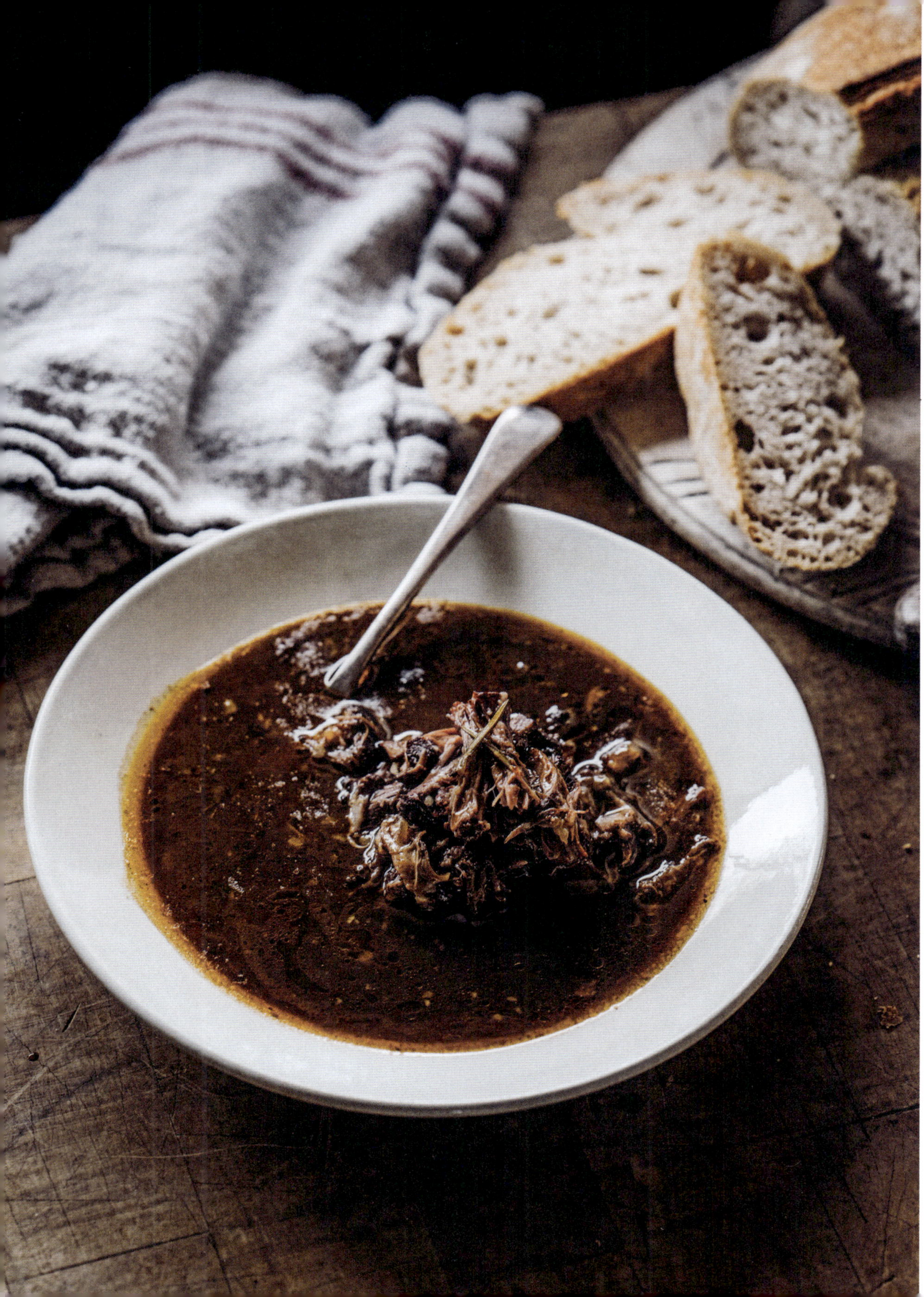

Steak & Kidney Pie

This recipe has been kindly contributed by my friend and food writer, Gill Meller. Not only is it a divine recipe, it also represents a huge part of how this book came to be.

I have been lucky enough to work alongside some of the country's most talented food producers and chefs, each one generous in opening up a world full of creativity, knowledge and passion for their craft. I have since, developed my own bank of knowledge and skills that I can share with you all. What a joy it is to honor those who have taught me and pass on their learnings to teach others.

grass-fed butter, for greasing
1 organic and/or free-range egg, beaten

For the pastry
175g (6oz) grass-fed butter, chilled and cut into small cubes
350g (12oz) stoneground unbleached plain flour, plus extra for dusting
a pinch of flaky sea salt
2–3 tablespoons iced water

For the filling
1kg (2lb 4oz) grass-fed braising beef
250g (9oz) grass-fed ox kidney
50g (1¾oz) stoneground unbleached plain flour
1 tablespoon beef dripping
2 onions, peeled and finely sliced
2 garlic cloves
2 sprigs of thyme
4 bay leaves
300ml (10fl oz) ale
1 litre (1¾ pints) beef stock
1 tablespoon Worcestershire sauce
1 tablespoon English mustard
flaky sea salt and freshly ground black pepper

To make the pastry, combine the butter, flour and salt in a bowl, then add just enough water to bring it together into a dough. Form into a rectangular shape with your hands and, on a well-floured surface, roll out in one direction away from you, so you have a rectangle about 1cm (½in) thick. Fold the two short ends into the middle so they overlap. Give the pastry a quarter turn and repeat the rolling-and-folding process five more times. Wrap the pastry, then rest it in the fridge for 30 minutes–1 hour.

Preheat the oven to 200°C/400°F/gas mark 6.

Season the beef and kidney pieces, then toss them in the flour, shaking off any excess.

Set a large, heavy-based pan over a low–medium heat and add half the dripping. Once hot, add the steak and kidney pieces. Brown well on all sides, then lift out to a plate and set aside. You'll need to do this in batches.

Add the remaining dripping to the pan, followed by the sliced onions and garlic. Season with salt and pepper and cook for 10–12 minutes, or until soft and fragrant. Return the meat to the pan, along with the thyme and bay leaves. Pour in the ale and the stock and bring to a simmer. Add the Worcestershire sauce and mustard and stir everything well.

Cover (with the lid ajar) and cook in the oven for 1½ –2 hours, or until the meat is tender and the sauce thickened. If it looks a little dry at any point, add a splash of water to loosen it up again. Let the pie filling cool once it's ready.

Remove the pastry from the fridge and cut it into two pieces of two-thirds and one-third. Lightly grease a 1.2-litre (2-pint) pie dish with a little butter. Roll out the larger piece of pastry and use it to line the pie dish. Don't worry if you have some overhang, this gets trimmed off. Spoon in the steak and kidney pie filling, making sure you remove the bay leaves and herb stalks from the mix as you go. Roll out the smaller piece of pastry to form a lid. Brush the edges of the pastry base with some egg wash, lay on the lid and crimp the edges together. Trim away any excess pastry. Brush with more egg, then cut a vent in the centre of the pie.

Bake in the oven at 200°C/400°F/gas mark 6 for 45–50 minutes, or until golden brown. Leave to cool for 15 minutes, then serve with mash, winter greens and English mustard.

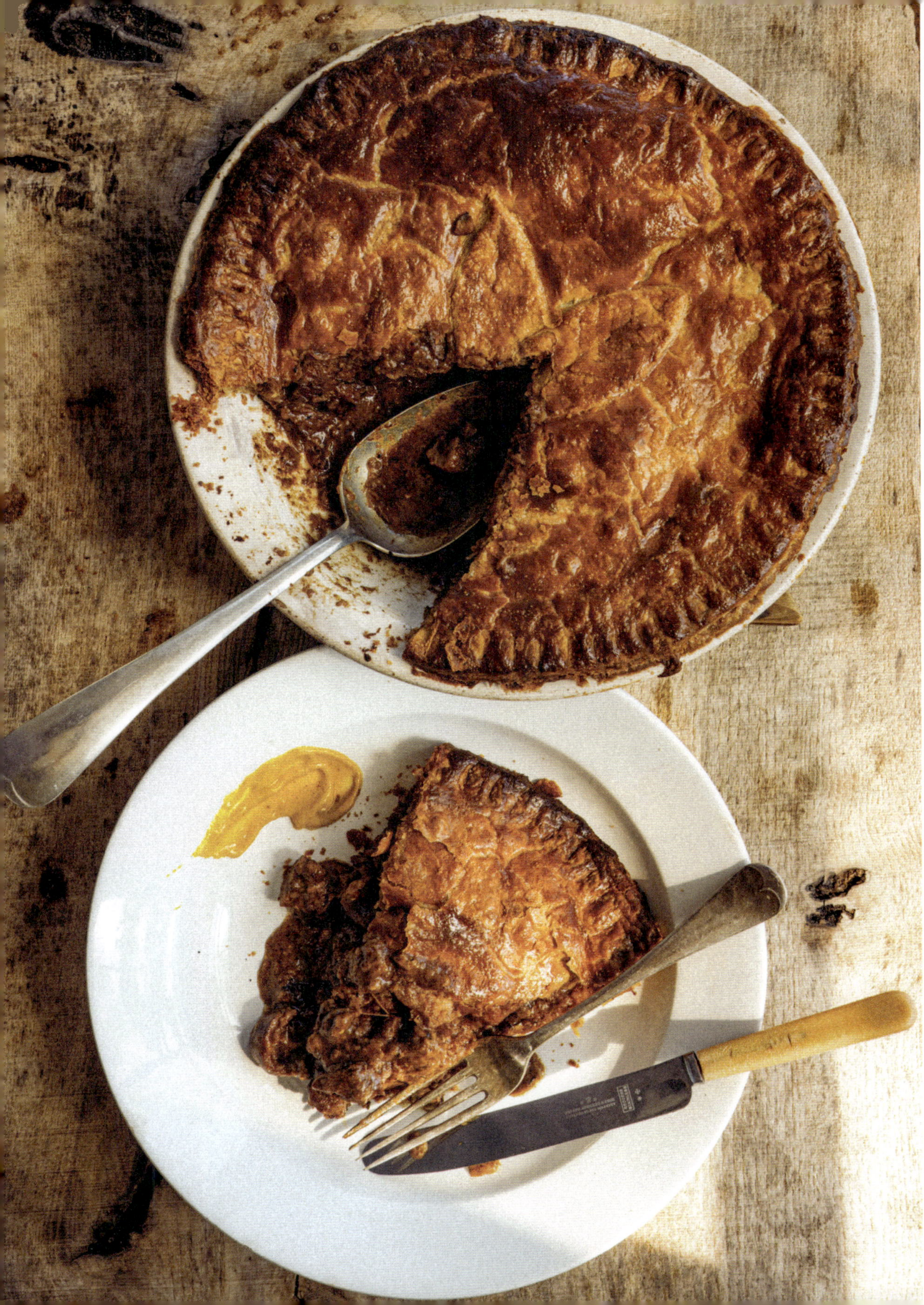

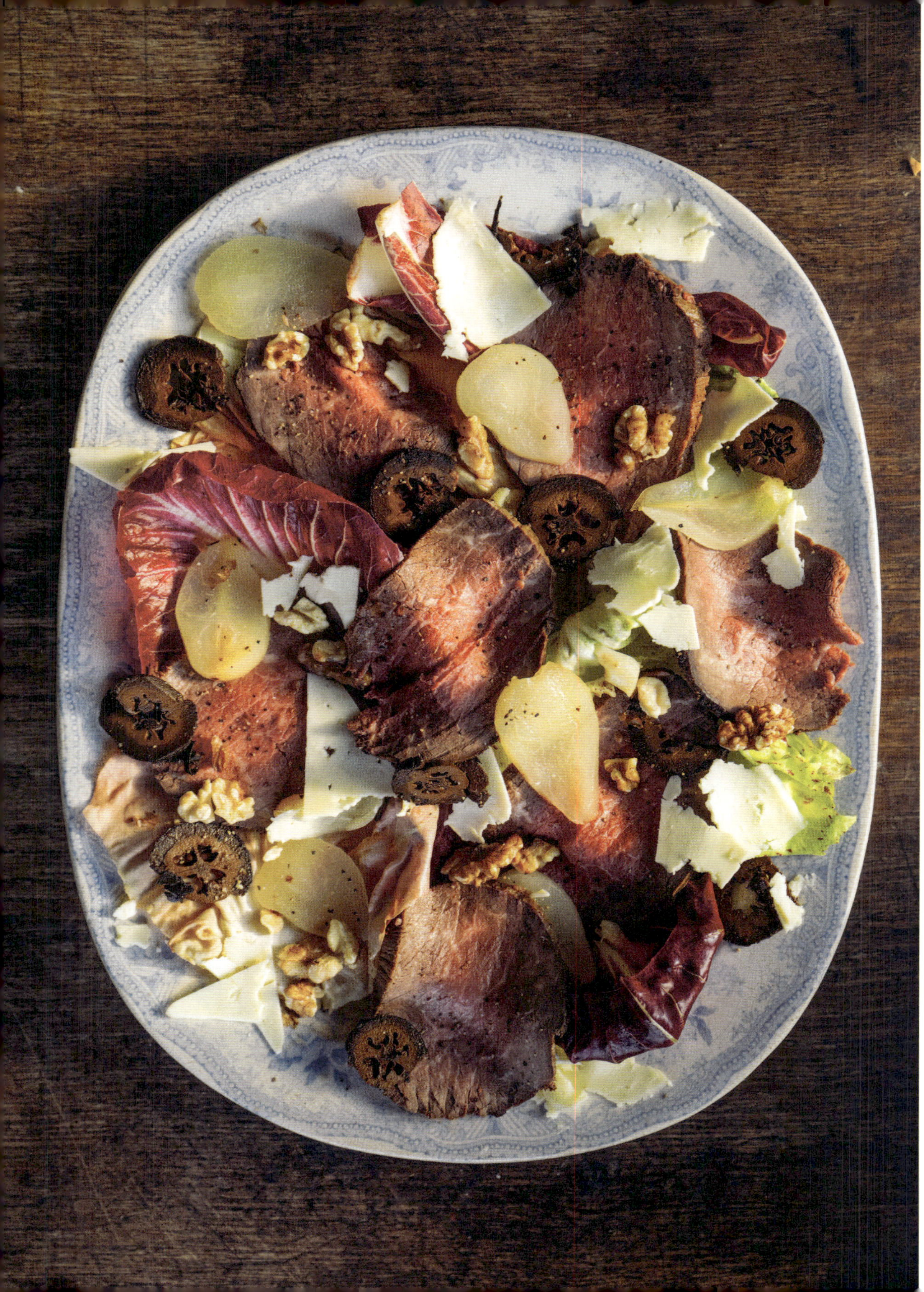

Rare Roast Beef with Radicchio, Pickled Pears & Wensleydale

Cheese was traditionally a way for farmers to preserve leftover milk, especially for the winter months. Britain once had thousands of farmhouse cheeses, but they dwindled first when the acts of enclosure pushed smallholders off the land, however it was the Second World War that led to the most existential crisis for small cheesemakers. During rationing, milk was reserved in greater amounts for drinking, and the only cheese that was made was 'Government Cheddar' – a homogenised block of cheddar-style cheese. Wensleydale, like most British cheeses, was almost destroyed in the post-war drive towards mass production. Fortunately, the centuries-old recipe for Wensleydale was preserved, and a growing number of artisans are starting to make it again. I love to make this recipe the day after a big roast, when there is beautiful, rare roast beef calling to me from the fridge. After the previous day's indulgence, I'm after something a little fresher, yet hearty nonetheless. The rich, buttery, yoghurty flavour of Wenslydale works so well alongside the sharp pickles, bitter leaves and meaty, minerally beef.

1 tablespoon grass-fed beef dripping
1kg (2lb 4oz) grass-fed beef topside (you can also use leftover rare roast beef from your Sunday roast – around 8–9 slices)
100g (3½oz) radicchio, separated into leaves
1–2 Pickled Pears (see page 148)
3–4 pickled walnuts
75g (2¾oz) raw milk Wensleydale cheese
50 whole walnuts, toasted
a drizzle of extra virgin olive oil
flaky sea salt and freshly ground black pepper

Take the beef out of the fridge an hour before you want to cook it, to let it come up to room temperature. Preheat the oven to 180°C/350°F/gas mark 4.

Generously season the beef with salt and pepper. Place a 25 x 35cm (10 x 14in) roasting tray on the hob over a high heat, add the beef dripping and allow to sizzle, then sear the beef for a few minutes until browned all over.

Transfer the roasting tray to the oven and roast for 25–30 minutes, keeping the beef rare to medium rare. If you are using a meat thermometer, aim for 50°C (120°F). Remove from the oven and leave to rest uncovered for 25 minutes before carving.

Once cooled and rested, very finely slice the beef and lay on to a platter along with the radicchio leaves. Slice the pickled pears, pickled walnuts and Wenslydale and lay onto the platter. Scatter over the toasted walnuts, giving them a little crush with your hand as you do so. Season the whole dish with a small pinch of salt and a more generous pinch of black pepper, then finish with a little drizzle of good quality extra virgin olive oil. Serve alongside some really good-quality bread.

Venison Shoulder with Bacon, Mushrooms & Chestnuts

While this recipe may look rather impressive, it is unbelievably simple to make. It's a case of bringing a few good ingredients together and letting the magic of time and heat turn the component parts into a rich, hearty meal that is both extremely nourishing and very delicious. Simply stick it all in the oven and forget about it until your rumbling tummy reminds you it's time to indulge.

a drizzle of rapeseed oil (or 1 teaspoon lard)
250g (9oz) smoked bacon lardons
1 onion, finely chopped
2 carrots, finely chopped
1 celery stick, finely chopped
3–4 bay leaves
2 sprigs of rosemary
4 garlic cloves, bashed, then chopped
100g (3½oz) dried porcini mushrooms
175ml (6fl oz) red wine
1.5 litres (2¾ pints) beef stock, warmed
1kg (2lb 4oz) venison shoulder
100g (3½oz) chestnut mushrooms, large ones quartered, small ones left whole or halved
100g (3½oz) chestnuts, chopped
flaky sea salt and freshly ground black pepper

Preheat the oven to 150°C/300°F/gas mark 2.

Set a large, lidded, cast-iron casserole pan over a medium heat. Drizzle in the fat, then add the bacon lardons. Sizzle the lardons for around 5–6 minutes until they have rendered down and become golden and crispy.

Turn the heat down and add the onion, carrots, celery, bay leaves, rosemary and a pinch of salt. Cook until the veg have softened and are smelling sweet, around 7–8 minutes. Add the garlic and cook for a further 3–4 minutes, ensuring you don't catch it.

Place the porcini mushrooms into a small bowl and pour over some boiling water. Leave them to soak for around 5 minutes, then drain and discard the water. Keeping most of them quite chunky, slice down any very large mushrooms and add them to the pan.

Turn the heat back up and pour in the red wine. Allow it to bubble up and reduce slightly, then pour in all the beef stock.

Generously season the venison shoulder all over and submerge in the pan. Cover with the lid and place into the oven. Cook gently for 2 hours.

Remove the casserole from the oven and carefully turn the venison shoulder over. Scatter in the chopped mushrooms and chestnuts. Top up the liquid if it is looking a little dry. Place the lid back on, slide the pan back into the centre of the oven and cook for another 1 hour.

Remove the casserole from the oven and check the texture of the meat. By now, it should be completely tender and falling off the bone. Spoon out generous portions of the tender meat, mushrooms and chestnuts into warmed bowls, with plenty of the rich sauce, and serve alongside buttery mash and seasonal greens.

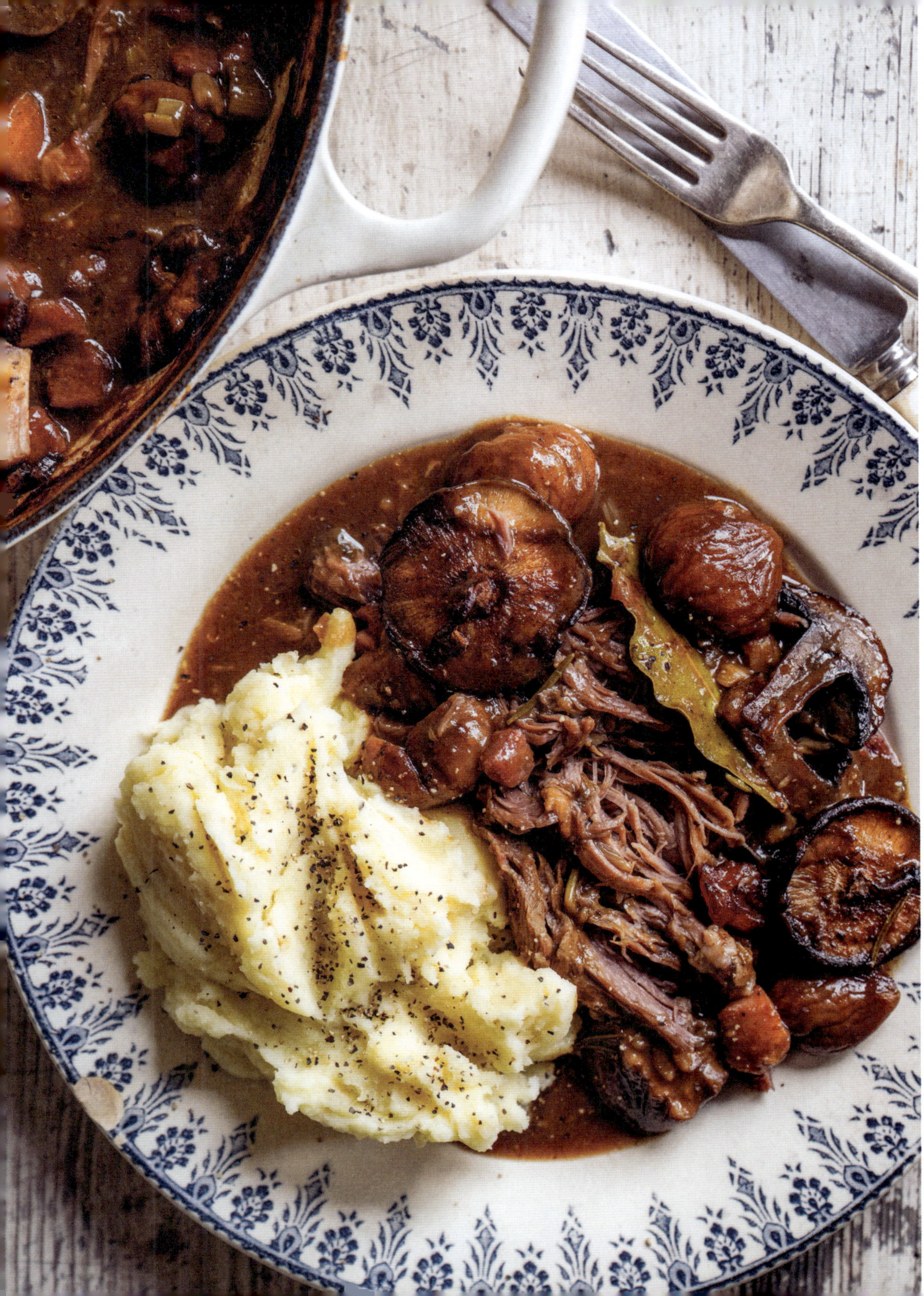

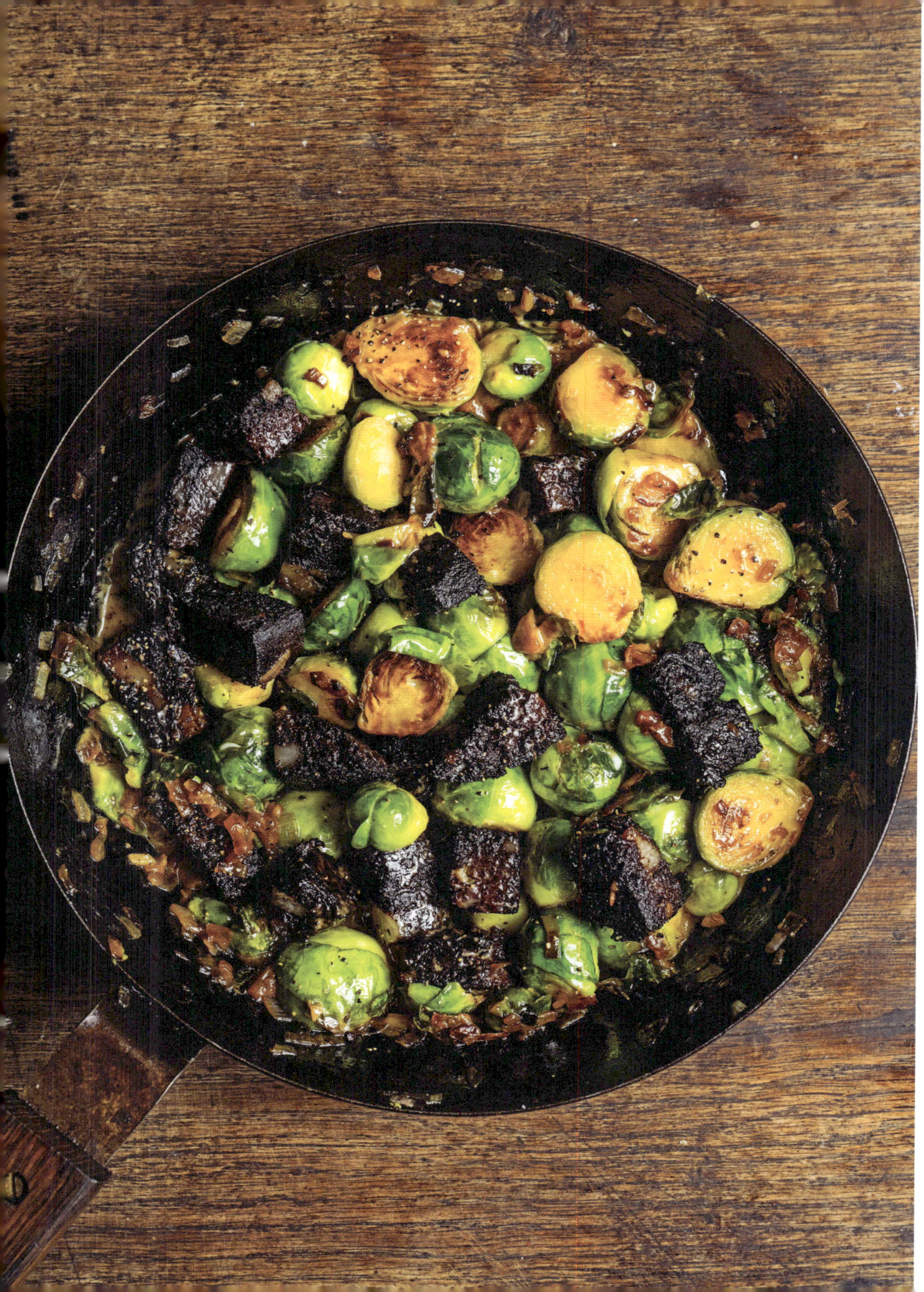

SERVES 4 Winter

Creamed Brussels Sprouts with Black Pudding

I live in a family of sprout haters. Often around the dinner table questions of my legitimacy arise due to my ardent adoration of this small, green, pungent brassica, to the rest of my family's fervent disdain. Never one to ignore a challenge, I have cooked sprouts in a multitude of ways to garner deserved affection by the dubious crowd. Grated raw, gratinated, roasted and tossed through cider vinegar, spiced, hidden in pasta … you name it, I've tried it. All of which efforts have been greeted with a roll of the eyes and a lukewarm reception. Frankly, I have given up. My beloved sprouts deserve better than this, some people are simply lacking in good taste! To cement my feelings, I have paired my delicious sprouts with another ingredient that many find troublesome, black pudding. It's a match made in heaven. These two oddballs co-exist wonderfully as an indulgent side dish perfect for a Henry VII-inspired festive banquet.

a knob of grass-fed butter
1 onion, finely sliced
5 garlic cloves, finely sliced
500g (1lb 2oz) Brussels sprouts, shredded
a few sprigs of thyme
a few sprigs of rosemary
100g (3½oz) black pudding
125ml (5fl oz) dry white wine
150ml (5fl oz) double cream
¼ teaspoon grated nutmeg
flaky sea salt and freshly ground black pepper

Place a cast-iron frying pan over a medium heat. Add the butter and let it sizzle slightly, then add the onion, garlic and a pinch of salt. Sweat the onion down for around 5–6 minutes. Increase the heat slightly and add the shredded Brussels sprouts and herbs. Once the sprouts have browned slightly, about 2 minutes, crumble in the black pudding and cook for a further minute, moving the black pudding around the pan. Pour in the wine and allow it to bubble up and reduce, then pour in the cream and allow it to thicken. This should take just a couple of minutes.

Remove from the heat, check the seasoning and adjust as necessary. Sprinkle over some nutmeg and serve warm as a super-indulgent side dish.

Winter

SERVES 4

Tuscan-style Sausagemeat Broth

This simple rustic soup is hearty and warming and packed full of vegetables, beans and peas, simply perfect to give your gut all the nourishment it needs to thrive during these brutal winter months. With a sprinkling of turmeric, rich in phytonutrients, this brothy soup is full to the brim with antioxidants, fibre and vitamins.

50g (1¾oz) lentils
50g (1¾oz) green split peas
25g (1oz) split marrowfat peas
25g (1oz) split fava beans
25g (1oz) barley flakes
1 litre (1¾ pints) chicken stock
a drizzle of olive oil
1 medium white onion
1 medium carrot
4 large garlic cloves
3 bay leaves
a few sprigs of rosemary
1 teaspoon turmeric
1 teaspoon cumin seeds
3–4 plain pork sausages
a small bunch of kale
flaky sea salt and freshly ground black pepper

The night before, put the lentils, peas, beans and barley flakes into a bowl and fill with cold water, then leave overnight to soak.

The next morning, tip the mix into a colander and give it a thorough rinse. Tip the mix into a saucepan and pour in the stock. Set the pan over a medium heat and bring to the boil, then immediately turn down the heat and leave the broth to simmer with the lid on for 40 minutes.

Meanwhile, set a cast-iron frying pan over a medium heat and drizzle in a little oil. Tip in the onions, carrots and garlic, along with a pinch of salt, and fry until soft. Add the bay leaves and rosemary along with the turmeric and cumin seeds, and cook for 2–3 minutes.

Take the sausages and slit the skins open. Squeeze the sausagemeat into the pan and discard the skins. Fry the sausage meat together with the veg and herbs until beautifully crisp, then scrape the sausagemeat, veg and herbs into the simmering broth.

Take the kale and strip the leaves from each stalk. Roughly chop the leaves and scatter into the broth, cooking for 2–3 minutes. Check the seasoning and adjust with a pinch of salt and pepper if required.

Remove the broth from the heat and ladle out into warmed bowls. Serve alongside some warm, buttery bread.

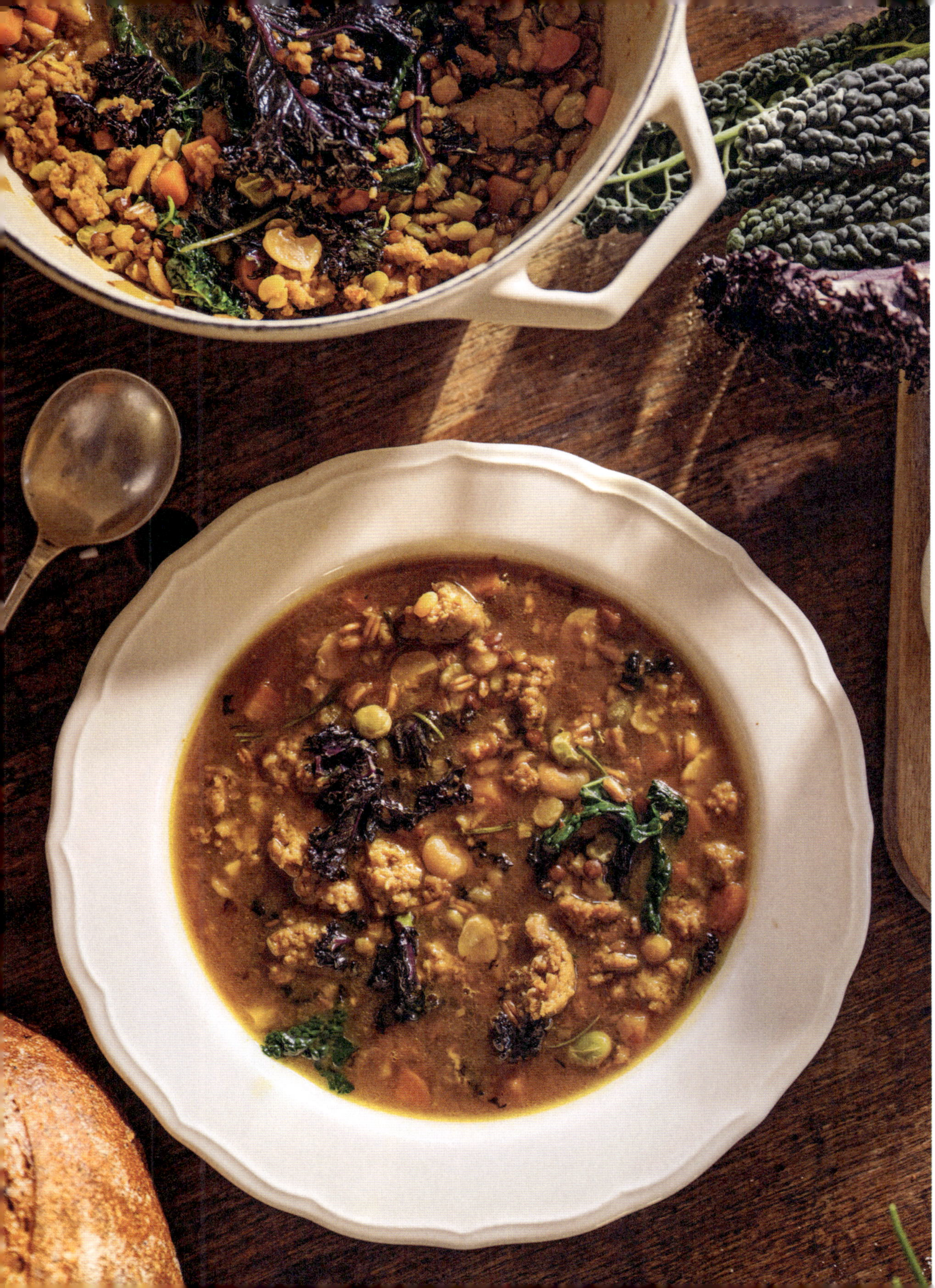

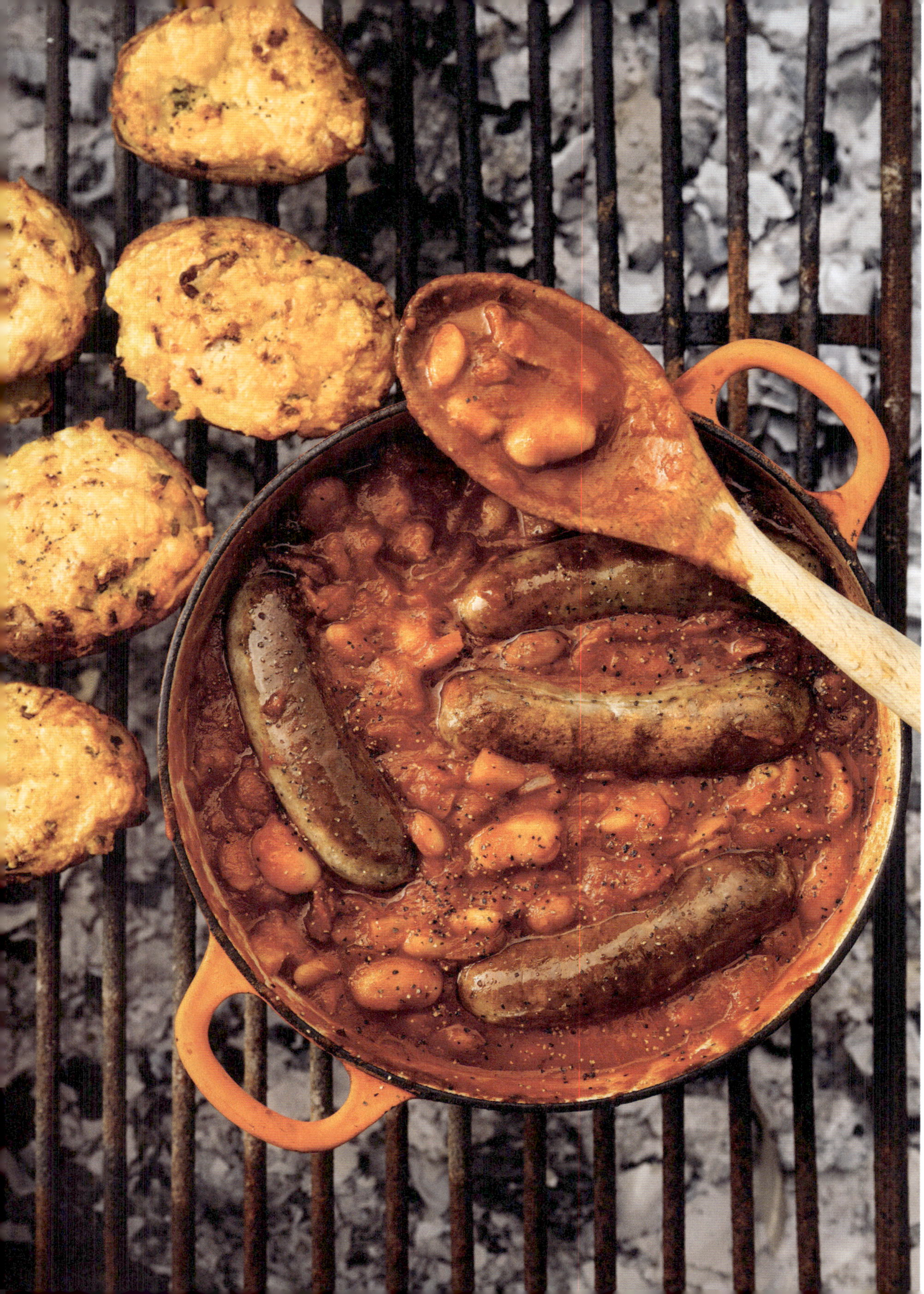

Loaded Baked Potatoes with Sausage & Bean Stew

This is the perfect feast to make ahead for chilly events, such as Bonfire Night or winter parties. Not only is this dish packed full of nourishment, but it is also so simple to put togethe – all you need to do is warm everything through and serve, leaving you time to gather with your friends and family.

For the loaded baked potatoes

4 baking potatoes (I like to use a variety called Triplo)
a drizzle of rapeseed oil
4 rashers of smoked streaky bacon
225g (8oz) clothbound Cheddar cheese, grated
175ml (6fl oz) sour cream
4 spring onions, finely sliced
1 tablespoon Worcestershire sauce
flaky sea salt and freshly ground black pepper

For the sausage and bean stew

a drizzle of rapeseed oil or ½ teaspoon free-range or organic pork lard
8 free-range or organic sausages
1 onion, finely chopped
2 celery sticks, finely chopped
2 carrots, finely chopped
3 garlic cloves, finely sliced
2–3 bay leaves
a few sprigs of thyme
3 teaspoons smoked paprika
1 teaspoon ground cumin
1 red pepper, deseeded and roughly chopped
1 teaspoon Dijon mustard
2 tablespoons cider vinegar
500ml (18fl oz) passata
400g (14oz) jar of Bold Bean Co butter beans
400g (14oz) jar of Bold Bean Co white beans
flaky sea salt and freshly ground pepper

To make the loaded baked potatoes, preheat the oven to 200°C/400°F/gas mark 6. Prick the potatoes all over, then place them in the oven for 1½ hours.

Meanwhile, make the sausage and bean stew. Set a large casserole dish over a medium heat, add a little fat and allow it to sizzle. Add the sausages and fry off for 2–3 minutes until caramelized, then remove from the pan and set aside.

Turn the heat down and add the onion, celery, carrots, garlic, bay leaves and thyme, along with a big pinch of salt. Gently fry until the veg is soft and smelling sweet. Add the paprika and cumin and leave it to toast for about a minute, then add the chopped pepper, mustard and cider vinegar, allowing the vinegar to bubble up and evaporate.

Pour in the passata along with the beans and their broth and give everything a good stir. Check the seasoning and make any adjustments with salt and pepper.

Place the sausages back into the pan and cook uncovered for about 30 minutes, or until the sauce has thickened and the flavours have intensified.

Turn your attention back to the jacket potatoes. Once the skins are crisp and the insides are fluffy, remove them from the oven and leave to cool a little.

Meanwhile drizzle a little oil into a frying pan and add the bacon, sizzling it until it is crispy and golden. Set to one side.

As soon as you can handle the hot potatoes, cut them in half lengthways and scoop the insides into a mixing bowl. Put the potato skins on to a tray and place back into the oven to crisp for a further 1–2 minutes. Remove from the oven and set aside.

To the mixing bowl, add the grated cheese, sour cream, spring onions, crispy bacon, Worcestershire sauce and a generous pinch each of salt and pepper. Combine the ingredients well, then fill each crispy potato skin with the mixture.

If you like, you could transfer the casserole dish filled with stew to a barbecue or campfire outside. Wrap the loaded potato skins in foil and nestle them in the coolest part of the fire or leave them on the grill to warm through. Gather your guests around and ladle out generous helpings of the stew into bowls and serve with a loaded potato on the side.

Slow-Cooked Kale & Celeriac Mash on Toast with Fried Eggs

Howling winds and angry lashings of rain spread wild across the countryside. Autumn is throwing a tantrum as she gives way to winter's frosty grip. Gone is her warm embrace, her gentle touch of golden light and softly falling leaves. Something darker and sharper is heading our way, forcing even the hardiest of us to spend more time inside. As the cold sets in and the morning light takes much longer to appear, it feels as though time has slowed. The outside world becomes still as I watch, warm mug in hand, from my kitchen window. The outside world can wait for a while; for now, I make the most of sluggish mornings with slowly stirred breakfasts, hearty enough to keep the biting cold at bay.

a knob of grass-fed butter
1 onion, finely sliced
4 garlic cloves, finely chopped
1 head of kale (I use cavolo nero), leaves stripped, stalks roughly chopped
150ml (5fl oz) chicken stock, warmed
1 tablespoon crème fraîche
50g (1¾oz) hard cheese (I like to use Old Winchester, but you could use Parmesan)
a pinch of grated nutmeg
flaky sea salt and freshly ground black pepper

For the celeriac mash
grass-fed butter
½ small celeriac, peeled and diced into small cubes
250ml (9fl oz) chicken stock, warmed
a pinch of grated nutmeg
flaky sea salt and freshly ground black pepper

To serve
2–4 eggs
2–4 slices of sourdough
a drizzle of extra virgin olive oil
1 garlic clove, peeled
a pinch of black pepper
a few sprigs of rosemary

Set a cast-iron pan over a medium heat, add a little butter along with the onion and gently sweat for 6–7 minutes until softened. Add the garlic and kale stalks and cook for 2–3 minutes, then add the shredded kale leaves along with a pinch of salt and half of the stock. Cook slowly over a low heat for about 15 minutes until the kale is tender. Add the rest of the stock and turn the heat up to let it bubble for a further 5–6 minutes. Remove from the heat and stir in the crème fraîche, cheese, nutmeg and some black pepper. Check the seasoning and set aside.

To make the celeriac mash, place a cast-iron pan over a medium heat and add a knob of butter along with the diced celeriac and a pinch of salt. Cook for 7–8 minutes, or until the celeriac has started to caramelise. Pour in the stock, stirring slowly, and cook until the liquid has been absorbed and the celeriac has started to collapse. Use a fork to gently mash the celeriac, then add a couple of knobs of butter, a pinch each of salt and pepper and the nutmeg. Set aside.

Fry the eggs and toast the bread.

When everything is ready, take a slice of toast and rub it with a little oil and the clove of garlic. Slather on a helping of buttery mash, then spoon on the slow-cooked kale and top with a fried egg. Finish with a pinch of black pepper and a few sprigs of rosemary. To make this a more carnivorous feast, you could top the toasts with crispy bacon, crumbled black pudding or even sliced sausage.

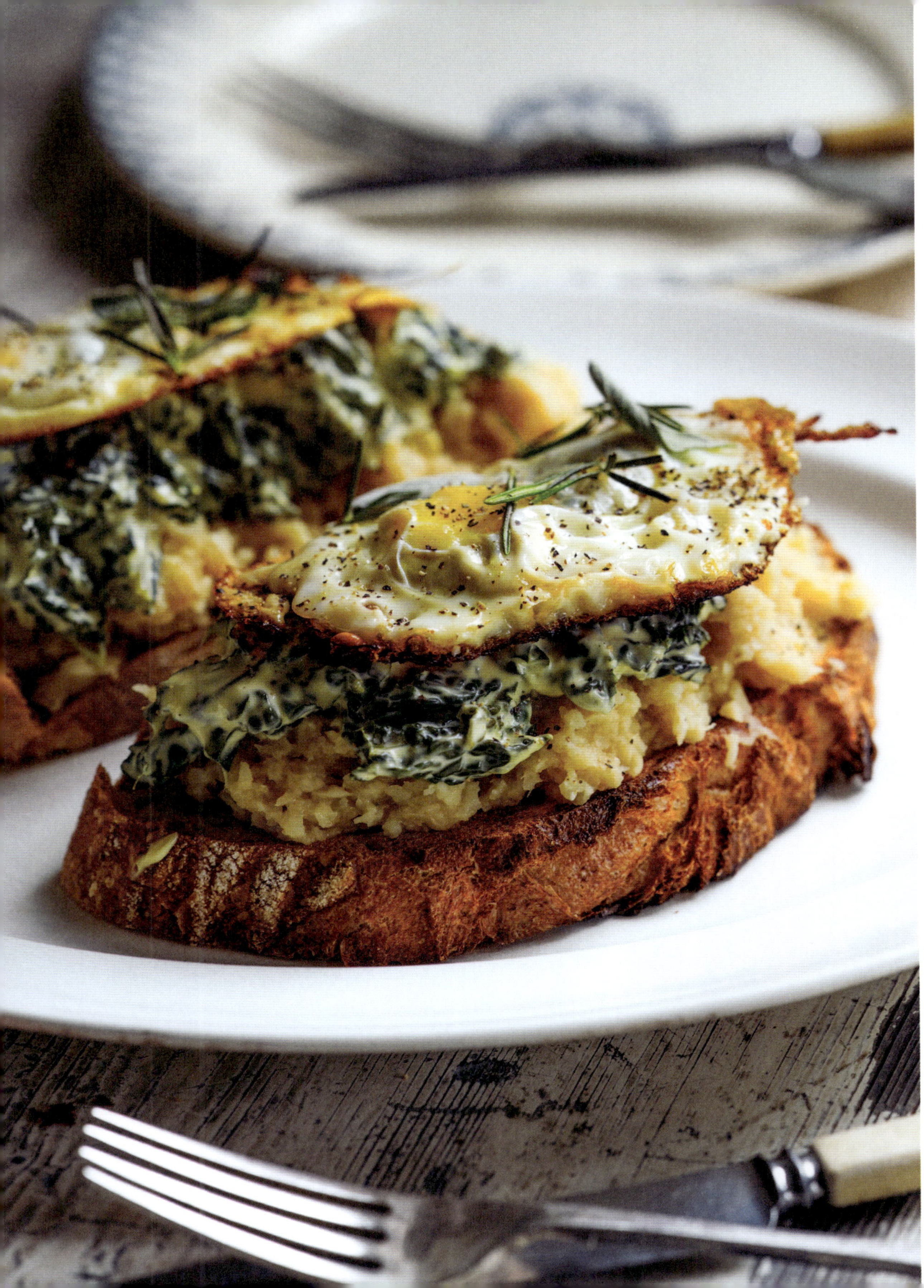

Winter

Smoked Haddock, Kale & Butter Bean Gratin

SERVES 4

One of the joys of living in Devon is the vast diversity of produce that one can find locally. With inshore fisheries active up and down my home county's coastline, I am never sort of beautiful, sparkling fresh fish. There are even a handful of traditional smokeries left, where sides of fish are meticulously prepared, carefully cured and kiln-smoked over woodchips.

A note on haddock. At the time of writing this, haddock stocks are strong, however haddock is a naturally fluctuating stock. It can easily be caught as bycatch, making it known as a 'choke species'. A choke species is a fish that is caught by accident while targeting other species, and if caught in excess of its quota, can cause fishing on the target species to stop. Unlike much of what we consume on land, the seasonality and sustainability of seafood fluctuates wildly, so it is important to check sustainability ratings regularly and make swaps to species that are in abundance. In this recipe, smoked haddock can easily be swapped for smoked pollack or smoked trout.

500ml (18fl oz) double cream
4 garlic cloves, peeled and finely sliced
a few sprigs of thyme
a big pinch of black pepper
a pinch of flaky sea salt
650g (1lb 7oz) sustainably caught smoked haddock
200g (7oz) kale
800g (1lb 12oz) canned butter beans
100g (3½oz) Lincolnshire Poacher cheese

Preheat the oven to 190°C/375°F/gas mark 5.

Set a saucepan over a medium heat. Pour in the cream, add the garlic, thyme sprigs and a pinch of black pepper and bring to the boil, taking care to swiftly remove the pan from the heat once it comes to a boil. Season the cream with a pinch of salt and let it sit for 10 minutes.

Remove the skin from the smoked haddock, then cut it into chunks. Slice the kale, stalks and all. Open the beans and drain away the liquid.

Place the smoked haddock, kale and butter beans in a casserole dish, then pour over the fragrant cream and grate the Lincolnshire Poacher over the top. Bake in the oven for 20 minutes until bubbling and lightly coloured on top.

Ladle into warmed bowls and serve alongside crusty bread, ready for dipping into the creamy sauce.

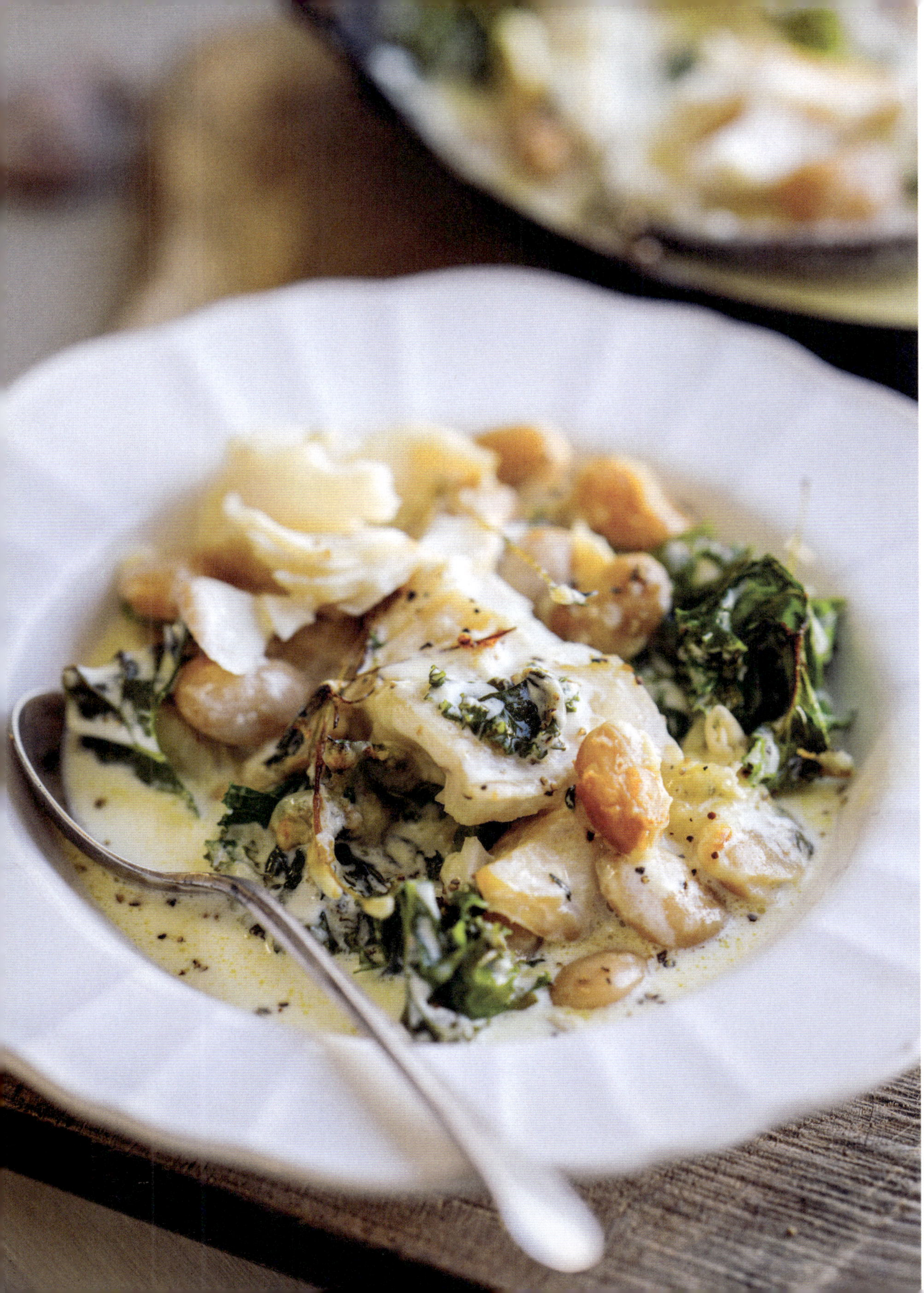

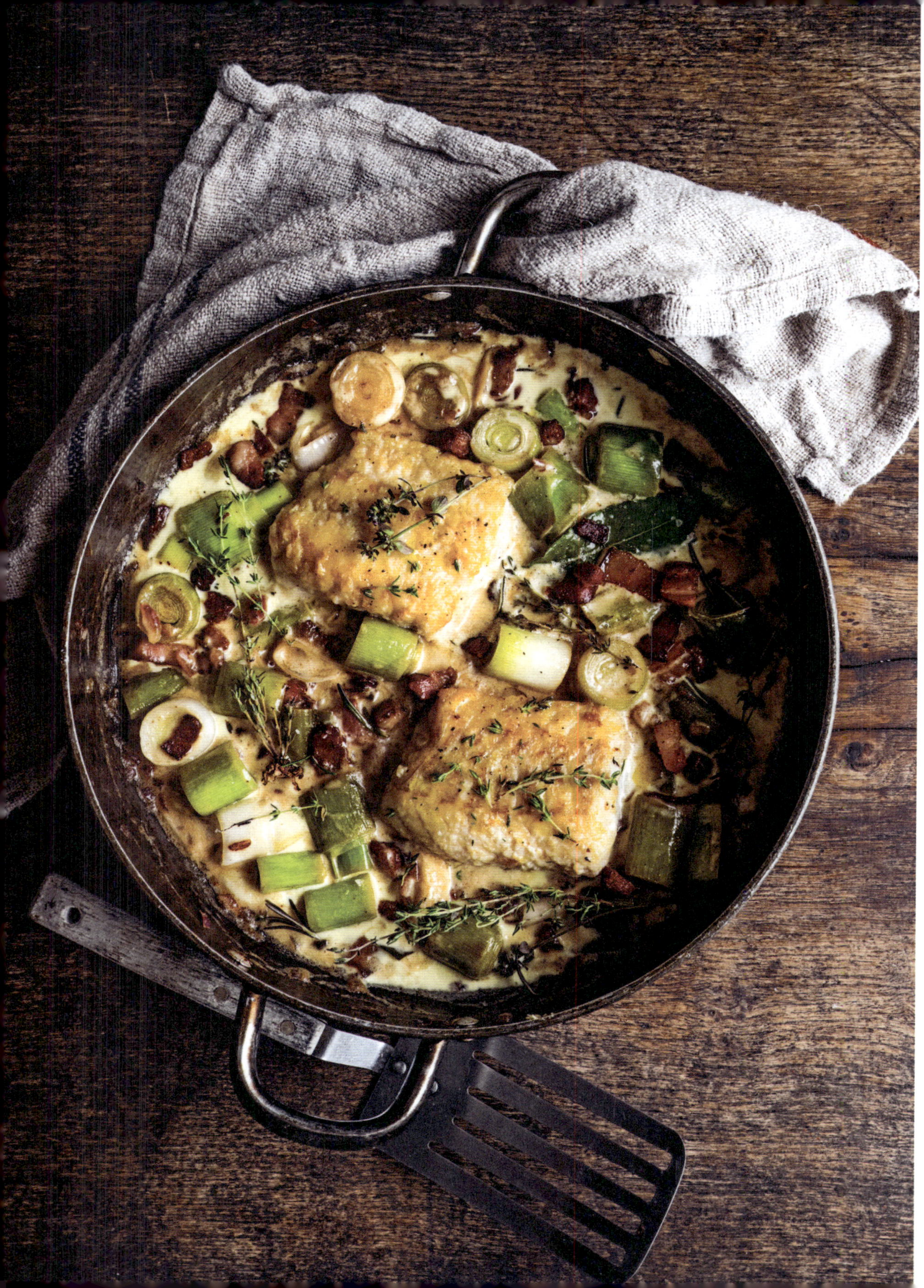

SERVES 4   Winter

Line-Caught Coley with Leeks & Bacon

Saithe, coalfish, pitlock, gilpin, Blockan, sillack, greylord ... the vast array of appellations for this special species of fish tells you something of its past. It was only a hundred years or so ago that coley was a central component of the British diet, however over time we have practically erased it from our consciousness. Coley has been replaced in our diets by the likes of cod, tuna, salmon and prawns, each hugely problematic in their vastly declining stocks, catch methods and use of modern-day slavery ever-present in large-scale fisheries around the world. A cold-water-loving fish, coley is similar in taste, texture and biology to pollack and cod. With sea temperatures rising, we are likely to see fewer of this once wildly abundant species in Devon and Cornwall, with larger catches now found amongst the Scottish isles.

2 sustainably caught coley fillets
25g (1oz) stoneground white flour, for dusting
a drizzle of organic rapeseed oil
a knob of grass-fed butter
250g (9oz) smoked bacon lardons
1 small onion, finely chopped
1 celery stick, finely chopped
2 leeks, finely sliced
4 garlic cloves, peeled and bashed
a sprig of thyme, leaves picked
2 bay leaves
a splash of cider vinegar
150ml (5fl oz) white wine
75ml (2½fl oz) double cream
flaky sea salt and freshly ground black pepper

Generously season the fish fillets with salt. Add the flour to a bowl and gently toss the fillets through it until each is lightly dusted.

Place a cast-iron pan over a medium–high heat, drizzle in a little oil and add a small knob of butter. Place the fish in the pan and fry on one side for 3 minutes until just golden, then flip over and fry on the other side for a further 2–3 minutes, or until just golden. Remove the fish from the pan and set aside.

To the same pan, add the bacon lardons and cook until they have rendered and are golden and crispy, this should take around 6–7 minutes. Remove the crispy lardons from the pan and set aside.

Add the onion, celery, leeks, garlic, thyme and bay leaves to the pan and cook until soft, about 7–8 minutes. Increase the heat and add the vinegar, allowing the liquid to evaporate and a sauce to begin to form. Add the wine and bubble over a high heat for a further 1–2 minutes until the alcohol has cooked off. Reduce the heat and add the cream. Allow the cream to bubble up before placing the fish and lardons back into the pan. Cover and simmer for 8–10 minutes.

Check the seasoning and add a generous pinch of black pepper. Serve alongside some crusty bread, which is perfect for mopping up the sauce.

Winter SERVES 4

Seafood Tagine

During the colder months I often turn to one-pot cooking, such as this enjoyable dish that sees sustainable coley and red mullet gently simmered in a richly spiced and fragrant tomato Moroccan tagine. A wonderful weeknight dinner that celebrates seafood in all its glory.

a drizzle of extra virgin olive oil
2 carrots, peeled and chopped
2 celery sticks, finely chopped
5cm (2in) knob of fresh root ginger, grated
2 garlic cloves, grated
2 green chillies, deseeded and sliced
200ml (7fl oz) boiling water
400g (14oz) Preserved Tomatoes (see page 77)
1 red pepper, deseeded and sliced
200g (7oz) preserved lemons, pith removed and rind sliced
a good pinch of flaky sea salt
a pinch of saffron
2 red mullet fillets, diced into cubes
1 coley fillet, skin removed and diced into cubes
200g (7oz) can of chickpeas, drained
80g (3oz) black olives
a bunch of fresh mint, leaves picked

For the tagine paste
2 red onions, chopped
3 garlic cloves
a small knob of fresh root ginger, peeled
100ml (3½fl oz) lemon juice (from about 3 lemons)
100ml (3½fl oz) extra virgin olive oil
1 tablespoon honey
1 tablespoon ground cumin
1 tablespoon paprika
1 tablespoon ground turmeric
1 tablespoon hot chilli powder
handful of fresh coriander, chopped

First make the tagine paste, simply tip all the paste ingredients into a blender and give them a good whizz for a couple of minutes.

Place a casserole dish over a medium heat, drizzle in a little olive oil, add the carrots and celery and gently cook for about 8–10 minutes until soft. Add the tagine paste and cook it out for 2–3 minutes, then add the ginger, garlic and chillies and cook for a couple of minutes. Add the boiling water, stir well and increase the heat to bring to a simmer. Add the tomatoes, pepper and preserved lemons and season well with salt. Stir in the saffron and leave for a couple of minutes until it starts to smell fragrant. Add the fish along with the chickpeas and olives and simmer for a further 4–5 minutes, or until the fish is cooked through.

Scatter a few mint leaves over the dish and serve with flatbreads or couscous.

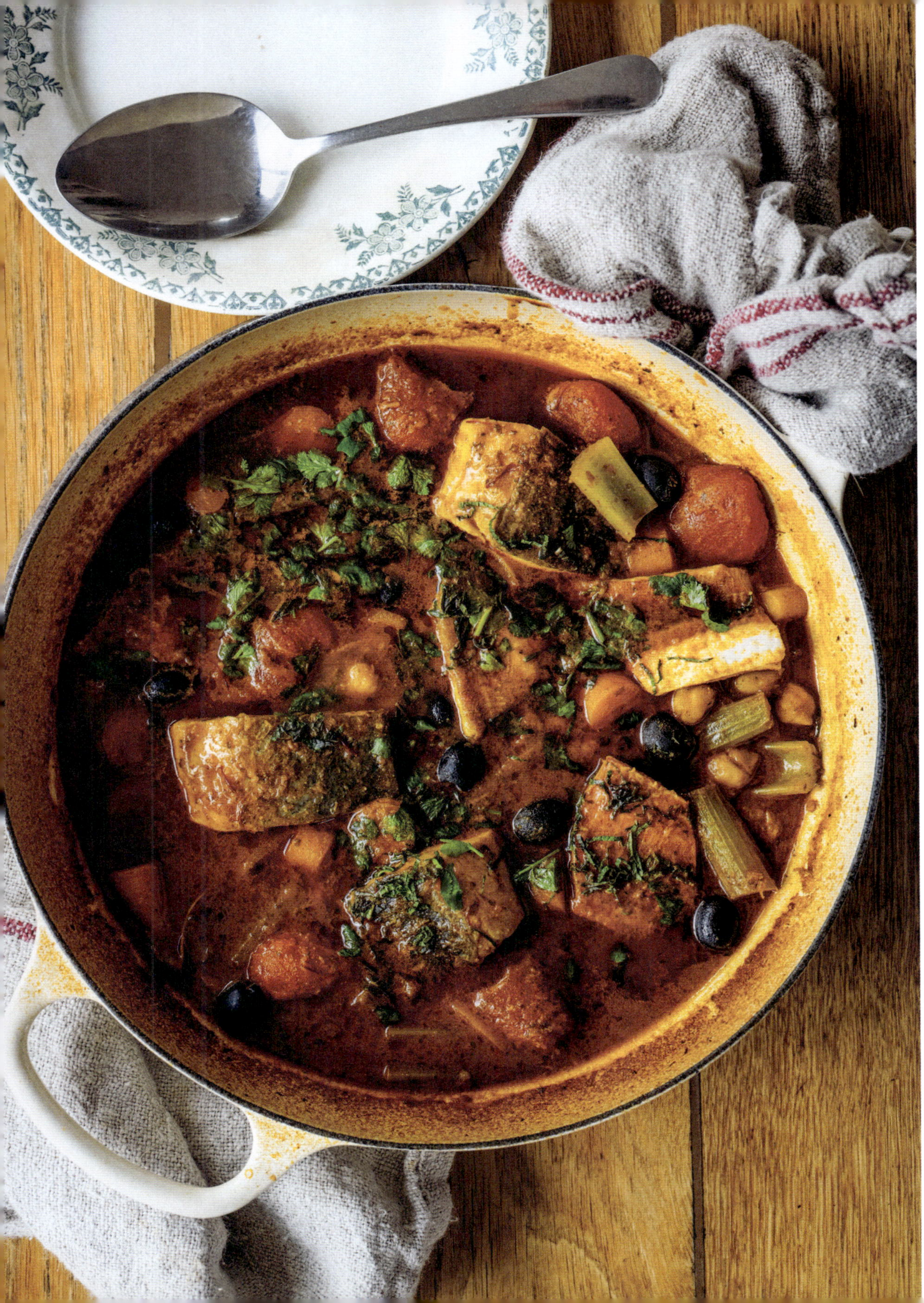

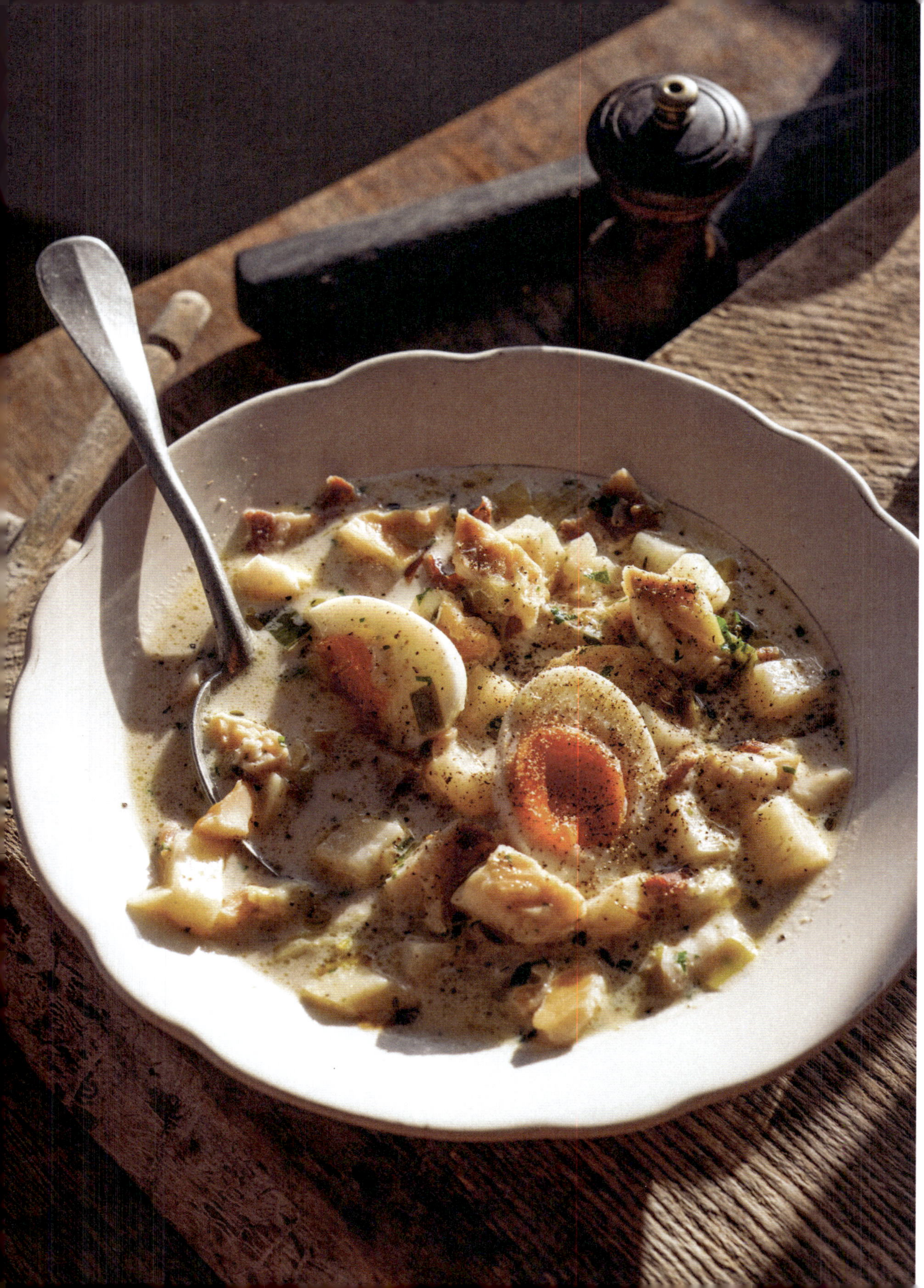

SERVES 4

Winter Fish Chowder

One could view fish chowder as a rather chaotic scene: meat, seafood, vegetables, hot stock and cream, each vying for center stage. What starts out as a jumbled crowd, with a little gentle coaxing soon becomes a harmonious chorus, as each carefully chosen ingredient makes its unique contribution to the finished dish.

2 tablespoons extra virgin olive oil
150g (5½oz) smoked bacon lardons
2 garlic cloves, finely chopped
2 leeks, finely chopped
a small bunch of thyme, leaves picked
400g (14oz) Maris Piper potatoes, peeled and cubed
750ml (1 1/3 pints) fish stock
175ml (6fl oz) double cream
1 sustainably caught British hake fillet, skin removed and cut into chunks
200g (7oz) sustainably caught British smoked haddock, skin removed and cut into chunks
a small bunch of parsley, roughly chopped
juice of 1 lemon
4 soft-boiled eggs, halved, to serve
flaky sea salt and freshly ground black pepper

Heat the oil in a large casserole dish over a medium heat and fry the lardons until completely crisp. Remove and set aside.

Add the garlic, leeks and thyme to the pan, along with a generous pinch of salt, and cook until soft and sweet. Return the lardons to the pan along with the potatoes. Fry for a minute, then tip in the stock and bring to the boil. Simmer for around 8 minutes, or until the potatoes have just started to become tender.

Add the cream and bring the contents of the pan back to a simmer, then add the fish and the chopped parsley and cook for a further 2–3 minutes until the fish is lightly cooked.

Remove the pan from the heat, squeeze in the lemon juice, then taste and adjust the seasoning.

Ladle the chowder into bowls, making sure that everyone gets an egg or two.

Warm Winter Cheese Board

You might think I'm bonkers, but I love cooking outside in winter. While a beautiful warm summer's day clearly has its charms, standing over a ferocious fire with its unrelenting heat isn't always the most practical activity. Come winter, it's the best seat in the house. With a deep, dark sky full of stars, the flicker of flames and smoke wafting through the crisp night air, cooking over fire takes on a bewitching quality in winter. In most other circumstances I am an advocate for cooking over sustainable charcoal, as it saves your eyes from the acrid intensity of wood. However, every so often a recipe calls for wood smoke – this one is such. Cooking over wood adds a depth of smokiness to the fruit and cheese that elevates this dish into something transcendent.

1–2 bunches black grapes
4 figs, sliced in half
2 Baron Bigod roundels (or any other British artisan brie-style cheese)
50g (1¾oz) walnuts
a few sprigs of rosemary
a few sprigs of thyme
4–6 tablespoons runny honey
crackers and sourdough bread, to serve

Light the campfire and wait until the wood has turned to embers and started to form a grey coating.

Take a large cast-iron pan and nestle in the grapes and figs. Place the pan directly over a low–medium heat away from any roaring flames and cook for around 5–6 minutes until the fruit has just started to give.

Remove the pan from the heat and squeeze the cheese in and around the softening fruit. Sprinkle over the walnuts and herbs and place back over the fire, this time nearer a smoky flame. Watch as the cheese begins to melt around the edges. Once this has begun, drizzle over your first 2 tablespoons of honey. Allow the cheese to vigorously bubble and the fruit to collapse and combine with the aromatic herbs, this may take around 7–8 minutes. Once the cheese is volcanic, gooey and gorgeous, remove from the heat and decently drizzle with a further 3–4 spoonfuls of honey.

Dive in with fresh bread and crackers, scooping up the luscious fruit, cheese and nuts. A little charcuterie also makes a delicious pairing, fondue-style. Get creative and enjoy being outside in the wild at this magical time of year.

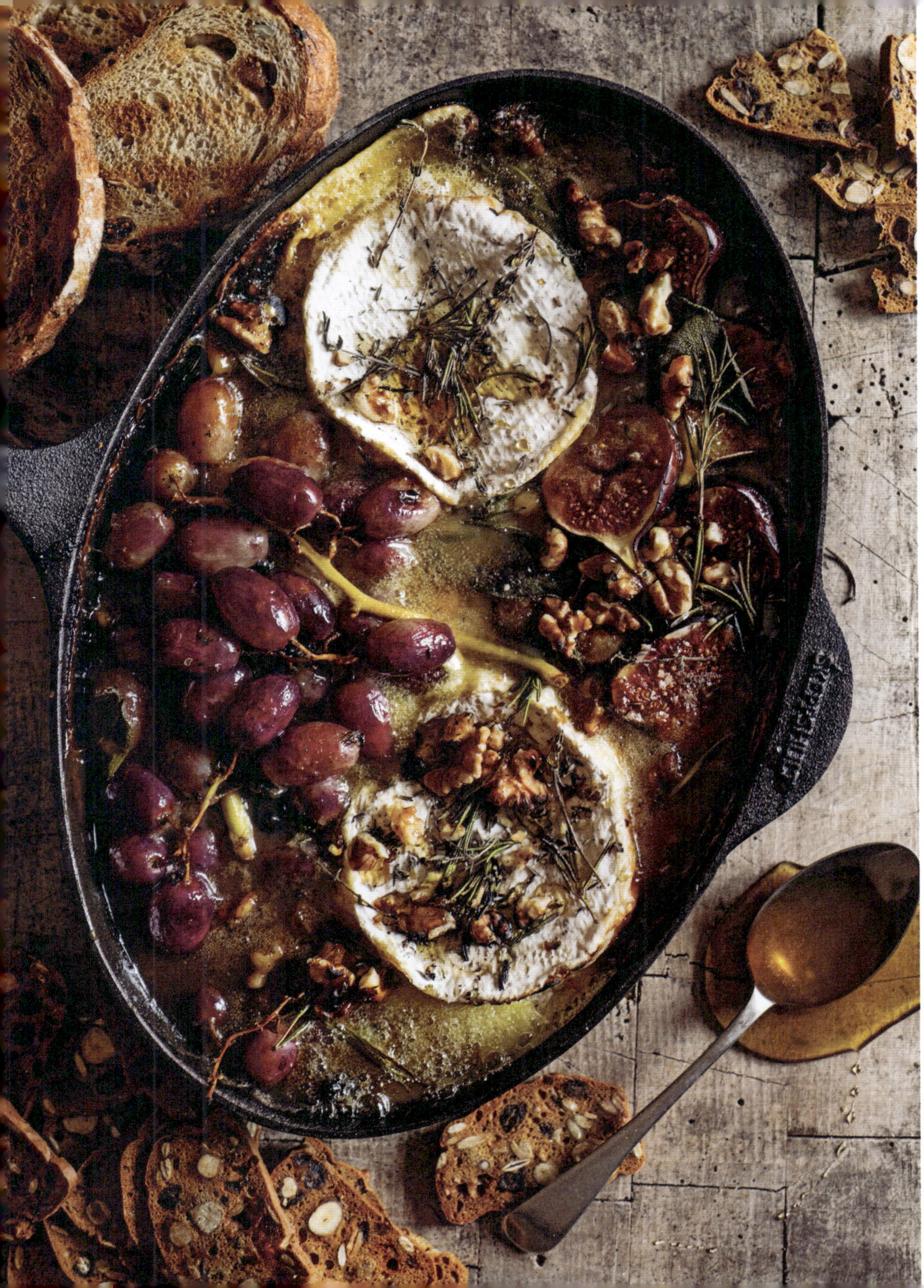

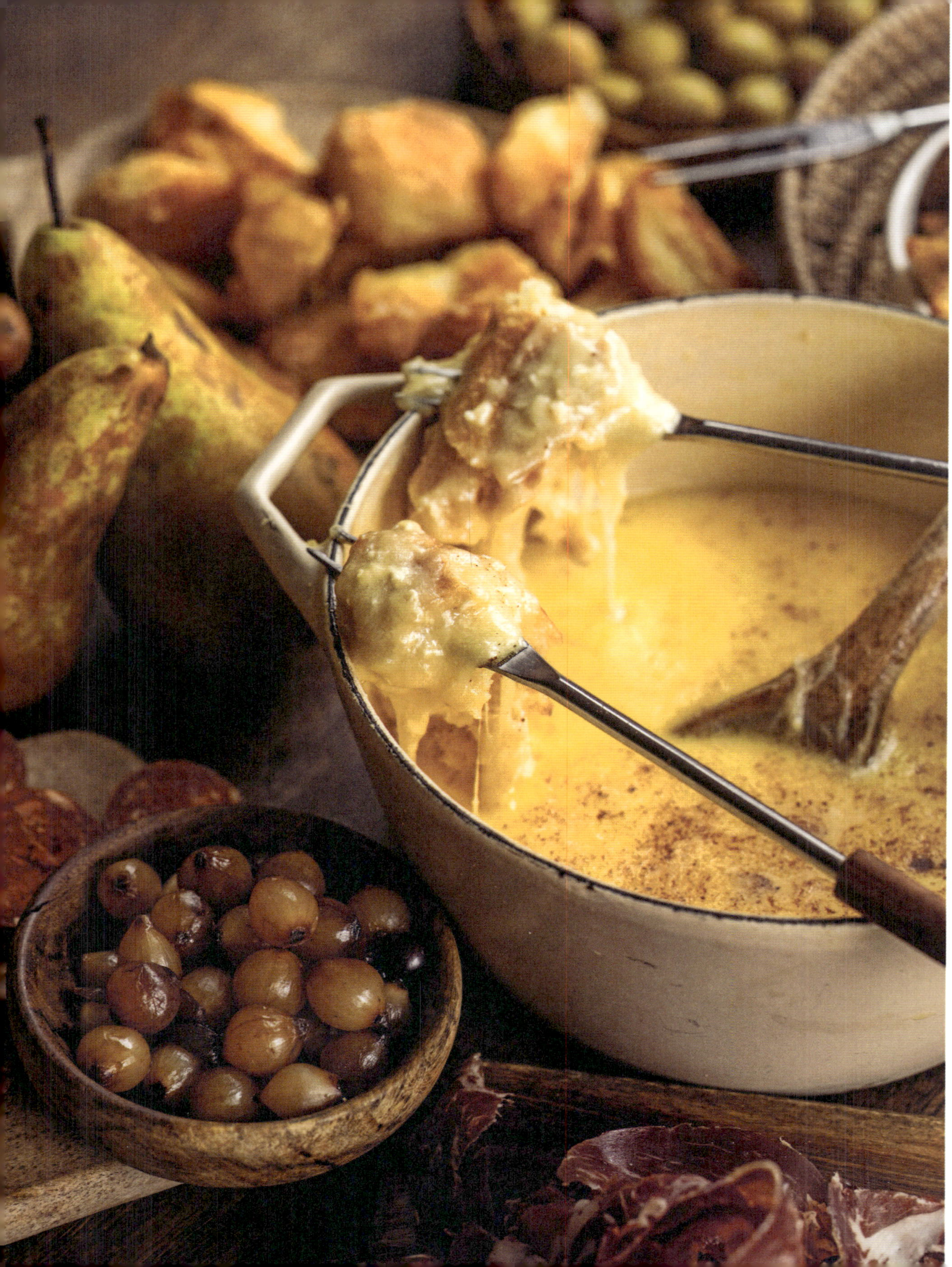

SERVES 4–6   Winter

Farmhouse Cheese Fondue

Like many of the best recipes from around the world, fondue was created by farmers. Its purpose was to use up stale bread and leftover cheese during the bleak winter months in the Swiss Alps. Today, we often think of it as a rather kitsch seventies dinner party dish. However, I'm here to change your mind. Fondue is simply a dish of softly bubbling cheese and white wine, scented with garlic and nutmeg and scooped up with chunks of bread. It doesn't need to be reserved as party food, although it is rather fun. There is something quite lovely about creating a coffee table picnic of all the component parts and devouring it while watching a good Friday night film. There are few better ways for keeping out the cold.

Here, I have selected some of my most beloved British cheeses that I believe rival those more traditionally used on the continent. Having a good mix of hard and soft cheeses is important for getting that perfect gooey, oozy consistency, but do have fun with it and use this as a guide rather than hard-and-fast rules.

1 large garlic clove, peeled and halved
1 tablespoon cornflour
300ml (10fl oz) dry English wine (look out for Bacchus)
350g (12oz) Lincolnshire Poacher (Swiss mountain-style British cow's milk cheese)
200g (7oz) Ogleshield (Raclette-style British cow's milk cheese)
200g (7oz) Tunworth (Camembert-style British cow's milk cheese)
150g (5½oz) Little Rollright (Reblochon-style British cow's milk cheese), torn
½ teaspoon grated nutmeg

To serve
British charcuterie
roast potatoes
sourdough bread
roasted cauliflower florets
sliced apples and pears
pickles

Set a fondue pan or a cast-iron casserole dish over a medium heat. Rub the cut side of the garlic clove all over the inside of the dish.

In a small jug, mix the cornflour with about 2 teaspoons of the wine to form a loose paste. Add the paste to the pan with the rest of the wine, stirring with a wooden spoon until simmering. Start to tip in the Lincolnshire Poacher and Oggleshield, then cook over a medium heat, whisking or stirring vigorously and allowing to melt before adding more. Do the same with the Tunworth, and finally the Rollright, continuing to stir until smooth. The cheese should steam but not boil. Whisk in the nutmeg.

Set the fondue pan or casserole dish over a tea light and tuck in immediately.

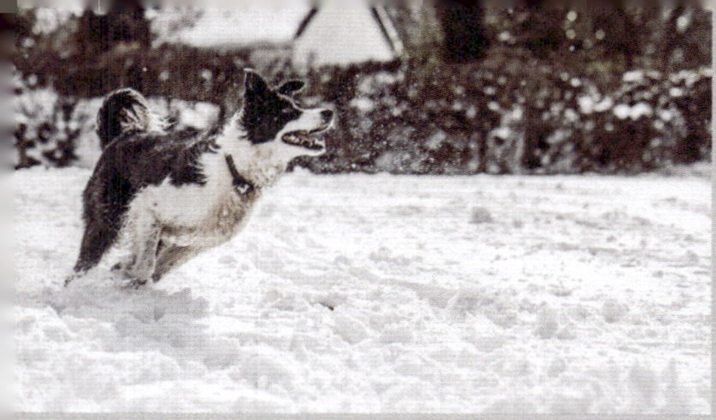
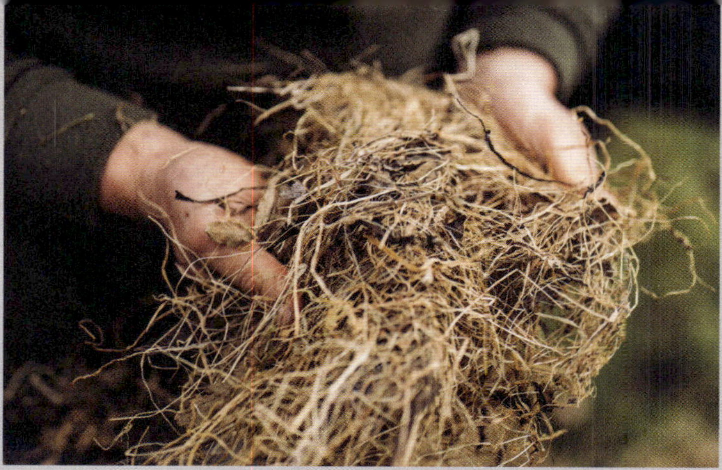
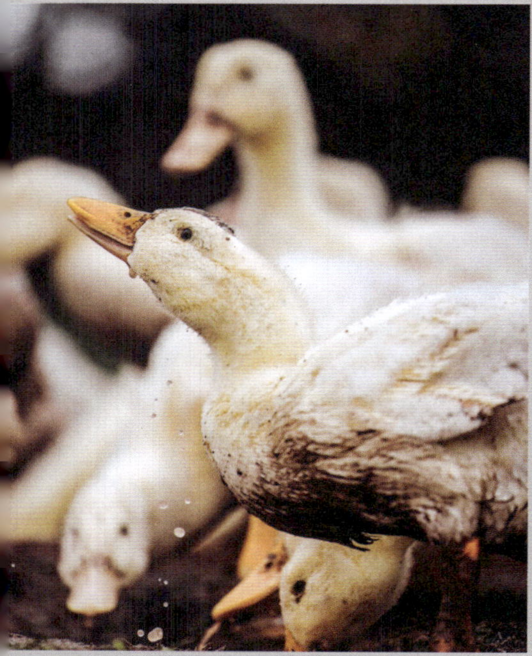
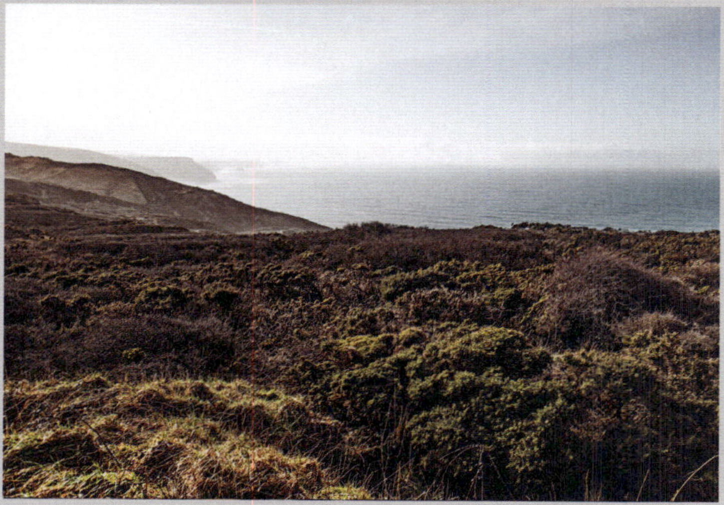
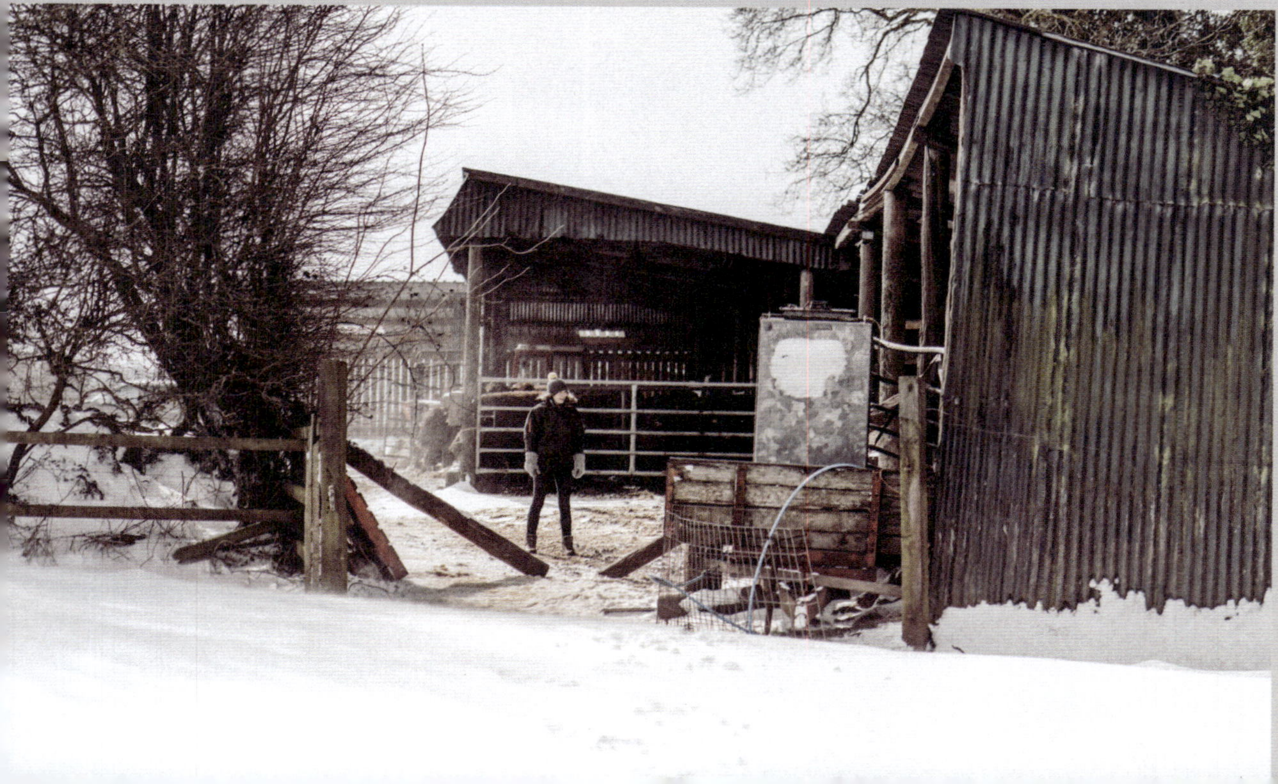

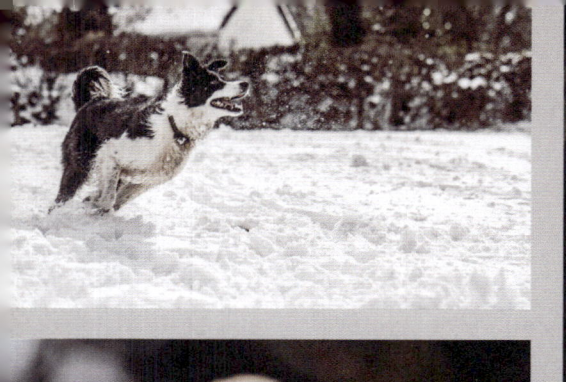

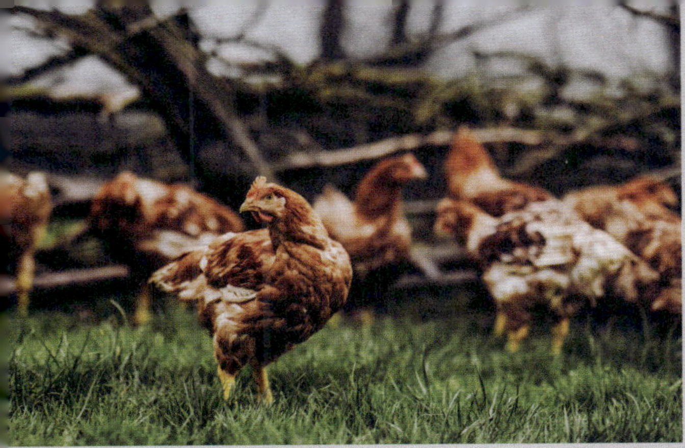
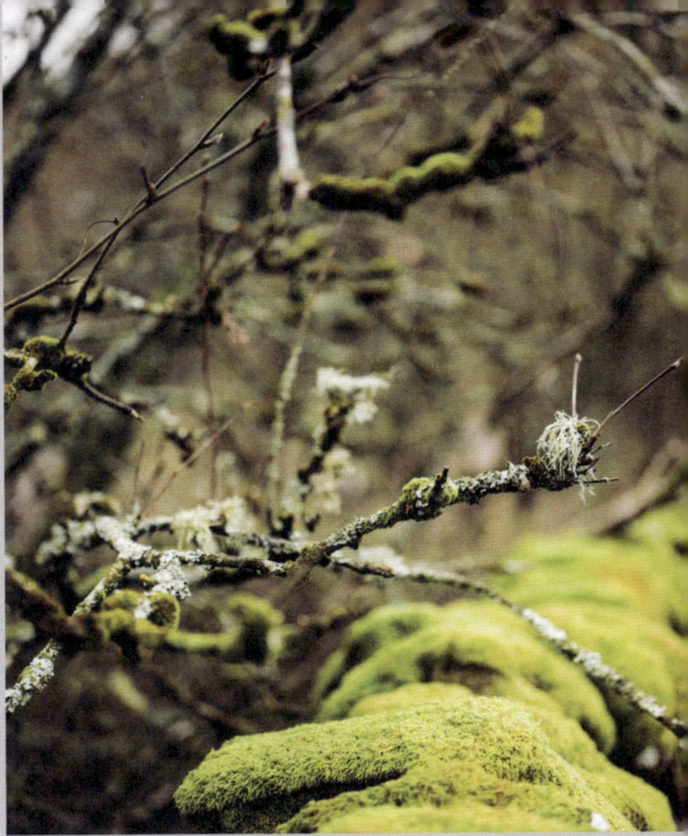
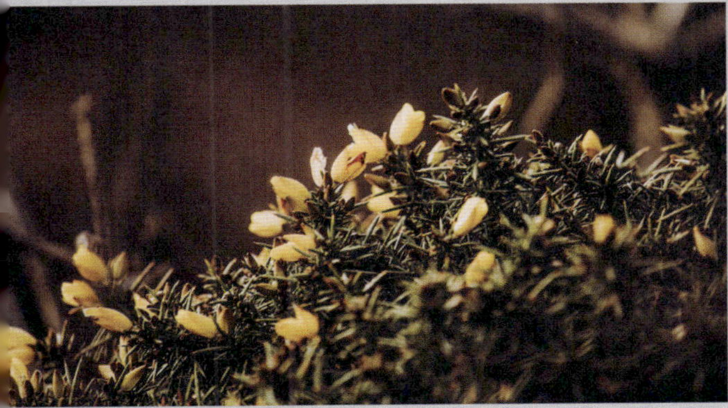
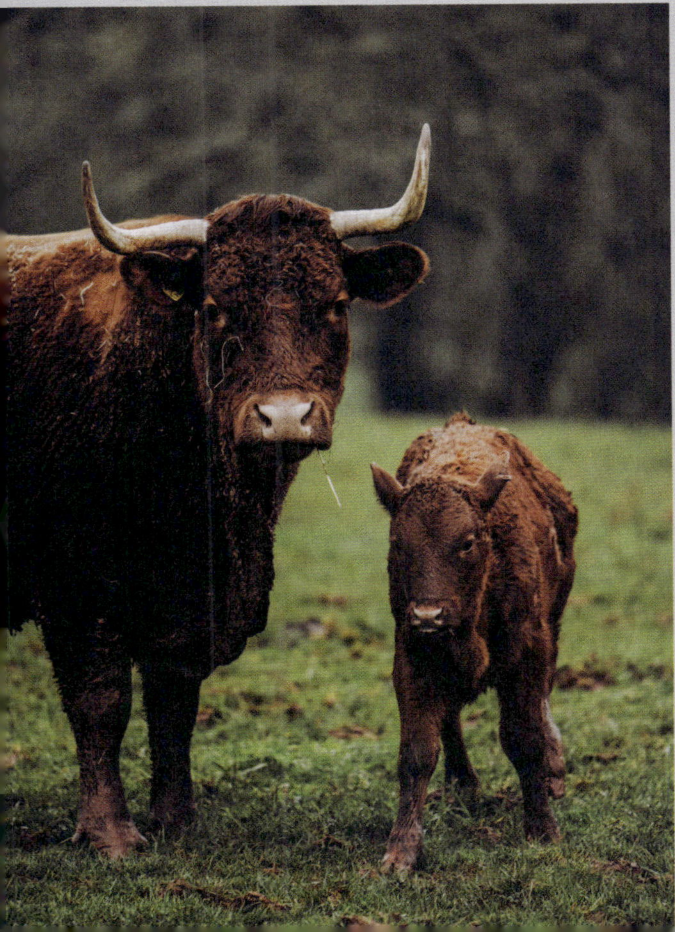
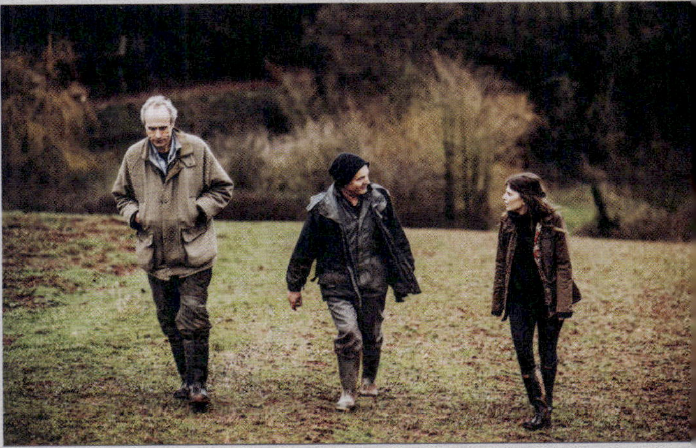
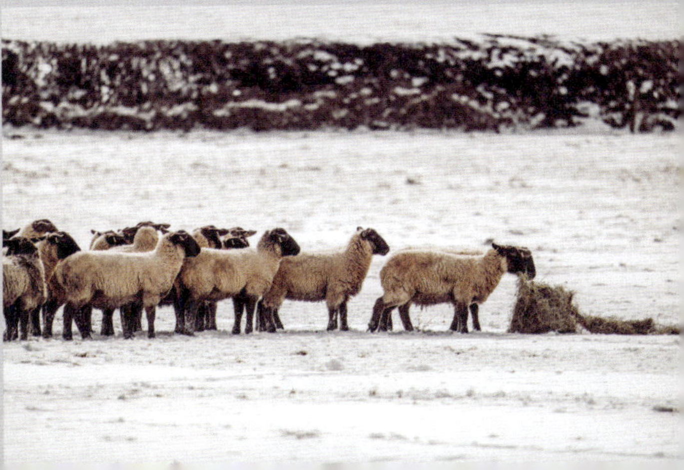

Index

agroecological farming 90–3
apples
  apple, leek, thyme & Cheddar toad in the hole 140, *141*
  apple, shallot, Cheddar & thyme galette *124*, 125
  chuck steak sandwich with smoky beetroot ketchup 151–2, *153*
  pork chops with apple ketchup *138*, 139
asparagus
  Jersey Royals with quail's eggs & asparagus *24*, 25
  new potato, sheep's cheese, asparagus, pea & mint frittata *18*, 19
aubergines
  grilled aubergines with honey, goat's curd, herbs and seeds *74*, *75*
  roasted red mullet with cherry tomatoes, aubergines & thyme *106*, 107
bacon
  Granny's cheese & bacon swirls 20–3
  line-caught coley with leeks & bacon 209
  pot-roast chicken with bacon & barley *34*, *35*
  rabbit, bacon, wild mushroom & spinach stuffed pancakes *184*, 185
  venison shoulder with bacon, mushrooms & chestnuts *196*, *197*
  wild rabbit pie 187–9, *188*
barley
  pot-roast chicken with bacon & barley *34*, *35*
beans
  broad bean, pea, mint, viola & sheep's cheese toasts *16*, *17*
  charred Cornish sardines on toast with bean mash & gremolata *104*, *105*
  chicken, chorizo & butter bean soup *136*, *137*
  harvest minestrone soup *122*, *123*
  loaded baked potatoes with sausage & bean stew *202*, 203
  pork chops with white beans, black pudding, kale and crispy sage *36*, 37
  rump pavé with green beans & salsa al dragoncello *98*, 99
  smoked haddock, kale & butter bean gratin 206, *207*
beef
  bavette steak with labneh & radishes *94*, *95*
  chuck steak sandwich with smoky beetroot ketchup 151–2, *153*
  côte de boeuf with peppercorn sauce & beef-fat chips *46*, 47
  flat-iron steak with romesco & charred spring onions on toast 87–9, *88*
  rare roast beef with radicchio, pickled pears & Wensleydale cheese *194*, 195
  rump pavé with green beans & salsa al dragoncello *98*, 99
  steak & kidney pie *192*, *193*
beetroot
  beetroot, celeriac, potato & thyme gratin *170*, 171
  chuck steak sandwich with smoky beetroot ketchup 151–2, *153*
black pudding
  creamed Brussels sprouts with black pudding *198*, 199
  pork chops with white beans, black pudding, kale and crispy sage *36*, 37
bread
  chuck steak sandwich with smoky beetroot ketchup 151–2, *153*
  farmhouse cheese fondue *216*, 217
  A British take on a Southern-style seafood boil *110*, 111
broccoli
  speltotto kedgeree with purple sprouting broccoli & kale *60*, 61
Brussels sprouts
  creamed Brussels sprouts with black pudding *198*, 199
butterflies 96

carrots
  hake & carrot dhal *156*, *157*
  venison steaks with honeyed carrots & spiced chickpeas *48*, *49*
cauliflower
  cauliflower soup with seared scallops *162*, 163
  farmhouse cheese fondue *216*, 217
celeriac
  beetroot, celeriac, potato & thyme gratin *170*, 171
  gamekeeper's pie *144*, 145
  slow-cooked kale & celeriac mash on toast with fried eggs *204*, *205*
cheese
  apple, leek, thyme & Cheddar toad in the hole 140, *141*
  apple, shallot, Cheddar & thyme galette *124*, 125
  baby leeks & ham on toast with ricotta parsley sauce *120*, 121
  baked new potatoes with chives, Cornish yarg & hot cheese sauce *26*, 27
  beetroot, celeriac, potato & thyme gratin *170*, 171
  broad bean, pea, mint, viola & sheep's cheese toasts *16*, *17*
  charred courgettes with mint, whipped ricotta & nasturtiums *68*, 69
  crab thermidor crumpets *158*, 159
  farmhouse cheese fondue *216*, 217
  field mushroom rarebit *130*, 131
  gardener's Bolognese *126*, 127
  Granny's cheese & bacon swirls 20, *21*–2, 23
  Hungry Gap canned seafood pasta *58*, *59*
  loaded baked potatoes with sausage & bean stew *202*, 203
  malloreddus with sausage & fennel seed ragu *38*, *39*
  mutton chops with beetroot hummus & dukkah 100, *101*
  mutton rump with roasted squash, sheep's cheese & pesto *154*, 155
  new potato, sheep's cheese, asparagus, pea & mint frittata *18*, 19
  rabbit, bacon, wild mushroom & spinach stuffed pancakes *184*, 185
  rare roast beef with radicchio, pickled pears & Wensleydale cheese *194*, 195
  slow-cooked kale & celeriac mash on toast with fried eggs *204*, *205*
  smashed cucumber with halloumi & tahini dressing *70*, *71*
  smoked haddock, kale & butter bean gratin 206, *207*
  spelt with charred summer veg, halloumi & kefir dressing *72*, 73
  turkey & ham Christmas crumble *178*, *179*
  venison steaks with honeyed carrots & spiced chickpeas *48*, *49*
  warm winter cheese board *214*, 215
chestnuts
  roast goose with sage & onion sausagemeat stuffing & crispy goose fat potatoes 174–7, *175*, *176*
  venison shoulder with bacon, mushrooms & chestnuts *196*, *197*
chicken
  chicken, chorizo & butter bean soup *136*, *137*
  chicken legs with lemon, potatoes, thyme and oregano *82*, *83*
  chicken schnitzel burger with cucumber pickle *84*, *85*–6
  chicken, spring greens & orzo broth *32*, *33*
  chicken stock 33
  pot-roast chicken with bacon & barley *34*, *35*
  roast cockerel with cider brandy & mushroom gravy *172*, *173*
chickpeas
  mutton chops with beetroot hummus & dukkah 100, *101*
  mutton rump with roasted squash 155

seafood tagine 210, *211*
venison steaks with honeyed carrots & spiced chickpeas 48, *49*

chorizo
chicken, chorizo & butter bean soup 136, *137*
scallop, chorizo & Padron pepper rosemary skewers 108, *109*

clams
A British take on a Southern-style seafood boil *110*, 111
Dorset clams with Coppa *50*, 51
A South-West bouillabaisse 160, *161*

cockerel
roast cockerel with cider brandy & mushroom gravy 172, *173*

coley
line-caught coley with leeks & bacon 209
seafood tagine 210, *211*

community and farming 180–3

courgettes
charred courgettes with mint, whipped ricotta & nasturtiums 68, *69*
gardener's Bolognese *126*, 127
mussels with saffron, cream & courgettes *56*, 57
spelt with charred summer veg, halloumi & kefir dressing *72*, 73

crab thermidor crumpets *158*, 159

cucumber
chicken schnitzel burger with cucumber pickle *84*, 85–6
smashed cucumber with halloumi & tahini dressing 70, *71*

Dorset clams with Coppa *50*, 51

eggs
creamy baked eggs with wild mushrooms & spinach 128, *129*
Jersey Royals with quail's eggs & asparagus *24*, 25
new potato, sheep's cheese, asparagus, pea & mint frittata *18*, 19
slow-cooked kale & celeriac mash on toast with fried eggs 204, *205*
speltotto kedgeree with purple sprouting broccoli & kale 60, *61*
winter fish chowder *212*, 213

farmhouse cheese fondue *216*, 217
farming and community 180–3

fennel
chuck steak sandwich with smoky beetroot ketchup 151–2, *153*
malloreddus with sausage & fennel seed ragu 38, *39*
A South-West bouillabaisse 160, *161*

figs
warm winter cheese board 214, *215*

fish
hake & carrot dhal 156, *157*
line-caught coley with leeks & bacon 209
pouting, leek & tarragon pie 52, *53*
roasted red mullet with cherry tomatoes, aubergines & thyme *106*, 107
seafood tagine 210, *211*
smoked haddock, kale & butter bean gratin 206, *207*
A South-West bouillabaisse 160, *161*
speltotto kedgeree with purple sprouting broccoli & kale 60, *61*
winter fish chowder *212*, 213

fondue, farmhouse cheese *216*, 217
food miles 134
food security 182
food waste 132

gamekeeper's pie *144*, 145
gardener's Bolognese *126*, 127

goat's curd
grilled aubergines with honey, goat's curd, herbs and seeds 74, *75*
minted hogget meatballs with peas & goat's curd *42*, 43

goose
roast goose with sage & onion sausagemeat stuffing & crispy goose fat potatoes 174–7, *175*, *176*

Granny's cheese & bacon swirls 20, *21*–2, 23

grapes
warm winter cheese board 214, *215*

growing your own food 28–31

hake
A South-West bouillabaisse 160, *161*
winter fish chowder *212*, 213

ham
baby leeks & ham on toast with ricotta parsley sauce *120*, 121
Dorset clams with Coppa *50*, 51
Jersey Royals with quail's eggs & asparagus *24*, 25
turkey & ham Christmas crumble 178, *179*

harvest minestrone soup 122, *123*

hogget
hogget liver on toast with creamed nettles 40, *41*
hogget shoulder cooked in milk with lemon & herbs *102*, 103
minted hogget meatballs with peas & goat's curd *42*, 43

Hungry Gap canned seafood pasta 58, *59*

jars, sterilizing 77
Jersey Royals with quail's eggs & asparagus *24*, 25

kale
pork chops with white beans, black pudding, kale and crispy sage *36*, 37
slow-cooked kale & celeriac mash on toast with fried eggs 204, *205*
smoked haddock, kale & butter bean gratin 206, *207*
speltotto kedgeree with purple sprouting broccoli & kale 60, *61*

kidneys
steak & kidney pie 192, *193*

labneh
bavette steak with labneh & radishes 94, *96*
roasted tomatoes with za'atar, labneh & oregano 78, *79*

langoustines
A British take on a Southern-style seafood boil *110*, 111

leeks
apple, leek, thyme & Cheddar toad in the hole 140, *141*
baby leeks & ham on toast with ricotta parsley sauce *120*, 121
line-caught coley with leeks & bacon 209
pouting, leek & tarragon pie 52, *53*
winter fish chowder *212*, 213

lemons
chicken legs with lemon, potatoes, thyme and oregano 82, *83*
hogget shoulder cooked in milk with lemon & herbs *102*, 103
winter fish chowder *212*, 213

lentils
gardener's Bolognese *126*, 127
hake & carrot dhal 156, *157*
harvest minestrone soup 122, *123*
Tuscan-style sausagemeat broth 200, *201*

liver
hogget liver on toast with creamed nettles 40, *41*
lobster roll with lemon & herb mayonnaise 112, *113*

lovage
hot or cold pea & lovage soup *14*, 15

mallard
gamekeeper's pie *144*, 145
malloreddus with sausage & fennel seed ragu 38, *39*

mint
broad bean, pea, mint, viola & sheep's cheese toasts 16, *17*
canned sardines on toast with wild garlic chimichurri 54, *55*
charred courgettes with mint, whipped ricotta & nasturtiums 68, *69*

minted hogget meatballs with peas & goat's curd 42, 43
new potato, sheep's cheese, asparagus, pea & mint frittata 18, 19
roast mutton leg with walnut & mint pesto 44, 45
mushrooms
creamy baked eggs with wild mushrooms & spinach 128, 129
field mushroom rarebit 130, 131
gamekeeper's pie 144, 145
gardener's Bolognese 126, 127
pot-roast chicken with bacon & barley 34, 35
rabbit, bacon, wild mushroom & spinach stuffed pancakes 184, 185
roast cockerel with cider brandy & mushroom gravy 172, 173
venison shoulder with bacon, mushrooms & chestnuts 196, 197
mussels
A British take on a Southern-style seafood boil 110, 111
mussels with saffron, cream & courgettes 56, 57
A South-West bouillabaisse 160, 161
mutton
mutton chops with beetroot hummus & dukkah 100, 101
mutton rump with roasted squash, sheep's cheese & pesto 154, 155
roast mutton leg with walnut & mint pesto 44, 45

nasturtiums
charred courgettes with mint, whipped ricotta & nasturtiums 68, 69
nature, reconnecting with 132–5
nettles
hogget liver on toast with creamed nettles 40, 41
washing 40

oregano
chicken legs with lemon, potatoes, thyme and oregano 82, 83
roasted tomatoes with za'atar, labneh & oregano 78, 79
orzo
chicken, spring greens & orzo broth 32, 33
oxtail soup 190, 191

pancakes
rabbit, bacon, wild mushroom & spinach stuffed pancakes 184, 185
parsley
baby leeks & ham on toast with ricotta parsley sauce 120, 121
canned sardines on toast with wild garlic chimichurri 54, 55

pasta
chicken, spring greens & orzo broth 32, 33
gardener's Bolognese 126, 127
Hungry Gap canned seafood pasta 58, 59
pearl barley
harvest minestrone soup 122, 123
pot-roast chicken with bacon & barley 34, 35
sausages with pearl barley, squash & mustard 142, 143
speltotto kedgeree with purple sprouting broccoli & kale 60, 61
pears
farmhouse cheese fondue 216, 217
rare roast beef with radicchio, pickled pears & Wensleydale cheese 194, 195
peas
broad bean, pea, mint, viola & sheep's cheese toasts 16, 17
harvest minestrone soup 122, 123
hot or cold pea & lovage soup 14, 15
minted hogget meatballs with peas & goat's curd 42, 43
new potato, sheep's cheese, asparagus, pea & mint frittata 18, 19
Tuscan-style sausagemeat broth 200, 201
peppers
flat-iron steak with romesco & charred spring onions on toast 87–9, 88
loaded baked potatoes with sausage & bean stew 202, 203
scallop, chorizo & Padron pepper rosemary skewers 108, 109
spelt with charred summer veg, halloumi & kefir dressing 72, 73
pigeon
gamekeeper's pie 144, 145
pigeon with roasted plums, red onion & crispy sage leaves 146, 147
pigeon schnitzel with pickled pears, hazelnuts & lemon mayo 148–50, 149
plastic pollution 134
plums
pigeon with roasted plums, red onion & crispy sage leaves 146, 147
pork
pork chops with apple ketchup 138, 139
pork chops with white beans, black pudding, kale and crispy sage 36, 37
pot-roast chicken with bacon & barley 34, 35
potatoes
baked new potatoes with chives, Cornish yarg & hot cheese sauce 26, 27
beetroot, celeriac, potato & thyme gratin 170, 171

A British take on a Southern-style seafood boil 110, 111
côte de boeuf with peppercorn sauce & beef-fat chips 46, 47
farmhouse cheese fondue 216, 217
gamekeeper's pie 144, 145
Jersey Royals with quail's eggs & asparagus 24, 25
loaded baked potatoes with sausage & bean stew 202, 203
new potato, sheep's cheese, asparagus, pea & mint frittata 18, 19
roast goose with sage & onion sausagemeat stuffing & crispy goose fat potatoes 174–7, 175, 176
roast mutton leg with walnut & mint pesto 44, 45
winter fish chowder 212, 213
pouting, leek & tarragon pie 52, 53
prawns
A South-West bouillabaisse 160, 161
pumpkin
harvest minestrone soup 122, 123
pigeon with roasted plums, red onion & crispy sage leaves 146, 147

rabbit
rabbit, bacon, wild mushroom & spinach stuffed pancakes 184, 185
wild rabbit pie 187–9, 188
radiccio
rare roast beef with radicchio, pickled pears & Wensleydale cheese 194, 195
radishes
bavette steak with labneh & radishes 94, 95
red mullet
roasted red mullet with cherry tomatoes, aubergines & thyme 106, 107
seafood tagine 210, 211
A South-West bouillabaisse 160, 161
red onions
grilled aubergines with honey, goat's curd, herbs and seeds 74, 75
mutton chops with beetroot hummus & dukkah 100, 101
pigeon with roasted plums, red onion & crispy sage leaves 146, 147
venison steaks with honeyed carrots & spiced chickpeas 48, 49
rewilding 93
ricotta
charred courgettes with mint, whipped ricotta & nasturtiums 68, 69
rosemary
beetroot, celeriac, potato & thyme gratin 170, 171
chicken, chorizo & butter bean soup 136, 137

côte de boeuf with peppercorn sauce & beef-fat chips 46, 47
creamed Brussels sprouts with black pudding 198, 199
hogget shoulder cooked in milk with lemon & herbs 102, 103
pork chops with apple ketchup 138, 139
roast goose with sage & onion sausagemeat stuffing & crispy goose fat potatoes 174–7, 175, 176
roast mutton leg with walnut & mint pesto 44, 45
sausages with pearl barley, squash & mustard 142, 143
scallop, chorizo & Padron pepper rosemary skewers 108, 109
turkey & ham Christmas crumble 178, 179
Tuscan-style sausagemeat broth 200, 201
warm winter cheese board 214, 215

saffron
mussels with saffron, cream & courgettes 56, 57

sage
pigeon with roasted plums, red onion & crispy sage leaves 146, 147
pigeon schnitzel with pickled pears, hazelnuts & lemon mayo 148–50, 149
pork chops with white beans, black pudding, kale and crispy sage 36, 37

sardines
canned sardines on toast with wild garlic chimichurri 54, 55
charred Cornish sardines on toast with bean mash & gremolata 104, 105
Hungry Gap canned seafood pasta 58, 59

sausages
apple, leek, thyme & Cheddar toad-in-the-hole 140, 141
malloreddus with sausage & fennel seed ragu 38, 39
sausages with pearl barley, squash & mustard 142, 143
Tuscan-style sausagemeat broth 200, 201

scallops
cauliflower soup with seared scallops 162, 163
scallops, chorizo & Padron pepper rosemary skewers 108, 109
seafood tagine 210, 211
seasonal eating 28–31

shallots
apple, shallot, Cheddar & thyme galette 124, 125
mussels with saffron, cream & courgettes 56, 57

sheep's cheese
broad bean, pea, mint, viola & sheep's cheese toasts 16, 17
mutton chops with beetroot hummus & dukkah 100, 101
mutton rump with roasted squash, sheep's cheese & pesto 154, 155
new potato, sheep's cheese, asparagus, pea & mint frittata 18, 19
venison steaks with honeyed carrots & spiced chickpeas 48, 49

smoked haddock
smoked haddock, kale & butter bean gratin 206, 207
speltotto kedgeree with purple sprouting broccoli & kale 60, 61
winter fish chowder 212, 213

soups
chicken, chorizo & butter bean soup 136, 137
chicken, spring greens & orzo broth 32, 33
harvest minestrone soup 122, 123
hot or cold pea & lovage soup 14, 15
oxtail soup 190, 191
Tuscan-style sausagemeat broth 200, 201
winter fish chowder 212, 213
A South-West bouillabaisse 160, 161

spelt
spelt with charred summer veg, halloumi & kefir dressing 72, 73
speltotto kedgeree with purple sprouting broccoli & kale 60, 61

spinach
creamy baked eggs with wild mushrooms & spinach 128, 129
rabbit, bacon, wild mushroom & spinach stuffed pancakes 184, 185

spring greens
chicken, spring greens & orzo broth 32, 33

spring onions
canned sardines on toast with wild garlic chimichurri 54, 55
flat-iron steak with romesco & charred spring onions on toast 87–9, 88

squash
mutton rump with roasted squash, sheep's cheese & pesto 154, 155
sausages with pearl barley, squash & mustard 142, 143

tahini
charred Cornish sardines on toast with bean mash & gremolata 104, 105
mutton chops with beetroot hummus & dukkah 100, 101
pork chops with white beans, black pudding, kale and crispy sage 36, 37

tarragon
pouting, leek & tarragon pie 52, 53

rump pavé with green beans & salsa al dragoncello 98, 99

thyme
apple, leek, thyme & Cheddar toad-in-the-hole 140, 141
apple, shallot, Cheddar & thyme galette 124, 125
beetroot, celeriac, potato & thyme gratin 170, 171
chicken legs with lemon, potatoes, thyme and oregano 82, 83
roasted red mullet with cherry tomatoes, aubergines & thyme 106, 107
toad-in-the-hole, apple, leek, thyme & Cheddar 140, 141

tomatoes
gardener's Bolognese 126, 127
Hungry Gap canned seafood pasta 58, 59
malloreddus with sausage & fennel seed ragu 38, 39
preserved 76, 77
gardener's Bolognese 126, 127
harvest minestrone soup 122, 123
seafood tagine 210, 211
A South-West bouillabaisse 160, 161
roasted red mullet with cherry tomatoes, aubergines & thyme 106, 107
roasted tomatoes with za'atar, labneh & oregano 78, 79
turkey & ham Christmas crumble 178, 179
Tuscan-style sausagemeat broth 200, 201

venison
gamekeeper's pie 144, 145
venison shoulder with bacon, mushrooms & chestnuts 196, 197
venison steaks with honeyed carrots & spiced chickpeas 48, 49

walnuts
grilled aubergines with honey, goat's curd, herbs and seeds 74, 75
rare roast beef with radicchio, pickled pears & Wensleydale cheese 194, 195
roast mutton leg with walnut & mint pesto 44, 45
warm winter cheese board 214, 215

wild garlic
canned sardines on toast with wild garlic chimichurri 54, 55
winter fish chowder 212, 213

yoghurt
bavette steak with labneh & radishes 94, 95
smashed cucumber with halloumi & tahini dressing 70, 71

Author's acknowledgements

I simply would not be where I am today without the kindness and support of those I have met along life's rich journey.

Will, you have held my hand every step along this rollercoaster we call life. I couldn't have achieved half the things I have if it wasn't for your love and encouragement. I am beyond lucky to have found you. This book exists because you believed in me.

Peter & Henri, your clear vision has paved the way for so many people to take back control of their health and their passion for producing food. Not only have you given me the most wonderful grounding, but your generosity has had such a ripple effect and touched more people than you could ever know. Thank you for inspiring us all to make change happen.

Matt and Marie, your beautiful images have brought to life the stories I have written for over a decade. I could ask for no better collaborator and partner to help me open the doors and share this wonderful world full of talented, passionate people whose mission is to produce nourishing food. You have brought my recipes to life, and I will forever be grateful for your help and your incredible talent.

Jo, you have championed our vision and values and supported me in creating not only the first book but these pages too. You believed in our little farm and a story of hope which has enabled us to connect with so many people around the world. Thank you for your patience and your unwavering support.